Scalable Modeling and Efficient Management of IoT Applications

Dharmendra Singh Rajput
Vellore Institute of Technology, India

Pushpendra Kumar
Central University of Jharkhand, India

Gotam Singh Lalotra
Government Degree College, Kathua, India

Harshita Patel
Vellore Institute of Technology, India

Vinod Kumar
Galgotias University, Greater Noida, India

Published in the United States of America by
IGI Global
701 E. Chocolate Avenue
Hershey PA, USA 17033
Tel: 717-533-8845
Fax: 717-533-8661
E-mail: cust@igi-global.com
Web site: https://www.igi-global.com

Library of Congress Cataloging-in-Publication Data

Names: Rajput, Dharmendra Singh, 1985- editor. | Lalotra, Gotam, 1983-
    editor. | Kumar, Vinod, 1986- editor. | Kumar, Pushpendra, 1989- editor.
    | Patel, Harshita, 1985- editor.
Title: Scalable modeling and efficient management of IoT applications /
    edited by: Dharmendra Rajput, Gotam Lalotra, Vinod Kumar, Pushpendra
    Kumar, Harshita Patel.
Description: Hershey PA : Information Science Reference, [2025] | Includes
    bibliographical references. | Summary: "The book aims to solve several
    problems: lack of guidance on intelligent modeling techniques;
    complexity in managing IoT applications; and keeping up with the rapidly
    evolving IoT landscape"-- Provided by publisher.
Identifiers: LCCN 2023055028 (print) | LCCN 2023055029 (ebook) | ISBN
    9798369316863 (hardcover) | ISBN 9798369316870 (ebook)
Subjects: LCSH: Internet of things--Industrial applications.
Classification: LCC TK5105.8857 .S34 2024 (print) | LCC TK5105.8857
    (ebook) | DDC 004.67/8--dc23/eng/20240826
LC record available at https://lccn.loc.gov/2023055028
LC ebook record available at https://lccn.loc.gov/2023055029

Vice President of Editorial: Melissa Wagner
Managing Editor of Acquisitions: Mikaela Felty
Managing Editor of Book Development: Jocelynn Hessler
Production Manager: Mike Brehm
Cover Design: Phillip Shickler

British Cataloguing in Publication Data
A Cataloguing in Publication record for this book is available from the British Library.

Editorial Advisory Board

Table of Contents

Detailed Table of Contents

Chapter 1
Predictive and Prescriptive Analytics for IoT Unlocking Insights 1
>   *Ravi Mohan Sharma, Makhanlal Chaturvedi National University of*
>   *Journalism and Communication, India*
>   *Sunita Dwivedi, Makhanlal Chaturvedi National University of*
>   *Journalism and Communication, India*
>   *Vinod Kumar, Galgotias University, India*

In today's information era, the use of internet of things (IOT) technologies and associated devices has multiplied, and they are now present in every sector. IOT technologies use sensors to sense data from the environment of deployment. Sensors generate a great deal of data that has valuable insights. Therefore, this chapter explores the intersection of predictive and prescriptive analytics within the context of the IoT. The chapter delves into the theoretical foundations, technological advancements, and practical applications of predictive and prescriptive analytics in the IoT domain. By understanding how these analytics techniques work synergistically, organisations can harness the power of IoT data to make informed decisions, optimize operations, and create value.

Chapter 2

Nagendra Singh Yadav, Engineering College, Bikaner, India
Vishal Kumar Goar, Engineering College, Bikaner, India

The incorporation of internet of things (IoT) technologies in the healthcare sector has ushered in a transformative era of patient care and medical practices. This chapter aims to share a thorough overview of the applications, benefits, challenges, and future prospects of IoT in healthcare and telemedicine. The chapter will explore the ways in which IoT is enhancing patient monitoring, diagnosis, treatment, and overall healthcare delivery. Additionally, it will delve into the ethical and security considerations linked with IoT in healthcare. This chapter will serve as an essential resource for healthcare professionals, researchers, policymakers, and technology enthusiasts seeking to understand and harness the potential of IoT in revolutionizing the healthcare industry.

Chapter 3

Venkat Narayana Rao T., Sreenidhi Institute of Science and Technology, India
M. Stephen, Sreenidhi Institute of Science and Technology, India
Rohan Kolachala, Sreenidhi Institute of Science and Technology, India

In an age where healthcare and telemedicine have never been more crucial, the rise of IoT has enhanced free use of healthcare systems around the world. This is accomplished by improving the decision making with the help of accessible data, ensuring that monitoring and consultation of patients is carried out by remote means. In order to efficiently use IoT in healthcare, scalable modelling and effective management of the application plays a critical role. Scalable modelling in healthcare and telemedicine involves the development of systems and that can flexibly respond to changing needs, induce quality, accessibility, and value-for-money. Management of IoT applications in healthcare comes with many challenges such as handling patient data on time, secured medical data, remote, ensure proper amount of medicine is taken by the patient, disease tracking, etc. This chapter aims to guide the readers to understand and develop their own frameworks for the scalable models which adapt to the needs in healthcare and enable readers to explore the potential of IoT in telemedicine.

Guillermo M. Limon-Molina, Universidad Politécnica de Baja California, Mexico

E. Ivette Cota-Rivera, Universidad Politécnica de Baja California, Mexico

Maria E. Raygoza-Limón, Universidad Politécnica de Baja California, Mexico

Fabian N. Murrieta-Rico, Universidad Politécnica de Baja California, Mexico

Jesus Heriberto Orduño-Osuna, Universidad Politécnica de Baja California, Mexico

Roxana Jimenez-Sánchez, Universidad Politécnica de Baja California, Mexico

Miguel E. Bravo-Zanoguera, Universidad Politécnica de Baja California, Mexico

Abelardo Mercado, Universidad Politécnica de Baja California, Mexico

Water scarcity is nowadays a global problem, which requires innovative and sustainable solutions to reduce waste. The main uses are in the agricultural sector where in most cases flood irrigation is still used. In a lower degree the domestic use is considered; here the "automated" irrigation is via temporized solenoids that turn on and off the water circulation. These kinds of systems have proved inefficiency due to not considering the real need of water for the plants and cultivations. Considering the above issues, the authors proposed Automatic Irrigation System (AIS) that uses a mobile app and microcontroller to monitor cultivations in real time; this allows the user to take informed decisions to avoid water waste. The proposed system uses moisture and temperature sensors to monitor each type of cultivation needs; with this information the system can work in automatic mode or in manual mode to be activated individually or by sections for maintenance purposes.

    Ravi Kant Kumar, Department of Computer Science and Engineering,
      SRM University, India
    Sobin C. C., Department of Computer Science and Engineering, SRM
      University, India

As technology continues to advance, the potential for IoT in healthcare (also called IoMT-Internet of Medical Things) is rising day by day. Innovations in telemedicine and remote patient monitoring are helping to improve the healthcare services, making them more accessible and efficient for patients. Contactless health monitoring can ensure better treatment of patients, especially in remote areas. It refers to the interconnection of medical devices, sensors, and systems to the internet. IoMT enables the collection, transmission, and analysis of patient's data in real-time, allowing for remote monitoring and early detection of health. IoMT systems present a promising opportunity for prevention, prediction, and monitoring of emerging infectious diseases. This technology also helps medical professionals make more informed treatment and deliver personalized care to patients. In this study, the authors focus on the emerging developments of IT-based telemedicine and remote patient monitoring including the definition, impact, importance, advantages, challenges, and future of IoT in healthcare.

    S. Aditi Apurva, Indian Institute of Information Technology, Ranchi,
      India

The modern era has become an era of machine learning as an essential tool for developing IoT (internet of things) application. Machine learning for IoT can be used to depict future trends, detect anomalies, and argument intelligence by ingesting images, videos, and audios. Introducing IoT and machine learning in agricultural has empowered farmers to make and take well informed decision in optimal resource utilization as well as mitigation of pest and disease control. IoT and machine learning has aided in revolutionizing the farming sector. IoT sensors placed in the soil measure parameters like moisture content, pH levels, and nutrient levels. This chapter delves into a comparative analysis of two deep learning architectures, the residual neural network (ResNet), and convolutional neural network (CNN), for detecting diseases in apple tree leaves. By employing these models, the study aims to determine their performance in accurately identifying and classifying diseased apple tree leaves against healthy ones.

Chapter 7

Parveen Sadotra, Central University of Himachal Pradesh, India
Pradeep Chouksey, Central University of Himachal Pradesh, India
Mayank Chopra, Central University of Himachal Pradesh, India
Rabia Koser, Government P.G. College, Rajouri, India
Rishikesh Rawat, Bansal College of Engineering, Mandideep, India

In green cloud computing, task scheduling entails assigning tasks to virtual machines in an approach that minimizes energy use whilst still reaching the performance targets. Green cloud computing is an evolving field that lowers the energy and carbon footprint of systems for using the cloud. In green cloud computing, task planning is a crucial problem because it determines how computational resources are allotted to workloads in order to decrease energy consumption and increase efficiency. Different task-scheduling techniques have been put forth in recent years for green cloud computing. The authors look at some current studies on task scheduling methods for green cloud computing in this overview of the literature.

Chapter 8
Unleashing IoT Data Insights Data Mining and Machine Learning
Techniques for Scalable Modeling and Efficient Management of IoT 153
    C. V. Suresh Babu, Hindustan Institute of Technology and Science, India
    Ganesh Moorthy A. V., Hindustan Institute of Technology and Science,
        India
    S. Lokesh, Hindustan Institute of Technology and Science, India
    Niranjan A. K., Hindustan Institute of Technology and Science, India
    Yuvaraja Manivannan, Hindustan Institute of Technology and Science,
        India

This chapter explores the era of unprecedented data creation propelled by the widespread adoption of internet of things (IoT) devices. The massive and diverse IoT data, while holding advantages, necessitates data mining and machine learning techniques to unveil concealed insights. Focusing on the integration of these techniques, the research explores scalable modeling and effective administration of IoT applications. It navigates through the challenges of scalability, data complexity, real-time processing, and security concerns within IoT data. The chapter emphasizes the necessity of feature engineering, data preparation, and model selection tailored to IoT data's particularities. By incorporating IoT capabilities for data gathering, real-time streaming, and comprehensive data analysis, the research promotes efficient handling of IoT data, fostering a new era of productivity and creativity. The findings contribute to the evolving landscape of IoT applications, presenting a roadmap for data-driven decision-making and enhanced operational efficiency.

Preface

Welcome to *Scalable Modeling and Efficient Management of IoT Applications*. The widespread adoption of Internet of Things (IoT) technologies has completely changed how society functions today, transforming entire industries, improving day-to-day life, and creating previously unheard-of levels of connectedness. Scalable modeling and effective IoT application management are becoming more and more necessary as the IoT ecosystem rapidly continues to grow.

The goal of this book is to provide readers with a thorough manual for negotiating the difficulties that arise when designing, implementing, and maintaining Internet of Things systems. Readers will walk through the foundational ideas, innovative approaches, and useful tactics that are necessary to fully utilize IoT technologies in a scalable and effective way within these pages.

The key to a successful IoT implementation in the fast-paced digital world of today is the capacity to create scalable models. Scalability is a crucial factor in Internet of Things applications, as it affects their ability to accommodate an increasing number of connected devices, remain sustainable in their performance, and adapt to changing requirements. This applies to both sensor networks and cloud platforms. This book gives readers the tools they need to build reliable and adaptable Internet of Things infrastructures by examining a wide range of scalable modeling approaches, including data management, architectural design, and communication protocols.

Ensuring the smooth functioning of Internet of Things apps requires equally important management practices. Effective management solutions are essential for maintaining data integrity, guaranteeing dependability, and optimizing resource utilization as the number and variety of IoT devices increase. This book explores the nuances of IoT application management through enlightening conversations and useful examples. It covers subjects including device provisioning, data analytics, security standards, and energy optimization, giving readers the tools, they need to optimize productivity and simplify operations.

This book also emphasizes the multidisciplinary character of IoT technology by incorporating ideas from a variety of disciplines, including business management, computer science, engineering, and mathematics. Whether you are an experienced IoT professional looking to expand your knowledge or a novice keen to learn the basics, the material provided here is designed to suit a wide range of skill levels and work experiences.

This book also emphasizes the multidisciplinary character of IoT technology by incorporating ideas from a variety of disciplines, including business management, computer science, engineering, and mathematics. Whether you are an experienced IoT professional looking to expand your knowledge or a novice keen to learn the basics, the material provided here is designed to suit a wide range of skill levels and work experiences.

Finally, we would like to thank the readers for traveling this journey with us. With the knowledge gained from these pages, may you be able to confidently traverse the IoT's intricacies, seizing new possibilities, overcoming obstacles, and realizing connected intelligence's full potential.

Several prominent researchers and practitioners in the fields of internet of this things (IoT) contributed to the book's 08 chapters. The book is organized in a logical progression from basic concepts to the corresponding technological solutions. The book's material is structured as follows:

In the rapidly evolving landscape of technology, the Internet of Things (IoT) stands out as a transformative force, reshaping industries, enhancing quality of life, and redefining the way we interact with our environments. This book is a comprehensive exploration into the critical aspects of designing, managing, and optimizing IoT applications to meet the demands of scalability and efficiency.

Chapter 1 introduces the foundational concepts of predictive and prescriptive analytics for IoT, illuminating how these methodologies unlock valuable insights from vast streams of IoT-generated data. From predictive maintenance in industrial settings to optimizing resource allocation in smart cities, the power of analytics is demonstrated across diverse applications.

Chapter 2 and Chapter 3 delve into the revolutionary impact of IoT in healthcare and telemedicine. These chapters explore how IoT technologies are revolutionizing patient care, enabling remote monitoring, improving diagnostics, and enhancing medical practices worldwide. The integration of IoT in healthcare not only improves efficiency but also expands access to healthcare services, particularly in remote and underserved areas.

Chapter 4 showcases the practical application of IoT in agriculture through an automatic irrigation system, illustrating how IoT sensors and data analytics can optimize water usage, enhance crop yield, and promote sustainable farming practices.

Chapter 5 continues the exploration of IoT in healthcare with a focus on telemedicine and remote patient monitoring. This chapter examines case studies and analyzes the impact of IoT-enabled solutions in transforming healthcare delivery, improving patient outcomes, and reducing healthcare costs.

In Chapter 6, the application of deep learning techniques (ResNet and CNN) for disease detection in apple tree leaves demonstrates how IoT can be leveraged for agricultural diagnostics, ensuring early detection and management of plant diseases through advanced image processing algorithms.

Chapter 7 shifts the focus to green cloud computing and the critical role of task scheduling algorithms in optimizing energy efficiency and resource utilization within IoT ecosystems. This research review provides insights into the state-of-the-art approaches for sustainable and environmentally friendly cloud-based IoT deployments.

Chapter 8 concludes the book by exploring data mining and machine learning techniques tailored for IoT environments. This chapter emphasizes scalable modeling approaches that empower organizations to extract actionable insights from IoT data, drive informed decision-making, and achieve operational excellence.

Throughout this book, our goal is to equip readers with a deep understanding of the methodologies, technologies, and best practices essential for harnessing the full potential of IoT applications. Whether you are a researcher, practitioner, or enthusiast, we invite you to embark on a journey through the dynamic world of scalable modeling and efficient management of IoT applications. Together, let us explore how IoT is shaping the future of industries, communities, and everyday life.

Anyone with even a basic understanding of IoT and its applications can easily understand this book because of its simple and succinct writing style. To aid readers in understanding the ideas and methods discussed in the book, each chapter contains a wealth of examples and pictures.

Scalable Modeling and Efficient Management of IoT Applications" is tailored for a diverse audience encompassing researchers, academics, industry professionals, and technology enthusiasts interested in advancing their understanding and capabilities within the realm of IoT.

1. **Researchers and Academics**: This book serves as a valuable resource for researchers and academics engaged in IoT-related disciplines such as computer science, electrical engineering, data analytics, and artificial intelligence. It provides comprehensive insights into advanced modeling techniques, data-driven approaches, and emerging trends in IoT applications, making it essential reading for those exploring the frontiers of technological innovation.

2. **Industry Professionals**: Professionals working in industries leveraging IoT technologies—including healthcare, agriculture, manufacturing, smart cities, and logistics—will find practical guidance and real-world case studies that

showcase best practices and successful implementations. The book equips industry leaders and decision-makers with the knowledge needed to optimize IoT deployments, improve operational efficiency, and drive business growth.

3. **IoT Practitioners**: Engineers, developers, and IoT solution architects involved in designing, developing, and deploying IoT applications will benefit from the detailed discussions on scalable modeling, efficient management strategies, and the integration of advanced analytics. The insights shared in the book empower practitioners to overcome technical challenges, enhance system reliability, and leverage IoT data to deliver impactful solutions.

4. **Technology Enthusiasts**: Enthusiasts with a keen interest in emerging technologies and their practical applications will find the book engaging and enlightening. It offers a deep dive into the transformative potential of IoT across various sectors, inspiring readers to explore new possibilities and contribute to the ongoing evolution of IoT ecosystems.

5. **Policy Makers and Innovators**: Policymakers, strategists, and innovators interested in the societal and economic implications of IoT adoption will gain valuable perspectives on governance, sustainability, and ethical considerations. The book encourages discussions on regulatory frameworks, privacy concerns, and the responsible deployment of IoT technologies to maximize benefits while minimizing risks.

Overall, *Scalable Modeling and Efficient Management of IoT Applications* caters to a broad audience seeking to deepen their knowledge, expand their skill set, and stay ahead in the rapidly evolving field of IoT. Whether you are delving into theoretical foundations, exploring practical applications, or envisioning future innovations, this book serves as an indispensable guide for navigating the complexities and unlocking the potential of IoT-driven transformation.

Dharmendra Singh Rajput
Vellore Institute of Technology, India

Gotam Singh Lalotra
Government Degree College, Basohli, India

Vinod Kumar
Galgotias University, Greater Noida, India

Pushpendra Kumar
Central University of Jharkhand, India

Harshita Patel

Vellore Institute of Technology, India

Acknowledgment

Scalable Modeling and Efficient Management of IoT Applications is an amazing result of many people's combined efforts and knowledge.

First of all, we would like to express my profound gratitude to each and every author for lending their knowledge, experience, and research to this book. It has been incredibly motivating to see how committed you are to expanding the field of IoT applications.

We owe a debt of gratitude to the reviewers for their insightful comments and recommendations, which have greatly influenced the book's substance and upheld its academic integrity.

We want to express my gratitude to the support personnel and editorial team for their careful effort overseeing the publication process. This project would not have been possible without the professionalism and meticulous attention to detail you have shown.

With special appreciation to the advisory board of this for their encouragement and assistance during the writing of this book. Finally, we want to thank my family and friends for their steadfast understanding and support during the writing and editing stages.

We are grateful to all of the contributors of this book. Thanks to your efforts, this is now a thorough and enlightening resource for students, practitioners, and academics studying IoT applications.

Introduction

The Internet of Things, or IoT, has become a transformative force in today's interconnected world, changing every aspect of our everyday lives, including industries and societies. In a variety of industries, including manufacturing, smart cities, healthcare, and agriculture, the spread of IoT devices, sensors, and networks has opened up previously unheard-of chances for creativity and efficiency.

Enabling scalable modeling and effective administration of Internet of Things applications is critical to this transition. The difficulties in managing these intricate ecosystems are increasing at an exponential rate as the number of linked devices reaches the billions. There is a great deal at stake, from preserving strong security protocols to guaranteeing dependable data transfer and storage.

This book, *Scalable Modeling and Efficient Management of IoT Applications*, provides guidance on how to deal with these difficulties. It offers insights into cutting-edge methods, best practices, and real-world case studies by bringing together a multitude of knowledge from top academics and industry professionals. This book looks to be a priceless resource for everyone interested in IoT, be they a novice, seasoned professional, or academic researcher.

This volume's chapters address a wide range of subjects that are crucial to comprehending and becoming an expert in IoT application efficiency and scalability. In addition to discussing cutting-edge methods for managing data security and privacy in an increasingly linked environment, they also delve into tactics for optimizing resource allocation and energy usage and advanced modeling techniques for Internet of Things systems.

As we stand on the precipice of a new era defined by the Internet of Things, the insights contained within these pages will be instrumental in shaping the future of IoT applications. I commend the editors and contributors for their dedication to advancing our understanding of this dynamic field and for their commitment to sharing their knowledge with the broader community.

Scalable Modeling and Efficient Management of IoT Applications looks to be a valuable travel companion, whether you are looking for helpful advice for implementing scalable IoT solutions or are excited to explore the boundaries of IoT research. I invite you to explore its pages, interact with its concepts, and help shape the further development of Internet of Things technology.

Dhamendra Singh Rajput
Vellore Institute of Technology, India

Gotam Singh Lalotra
Government Degree College, Basohli, India

Vinod Kumar
Galgotias University, Greater Noida, India

Pushpendra Kumar
Central University of Jharkhand, India

Harshita Patel
Vellore Institute of Technology, India

Introduction

1. INTRODUCTION

The way we connect with the physical world is being revolutionized by the Internet of Things (IoT). The Internet of Things (IoT) transforms common things into intelligent devices with data gathering and communication capabilities by integrating computational power and connectivity into them. With billions of sensors, devices, and systems connected, this network of networks provides unmatched insight and control, spurring innovation in a variety of industries, including smart cities, smart homes, industrial automation, and healthcare. To fully utilize the promise of IoT applications, advanced methods for scalable modeling and effective administration are required due to the exponential growth of IoT devices and data volume. IoT poses major hurdles as it grows, especially in the areas of scalable modeling and effective management.

Designing systems with scalability in mind ensures that they can handle the exponential rise of IoT devices and data without sacrificing functionality. The basic goals of effective management are to maximize resources, guarantee data integrity, and continue to run smoothly under changing circumstances. Figure 1 depicts the essential elements of the Internet of Things (IoT) in visual form. This chapter offers a thorough overview of these crucial topics, highlighting their significance within the larger IoT ecosystem and laying the groundwork for in-depth discussions in the parts that follow.

Figure 1. Key components of IoT

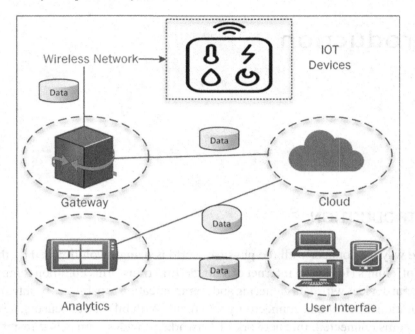

2. THE GROWTH AND IMPACT OF IOT

2.1 Rapid Expansion of IoT

The Internet of Things (IoT) has grown at an unprecedented rate due to developments in data analytics, wireless connectivity, and sensor technologies. Forecasts indicate that by 2025, there will be more than 75 billion linked IoT devices, demonstrating the vast scope and impact of this technology (Statista, 2021). The need for intelligent systems that boost productivity, lower operating expenses, and enhance user experiences across a variety of industries is driving this rise.

IoT has an influence on societal and economic aspects in addition to going much beyond technology innovation. IoT, for example, makes it possible to establish "smart factories" in the industrial sector, where networked systems improve production procedures, streamline supply chains, and lower downtime through preventative maintenance (Gilchrist, 2016). IoT enables precision farming in agriculture, where sensors track crop health, weather patterns, and soil conditions to maximize productivity and minimize resource usage (Wolfert et al., 2017). IoT applications change patient care in the healthcare industry by enhancing results and operational efficiency. Examples of these applications include wearable health devices, remote patient monitoring, and smart hospital systems (Hassanalieragh et al., 2015).

2.2 Economic and Societal Impact

The economic sphere is also affected by IoT, since it stimulates innovation, increases production, and creates new company prospects. McKinsey & Company (2020) asserts that via enhancing operational efficiency, opening up new services, and encouraging data-driven decision-making, IoT has the potential to provide considerable economic value across a range of sectors. IoT, for instance, may automate inventory management, save costs, and speed up delivery by streamlining supply chain operations through real-time tracking, predictive analytics, and automated inventory management (Wamba & Akter, 2019).

In terms of society, IoT helps create "smart cities," which are communities with networked systems that improve urban life by encouraging citizen participation, streamlining resource management, and enhancing public services. In order to create sustainable and habitable urban settings, smart city efforts use IoT technology to monitor environmental conditions, control traffic flow, and increase energy efficiency (Zanella et al., 2014).

In addition, IoT is essential for tackling global issues including food security, healthcare accessibility, and climate change. To help with disaster management and environmental conservation efforts, IoT-based environmental monitoring systems, for example, can offer real-time data on air quality, water levels, and meteorological conditions (Wang et al., 2020). IoT applications in the healthcare industry can expand access to medical services to poor and rural areas, closing access gaps and enhancing general public health outcomes (Islam et al., 2015).

3. CHALLENGES IN IOT APPLICATIONS

Even though the Internet of Things has a lot of potential, managing and deploying it will be difficult. There are several facets to these issues, including technological, operational, and strategic aspects. The main obstacles consist of:

3.1 Scalability

In the Internet of Things, scalability is a basic concern because of the rapid expansion of devices and data. It's crucial to make sure IoT systems can grow effectively to handle more devices and bigger data volumes without experiencing performance degradation. In order to achieve scalability, problems with computing loads, data storage capacity, and network congestion must be resolved (Atzori et al., 2010).

For instance, the enormous amount of data produced by IoT devices may be too much for conventional centralized cloud architectures to manage, resulting in bottlenecks and latency problems. Edge computing, which distributes data processing closer to the source of data generation to reduce latency and network congestion, has emerged as a scalable option to solve this (Shi et al., 2016). Furthermore, managing the massive amounts of data created by IoT devices requires scalable data management approaches like distributed databases and decentralized storage systems (Nath et al., 2020).

3.2 Interoperability

In IoT ecosystems, where devices are frequently heterogeneous and have different operating systems, data formats, and communication protocols, interoperability is yet another crucial problem. According to Bandyopadhyay and Sen (2011), constructing cohesive and effective Internet of Things systems requires ensuring smooth interaction and data flow among these diverse components.

Interoperability in the Internet of Things is greatly aided by standards and protocols. For example, MQTT (Message Queuing Telemetry Transport) is a widely-used protocol in Internet of Things applications for lightweight, publish-subscribe messaging that facilitates effective communication between devices with constrained processing and bandwidth (Hunkeler et al., 2008). In a similar vein, middleware platforms like OpenIoT and Node-RED offer integration frameworks that make it easier to create and implement interoperable IoT solutions (Perera et al., 2014).

3.3 Security and Privacy

Sensitive data is often included in the massive amounts of data created by IoT devices, thus security and privacy are top priorities. IoT systems are prone to many dangers by nature, such as malicious attacks, illegal access, and data breaches. To preserve confidence and protect sensitive data, it is essential to guarantee the security and privacy of IoT data (Roman et al., 2013).

IoT security presents a variety of security problems, including data security, network security, and device security. For example, IoT devices frequently have little processing power, which makes it difficult to put strong security measures like intrusion detection systems and encryption in place (Fernandes et al., 2017). Furthermore, the deployment of uniform security rules and procedures is made more difficult by the dispersed and diverse character of Internet of Things networks.

The massive data collecting and processing operations in the Internet of Things give rise to privacy issues. Without their express agreement, users' behavioral and personal data may be gathered and analyzed, creating moral and legal quandaries (Sicari et al., 2015). Using data anonymization techniques, guaranteeing user permission and management over data, and adhering to privacy laws like the General Data Protection Regulation (GDPR) are all necessary to address privacy concerns in the Internet of Things (European Parliament, 2016).

3.4 Resource Management

Sustaining IoT system performance and sustainability requires effective resource management, including electricity, bandwidth, and computing power. IoT devices frequently have limited power and processing capacity, making them resource-constrained. In order to balance availability and demand, this calls for dynamic allocation and optimization techniques (Zanella et al., 2014).

Since many IoT devices run on batteries and are placed in hard-to-reach places, energy management is very important. According to Centenaro et al. (2016), energy-efficient communication protocols like Bluetooth Low Energy (BLE) and Low Power Wide Area Networks (LPWAN) are crucial for extending device battery life and guaranteeing sustainable operation. Moreover, methods like energy harvesting and duty cycling can lower energy usage and increase the lifespan of Internet of Things devices (Elsts et al., 2018).

Another crucial component of IoT resource management is bandwidth control. As more devices become linked, effective bandwidth management and allocation are necessary to avoid network congestion and guarantee dependable communication. Effective management of bandwidth resources may be achieved by methods including traffic shaping, data compression, Quality of Service (QoS) prioritizing, and data compression (Gupta et al., 2016).

3.5 Data Management

Strong data management techniques are necessary due to the constant stream of data coming from IoT devices. Real-time data processing, scalable storage options, sophisticated data analytics, and guaranteeing data quality and integrity are all necessary for effective data management in the Internet of Things (Gubbi et al., 2013).

For Internet of Things applications that need to react instantly, including industrial automation and driverless cars, real-time data processing is essential. IoT systems that need low-latency decision-making might benefit from stream processing frameworks like Apache Kafka and Apache Flink, which provide real-time data intake, processing, and analysis (Kreps et al., 2011).

To handle the enormous amounts of data produced by Internet of Things devices, scalable storage solutions are required. According to Ghemawat et al. (2003), distributed storage systems, like Amazon S3 and the Hadoop Distributed File System (HDFS), offer scalable and fault-tolerant storage solutions that can manage the high data throughput and storage needs of Internet of Things applications.

To extract useful insights from IoT data, advanced data analytics techniques such as machine learning and big data analytics are necessary. IoT data patterns and trends may be analyzed by machine learning algorithms, allowing for anomaly identification, predictive maintenance, and customized services (Zhou et al., 2019). Large-scale data processing and analysis are supported by big data analytics platforms like Google BigQuery and Apache Spark, which enable data-driven decision-making in the Internet of Things (Zaharia et al., 2010).

In IoT, ensuring data integrity and quality is also essential. IoT device data can be noisy, lacking, or inconsistent, therefore rigorous data cleaning and validation procedures are required. IoT application dependability may be increased and data quality can be enhanced with the use of strategies including data fusion, anomaly detection, and data reconciliation (Aggarwal et al., 2013).

4. OBJECTIVES OF SCALABLE MODELING AND EFFICIENT MANAGEMENT

To address the challenges outlined above, advanced modeling and management techniques are required. The primary objectives in the context of IoT include:

4.1 Developing Scalable Architectures

One of the primary goals is to design Internet of Things systems that can easily grow and adapt to the rising number of devices and data traffic while preserving dependability and performance. According to Bonomi et al. (2012), scalable architectures are distributed and modular systems that are capable of managing the dynamic nature of IoT contexts.

One scalable design method is microservices architecture, in which programs are made up of independently deployable, loosely connected services. This facilitates the creation of reliable and maintainable Internet of Things systems by allowing for the flexible scaling of individual components in response to demand (Newman, 2015). In a similar vein, serverless computing provides an affordable and scalable option for Internet of Things applications by having cloud providers handle the infrastructure and dynamically scale resources based on demand (Roberts, 2017).

4.2 Ensuring Efficient Resource Utilization

Sustaining the functionality and longevity of IoT systems requires putting ideas for efficient resource utilization into practice. This includes dynamic bandwidth control, energy-efficient protocols, and practical data storage options (Gupta et al., 2016).

Zigbee and Z-Wave are two examples of energy-efficient protocols that are intended to reduce power usage and increase the battery life of Internet of Things devices. According to Shang et al. (2015), these protocols are appropriate for low-power communication applications including industrial monitoring and home automation. IoT systems may distribute and optimize bandwidth resources depending on application needs and real-time conditions thanks to dynamic bandwidth management techniques like network slicing and adaptive bitrate streaming (Foukalas et al., 2019).

Using hierarchical and distributed storage systems that can manage the massive data requirements of Internet of Things applications is a key component of effective data storage solutions. Storage resource optimization and latency reduction are possible with hierarchical storage management, where data is processed and stored at several tiers (such as edge, fog, and cloud) (Vaquero & Rodero-Merino, 2014).

4.3 Enhancing Security and Privacy

It is imperative to implement strong security frameworks and privacy-preserving techniques in order to safeguard IoT data and guarantee safe network interactions. According to Sicari et al. (2015), this entails putting security measures in place at several levels, including the device, network, and application.

Device-level security is concerned with defending individual Internet of Things devices from virus, physical manipulation, and illegal access. IoT device security requires methods like hardware-based security modules, secure boot, and device authentication (Alrawais et al., 2017). Securing communication channels and thwarting assaults like denial-of-service (DoS) attacks, man-in-the-middle attacks, and eavesdropping are all part of network-level security. In order to guarantee safe network connections in the Internet of Things, intrusion detection systems, virtual private networks (VPNs), and encryption are essential (Rayes & Salam, 2019).

Application-level security addresses the protection of IoT applications and data from vulnerabilities and breaches. This includes implementing secure coding practices, access control mechanisms, and data encryption. Privacy-preserving techniques, such as data anonymization, differential privacy, and user consent management, are essential for protecting user data and ensuring compliance with privacy regulations (Zhou et al., 2017).

4.4 Facilitating Interoperability

Building cohesive and effective IoT ecosystems requires developing standards and protocols that provide interoperability and integration across various IoT devices and systems (Kortuem et al., 2010).

Adopting standard data formats, integration frameworks, and communication protocols can help achieve interoperability. Constrained Application Protocol (CoAP) is a lightweight protocol that facilitates effective communication and interoperability in Internet of Things networks, particularly in devices with limited resources (Shelby et al., 2014). IoT devices and apps may describe and exchange data in standardized ways using formats like XML (eXtensible Markup Language) and JSON (JavaScript Object Notation) (Marrs, 2016).

IoT middleware platforms and other integration frameworks offer services and solutions for coordinating, administering, and integrating disparate IoT systems and devices. By abstracting the complexities of data integration and device connectivity, these platforms make it easier to create and implement interoperable Internet of Things solutions (Zhou et al., 2019).

4.5 Advancing Data Management Techniques

To manage the massive amounts of data created by Internet of Things applications, techniques for real-time data processing, advanced analytics, and effective storage must be developed (Tsai et al., 2014).

Analyzing and responding to data as it is created is known as real-time data processing, and it is used to assist applications like smart grid systems and autonomous cars that need quick decisions. Low-latency decision-making in the Internet of Things is made possible by stream processing frameworks like Apache Storm and Spark Streaming, which offer tools for ingesting, processing, and analyzing real-time data streams (Toshniwal et al., 2014).

To get useful insights from IoT data, advanced analytics methods like artificial intelligence (AI) and machine learning are crucial. IoT data patterns and trends may be analyzed by machine learning algorithms, allowing for anomaly detection, predictive maintenance, and customized services. By offering sophisticated skills for data analysis and decision-making, AI approaches like deep learning and reinforcement learning can significantly improve Internet of Things applications (Zhou et al., 2019).

To handle the enormous volumes of data produced by Internet of Things devices, effective storage options are required. The high data throughput and storage needs of Internet of Things applications may be met by distributed storage systems like HDFS and Cassandra, which offer scalable and fault-tolerant storage choices.

Storage resource optimization and latency reduction are possible with hierarchical storage management, where data is processed and stored at several tiers (such as edge, fog, and cloud) (Vaquero & Rodero-Merino, 2014).

5. SCALABLE IOT ARCHITECTURES

Developing scalable architectures is essential to manage the increasing complexity, data volume, and connectivity needs as the number of IoT devices continues to expand dramatically. The scalability and efficiency of IoT systems are supported by a variety of architectural models and design ideas that are examined in this segment.

5.1 Architectural Models for IoT

Several architectural models have been proposed for IoT systems, each with unique characteristics and advantages. Key models include:

5.1.1 Centralized Architecture

A central server or cloud platform gathers and processes data from devices in a centralized Internet of things architecture. Although this architecture makes management and control easier, when the number of devices and data volume increase, scalability problems may arise (Bonomi et al., 2012).

Applications like smart city platforms and industrial monitoring systems, which demand large-scale data processing and analytics, are well-suited for centralized architectures. Nevertheless, single points of failure, bandwidth restrictions, and latency might be issues.

5.1.2 Distributed Architecture

In distributed IoT systems, a number of nodes gather, process, and distribute data throughout the network. By dispersing the burden and preventing single points of failure, this architecture improves fault tolerance and scalability (Bonomi et al., 2012).

Applications like autonomous cars and smart grids that demand real-time processing, quick reactions, and local decision-making are ideal candidates for distributed architectures. They could, however, run into issues with security, synchronization, and consistency of data.

5.1.3 Hybrid Architecture

Hybrid Internet of Things designs offer a balanced approach to scalability, performance, and reliability by combining components of distributed and centralized approaches. Both central and peripheral levels of data processing and decision-making are supported by this approach (Vaquero & Rodero-Merino, 2014).

Applications that need to handle large amounts of data and respond quickly, such intelligent transportation networks and healthcare systems, are best suited for hybrid architectures. They are resilient and flexible, but their design and administration may be more complicated.

6. DESIGN PRINCIPLES FOR SCALABLE IOT SYSTEMS

To support the development of scalable IoT systems, several key design principles should be considered:

6.1 Modularity

By dividing the system into smaller, more manageable parts or modules that can be designed, implemented, and scaled separately, modular design allows for greater flexibility. According to Newman (2015), this strategy improves scalability, maintainability, and adaptability.

For instance, separate modules in a smart home system can manage various tasks like temperature management, lighting control, and security monitoring. The ability to grow and upgrade each module individually makes it possible to integrate new devices and services with ease (Rayes & Salam, 2019).

6.2 Service-Oriented Architecture (SOA)

A design approach known as service-oriented architecture (SOA) arranges system parts as loosely connected services that communicate via well defined interfaces. Interoperability, reusability, and scalability are encouraged by this strategy (Papazoglou & van den Heuvel, 2007).

By offering a standard foundation for communication and interaction, SOA in the Internet of Things might make it easier to integrate various devices and applications. For example, autonomous development and deployment of traffic control, garbage collection, and energy monitoring services allows for flexible scalability and integration within a smart city platform (Zanella et al., 2014).

6.3 Microservices Architecture

By breaking down programs into tiny, independently deployable services that can be scaled and maintained independently, microservices architecture expands on the concepts of service-oriented architecture (SOA). Every microservice concentrates on a particular purpose and employs lightweight protocols to interact with other services (Newman, 2015).

By providing fine-grained scaling and fault separation, microservices architecture in the Internet of Things facilitates the construction of scalable and robust systems. Microservices, for instance, may control operations like order processing, inventory monitoring, and payment processing in an e-commerce platform with IoT-enabled inventory management, enabling flexible scaling and reliable performance (Newman, 2015).

6.4 Edge Computing

By processing data closer to the point of creation, edge computing lowers latency, bandwidth consumption, and network congestion. IoT applications that demand real-time processing and low latency responses would benefit most from this strategy (Shi et al., 2016).

For instance, edge computing allows real-time equipment monitoring and management in smart manufacturing systems, which improves operational efficiency and reaction times. According to Kumari et al. (2020), the system can improve safety and productivity by promptly identifying and addressing abnormalities using local data processing at the edge.

6.5 Serverless Computing

A cloud computing architecture known as "serverless computing" allows cloud providers to autonomously scale resources in response to demand and manage the infrastructure. With this method, developers may concentrate on creating code and implementing features rather than worrying about server administration (Roberts, 2017).

Serverless computing in the Internet of Things facilitates the scalable and economical implementation of event-driven applications. Serverless functions, for example, can evaluate sensor data in a smart building system and then initiate actions, such changing the HVAC or lighting settings based on occupancy and outside circumstances. According to Roberts (2017), the serverless paradigm guarantees that resources are scaled and allocated effectively in response to current demands.

7. APPLICATIONS AND CASE STUDIES

We will examine a number of real-world applications and case studies from various fields to demonstrate the ideas of scalable modeling and effective management in the Internet of Things. These illustrations show how cutting-edge methods and approaches are used to overcome obstacles and accomplish the previously mentioned goals.

7.1 Smart Cities

By maximizing resource management, enhancing public services, and encouraging citizen involvement, smart cities use IoT technology to improve urban living. Intelligent transportation systems, intelligent lighting, waste management, and environmental monitoring are some of the IoT applications seen in smart cities (Zanella et al., 2014).

For instance, a complete smart city effort that incorporates IoT technology across several sectors has been implemented in Barcelona, Spain. By monitoring and controlling traffic flow, the city lowers congestion and boosts the effectiveness of transportation through the use of IoT sensors. By adjusting street lighting in response to current conditions, smart lighting systems lower operating costs and energy usage. Garbage collection routes and timetables are optimized using IoT-enabled trash management systems, increasing efficiency and lessening environmental effect (Chourabi et al., 2012).

7.2 Industrial IoT

The application of IoT technology to improve industrial and manufacturing processes is known as industrial IoT, or IIoT. Predictive maintenance, asset tracking, and process optimization are examples of IIoT applications that increase productivity, safety, and efficiency (Gilchrist, 2016).

For example, Predix, an IIoT platform developed by General Electric (GE), links and tracks industrial equipment in a variety of sectors. Predix reduces downtime and facilitates predictive maintenance by gathering and analyzing data from sensors integrated into machines. According to Dawson et al. (2015), the platform further allows real-time monitoring and improvement of industrial operations, hence improving operating efficiency and cutting costs.

7.3 Healthcare

Applications of IoT in healthcare have the potential to completely transform patient care by enhancing results and streamlining operations. Wearable medical technology, smart hospital systems, and remote patient monitoring are examples of healthcare IoT (Hassanalieragh et al., 2015).

An example of an Internet of Things-based patient monitoring system that gathers and analyzes data from wearable sensors is Massachusetts General Hospital in the United States. Real-time vital sign monitoring by the system allows for the early identification of health problems and prompt care. In order to maximize patient comfort and lower the danger of pressure ulcers, the hospital also employs Internet of Things-enabled smart beds that adapt automatically (Islam et al., 2015).

7.4 Agriculture

Precision farming, sometimes referred to as smart agriculture, uses the Internet of Things (IoT) to improve yield optimization, resource efficiency, and crop management. Soil moisture sensors, weather monitoring systems, and controlled irrigation systems are examples of IoT technology in agriculture (Wolfert et al., 2017).

For example, the well-known agricultural machinery manufacturer John Deere has created the John Deere Operations Center, an Internet of Things-based precision farming platform. Through the collection and analysis of data from sensors and machines, the platform offers farmers information into weather patterns, crop health, and soil conditions. This makes it possible to optimize farming operations and make decisions based on data, which raises productivity and increases resource efficiency (Wolfert et al., 2017).

8. FUTURE TRENDS AND DIRECTIONS

The future of scalable modeling and effective management in IoT applications is being shaped by a number of new trends and directions that are developing as IoT continues to develop. Among these tendencies are:

8.1 Edge Computing

A new concept called "edge computing" includes processing data closer to the point of origination instead of depending on cloud servers that are centralized. Edge computing is ideal for Internet of Things applications that need real-time processing and low-latency responses as it lowers latency, bandwidth consumption, and network congestion (Shi et al., 2016).

For instance, edge computing allows for the real-time processing of sensor data in autonomous cars to assist essential operations like collision avoidance, object identification, and navigation. Autonomous cars can improve safety and performance by processing data locally at the edge, enabling them to make judgments instantly without depending on cloud connectivity (Kumari et al., 2020).

8.2 5G Networks

It is anticipated that the introduction of 5G networks would greatly improve the functionality and efficiency of Internet of Things devices. According to Shafi et al. (2017), 5G networks provide large device connectivity, high-speed, low-latency communication, and support for the scalability and real-time requirements of Internet of Things applications.

For example, 5G networks can facilitate the implementation of dense IoT sensor networks in smart cities, enabling real-time monitoring and control of urban processes like electricity, public safety, and transportation. The creation of sophisticated smart city services and applications is made easier by 5G's high speed and low latency capabilities, which allow for rapid and dependable communication (Zanella et al., 2014).

8.3 Artificial Intelligence and Machine Learning

In order to improve automation, decision-making, and data analysis, machine learning (ML) and artificial intelligence (AI) are being included into Internet of Things (IoT) systems more and more. Large amounts of IoT data may be analyzed using AI and ML approaches, which can also be used to enhance prescriptive and predictive analytics by finding patterns and anomalies (Zhou et al., 2019).

In the healthcare industry, for instance, AI and ML algorithms may evaluate data from electronic health records and wearable medical devices to forecast disease outbreaks, improve treatment regimens, and customize patient care. AI and ML may help predictive maintenance, process optimization, and quality control in industrial IoT, increasing productivity and lowering operating costs (Daugherty et al., 2015).

8.4 Blockchain and Distributed Ledger Technologies

Distributed ledger technologies (DLTs) and blockchain are viable ways to improve the security, transparency, and trustworthiness of Internet of Things networks. Blockchain is appropriate for applications that need safe and transparent data sharing because it offers a decentralized, tamper-resistant ledger for recording and validating transactions (Christidis & Devetsikiotis, 2016).

Blockchain, for example, may offer end-to-end product visibility and traceability in supply chain management, increasing transparency and lowering the risk of fraud and counterfeiting. Blockchain can provide reliable and safe communication between devices in the Internet of Things, guaranteeing data integrity and guarding against tampering and unwanted access (Moin et al., 2019).

8.5 Sustainability and Green IoT

When designing and implementing Internet of Things systems, sustainability and energy efficiency are becoming more and more crucial factors to take into account. The goal of green IoT is to lessen the negative effects of IoT technology on the environment by using eco-friendly designs, sustainable resource management, and energy-efficient practices (Atzori et al., 2017).

Green IoT activities in smart cities, for instance, include the installation of waste management programs, environmental monitoring networks, and energy-efficient lighting systems. By maximizing water use, cutting chemical inputs, and limiting environmental effect, green IoT technologies in agriculture promote sustainable farming practices (Wolfert et al., 2017).

9. CONCLUSION

The Internet of Things, or IoT, is revolutionizing our interactions with the real world by enabling intelligent systems that improve productivity, quality of life, and efficiency in a variety of fields. However, scalable modeling and effective management face substantial hurdles due to the Internet of Things' fast expansion and complexity. In order to overcome these obstacles, sophisticated methods and strategies that consider the dynamic and diverse character of IoT ecosystems are needed. The main goals and problems of scalable modeling and effective administration in Internet of Things applications have been outlined in this chapter. We have demonstrated the practical implementations of these ideas as well as their potential for future advancements by examining rising trends and real-world applications.

We will go into these subjects in more detail in the upcoming sections of this book, looking at the most recent methods, research, and case studies that help to build scalable and effective IoT systems.

Vinod Kumar

Galgotias University, Greater Noida, India

Gotam Singh Lalotra

Government Degree College, Basohli, India

REFERENCES

Aggarwal, C. C., Ashish, N., & Sheth, A. (2013). The Internet of Things: A Survey from the Data-Centric Perspective. In *Managing and Mining Sensor Data* (pp. 383–428). Springer. DOI: 10.1007/978-1-4614-6309-2_12

Alrawais, A., Alhothaily, A., Hu, C., & Cheng, X. (2017). Fog Computing for the Internet of Things: Security and Privacy Issues. *IEEE Internet Computing*, 21(2), 34–42. DOI: 10.1109/MIC.2017.37

Atzori, L., Iera, A., & Morabito, G. (2010). The Internet of Things: A Survey. *Computer Networks*, 54(15), 2787–2805. DOI: 10.1016/j.comnet.2010.05.010

Bandyopadhyay, D., & Sen, J. (2011). Internet of Things: Applications and Challenges in Technology and Standardization. *Wireless Personal Communications*, 58(1), 49–69. DOI: 10.1007/s11277-011-0288-5

Bonomi, F., Milito, R., Zhu, J., & Addepalli, S. (2012). Fog Computing and Its Role in the Internet of Things. In *Proceedings of the First Edition of the MCC Workshop on Mobile Cloud Computing* (pp. 13-16). DOI: 10.1145/2342509.2342513

Centenaro, M., Vangelista, L., Zanella, A., & Zorzi, M. (2016). Long-Range Communications in Unlicensed Bands: The Rising Stars in the IoT and Smart City Scenarios. *IEEE Wireless Communications*, 23(5), 60–67. DOI: 10.1109/MWC.2016.7721743

Chourabi, H., Nam, T., Walker, S., Gil-Garcia, J. R., Mellouli, S., Nahon, K., & Scholl, H. J. (2012). Understanding Smart Cities: An Integrative Framework. In *Proceedings of the 45th Hawaii International Conference on System Sciences* (pp. 2289-2297).

Christidis, K., & Devetsikiotis, M. (2016). Blockchains and Smart Contracts for the Internet of Things. *IEEE Access : Practical Innovations, Open Solutions*, 4, 2292–2303. DOI: 10.1109/ACCESS.2016.2566339

Daugherty, P., Banerjee, P., Negm, W., & Alter, A. E. (2015). *Driving Unconventional Growth through the Industrial Internet of Things*. Accenture.

Elsts, A., Fafoutis, X., Oikonomou, G., Piechocki, R., & Craddock, I. (2018). An Energy Efficient IoT Data Collection System for Structural Health Monitoring. *IEEE Internet of Things Journal*, 5(6), 4943–4954.

European Parliament. (2016). General Data Protection Regulation (GDPR). Retrieved from https://gdpr-info.eu/

Fernandes, E., Rahmati, A., Paupore, R., Simion, S., Fernandes, D., Jung, J., & Prakash, A. (2017). FlowFence: Practical Data Protection for Emerging IoT Application Frameworks. In *Proceedings of the 25th USENIX Security Symposium* (pp. 531-548).

Foukalas, F., Gazis, V., & Glitho, R. (2019). Network Slicing in 5G: Survey and Challenges. *IEEE Communications Magazine*, 55(5), 94–100. DOI: 10.1109/MCOM.2017.1600951

Ghemawat, S., Gobioff, H., & Leung, S. T. (2003). The Google File System. In *Proceedings of the Nineteenth ACM Symposium on Operating Systems Principles* (pp. 29-43). DOI: 10.1145/945445.945450

Gilchrist, A. (2016). *Industry 4.0: The Industrial Internet of Things*. Apress. DOI: 10.1007/978-1-4842-2047-4

Gubbi, J., Buyya, R., Marusic, S., & Palaniswami, M. (2013). Internet of Things (IoT): A Vision, Architectural Elements, and Future Directions. *Future Generation Computer Systems*, 29(7), 1645–1660. DOI: 10.1016/j.future.2013.01.010

Gupta, A., Harsh, A., & Kumar, V. (2016). Bandwidth Management Techniques for Large Scale Systems. *Procedia Computer Science*, 78, 13–18.

Hassanalieragh, M., Page, A., Soyata, T., Sharma, G., Aktas, M. S., Mateos, G., & Andreescu, S. (2015). Health Monitoring and Management Using Internet-of-Things (IoT) Sensing with Cloud-Based Processing: Opportunities and Challenges. In *Proceedings of the 2015 IEEE International Conference on Services Computing* (pp. 285-292). DOI: 10.1109/SCC.2015.47

Hunkeler, U., Truong, H. L., & Stanford-Clark, A. (2008). MQTT-S—A Publish/Subscribe Protocol for Wireless Sensor Networks. In 2008 3rd International Conference on Communication Systems Software and Middleware and Workshops (pp. 791-798).

Islam, S. M. R., Kwak, D., Kabir, M. H., Hossain, M., & Kwak, K. S. (2015). The Internet of Things for Health Care: A Comprehensive Survey. *IEEE Access: Practical Innovations, Open Solutions*, 3, 678–708. DOI: 10.1109/ACCESS.2015.2437951

Kortuem, G., Kawsar, F., Fitton, D., & Sundramoorthy, V. (2010). Smart Objects as Building Blocks for the Internet of Things. *IEEE Internet Computing*, 14(1), 44–51. DOI: 10.1109/MIC.2009.143

Kumari, P., De, D., & Das, M. L. (2020). Multi-Layer Security of IoT-Enabled Autonomous Vehicles in a 5G Environment. *IEEE Internet of Things Journal*, 7(5), 4178–4187.

Marrs, T. (2016). *JSON at Work*. O'Reilly Media, Inc.

Moin, A., Karim, M., Khan, A., Akram, R., & Abbasi, M. (2019). Blockchain Based Decentralized IoT Framework. In *Proceedings of the 2019 IEEE International Conference on Electronics, Information, and Communication* (pp. 1-4).

Newman, S. (2015). *Building Microservices*. O'Reilly Media, Inc.

Rayes, A., & Salam, S. (2019). *Internet of Things from Hype to Reality: The Road to Digitization*. Springer.

Roberts, M. (2017). *Serverless Architectures on AWS*. Manning Publications.

Shafi, M., Molisch, A. F., Tufvesson, F., Benjebbour, A., Wunder, G., Sahin, O., & Hälsig, S. (2017). 5G: A Tutorial Overview of Standards, Trials, Challenges, Deployment, and Practice. *IEEE Journal on Selected Areas in Communications*, 35(6), 1201–1221. DOI: 10.1109/JSAC.2017.2692307

Shang, W., Wahle, S., Puzar, G., & Strassner, J. (2015). Low-Power Wireless Communication for the Internet of Things: A Comparative Study. *IEEE Communications Magazine*, 53(10), 90–97.

Shelby, Z., Hartke, K., Bormann, C., & Frank, B. (2014). The Constrained Application Protocol (CoAP). IETF RFC 7252.

Shi, W., Cao, J., Zhang, Q., Li, Y., & Xu, L. (2016). Edge Computing: Vision and Challenges. *IEEE Internet of Things Journal*, 3(5), 637–646. DOI: 10.1109/JIOT.2016.2579198

Sicari, S., Rizzardi, A., Grieco, L. A., & Coen-Porisini, A. (2015). Security, Privacy and Trust in Internet of Things: The Road Ahead. *Computer Networks*, 76, 146–164. DOI: 10.1016/j.comnet.2014.11.008

Toshniwal, A., Taneja, S., Shukla, A., Ramasamy, K., Patel, J., Kulkarni, S., & Fu, M. (2014). Storm@Twitter. In *Proceedings of the 2014 ACM SIGMOD International Conference on Management of Data* (pp. 147-156). DOI: 10.1145/2588555.2595641

Tsai, C. W., Lai, C. F., Chao, H. C., & Vasilakos, A. V. (2014). Big Data Analytics: A Survey. *Journal of Big Data*, 1(1), 1–32.

Vaquero, L. M., & Rodero-Merino, L. (2014). Finding Your Way in the Fog: Towards a Comprehensive Definition of Fog Computing. *Computer Communication Review*, 44(5), 27–32. DOI: 10.1145/2677046.2677052

Wolfert, S., Ge, L., Verdouw, C., & Bogaardt, M. J. (2017). Big Data in Smart Farming—A Review. *Agricultural Systems*, 153, 69–80. DOI: 10.1016/j. agsy.2017.01.023

Zaharia, M., Chowdhury, M., Franklin, M. J., Shenker, S., & Stoica, I. (2010). Spark: Cluster Computing with Working Sets. In *Proceedings of the 2nd USENIX Conference on Hot Topics in Cloud Computing* (pp. 10-10).

Zanella, A., Bui, N., Castellani, A., Vangelista, L., & Zorzi, M. (2014). Internet of Things for Smart Cities. *IEEE Internet of Things Journal*, 1(1), 22–32. DOI: 10.1109/JIOT.2014.2306328

Zhou, J., Cao, Z., Dong, X., Lin, X., & Li, X. (2017). Securing mHealth Apps in Bring-Your-Own-Device Era: A Survey. *IEEE Access : Practical Innovations, Open Solutions*, 5, 26508–26536.

Zhou, X., Li, H., Liu, X., Zhang, Z., & Xu, F. (2019). Edge Computing in IoT: Technologies, Applications, and Challenges. *IEEE Internet of Things Journal*, 6(3), 4691–4709.

Chapter 1
Predictive and Prescriptive Analytics for IoT
Unlocking Insights

Ravi Mohan Sharma

https://orcid.org/0000-0001-5750-0450

Makhanlal Chaturvedi National University of Journalism and Communication, India

Sunita Dwivedi

Makhanlal Chaturvedi National University of Journalism and Communication, India

Vinod Kumar

https://orcid.org/0000-0002-3495-2320

Galgotias University, India

ABSTRACT

In today's information era, the use of internet of things (IOT) technologies and associated devices has multiplied, and they are now present in every sector. IOT technologies use sensors to sense data from the environment of deployment. Sensors generate a great deal of data that has valuable insights. Therefore, this chapter explores the intersection of predictive and prescriptive analytics within the context of the IoT. The chapter delves into the theoretical foundations, technological advancements, and practical applications of predictive and prescriptive analytics in the IoT domain. By understanding how these analytics techniques work synergistically, organisations can harness the power of IoT data to make informed decisions, optimize operations, and create value.

DOI: 10.4018/979-8-3693-1686-3.ch001

INTRODUCTION

Predictive analytics is a branch of advanced analytics that uses historical data, statistical algorithms, and machine learning techniques to identify the likelihood of future outcomes based on historical data. In simpler terms, predictive analytics predicts what might happen in the future based on patterns found in past and present data. It's widely used in various fields including business, finance, healthcare, and marketing for making informed decisions and optimizing processes (Bhatia et al., 2022).

Predictive analytics (Kumar & Lalotra,2021) in the context of the Internet of Things (IoT) involves leveraging data generated by IoT devices and sensors to predict future events or trends. By applying sophisticated algorithms and machine learning techniques to IoT data, businesses and organizations can anticipate issues, optimize operations, and improve decision-making processes (Adi et al., 2020).

Prescriptive analytics (Frazzetto et al., 2019) in the context of the Internet of Things (IoT) takes predictive analytics a step further. While predictive analytics predicts what might happen based on historical data and current conditions, prescriptive analytics goes beyond that by suggesting specific actions or strategies to optimize outcomes. It not only predicts future events but also provides recommendations on what should be done to achieve desired results in IoT applications.

The role of IoT in sustainable development for building a Smarter and greener future is today's prime need (Memić, et al. 2022). In the pursuit of a sustainable future, the integration of innovative technologies has become crucial. One such transformative force is the Internet of Things (IoT), which plays a pivotal role in reshaping industries, enhancing efficiency, and promoting sustainable development. IoT refers to the interconnected network of devices, sensors, and systems that communicate and share data, leading to smarter and more efficient processes.

The introduction provides a comprehensive overview of the Internet of Things (IoT), highlighting its exponential growth and the challenges faced due to the vast volume of generated data. It introduces predictive analytics as the practice of using historical data to predict future outcomes, and prescriptive analytics as the process of recommending actions for desired outcomes. An example of predictive analytics in IoT (Kumar & Lalotra, 2023) could be predicting equipment failures based on sensor data trends. Prescriptive analytics, on the other hand, could recommend maintenance schedules or optimal operating conditions to prevent those failures. We discuss the challenges faced by organizations in handling vast IoT data and introduce predictive and prescriptive analytics as solutions.

Table 1 contains the highlighting key differences between predictive and prescriptive analytics in the context of IoT (Internet of Things) (Deshpande, et al., 2019).

Table 1. Predictive and prescriptive analytics in the context of IoT (Internet of Things)

Feature	Predictive Analytics	Prescriptive Analytics
Objective	Forecasts future trends and outcomes based on patterns and historical data.	Recommends actions to optimize outcomes based on predictions and current data.
Focus	Identifying potential future events and trends.	Providing actionable recommendations for decision-making.
Data Usage	Relies on historical and real-time data to make predictions.	Utilizes predictions and current data to suggest optimal actions.
Output	Predictions, probabilities, and likelihoods of future events.	Prescribed actions, recommendations, and decision support.
Timing	Future-oriented, focusing on what might happen.	Present and future-oriented, suggesting what should be done.
Example Applications	Predicting equipment failures, forecasting demand, and anomaly detection (Poornima et al., 2020)	Recommending maintenance schedules, optimizing resource allocation, and suggesting process improvements.
Decision Support	Provides information to support decision-making processes (Divakar et al., 2022).	Offers specific actions or strategies to improve outcomes.
Flexibility	Less prescriptive, leaving room for interpretation and decision-making.	More prescriptive, providing specific guidance for optimal outcomes (Basu, 2013).
Feedback Loop	Typically feeds into decision-making processes and informs strategy.	Integrates feedback from actions taken to continuously improve recommendations.

Predictive analytics and prescriptive analytics are two distinct categories of analytical techniques, each serving different purposes in extracting insights and informing decision-making. Here's an overview of the methods within each category:

Predictive Analytics (Menezes, et al. 2019)

1. **Regression Analysis**
   - **Description:** Predicts a numerical outcome based on the relationship between variables.
   - **Use Cases:** Sales forecasting, demand prediction, financial modeling.
2. **Time Series Analysis**
   - **Description:** Analyzes data points collected over time to identify patterns and trends.
   - **Use Cases:** Stock price forecasting, weather prediction, energy consumption forecasting.
3. **Machine Learning Algorithms**
   - **Description:** Utilizes algorithms to learn patterns from data and make predictions.
   - **Use Cases:** Classification and regression tasks, such as customer churn prediction, fraud detection.

4. **Decision Trees**
   - **Description:** Hierarchical tree-like structures used to make decisions based on input features.
   - **Use Cases:** Customer segmentation, product recommendation systems.
5. **Clustering Analysis**
   - **Description:** Groups similar data points together to identify patterns or associations.
   - **Use Cases:** Market segmentation, anomaly detection.
6. **Neural Networks**
   - **Description:** Mimics the structure and functioning of the human brain to recognize patterns.
   - **Use Cases:** Image and speech recognition, complex pattern analysis.
7. **Ensemble Learning**
   - **Description:** Combines multiple models to improve predictive performance.
   - **Use Cases:** Random Forests, Gradient Boosting for improved accuracy.
8. **ARIMA (AutoRegressive Integrated Moving Average)**
   - **Description:** Models time series data by considering its autocorrelations.
   - **Use Cases:** Financial market analysis, economic forecasting.

Prescriptive Analytics (Vanani & Majidian, 2021)

1. **Optimization Models**
   - **Description:** Identifies the best solution from a set of alternatives by optimizing certain criteria.
   - **Use Cases:** Supply chain optimization, resource allocation.
2. **Simulation Models**
   - **Description:** Mimics the operation of a system over time to assess its behavior under different conditions.
   - **Use Cases:** Risk analysis, process optimization.
3. **Game Theory**
   - **Description:** Analyzes strategic interactions between different entities to predict their decisions.
   - **Use Cases:** Pricing strategy, competitive analysis.
4. **Decision Analysis**
   - **Description:** Evaluates decision-making processes and considers uncertainties and risks.
   - **Use Cases:** Investment decisions, project planning.
5. **Prescriptive Machine Learning**

- **Description:** Recommends actions to optimize outcomes based on predictive models.
- **Use Cases:** Dynamic pricing, personalized marketing.

6. **Expert Systems**
   - **Description:** Utilizes rule-based systems and knowledge bases to make decisions.
   - **Use Cases:** Diagnosis and treatment recommendation in healthcare, troubleshooting systems.
7. **Linear Programming**
   - **Description:** Models real-world problems with linear relationships to optimize resource allocation.
   - **Use Cases:** Supply chain optimization, production scheduling.
8. **Heuristic Methods**
   - **Description:** Uses practical rules of thumb or trial-and-error approaches to find solutions.
   - **Use Cases:** Vehicle routing, job scheduling.

Predictive analytics focuses on forecasting future trends and outcomes, while prescriptive analytics goes a step further by recommending actions to optimize those outcomes. Often, these two types of analytics are used in tandem to create a comprehensive data-driven decision-making process. Figure 1 and Figure 2 shows the more detailed categories of methods for predictive analytics and prescriptive analytics respectively (Lepenioti et al., 2020).

Figure 1. Types of approaches for predictive analytics (Lepenioti et al., 2020)

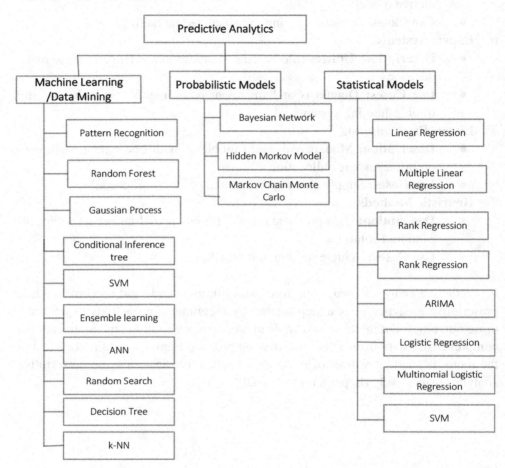

Figure 2. Types of approaches for prescriptive analytics (Lepenioti et al., 2020)

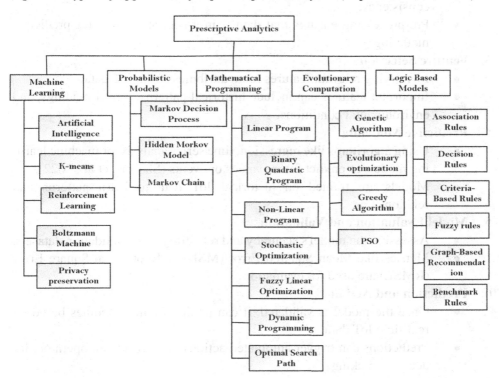

METHODOLOGY

In this section, the methodology for predictive (G. S. Lalotra et al., 2021) and prescriptive analytics for IoT to help in decision-making has been discussed.

Key Components of Predictive Analytics in IoT

1. **Data Collection from IoT Devices**
   - Sensors, actuators, and devices in IoT networks collect vast amounts of data.
   - Data can include temperature readings, motion sensor data, location information, and much more.
2. **Data Pre-processing**

- Raw IoT data often requires cleaning, filtering, and normalization for consistency.
- Pre-processing ensures that data is in a suitable format for predictive modeling.

3. **Feature Selection**
   - Identifying relevant features (data attributes) from IoT data.
   - Important features can include historical patterns, sensor readings, and environmental conditions.

4. **Predictive Modeling**
   - Using algorithms like regression, time series analysis, or machine learning models to predict future values or events (Sharma, et al., 2022).
   - Models are trained on historical IoT data to learn patterns and relationships.

5. **Model Evaluation and Validation**
   - Assessing the model's accuracy and reliability using validation datasets.
   - Metrics like Mean Squared Error (MSE) or Root Mean Square Error (RMSE) are used for evaluation.

6. **Prediction and Action**
   - Once the model is validated, it can predict future outcomes based on real-time IoT data.
   - Predictions can trigger automated actions or alert human operators for decision-making.

Predictive Maintenance in Industrial IoT

Consider a manufacturing plant equipped with various IoT sensors to monitor the health of machines. Predictive maintenance using IoT data can prevent unexpected breakdowns and improve operational efficiency.

1. **Data Collection**
   - Sensors collect data on machine temperature, vibration, and usage patterns.
   - Historical data includes records of machine failures and maintenance activities.

2. **Data Pre-processing**
   - Cleaning the data to remove outliers and inconsistencies.
   - Normalizing sensor readings to a standardized scale.

3. **Feature Selection**

- Relevant features include temperature trends, vibration patterns, and historical failure records.

4. **Predictive Modelling**
   - Machine Learning Algorithm: Decision Trees for classification (healthy vs. faulty state).
   - The model is trained on historical data to identify patterns indicating an impending machine failure.

5. **Model Evaluation and Validation**
   - Validation data, collected from real-time sensors, is used to evaluate the model's accuracy.
   - The model is evaluated based on its ability to correctly predict machine failures.

6. **Prediction and Action**
   - When the model predicts an increased likelihood of machine failure based on real-time sensor data, it triggers a maintenance alert.
   - Maintenance teams receive notifications, enabling them to perform pro-active maintenance, preventing costly breakdowns.

Fundamentals of Predictive Analytics

- **Data Collection and Preprocessing in IoT**

The data accumulated from various sensors are not in appropriate format to directly apply for predictive analysis. Therefore, it needs the proper treatment to make it appropriate for further course of action. Various techniques such as missing value imputation, Data cleaning, Data Transformation, Dimensionality reduction, attribute reduction, normalization etc are key techniques in the process (Onal, et al., 2017).

- *Example*: Temperature, humidity, and vibration data collected from industrial sensors.
- *Preprocessing*: Normalization equation:

$$X_{normalized} = (X - X_{min})/(X_{max} - X_{min})$$

- **Predictive Modeling Techniques**
- *Regression Analysis*: Linear Regression Equation: $y = mx + b$ where m is the slope, b is the intercept.

- *Time Series Forecasting*: ARIMA Equation: $Y_t = c + \phi_1 Y_{t-1} + \theta_1 \epsilon_{t-1} + \epsilon_t$.
- *Machine Learning Algorithms*: Neural Network Equation: $y = f(w_1 x_1 + w_2 x_2 + ... + w_n x_n + b)$ where f is the activation function.

Prescriptive Analytics: From Data to Decisions

Optimization Techniques in IoT

Optimization techniques in the context of the Internet of Things (IoT) involve using mathematical algorithms and computational methods to find the best solution to a problem. These techniques are crucial for maximizing efficiency, minimizing costs, and improving decision-making processes in IoT applications (Bertsimas & Kallus, 2020). Here are some optimization techniques commonly used in IoT scenarios:

Linear programming (LP) is used to optimize a linear objective function subject to a set of linear constraints. In IoT, it can be applied to problems like resource allocation, energy management, and scheduling.

Example: Optimizing the allocation of IoT devices in a smart grid to minimize energy loss during transmission.

Example: Maximize $Z = 3x + 2y$ subject to $2x + y \leq 20$ and $4x - 5y \geq -10$.

- *Genetic Algorithms* Genetic algorithms are a class of evolutionary algorithms inspired by the process of natural selection. They are used for optimization and search problems. Solutions evolve over generations to find the optimal solution.

Steps such as Selection, Crossover, and Mutation operators applied to evolve solutions.
Case: Optimizing the configuration parameters of IoT devices in a smart home system to minimize energy consumption.

- Constraint Programming (CP) solves combinatorial problems over variables that are subject to constraints. It is used in IoT for problems involving complex constraints where variables are interdependent.

Example: Constraint Satisfaction Problem (CSP) with variables and constraints.
Example: Constraint satisfaction problem where variables have constraints like $x \neq y$ and $x < z$.
Case: Optimizing the scheduling of IoT sensors in a wildlife monitoring system considering constraints like power supply, communication range, and data synchronization.

Decision Support Systems (DSS)

Example: DSS integrating weather data and crop health sensors recommends irrigation schedules to farmers.

- Example: A DSS integrating IoT data recommends optimal settings for greenhouse climate control based on predictive analytics.

INTEGRATION OF PREDICTIVE AND PRESCRIPTIVE ANALYTICS IN IOT

• Case Studies

With the help of predictive maintenance (PdM) can spot possible equipment flaws and operating irregularities in advance of failures, allowing for prompt repairs. By reducing the frequency of maintenance, it seeks to reduce unplanned outages and needless preventive maintenance expenses.

- *Predictive Maintenance in Industrial IoT*:

Figure 3. Predictive maintenance by locating the failure point by sensing data

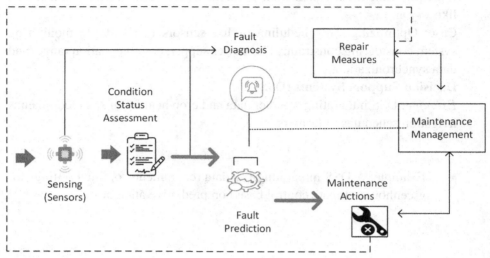

- *Smart Healthcare Systems*:
- *Example*: Predictive model detects anomalies in patient vital signs; prescriptive model recommends medication adjustments.
- *Smart Cities*:
- Map illustrating traffic flow predictions; prescriptive model suggests optimal traffic light timings.

• Ethical and Privacy Implications

The vast amount of data generated by IoT devices has led to significant advancements in various fields, but it has also raised ethical and privacy concerns.

Example: Bias in predictive models leading to unfair treatment, necessitating fairness-aware algorithms.

• *Privacy Concerns*: Ensuring data anonymization using techniques like differential privacy.

TOOLS AND TECHNOLOGIES FOR PREDICTIVE AND PRESCRIPTIVE ANALYTICS IN IOT

• Data Analytics Platforms and Frameworks

When it comes to predictive and prescriptive analytics in the Internet of Things (IoT), several tools and technologies play a crucial role in processing and analyzing vast amounts of data. Here are some tools and frameworks commonly used in this domain:

1. **Apache Spark**
   - **Use:** General-purpose distributed data processing engine.
   - **Why:** Spark is well-suited for processing large-scale data sets and is commonly used for real-time stream processing, which is essential in IoT applications.
2. **TensorFlow and PyTorch**
   - **Use:** Deep learning frameworks.
   - **Why:** These frameworks are used for building and training machine learning models, including neural networks, which are often used in predictive analytics for IoT.
3. **Hadoop**
   - **Use:** Distributed storage and processing of large data sets.
   - **Why:** Hadoop is used for storing and managing the vast amounts of data generated by IoT devices, making it accessible for analytics.
4. **Apache Flink**
   - **Use:** Stream processing framework.
   - **Why:** Flink is designed for real-time analytics on data streams. It is used in IoT applications where timely insights and responses are crucial.
5. **KNIME**
   - **Use:** Open-source data analytics platform.
   - **Why:** KNIME provides a visual interface for building data workflows, making it accessible for users with varying levels of technical expertise.
6. **RapidMiner**
   - **Use:** Data science platform for building predictive analytics models.
   - **Why:** RapidMiner allows users to design, evaluate, and deploy predictive models, making it suitable for IoT applications that require predictive analytics.
7. **Microsoft Azure Machine Learning**
   - **Use:** Cloud-based machine learning service.

- **Why:** Azure ML provides tools for building, training, and deploying machine learning models. It integrates well with other Azure services and can handle large-scale data processing.

8. **IBM Watson IoT Platform**
   - **Use:** IoT platform with analytics capabilities.
   - **Why:** IBM Watson IoT Platform enables the integration of IoT data with advanced analytics, facilitating predictive and prescriptive analytics for IoT applications.

9. **Databricks**
   - **Use:** Unified analytics platform.
   - **Why:** Databricks provides a collaborative environment for big data analytics and machine learning. It often leverages Apache Spark for distributed processing.

10. **Elasticsearch**
    - **Use:** Distributed search and analytics engine.
    - **Why:** Elasticsearch is used for indexing and searching data in real-time. It can be valuable in IoT scenarios where quick access to data is crucial for decision-making.

11. **MATLAB**
    - **Use:** Numerical computing environment.
    - **Why:** MATLAB is widely used for mathematical modeling and simulation. It can be applied to analyze and model data in various IoT applications.

• IoT Protocols and Standards

- *Example*: MQTT message structure - Topic, Message, QoS Level, Retained Flag.

• IoT Security Considerations

- Encryption process flow ensures data integrity and confidentiality.

FUTURE TRENDS AND CHALLENGES

- **Advancements in AI and Machine Learning**
- *Example*: Reinforcement Learning agent controlling smart home devices for energy efficiency (vassakis, et al., 2018).

- *GANs for IoT*: Generating synthetic IoT sensor data for training predictive models.
- **Edge Computing and Real-time Analytics**
- *Example*: Smart grid with edge devices adjusting power distribution based on real-time consumption data.
- *Autonomous Vehicles*: Making split-second decisions using edge analytics.
- **Blockchain Technology**
- Blockchain architecture ensures data integrity in a supply chain.
- **Ethical AI**

    Ethical AI is important because it ensures that artificial intelligence is developed and used in a manner that respects human values, promotes fairness, and minimizes the potential for harm to individuals and society at large. This approach is essential for realizing the full potential of AI while addressing its challenges responsibly. It is important for bias detection and mitigation in machine learning models.

CONCLUSION

This chapter focuses on the principles of predictive and prescriptive analytics approaches, as well as their crucial role in defining IoT's future. It also highlights the current tools and technology for predictive and prescriptive analytics in the IOT field. It emphasizes the significance of continuous research in addressing emergent issues, as well as the significance of ethical considerations in AI-driven decision-making processes. In the subsequent portion, we outline major findings and their implications for the future of IoT analytics. In the developing horizon of predictive and prescriptive analytics for IoT, the significance of continual research, issue solving, and ensuring ethical standards is stressed.

REFERENCES

Adi, E., Anwar, A., Baig, Z., & Zeadally, S. (2020). Machine learning and data analytics for the IoT. *Neural Computing & Applications*, 32(20), 16205–16233. DOI: 10.1007/s00521-020-04874-y

Basu, A. T. A. N. U. (2013). Five pillars of prescriptive analytics success. Analytics Magazine, 8, 12.

Bertsimas, D., & Kallus, N. (2020). From predictive to prescriptive analytics. *Management Science*, 66(3), 1025–1044. DOI: 10.1287/mnsc.2018.3253

Bhatia, J., Italiya, K., Jadeja, K., Kumhar, M., Chauhan, U., Tanwar, S., Bhavsar, M., Sharma, R., Manea, D. L., Verdes, M., & Raboaca, M. S. (2022). An overview of fog data analytics for IoT applications. *Sensors (Basel)*, 23(1), 199. DOI: 10.3390/s23010199 PMID: 36616797

Deshpande, P. S., Sharma, S. C., & Peddoju, S. K. (2019). Predictive and Prescriptive Analytics in Big-data Era. In *Security and Data Storage Aspect in Cloud Computing. Studies in Big Data* (Vol. 52). Springer. DOI: 10.1007/978-981-13-6089-3_5

Divakar, R., Sowmya, P., Suganya, G., & Primya, T. (2022, March). Prescriptive and Predictive Analysis of Intelligible Big Data. In *2022 6th International Conference on Computing Methodologies and Communication (ICCMC)* (pp. 845-851). IEEE.

Frazzetto, D., Nielsen, T. D., Pedersen, T. B., & Šikšnys, L. (2019). Prescriptive analytics: A survey of emerging trends and technologies. *The VLDB Journal*, 28(4), 575–595. DOI: 10.1007/s00778-019-00539-y

Kumar, V., & Lalotra, G. S. (2021). predictive model based on supervised machine learning for heart disease diagnosis. In *2021 IEEE International Conference on Technology, Research, and Innovation for Betterment of Society (TRIBES)* (pp. 1-6). IEEE. DOI: 10.1109/TRIBES52498.2021.9751644

Kumar, V., & Lalotra, G. S. (2023). Blockchain-Enabled Secure Internet of Things. In Research Anthology on Convergence of Blockchain, Internet of Things, and Security (pp. 133-141). IGI Global.

Lalotra, G. S., Kumar, V., & Rajput, D. S. (2021). Predictive performance analysis of ensemble learners on bcd dataset. In *2021 IEEE International Conference on Technology, Research, and Innovation for Betterment of Society (TRIBES)* (pp. 1-6). IEEE. DOI: 10.1109/TRIBES52498.2021.9751648

Lepenioti, K., Bousdekis, A., Apostolou, D., & Mentzas, G. (2020). Prescriptive analytics: Literature review and research challenges. *International Journal of Information Management*, 50, 57–70. DOI: 10.1016/j.ijinfomgt.2019.04.003

Memić, B., Hasković Džubur, A., & Avdagić-Golub, E. (2022). Green IoT: Sustainability environment and technologies. Science. *Engineering and Technology*, 2(1), 24–29.

Menezes, B. C., Kelly, J. D., Leal, A. G., & Le Roux, G. C. (2019). Predictive, prescriptive and detective analytics for smart manufacturing in the information age. *IFAC-PapersOnLine*, 52(1), 568–573. DOI: 10.1016/j.ifacol.2019.06.123

Onal, A. C., Sezer, O. B., Ozbayoglu, M., & Dogdu, E. (2017). Weather data analysis and sensor fault detection using an extended IoT framework with semantics, big data, and machine learning. In *2017 IEEE International Conference on Big Data (Big Data)* (pp. 2037-2046). IEEE. DOI: 10.1109/BigData.2017.8258150

Pattnaik, P., Mishra, S., & Mishra, B. S. P. (2020). Optimization techniques for intelligent iot applications. *Fog, Edge, and Pervasive Computing in Intelligent IoT Driven Applications*, 311-331.

Poornima, S., & Pushpalatha, M. (2020). A survey on various applications of prescriptive analytics. *International Journal of Intelligent Networks*, 1, 76–84. DOI: 10.1016/j.ijin.2020.07.001

Raeesi Vanani, I., & Majidian, S. (2021). Prescriptive Analytics in Internet of Things with Concentration on Deep Learning. In García Márquez, F. P., & Lev, B. (Eds.), *Introduction to Internet of Things in Management Science and Operations Research. International Series in Operations Research & Management Science* (Vol. 311). Springer. DOI: 10.1007/978-3-030-74644-5_2

Sharma, A. K., Sharma, D. M., Purohit, N., Rout, S. K., & Sharma, S. A. (2022). Analytics Techniques: Descriptive Analytics, Predictive Analytics, and Prescriptive Analytics. In Jeyanthi, P. M., Choudhury, T., Hack-Polay, D., Singh, T. P., & Abujar, S. (Eds.), *Decision Intelligence Analytics and the Implementation of Strategic Business Management. EAI/Springer Innovations in Communication and Computing*. Springer. DOI: 10.1007/978-3-030-82763-2_1

Vassakis, K., Petrakis, E., & Kopanakis, I. (2018). Big data analytics: Applications, prospects and challenges. Mobile big data: A roadmap from models to technologies, 3-20.

KEY TERMS AND DEFINITIONS

IoT: This refers to the network of interconnected physical devices or "things" embedded with sensors, software, and other technologies to collect and exchange data over the internet.

Predictive Analytics: Predictive analytics involves using data, statistical algorithms, and machine learning techniques to identify the likelihood of future outcomes based on historical data.

Prescriptive Analytics: Prescriptive analytics is the process of analyzing data to make decisions and then prescribing actions to achieve desired outcomes. It suggests the best course of action.

Sensor: A sensor is a device that detects or measures physical properties (like temperature, light, motion, etc.) and converts them into signals that can be interpreted or processed by other devices.

Chapter 2
IoT in Healthcare and Telemedicine:
Revolutionizing Patient Care and Medical Practices

Nagendra Singh Yadav
https://orcid.org/0000-0002-9591-4491
Engineering College, Bikaner, India

Vishal Kumar Goar
Engineering College, Bikaner, India

ABSTRACT

The incorporation of internet of things (IoT) technologies in the healthcare sector has ushered in a transformative era of patient care and medical practices. This chapter aims to share a thorough overview of the applications, benefits, challenges, and future prospects of IoT in healthcare and telemedicine. The chapter will explore the ways in which IoT is enhancing patient monitoring, diagnosis, treatment, and overall healthcare delivery. Additionally, it will delve into the ethical and security considerations linked with IoT in healthcare. This chapter will serve as an essential resource for healthcare professionals, researchers, policymakers, and technology enthusiasts seeking to understand and harness the potential of IoT in revolutionizing the healthcare industry.

DOI: 10.4018/979-8-3693-1686-3.ch002

1. INTRODUCTION

Brief Overview of IoT Technology

The Internet of Things is synonymous with the interconnectedness of everyday objects and devices through the internet. These 'things' encompass a wide spectrum, spanning from everyday household gadgets and wearable technology to heavy-duty industrial machinery and intricate sensor networks. The fundamental aim of IoT is to empower these devices to gather, exchange, and act upon data, thereby facilitating intelligent decision-making and automation.

The idea of the IoT revolves around an intricate web of liked devices that seamlessly interact and exchange data amongst themselves and with cloud-based systems (Al-Fuqaha et al., 2015). These IoT devices are usually equipped with advanced technology, encompassing an array of sensors, software, and can span across both mechanical and digital machinery, as well as everyday consumer items.

The concept of the Internet of Things (IoT) seamlessly connects our everyday objects to the vast realm of the internet. This groundbreaking integration of technology and the physical world has been an ongoing journey for computer engineers since the 1990s.

In 1999, Kevin Ashton, a co-founder of the Auto-ID Center located at the prestigious MIT (Massachusetts Institute of Technology) introduced a groundbreaking concept during a presentation to the executives at Procter & Gamble (P&G). His primary goal was to capture the attention of P&G's senior leadership and highlight the potential of radio frequency identification (RFID) technology. To make the idea more captivating, Ashton decided to christen his presentation "The Internet of Things," drawing inspiration from the burgeoning trend of that era: the internet.

Around the same time, MIT's distinguished professor Neil Gershenfeld contributed to the IoT movement with his influential book titled "When Things Start to Think," which also debuted in 1999. While Gershenfeld's book did not explicitly employ the phrase "Internet of Things," it painted a vivid picture of the direction in which the Internet of Things was poised to evolve.

IoT has emerged as a result of the fusion of wireless technologies, microelectromechanical systems, microservices, & the internet. This fusion has played a pivotal role in breaking down the traditional barriers that separated operational technology from information technology.

While Kevin Ashton's name is often associated with the coining of the term IoT, the concept of interconnected devices has been circulating since the 1970s, known by various names like embedded internet and pervasive computing.

An interesting historical example of IoT's early roots can be found in the form of the first internet-connected appliance. Surprisingly, it wasn't a high-tech gadget but rather a humble Coke machine located at Carnegie Mellon University during the early 1980s. This pioneering device allowed programmers to access its status remotely via the web. They could ascertain whether a refreshing beverage was available, thus helping them decide whether to make the journey to the machine.

The genesis of IoT can be traced back to M2M communication, where machines established connections amongst themselves through a network, devoid of any human intervention. M2M, or Machine-to-Machine communication, was the initial step in linking devices to the cloud, overseeing their operations, and gathering data.

Building upon the principles of M2M, IoT has emerged as a sprawling network of countless smart devices. These interconnected devices serve as sensors, linking individuals, computer systems, and various applications, facilitating the seamless exchange of data (Kashani et al., 2021).

The concept of IoT seamlessly builds upon the foundations of Supervisory Control and Data Acquisition (SCADA), an established category of software applications designed for process control and real-time data collection from remote locations to manage equipment and environmental conditions (Mathew et al., 2017). SCADA systems are comprised of hardware and software components that work in harmony to Guarantee smooth operations. The hardware serves as the data collection hub, transmitting information to a dedicated desktop computer equipped with SCADA software.

As technology evolved, late-generation SCADA systems naturally transitioned into the pioneering era of the Internet of Things. In this new paradigm, the boundaries of data collection and control expanded exponentially, incorporating a broader range of devices and technologies interconnected through the internet. IoT has emerged as the next logical step in the evolution of SCADA, offering enhanced connectivity, automation, and data analysis capabilities that empower businesses and industries in unprecedented ways.

The IoT ecosystem, however, remained somewhat dormant until a pivotal moment in 2010. This turning point can be attributed, in part, to China's government, which declared IoT a strategic priority within its comprehensive five-year plan.

From 2010 to 2019, the landscape of IoT underwent a remarkable transformation, extending its influence to an ever-widening audience of consumers. People began to embrace internet-connected devices with increasing fervor, encompassing a spectrum ranging from ubiquitous smartphones to the ingenious world of smart TVs.

The year 2020 marked yet another milestone in the IoT narrative as the number of IoT devices continued its exponential growth. The proliferation extended its reach to encompass cellular IoT, now operating across a gamut of generations - from the venerable 2G and 3G to the formidable 4G and 5G, not to mention the ascendant

LoRaWAN and the innovation of long-term evolution for machines, known colloquially as LTE-M. This burgeoning diversity in connectivity options further solidified IoT's standing as an omnipresent force in the digital age.

In the year 2023, an extraordinary proliferation of internet-connected technological advancements has heralded a fresh era of data exchange, shaping both consumer experiences and industrial landscapes. This era has seen the emergence of a transformative concept known as the 'Digital Twin,' which essentially embodies a virtual mirror image of tangible real-world entities or intricate processes.

In the nascent days of IoT, engineers initially turned to low-power computer chips known as RFID tags to monitor and trace valuable equipment (S et al., 2021). These unobtrusive chips marked a significant step forward, albeit small in size themselves. However, as the world of computing underwent remarkable transformations, these chips followed suit, shrinking in size, accelerating in processing power, and growing increasingly intelligent over time.

The affordability of incorporating computing power into compact devices has significantly decreased. To illustrate, you can now imbue MCUs with Alexa voice services and connectivity features using less than 1MB of embedded RAM, even for something as simple as a light switch. This phenomenon has spawned an entire industry centered around enriching our living spaces, workplaces, and commercial establishments with IoT devices. These ingenious gadgets possess the capability to seamlessly exchange data with the internet.

The Internet of Things (IoT) revolutionizes the way we live & work, Introducing a fresh beginning of enhanced convenience and productivity. In day-to-day lives, consumers can harness the power of IoT-embedded devices i.e. cars, smartwatches, to elevate their overall quality of life. For instance, imagine returning home after a long day: your car seamlessly communicates with your garage, effortlessly opening the door as you approach. Simultaneously, your thermostat anticipates your arrival, adjusting the temperature to your preferred setting, while your lighting gracefully transitions to a soothing, lower intensity and your chosen color scheme.

IoT equips organizations with real-time insights into the inner workings of their systems, offering a profound understanding of machine performance and streamlining supply chain and logistics operations. This invaluable data empowers companies to make informed decisions, optimize processes, and enhance efficiency, ultimately contributing to their bottom line and competitive advantage in today's dynamic marketplace.

Within the vast landscape of the Internet of Things, entities can encompass a diverse span of elements. These might include individuals equipped with heart monitor implants, livestock embedded with biochip transponders, vehicles featuring integrated sensors capable of notifying the driver about low tire pressure, or indeed any conceivable entity, whether organic or artificial, eligible for an Internet Protocol address assignment and endowed with the ability to transmit data using the network.

The Internet of Things empowers machines to handle repetitive tasks autonomously, sparing humans from the burden of manual intervention. This technological marvel equips companies with the ability to streamline operations, slash labor expenses, minimize wastage, and enhance service delivery. Moreover, IoT plays a pivotal role in driving cost-efficiency throughout the manufacturing and supply chain processes, granting invaluable insights into customer interactions.

How Does IoT Work?

In the realm of IoT, a web of interconnected intelligent gadgets thrives, each boasting embedded systems, complete with processors, sensors, and communication components. Utilizing their web connectivity, these smart devices are engineered to collect, transmit, and react to information sourced from their environment.

In the world of IoT, sensor-laden devices collaborate by linking up with an IoT gateway, essentially serving as a central nexus where IoT gadgets transmit their gathered data. Prior to sharing this data, it often makes a pit stop at an edge device, where it undergoes local analysis. This localized data crunching serves to trim down the data payload headed for the cloud, effectively curtailing the strain on bandwidth resources.

Intriguingly, these devices occasionally engage in conversations with their counterparts, exchanging valuable insights that prompt coordinated actions. Remarkably, the lion's share of tasks is accomplished autonomously, sparing humans from the need for constant intervention. Nevertheless, individuals retain the ability to interact with these devices as needed, be it for setup, providing instructions, or accessing the troves of data they generate.

"The choice of connectivity, networking, and communication protocols for web-enabled devices in the IoT ecosystem heavily relies on the particular applications they are employed for.

Furthermore, IoT can harness the power of artificial intelligence and machine learning to enhance information gathering procedures, making them further seamless and adaptive (Fuller et al., 2020).

Figure 1. Inner workings of IoT

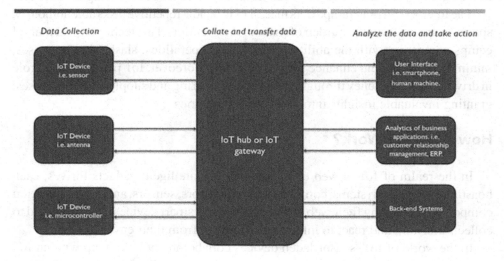

Components of IoT

- **Sensors and Actuators** - At the heart of IoT are sensors & actuators. Sensors are devices that are capable of detecting and measuring tangible or environmental conditions, i.e. temperature & humidity. Actuators, are mechanisms capable of performing decisions rooted in the data received from sensors, i.e. controlling a robotic arm.
- **Connectivity** - IoT devices depend on a multitude of communication technologies for establishing connectivity to the internet & exchanging data. These technologies consist of Wi-Fi, cellular networks, Bluetooth. The selection of connectivity options hinges on considerations like range and power efficiency, and data transfer speed.
- **Data Processing** - Data produced by IoT devices is often vast & diverse. To make this data meaningful and actionable, it must undergo processing. This involves filtering, aggregating, and analyzing the data either on the device itself (edge computing) or in the cloud (cloud computing). Machine learning algorithms are frequently used to extract valuable revelations drawn using IoT data (Sworna et al., 2021).
- **Cloud Computing** - Cloud platforms play a critical aspect in IoT by supplying scalable storage & computing resources. They allow for the centralized management of IoT devices, data storage, and analysis. Cloud services also

enable remote device management and software updates, making IoT systems more flexible and adaptable.

The Applications of IoT in Healthcare

- **Remote Patient Monitoring -** Remote patient monitoring stands as a beacon of innovation within healthcare, showcasing the power of IoT (Alshamrani, 2022). IoT devices, i.e. wearable fitness trackers, continuously gather patient information and securely share it with medical professionals. Continuous live monitoring plays a vital role in the care of individuals managing chronic illnesses, as it allows for early intervention and personalized care plans.
- **Telemedicine Consultations -** IoT enables telemedicine consultations, which have become increasingly popular, especially in rural or underserved areas. By utilizing video conferencing, individuals can access medical advice and consultations from healthcare experts, share symptoms, and receive medical advice without the need for in-person visits (Haleem et al., 2021).
- **Medication Adherence -** Medication adherence is significantly improved through the use of IoT-enabled dispensers and accompanying apps, which not only send timely reminders but also monitor medication consumption. This technology not only improves patient end results but also reduces healthcare costs associated with non-adherence.
- **Asset and Inventory Management -** Hospitals and healthcare facilities use IoT to manage assets and inventory efficiently. Smart tags and sensors help monitor the location and status of equipment and supplies, reducing waste and enhancing resource allocation (Al-Fuqaha et al., 2015b).

The Benefits of IoT in Healthcare

- **Improved Patient Outcomes -** IoT-driven data collection and analysis provide medical practitioners with valuable data on patient health trends. This results in enhanced precision in diagnoses, customized treatment strategies, and, in the end, better health end results for patients (Elhoseny et al., 2018).
- **Cost Reduction -** IoT can reduce healthcare costs through the prevention of hospital readmissions, early disease detection, and optimized resource allocation. Shifting care from hospitals to homes also lowers the burden on healthcare infrastructure.
- **Enhanced Access to Care -**Telemedicine powered by IoT improves access to medical services. Patients can consult with specialists and receive expert care without traveling long distances.

- **Real-time Monitoring -** Continuous, real-time monitoring through IoT devices allows for immediate intervention in emergencies or when vital signs deviate from normal ranges, potentially saving lives (Laplante & Laplante, 2016).

IoT in Telemedicine: A Perfect Match

- **Remote Patient Monitoring -** IoT devices have empowered healthcare professionals to efficiently track patient's vital parameters and health status from a distance. These devices continuously gather live data, encompassing heart rate, blood pressure, and glucose readings, and even activity levels, and share this information with medical professionals through secure channels. This continuous monitoring allows for the timely identification of medical concerns, enabling timely actions and reducing the risk of complications (Chunara et al., 2020).
- **Teleconsultations -** IoT facilitates seamless teleconsultations by providing the necessary infrastructure for high-quality video conferencing and data exchange between individuals and healthcare professionals. Through secure and reliable IoT connectivity, physicians can conduct virtual appointments, assess symptoms, and provide medical advice in real-time. This not only enhances patient convenience but also reduces the burden on healthcare facilities, making healthcare more accessible to those in remote areas or with limited mobility.
- **Medication Adherence -** Non-adherence to medication regimens is a current problem in healthcare, leading to treatment failure & growing healthcare costs. IoT-enabled smart pill dispensers and medication reminder apps help patients adhere to their prescribed medications. These devices send reminders, dispense pills at the correct times, and track medication consumption. Additionally, they can notify medical professionals or families in case of missed doses, enabling timely interventions and improving treatment outcomes.
- **Emergency Response -** IoT devices equipped with GPS and fall detection capabilities are invaluable in emergency situations, especially for elderly or vulnerable patients. Wearable devices can detect falls or sudden health deteriorations and automatically alert healthcare providers.

2. IOT APPLICATIONS IN HEALTHCARE

2.1. Remote Patient Monitoring: Wearable Devices and Sensors

Lately, the healthcare landscape has seen a transformative shift towards patient-centric care & the integration of technology into healthcare delivery. Remote Patient Monitoring has appeared as a powerful tool for achieving these goals, enabling healthcare providers to supervise the well-being of patients remotely and allowing patients to engage proactively in managing their well-being. At the forefront of RPM technology are wearable devices and sensors, which have rapidly evolved to become indispensable tools in modern healthcare.

Evolution of Wearable Devices and Sensors

Wearable devices and sensors have come a long way since their inception. Initially, simple pedometers and heart rate monitors were the primary wearables used for tracking physical activity and basic health metrics. However, with advancements in technology, these devices have evolved into sophisticated tools capable of measuring a wide range of physiological parameters.

The introduction of smartphones and the miniaturization of electronic components played a crucial role in this evolution. Today, wearable devices can track essential health metrics like heart rate & body temperature. They can also track sleep patterns, physical activity, and even assess more specialized metrics like glucose levels for patients with diabetes.

The development of sensors that can measure biometric data accurately and transmit it wirelessly to healthcare providers has revolutionized patient monitoring. These sensors have become smaller, more energy-efficient, and increasingly affordable, making them accessible to a wider range of patients.

Benefits of Wearable Devices and Sensors in RPM

The acquiring of wearable devices & sensors in remote patient monitoring offers a multitude of benefits to both patients and healthcare providers:

- **Real-Time Monitoring** - Through wearable devices, patients can stay continuously connected, receiving real-time updates on their health condition. This continuous data collection allows healthcare providers to detect subtle shifts in a patient's condition promptly.
- **Improved Patient Engagement** - Patients become active participants in their healthcare journey through wearable devices. They can track their progress,

set goals, & receive immediate feedback, fostering a sense of empowerment and engagement in their own well-being.

- **Early Intervention** - Timely recognition of health concerns is a critical aspect of remote patient monitoring. Wearable devices can provide early warning signs, allowing healthcare providers to step in proactively and prevent a condition from deteriorating, reducing hospital readmissions and improving patient outcomes.
- **Enhanced Data Accuracy** - Wearable sensors provide highly accurate and objective data, reducing the potential for human error in data collection. This accuracy is particularly critical in chronic disease management and clinical research.
- **Cost Savings** - Remote patient monitoring with wearables can result in expense reduction for healthcare systems by reducing the frequency of in-person visits, hospital admissions, & associated healthcare costs (Kakhi et al., 2022).

Continuous Data Collection and Analysis in Remote Patient Monitoring

Remote Patient Monitoring has appeared as a transformative approach to healthcare, enabling healthcare providers to monitor and oversee patient's well-being beyond the confines of conventional medical environments. One of the cornerstones of RPM is the continuous data collection and analysis, which provides healthcare professionals with instantaneous updates on a patient's current health condition.

The Significance of Continuous Data Collection

Continuous data collection in continuous tracking of a patient's vital signs is an integral part of Remote Patient Monitoring. This approach offers several key advantages:

- **Early Detection of Health Deterioration** - Continuous data collection allows healthcare providers to detect subtle shifts in a patient's health status as soon as they occur. This early detection allows for prompt intervention, minimizing the likelihood of adverse outcomes and unplanned hospital stays.
- **Personalized Care** - RPM allows for the creation of custom healthcare strategies designed to address the individual requirements of every patient. Uninterrupted data collection equips healthcare professionals with a treasure trove of patient-specific data, allowing them to make informed decisions and adjustments to treatment plans.

- **Enhanced Patient Engagement** - Patients are more involved in self-care when they have real-time data accessibility about their health. Continuous data collection empowers patients to engage proactively in managing their conditions, resulting in better adherence to treatment plans and improved outcomes.

Technologies for Continuous Data Collection

Various technological advancements are pivotal in continuous data collection in RPM:

- **Wearable Devices** - Wearable devices can continuously track essential indicators i.e. heart rate. These devices send data wirelessly to healthcare providers for analysis.
- **Home Monitoring Equipment** - Patients can use home monitoring equipment like blood glucose monitors, spirometers, and electrocardiogram (ECG) machines to collect data on specific health parameters. This data is typically transmitted to healthcare providers through secure connections.
- **Mobile Applications** - Mobile apps designed for RPM enable patients to log symptoms, medications, and activities. They can also receive educational materials and reminders. These apps are often integrated with wearable devices to offer a holistic perspective on a patient's well-being.
- **Telehealth Platforms** - Telehealth platforms provide virtual appointments connecting patients with healthcare professionals. During these virtual visits, providers can review data collected by wearable devices and discuss the patient's health status and treatment plan.

Data Analysis in Remote Patient Monitoring

Continuous data collection is only valuable if the data is analyzed effectively. Data analysis in RPM involves several key steps:

- **Data Aggregation** – Data gathered from diverse origins i.e, home monitoring equipment, and mobile apps, are aggregated into a single, centralized platform. This ensures that healthcare providers can tap into an extensive reservoir of data.
- **Data Integration** - Data integration is the art of merging information from various origins to create a holistic view of a patient's health. For example, combining heart rate data from a wearable device with blood glucose read-

ings from a glucose monitor can provide insights into the relationship between these parameters.

- **Real-Time Alerts** - Sophisticated algorithms can continuously examine the data to pinpoint trends & anomalies. When a concerning change is detected, healthcare providers receive instant alerts, allowing them to take immediate action (Aghdam et al., 2021).
- **Predictive Analytics** - Machine learning & predictive analytics can be utilized to forecast future health events based on historical data. This enables proactive interventions to prevent complications.

2.2 Smart Healthcare Facilities: IoT-Enabled Equipment and Infrastructure

Smart Infrastructure for Healthcare

Creating a smart healthcare facility goes beyond just connecting medical devices. It involves a comprehensive approach to the infrastructure to ensure seamless data flow and optimal operations.

- **Building Automation Systems (BAS)** - BAS, powered by IoT, manages and oversees critical building infrastructure, including heating, ventilation, air conditioning, and security systems. These systems can automatically adjust environmental conditions for patient comfort and energy efficiency.
- **EHR (Electronic Health Records) Integration** - Integrating EHR systems with IoT infrastructure enables healthcare professionals to swiftly and confidently retrieve patient information. This ensures that physicians have the latest data, facilitating more informed choices and enhancing the quality of patient treatment.
- **Security and Privacy Measures** - The healthcare industry is highly regulated, with strict privacy and security requirements. IoT-enabled healthcare facilities must prioritize data security through encryption, access control, and robust authentication methods to protect patient information.

Use Cases of IoT in Smart Healthcare Facilities

- **Remote Patient Monitoring** - IoT-enabled wearable devices and sensors offer continuous monitoring of vital signs, delivering instant health data to medical professionals. This remote monitoring is particularly beneficial for patients having chronic illnesses, allowing them to live more independently while ensuring prompt medical intervention when necessary.

- **Telemedicine** -Telemedicine has become a vital component of healthcare, especially during moments of turmoil such as the COVID-19 pandemic. IoT-enabled video conferencing tools and remote diagnostic equipment facilitate virtual consultations, minimizing the necessity for in-person appointments while enhancing healthcare accessibility (Sarhan, 2009).
- **Medication Management -** Medication dispensers connected to the Internet of Things (IoT) ensure timely medication reminders for patients following their prescribed schedules. These gadgets also have the capability to alert healthcare providers if doses are overlooked, enhancing medication adherence and patient safety.
- **Infection Control -**Smart healthcare facilities use IoT to monitor and manage infection control measures. Sensors can track hand hygiene compliance, monitor air quality, and provide real-time data on patient and staff movements to help prevent the spread of infections.

Improved Resource Management

Healthcare is a resource-intensive industry. From medical equipment to skilled healthcare professionals, hospitals and clinics require a multitude of resources to deliver quality patient care. However, the rising demand for healthcare services, coupled with the increasing costs associated with them, has made resource management a pressing concern.

Traditionally, resource management in healthcare facilities was done manually, relying on experience and historical data. This approach often led to inefficiencies, including underutilized resources, long wait times, and suboptimal patient outcomes.

The IoT assumes a central position in enhancing resource management in smart healthcare facilities. IoT devices i.e. smart sensors & wearable devices are deployed throughout the facility to gather up-to-the-minute information on diverse metrics. This data is then analyzed to make informed decisions about resource allocation.

- **Asset Tracking -** An essential use case for IoT technology in smart healthcare facilities is asset tracking. Hospitals & clinics have a vast inventory of medical equipment, from ventilators to MRI machines. IoT sensors can track the location & usage of these assets, making sure that they are always available when needed. This prevents equipment hoarding in certain areas while others face shortages, ultimately leading to better resource utilization.
- **Patient Monitoring -** Continuous patient monitoring is crucial, especially in critical care units. IoT-enabled devices can monitor vital signs & notify healthcare providers instantly if any abnormality is detected. This not only

enhances patient safety but also optimizes the allocation of nursing staff who can prioritize patients requiring immediate attention.

Predictive Analytics for Staffing and Inventory

Smart healthcare facilities leverage predictive analytics to forecast resource requirements accurately. By analyzing past data and simultaneous information, these systems can project patient admission rates, the need for specific medications, and even staff scheduling requirements.

- **Staffing Optimization -** Predictive analytics can aid hospitals in enhancing their staffing strength. By forecasting patient admissions and the required skill mix, healthcare facilities can ensure that they have the right number of healthcare professionals on hand at all times. This reduces the strain on staff and improves patient care quality.
- **Inventory Management -** Accurate inventory management is crucial for ensuring that medications and medical supplies are always available. Predictive analytics can help healthcare facilities maintain optimal inventory levels, reducing the risk of shortages or overstocking. This, in turn, leads to cost savings and ensures that patients receive the necessary treatments without delays.

Telemedicine and Remote Monitoring

The adoption of telemedicine & remote monitoring has also revolutionized resource management in healthcare facilities. These technologies enable healthcare providers to increase their availability far from the physical location of the facility, reducing the strain on in-house resources (Charles, 2000).

- **Telemedicine -**Telemedicine enables patients to work with healthcare professionals distantly, minimizing the number of physical meetings. This not only improves resource allocation within the facility but also enhances patient convenience and access to care.
- **Remote Monitoring -** Remote monitoring solutions enable healthcare providers to keep tabs on patients' health status even when they are at home. For patients having chronic illness, this minimizes the requirement for prompt hospital visits & ensures that resources are directed toward those who need them the most.

2.3. Medication Management: Smart Pill Dispensers

Medication non-adherence, where patients fail to take their prescribed medications as directed, is a significant concern in healthcare. This issue not only leads to poor health outcomes but also increases healthcare costs due to hospitalizations and complications.

Several factors contribute to medication non-adherence, including forgetfulness, complex dosing schedules, fear of side effects, and the absence of knowledge about the significance of medication standards. Traditional methods to address this problem have included pill organizers and medication alarms, but these solutions are often insufficient for patients with multiple medications and those requiring precise dosing schedules.

The advent of smart pill dispensers represents a promising step forward in the battle against medication non-adherence. These devices leverage cutting-edge technology to simplify medication management for patients while providing healthcare providers and caregivers with valuable insights into patient adherence patterns.

Smart pill dispensers are equipped with a range of features that make medication management more accessible and efficient. These features typically include:

- **Automated Dispensing** -Smart pill dispensers can automatically dispense medications at the prescribed times, eliminating the need for manual sorting and administration. This automation reduces the risk of human error and ensures that doses are taken on time.
- **Medication Reminders** - Many smart pill dispensers are equipped with reminder systems that use alarms, lights, or even smartphone notifications to alert patients when the moment arrives to take their prescribed medicine. These reminders help combat forgetfulness, a common cause of non-adherence.
- **Dose Verification** - Some smart pill dispensers incorporate technology to verify that the correct dose has been taken. This verification can be essential for patients who require precise dosing.
- **Connectivity** - Many smart pill dispensers are designed to connect to the internet or mobile applications, enabling patients, caregivers, & healthcare providers to track medication adherence remotely. This connectivity enables real-time tracking of adherence and provides valuable data for healthcare professionals to make informed decisions.

Benefits of Smart Pill Dispensers

The adoption of smart pill dispensers offers numerous benefits for patients, caregivers, and healthcare systems (Yin et al., 2016):

- **Improved Adherence -** Smart pill dispensers significantly enhance medication adherence by automating the process, sending reminders, and providing added accountability.
- **Enhanced Safety -** With dose verification and automated dispensing, the risk of medication errors is minimized, reducing the potential for adverse drug reactions.
- **Data-Driven Insights -** The data captured with the help of smart pill dispensers can be shared with healthcare providers, enabling better-known treatment decisions and adjustments to medication regimens.
- **Peace of Mind -** For both patients and caregivers, smart pill dispensers offer peace of mind by ensuring that medications are taken correctly and on time.

Medication Adherence Monitoring

Medication adherence is fundamental to achieving successful treatment outcomes. Poor adherence can result in treatment failure, progression of diseases, increased hospitalizations, and even death. It also places a substantial financial burden on healthcare systems worldwide (Goar et al., 2021).

Figure 2. Medication adherence monitoring

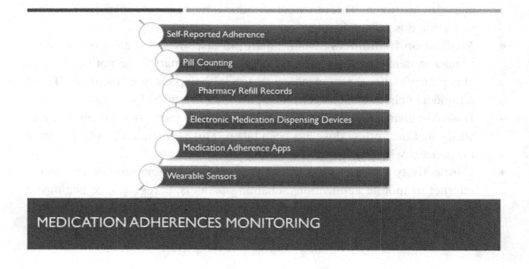

Therefore, it is crucial to assess and improve medication adherence to optimize patient health. Below are the methods for Medication Adherence Monitoring -

- **Self-Reported Adherence -** One of the simplest methods for monitoring medication adherence is to rely on self-reports from patients. Healthcare providers can ask patients about their medication-taking behaviors during clinic visits. However, self-reported adherence may not always be accurate, as patients may overestimate their adherence to please their healthcare providers or feel embarrassed about non-adherence.
- **Pill Counting -** Pill counting involves counting the remaining pills in a medication container to estimate a patient's adherence. This method is inexpensive and straightforward but is subject to human error. Patients may forget to take doses or discard pills, making pill counting less reliable for long-term adherence monitoring.
- **Pharmacy Refill Records -** Pharmacy refill records provide a valuable source of data for medication adherence assessment. By tracking when patients refill their prescriptions, healthcare providers can estimate adherence indirectly. However, this method does not account for patients who have extra medication on hand or who obtain medications from multiple pharmacies.
- **Electronic Medication Dispensing Devices -** Electronic medication dispensing devices, such as smart pill bottles or blister packs, offer a more advanced approach to monitoring adherence. These devices dispense medication at scheduled times and record the date and time of each dose taken. They can share real-time adherence data with both patients & healthcare providers, helping identify non-adherence promptly.
- **Medication Adherence Apps -** Mobile applications designed for medication adherence tracking have gained popularity in recent years. These apps provide patients with medication reminders, educational content, and the ability to log their doses. Healthcare providers can access adherence data through these apps, facilitating remote monitoring and interventions.
- **Wearable Sensors -** Wearable devices, such as smartwatches and sensors embedded in medication packaging, offer continuous monitoring of patient behavior. These devices can detect when medication is taken and relay this information to healthcare providers. They also allow for real-time feedback and interventions.

Benefits of Medication Adherence Monitoring

- **Improved Patient Outcomes -** Monitoring medication adherence can lead to good health results by making sure that patients get the full benefits of their medications.

- **Personalized Interventions** - Healthcare providers can tailor interventions based on individual patient adherence patterns, focusing on those at higher risk of non-adherence.
- **Reduction in Healthcare Costs** - Improved adherence can lead to reduced hospitalizations and complications, ultimately lowering healthcare costs.
- **Data-Driven Decision-Making** - Adherence data can inform treatment decisions, helping healthcare providers make more informed choices about medication regimens.

2.4. Telemedicine and Virtual Health: Real-Time Video Consultations

Telemedicine, broadly defined as the provision of healthcare services remotely using technology, has a rich history dating back to the early 20th century when radio and telephone communications were first explored for medical purposes. However, it wasn't until the advent of the internet and high-speed connectivity that telemedicine truly began to flourish. The evolution of telemedicine can be divided into several phases:

- **Early Telemedicine** - The early years of telemedicine were characterized by simple voice & video transmissions among healthcare providers & patients. These consultations were limited by low-quality technology and often lacked the necessary infrastructure for widespread adoption (Bollmeier et al., 2020).
- **Store-and-Forward Telemedicine** - As technology improved, so did the capabilities of telemedicine. The "store-and-forward" method allowed healthcare providers to share patient data, electronically, enabling more comprehensive consultations. However, this method was still asynchronous and did not facilitate real-time communication (Losorelli et al., 2021).
- **Real-time Video Consultations** - The advent of high-speed internet and advancements in video conferencing technology paved the way for real-time video consultations. These virtual visits enable face-to-face interactions among patients and healthcare providers, simulating the experience of a physical appointment.

Benefits of Real-Time Video Consultations

Real-time video consultations offer a myriad of advantages for both patients and healthcare providers, making them a valuable addition to modern healthcare delivery.

- **Improved Access to Care** - Geography and mobility are no longer significant barriers to healthcare access. Patients can connect with specialists and primary care providers from home, lowering travel time and expenses. This is fruitful for individuals in rural locations.
- **Convenience** - Patients appreciate the convenience of real-time video consultations. They can schedule appointments at times that suit their busy lives, reducing the need to get transportation to a clinic. This convenience also extends to healthcare providers, who can offer flexible scheduling.
- **Enhanced Continuity of Care** - Real-time video consultations facilitate ongoing care by empowering patients to foster enduring connections with their healthcare professionals. This continuity of care is particularly crucial for managing chronic conditions and ensuring that patients receive personalized treatment plans.
- **Reduced Healthcare Costs** - Telemedicine has the ability to lower healthcare expenses notably. By eliminating the need for physical infrastructure and streamlining administrative processes, healthcare providers can offer services at a lower cost. Additionally, patients save on transportation and related expenses (Bashshur, 1995).

Benefits of IoT-Supported Telehealth Platforms

- **Remote Monitoring** - Healthcare providers can securely track patients' vital signs from a distance including chronic conditions, & medication adherence. This continuous monitoring enables the timely identification of medical concerns and interventions, lowering hospital readmissions & enhancing patient outcomes.
- **Improved Patient Engagement** -Through mobile apps and wearable devices, patients actively participate in their healthcare journey. They gain permission to view their medical information, receive educational resources, & communicate with healthcare professionals. This increased engagement fosters better compliance with prescribed regimens and the adoption of well-being-focused habits.
- **Enhanced Access to Care** -IoT-supported telehealth platforms break down geographical hurdles, sharing healthcare services to distant areas. Patients can consult with specialists, obtain second opinions, and access healthcare services without the need for travel.
- **Data-Driven Decision Making** - IoT-generated data provides key insights for healthcare providers. Machine learning algorithms and data analytics help identify patterns, predict health trends, and tailor treatment plans, ultimately leading to more effective and efficient care.

3. BENEFITS AND ADVANTAGES

3.1. Improved Patient Outcomes: Improved Patient Outcomes

Amid the ever-changing terrain of the healthcare domain, the pursuit of improved patient outcomes is a fundamental goal. Advances in medical science, technology, and data analytics have opened new avenues for enhancing the quality of care.

Early Detection of Health Issues

Timely identification of health concerns is a cornerstone of modern healthcare. It encompasses a range of practices, from routine screenings to advanced diagnostic tools, aimed at identifying potential health problems before they become severe. The benefits of early detection are manifold:

- **Prevention of Disease Progression** - Identifying medical conditions in their initial phases often allows for more effective intervention and treatment, preventing diseases from advancing to a point where they are difficult or impossible to manage.
- **Improved Survival Rates** - Many medical conditions, such as cancer, cardiovascular diseases, and diabetes, have significantly better survival rates when diagnosed early. Early treatment can increase the chances of a full recovery.
- **Reduced Healthcare Costs** - Preventive measures and early intervention are often less expensive than treating advanced diseases. By catching health issues early, healthcare systems can reduce the economic burden on patients and society.
- **Enhanced Quality of Life** - Early detection can lead to less invasive treatments, shorter recovery times, and fewer complications, ultimately resulting in a better quality of life for patients.

Personalized Treatment Plans

Once a health issue is detected, the next crucial step is the development of a personalized treatment plan. Generic, one-size-fits-all approaches are being replaced by strategies that take into account an individual's unique genetic makeup, lifestyle, and preferences. Here's why personalized treatment plans are essential:

- **Tailored Interventions** - Personalized treatment plans consider a patient's genetic profile and other individual factors to identify the optimal treatments. This results in better outcomes and fewer adverse effects.

- **Enhanced Adherence** -When patients feel that their treatment plans are customized to their needs, they are more likely to adhere to them. This improves the chances of successful outcomes.
- **Optimized Resource Allocation** - By avoiding trial-and-error approaches, personalized treatment plans can reduce the use of resources on ineffective treatments and focus on those most likely to benefit the patient.
- **Improved Patient Satisfaction** - Individualized healthcare approaches frequently lead to increased patient contentment, contributing to a more favorable influence on their holistic health and wellness.

3.2. Enhanced Efficiency in Healthcare: Streamlined Workflows and Reduced Hospital Readmissions

Streamlined Workflows

- **Remote Patient Monitoring** – The most notable advancement brought about by IoT in healthcare is remote patient monitoring (IoT in Healthcare and Ambient Assisted Living, 2021). This enables healthcare professionals to monitor patients' health & other health metrics from the comfort of their homes. Patients wear devices like smartwatches or patches that continuously collect data and send it to healthcare providers.
- **Asset Management and Inventory Control** - IoT-enabled asset tracking and inventory management systems have streamlined hospital workflows. Hospitals can now track the location & status of medical hardware, making sure that they are always accessible when needed.
- **Workflow Automation** - IoT can automate routine tasks within healthcare facilities. For example, intelligent lighting and climate management systems can automatically adapt configurations in response to occupancy, effectively lowering energy expenses. Automated medication dispensing systems can reduce errors and ensure patients receive their medications on time.

Reduced Hospital Readmissions

Hospital readmissions are not only costly but also an indicator of suboptimal patient care. IoT technologies play a crucial role in reducing hospital readmissions by:

- **Medication Adherence** - IoT-connected pill dispensers and medication reminder systems help patients adhere to their treatment plans. These devices send reminders and monitor whether medications are taken as prescribed. If a patient misses a dose, healthcare providers have the opportunity to step in promptly, mitigating risks that could result in a return visit.

- **Post-discharge monitoring-** After patients are discharged from the hospital, IoT devices can continue to track their health. Wearables & sensors can track vital signs and symptoms, providing early warnings of potential complications. This continuous monitoring allows for timely interventions, reducing the risk of readmission.
- **Personalized Care Plans -** IoT-driven analytics can assist healthcare professionals in developing tailored treatment strategies for individuals by leveraging their health information. These plans take into account the patient's unique medical history, lifestyle, & risk factors. By tailoring care to the individual, providers can better manage chronic conditions and prevent readmissions.

3.3. Cost Savings: Lower Healthcare Expenses and Preventive Care and Reduced Hospitalization

Lowering Healthcare Expenses

One of the most compelling advantages of IoT in healthcare is its capacity to lower costs across the board. Here's how:

- **Remote Patient Monitoring -** IoT devices allow for remote patient monitoring. Patients can be continuously tracked in the comfort of their own homes, lowering the requirement for prompt doctor visits. This not only improves patient comfort but also cuts down on transportation costs and the strain on healthcare institutions.
- **Predictive Maintenance -** In healthcare, downtime of critical medical equipment can be costly and life-threatening. IoT-enabled equipment can self-diagnose issues and alert maintenance personnel before a breakdown occurs. This proactive approach to maintenance reduces equipment repair costs and minimizes the risk of costly emergencies.
- **Streamlined Operations -** IoT in healthcare also optimizes operational efficiency. Hospital administrators can use IoT data to manage inventory, allocate resources more effectively, and improve energy efficiency. By reducing waste and improving resource allocation, healthcare facilities can lower their operational costs (Bhatt et al., 2017).
- **Personalized Medicine -** IoT facilitates the collection of patient-specific data, allowing for the delivery of more personalized treatment plans. Personalized medicine can reduce the trial-and-error approach to treatment, potentially

decreasing the overall cost of care by avoiding ineffective treatments and adverse reactions.

Preventive Care and Reduced Hospitalization

Preventive care is the cornerstone of a sustainable healthcare system. IoT plays a vital role in recognizing and tackling medical concerns proactively to prevent complications, thereby reducing the requirement for hospitalization:

- **Early Disease Detection** - IoT sensors can continuously monitor vital signs, detect anomalies, and deliver timely alerts to healthcare professionals. For instance, a wearable ECG monitor can alert a patient and their physician to irregular heart rhythms, enabling timely intervention to prevent a heart attack.
- **Medication Adherence** - Failure to follow prescribed medication regimens is a significant contributor to hospital readmissions. IoT-powered medication dispensers ensure patients never miss a dose by sending timely reminders and automatically alerting healthcare professionals when doses are skipped. This technology helps patients stay on track with their treatments, reducing the likelihood of hospitalization due to uncontrolled conditions.
- **Chronic Disease Management** - Chronic diseases like diabetes and hypertension often lead to costly hospitalizations. IoT devices can aid patients in managing such conditions more effectively by sharing live data and feedback to both patients and healthcare providers. By proactively managing chronic illnesses, patients can avoid acute exacerbations that might necessitate hospitalization.
- **Telemedicine and Virtual Consultations** - IoT-powered telemedicine platforms have become increasingly popular, allowing patients to connect with healthcare experts from home. This not only enhances access to care but also reduces the necessity of in-person healthcare appointments. Telemedicine has been particularly valuable during public health emergencies i.e. COVID-19.

4. CHALLENGES AND CONSIDERATIONS

In recent years, the integration of IoT and telemedicine has transformed the healthcare domain. These innovations have the capacity to enhance the quality of patient treatment, lower costs, & grow accessibility to medical services. However, as with any technological advancement, they come with their own set of challenges, particularly in the realms of privacy and data security.

4.1. Privacy Challenges

- **Data Sensitivity** - Patient data, including medical records, treatment plans, and personal information, is highly sensitive and must be handled with extreme care. IoT devices and telemedicine platforms often collect and transmit this data, raising concerns about unauthorized access or breaches.
- **Consent and Control** - IoT devices, such as wearable health trackers, may continuously collect data without explicit patient consent. Telemedicine platforms must also ensure patients can manage their own data, including who can view it and for what purposes.
- **Data Ownership** - Identifying who owns patient data generated by IoT devices or shared during telemedicine consultations can be murky. Clear guidelines are needed to establish data ownership rights and responsibilities.
- **Vulnerable IoT Devices** - IoT devices are notorious for their security vulnerabilities. Hackers may exploit these weaknesses to gain access to sensitive patient data or compromise device functionality.
- **Encryption and Authentication** - Securing data in transit and ensuring that only authorized personnel can access it are paramount. Encryption and strong authentication methods are critical to protect data from interception or unauthorized access.
- **Data Retention** - Clear policies must dictate how long patient data is retained and when it should be securely deleted or anonymized. Storing data for too long increases the risk of exposure in the event of a breach.

4.2. Cybersecurity Threats

- **Ransomware Attacks** - Ransomware attacks are on the rise, with hospitals and healthcare providers becoming a frequent bull's-eye. Cybercriminals lock patient records behind encryption, then extort a ransom to unlock them, putting patient care at risk.
- **Phishing** - Phishing attacks often target healthcare professionals to gain access to patient data. Training staff to recognize and avoid phishing attempts is crucial.
- **IoT Botnets** - IoT devices can be commandeered into botnets, formerly employed to initiate offensives on healthcare systems. Implementing strong security measures for IoT devices is essential.
- **Data Theft and Sale** - Stolen patient data can be sold on the dark web, leading to identity theft and fraud. Protecting patient data from theft is critical to avoid these consequences.

4.3. Interoperability: The Bedrock of IoT and Telemedicine

Interoperability is the linchpin upon which the success of both IoT anu telemedicine hinges. It refers to the capacity of disparate devices, systems, and applications to communicate & work together harmoniously. In the context of telemedicine, seamless connectivity enables the link of various medical devices, patient information systems, electronic health records (EHRs), and remote monitoring tools, enabling healthcare providers to deliver efficient, patient-centric care.

- **Device Diversity and Heterogeneity** - One of the foremost challenges in achieving interoperability in IoT and telemedicine is the sheer diversity and heterogeneity of devices and systems. Medical devices, sensors, and IoT gadgets come from myriad manufacturers, each with its own proprietary protocols, data formats, and communication methods. Bridging this chasm of device diversity requires standardized protocols and communication interfaces.
- **Legacy Systems and Infrastructure** - Many healthcare organizations still depend on legacy systems and infrastructure, which were not designed with interoperability in mind. As a result, the integration of modern IoT devices and telemedicine solutions can be a daunting task. Transitioning from these legacy systems to more interoperable ones often necessitate substantial investments in time and resources.

4.4. Data Standardization: A Necessity for Cohesive Healthcare

Data standardization is the process of establishing consistent data formats, structures, and semantics, ensuring that information can be uniformly interpreted and exchanged across systems. In telemedicine, data standardization is vital for accurate diagnosis, treatment planning, and information sharing among healthcare providers.

- **Medical Terminologies and Ontologies** - The healthcare domain is replete with specialized terminologies and ontologies. For instance, diagnostic codes (e.g., ICD-10), medication classifications, and procedural codes (e.g., CPT) all have their unique standards. Achieving data standardization necessitates mapping and harmonizing these disparate vocabularies to facilitate meaningful data exchange.
- **Semantic Interoperability** - Semantic interoperability transcends syntactic uniformity and delves into the meaning and context of data. Ensuring semantic interoperability in telemedicine requires establishing a common understanding of medical concepts, diagnoses, and treatments. Standards like HL7 FHIR (Fast Healthcare Interoperability Resources) aim to address this chal-

lenge by providing a framework for sharing healthcare data in a semantically meaningful way.

- **Patient Identifiers and Consent Management -** Accurate patient identification and consent management are critical in telemedicine. Data standardization efforts should include standardized patient identifiers and consent frameworks to ensure that healthcare information is linked to the correct individual and that their preferences regarding data sharing are respected.

4.5. Ethical Concerns: Informed Consent

Informed consent is a foundational ethical principle in medical practice, guaranteeing that patients are well-informed about the possible advantages and drawbacks linked to their healthcare decisions. In the digital age, where healthcare increasingly relies on interconnected devices and telemedicine platforms, obtaining informed consent presents unique challenges and considerations.

Challenges

- **Digital Literacy Gap -** One of the foremost challenges in obtaining informed consent in IoT and telemedicine is the digital literacy gap. Patients may not fully comprehend the complexities of the technology involved or the data-sharing processes. This gap can lead to misunderstandings and hinder their ability to provide truly informed consent.
- **Continuous Data Collection -** IoT devices continuously collect data, often without the patient's explicit consent for every data point. The challenge is determining how to strike a balance between collecting essential health information and respecting patient autonomy.
- **Dynamic Consent -** Telemedicine services and IoT devices may evolve over time, requiring consent for new features, data sharing, or partnerships. Ensuring that patients remain informed and have the ability to revoke consent at any point is a significant challenge.

Considerations

- **Education and Transparency -** Healthcare providers and technology companies must prioritize patient education and transparency. This involves explaining in simple terms how IoT and telemedicine work, what data is collected, and how it is used. Patient portals and educational materials can be valuable tools in achieving this goal.

- **Dynamic Consent Mechanisms** - Developing dynamic consent mechanisms that allow patients to easily manage their preferences and revoke consent when necessary is crucial. These mechanisms should be user-friendly and accessible.
- **Ethical Oversight** - Regulatory bodies and ethical committees should play an active role in overseeing the utilization of IoT and telemedicine in healthcare. They can aid in setting guidelines and standards for informed consent and ensure that healthcare providers and technology companies adhere to them.

4.6. Data Ownership

The huge volume of data produced by IoT devices and telemedicine platforms has raised questions about data ownership and how this information is used. Balancing the advantages of data-driven healthcare with patient privacy & security concerns is paramount (Chacko & Hayajneh, 2018).

Challenges

- **Ownership Ambiguity** - Determining who owns healthcare data in IoT and telemedicine ecosystems can be challenging. Is it the patient, the healthcare provider, the technology company, or a combination of these stakeholders? This ambiguity can lead to disputes and mistrust.
- **Data Security** - The threat of data breaches & unapproved access to sensitive medical information is a significant concern. Patients worry about the security of their data, especially when it is transmitted or stored on interconnected devices.
- **Secondary Use of Data** - Healthcare data can be valuable for research and commercial purposes. However, the line between responsible data use and exploitation can be blurry. Patients may be uncomfortable with their data being used for purposes beyond their immediate care.

Considerations

- **Clear Data Ownership Policies** - Stakeholders involved in IoT and telemedicine should define explicit data ownership guidelines, outlining the rights and responsibilities of each party. Patients should maintain authority over their information and the capability to retrieve, alter, or erase it.
- **Robust Data Security Measures** - Data security should be a top priority, with robust encryption, authentication, & access control mechanisms in place

to protect patient information. Regular audits and assessments of data security should be undertaken to pinpoint and rectify weaknesses.

- **Ethical Data Use Frameworks** - Healthcare organizations and technology companies should adopt ethical data use frameworks that specify how patient data will be used and shared. Transparency in these practices is essential to building and maintaining trust.

5. CASE STUDIES

Healthcare, known for its propensity to embrace cutting-edge technology, remains at the forefront of innovation by harnessing the boundless potential of the IoT.

Incorporating IoT into healthcare has paved the way for seamless connections between patients and physicians through remote monitoring and virtual consultations. This transformative technology is not limited to telehealth alone; it also holds the power to revolutionize pharmaceutical manufacturing, providing opportunities to enhance efficiency and precision in drug production. Furthermore, healthcare providers can tap into the wealth of patient data made accessible by IoT, enabling them to swiftly access and utilize critical information.

By integrating IoT solutions, healthcare organizations can streamline various facets of the industry, from patient care to medication refills and manufacturing processes. The result? A more efficient and cost-effective healthcare ecosystem that benefits both patients and providers.

The healthcare sector has witnessed a remarkable transformation kudos to the diverse applications of the IoT. From cutting-edge medical devices to innovative public health services, from intelligent sleep technology to streamlined medication refills & remote monitoring solutions, a multitude of companies are at the forefront of reshaping the landscape of healthcare technology through IoT.

IoT Medical Devices

Figure 3. IoT medical devices

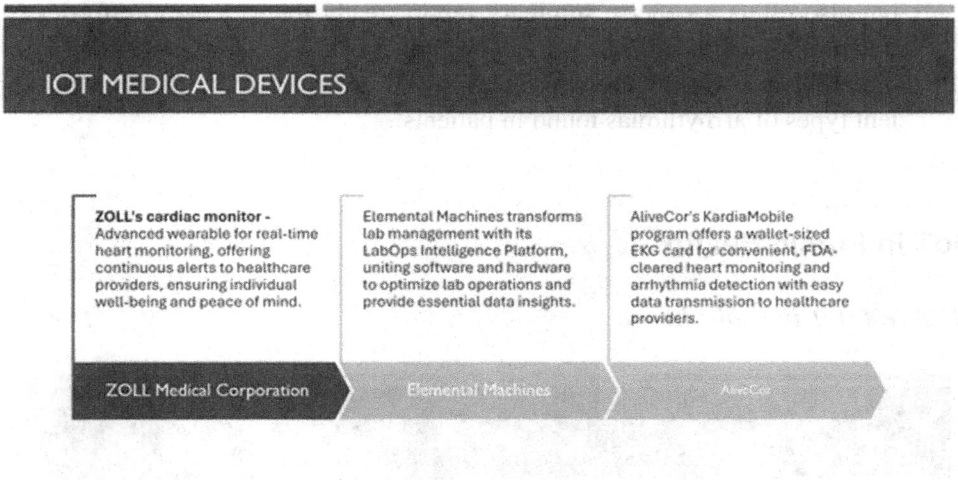

IOT MEDICAL DEVICES

| ZOLL's cardiac monitor - Advanced wearable for real-time heart monitoring, offering continuous alerts to healthcare providers, ensuring individual well-being and peace of mind. | Elemental Machines transforms lab management with its LabOps Intelligence Platform, uniting software and hardware to optimize lab operations and provide essential data insights. | AliveCor's KardiaMobile program offers a wallet-sized EKG card for convenient, FDA-cleared heart monitoring and arrhythmia detection with easy data transmission to healthcare providers. |

ZOLL Medical Corporation — Elemental Machines — AliveCor

- **ZOLL Medical Corporation** - ZOLL provides a broad spectrum of cutting-edge devices & wearables designed to empower individuals to manage their health while on the move. Among various innovative offerings is the ZOLL cardiac monitor, a remarkable device that tirelessly monitors heart rhythms and meticulously documents any clinical arrhythmias that may arise. The goal is to ensure that patients remain seamlessly connected with their healthcare providers. To this end, the ZOLL cardiac monitor goes above and beyond by automatically transmitting alerts to the corresponding healthcare professional whenever a cardiac event is detected. This continuous monitoring and instant reporting not only provide individuals with peace of mind but also enable the healthcare team to offer prompt and personalized care, ultimately enhancing the well-being of individuals.

- **Elemental Machines** - Elemental Machines revolutionizes laboratory management with its cutting-edge cloud-based software and hardware ecosystem, designed to streamline operations in research and development, clinical, quality control, and diagnostic labs. Renamed as the LabOps Intelligence Platform, this innovative solution offers invaluable data insights into critical parameters such as temperature, humidity, and equipment performance. Furthermore, the company facilitates seamless integrations of both software and hardware to enable enhanced data extraction capabilities.

- **AliveCor** - AliveCor specializes in crafting cutting-edge heart monitoring solutions. One of their standout innovations is the KardiaMobile program, which boasts an EKG card designed to conveniently slip into the wallet. This remarkable, FDA-cleared device not only securely stores vital patient data but also offers a concise summary report, ready for patients to effortlessly transmit to their healthcare providers. Notably, this personal EKG device exhibits the remarkable ability to identify and report on six of the most prevalent types of arrhythmias found in patients.

IoT in Public Health

Figure 4. IoT in public health

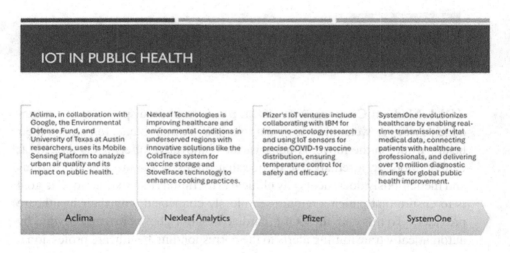

IOT IN PUBLIC HEALTH

Aclima, in collaboration with Google, the Environmental Defense Fund, and University of Texas at Austin researchers, uses its Mobile Sensing Platform to analyze urban air quality and its impact on public health.

Nexleaf Technologies is improving healthcare and environmental conditions in underserved regions with innovative solutions like the ColdTrace system for vaccine storage and StoveTrace technology to enhance cooking practices.

Pfizer's IoT ventures include collaborating with IBM for immuno-oncology research and using IoT sensors for precise COVID-19 vaccine distribution, ensuring temperature control for safety and efficacy.

SystemOne revolutionizes healthcare by enabling real-time transmission of vital medical data, connecting patients with healthcare professionals, and delivering over 10 million diagnostic findings for global public health improvement.

Aclima   Nexleaf Analytics   Pfizer   SystemOne

- **Aclima** - Collaborating alongside Google, the Environmental Defense Fund, & researchers from the University of Texas at Austin, Aclima harnesses its innovative Mobile Sensing Platform to gain profound insights into the very essence of urban life, examining the intricate rhythms of air quality. This pioneering technology allows us to gauge the delicate balance of urban ecosystems, with a particular focus on the nexus of factors influencing air quality, such as transportation, energy consumption, and meteorological conditions.

  The significance of this endeavor extends beyond mere scientific curiosity. By amassing precise and up-to-date air quality data, Aclima empowers the healthcare industry to not only detect but also preemptively combat diseases. Air pollution, a potent catalyst for increased cardiovascular and respiratory ailments, is a challenge we must confront head-on. Our commitment to providing actionable insights is poised to make a significant impact on public health.

- **Nexleaf Analytics** - Nexleaf Technologies is on a mission to enhance living conditions in underserved regions by focusing on advancements in both vaccine storage and cooking practices. Through its innovative solutions, Nexleaf is determined to create a beneficial influence on the healthcare sector and the environment.

  One of Nexleaf's groundbreaking offerings is the ColdTrace system, designed to revolutionize vaccine storage in remote clinics and healthcare facilities. By employing remote temperature monitoring without the hassle of wires, ColdTrace ensures that vaccine refrigerators in these rural areas maintain the required temperature levels. This not only safeguards the integrity of vaccines but also enables healthcare workers to administer crucial disease-preventing and life-saving injections with confidence. Within the system, a sensor probe is kept inside the refrigeration unit, continuously uploading temperature and power grid data. This information is then relayed through text updates to monitoring personnel, guaranteeing the reliability and safety of vaccines in these resource-constrained settings. In parallel, Nexleaf introduces its StoveTrace technology, a cloud-based remote monitoring system designed to enhance cooking practices in rural households. StoveTrace empowers users by providing real-time measurements of cookstove usage, promoting the adoption of safer, cleaner-burning appliances that emit less carbon dioxide and do not rely on wood fuel.

- **Pfizer** - Pfizer's foray into the world of IoT has been multifaceted, manifesting through various initiatives. One noteworthy endeavor is its collaboration with IBM, aimed at advancing immuno-oncology research. Simultaneously, Pfizer has been harnessing digital IoT technology to optimize the manufacturing and distribution processes of COVID-19 vaccines.

  In the context of vaccine distribution, Pfizer has been at the forefront of innovation. They have seamlessly integrated IoT sensors into their logistics framework, leveraging cold chain capabilities. These IoT sensors play a pivotal role in meticulously tracking and monitoring the shipments of COVID-19 vaccines, safeguarding their integrity by ensuring they remain within the prescribed temperature range throughout their journey.

- **SystemOne** - SystemOne, a specialist in barcode and label systems, has transformed the healthcare domain by enabling real-time transmission of crucial medical diagnostic data to physicians and healthcare professionals. With a mission to bridge the healthcare gap in technology-deprived regions across the globe, the company is dedicated to linking patients with healthcare providers to enhance the management of public health crises, including infectious diseases. To date, SystemOne has delivered over 10 million diagnostic findings across a diverse spectrum of conditions, i.e. TB, Ebola, HIV, and more, positively impacting patients worldwide.

6. FUTURE TRENDS AND PROSPECTS

6.1. Emerging IoT Technologies and Its Integration With Artificial Intelligence (AI) and Machine Learning (ML)

The IoT has rapidly evolved over the years, becoming a ubiquitous part of our everyday lives. It encompasses an extensive web of linked gadgets, sensors, & systems that communicate and share data to improve efficiency, productivity, and overall quality of life. As we move forward into the future, the future holds an even more prominent position for IoT, especially when integrated with Artificial Intelligence (AI) and Machine Learning (ML) (Jiang et al., 2017).

AI and ML have been transformative in their own right. AI algorithms enable machines to complete activities that traditionally demand human-like cognitive abilities, like understanding and working with human languages and computer vision. ML, a component of artificial intelligence, allows machines to acquire knowledge from data and enhance their capabilities through continuous learning. When integrated with IoT, AI and ML can make sense of the vast volumes of data produced by IoT devices, providing actionable insights & automating decision-making processes (Davenport & Kalakota, 2019).

Integration With AI and ML

The integration of IoT with AI and ML increases the capabilities of telemedicine exponentially. Here are some key trends and prospects in this domain:

- **Predictive Analytics for Early Intervention** - AI and ML algorithms can analyze historical patient data combined with live IoT-generated data to forecast the course of the illness and pinpoint potential adverse developments. This empowers healthcare professionals to take proactive action & offer personalized treatment plans.
- **Remote Diagnostics** - IoT-enabled devices and wearables can collect comprehensive health data, including ECG readings, blood pressure, and blood glucose levels. AI algorithms can interpret this data, supporting healthcare

professionals in achieving precise medical assessments without the need for physical appointments.

- **Personalized Treatment Plans** - By analyzing a patient's health data & medical history, AI-driven systems can recommend tailored treatment plans and medication dosages. This personalized approach improves patient outcomes and reduces the risk of adverse reactions.
- **Telemedicine Chatbots** - AI-powered chatbots integrated with IoT devices can provide real-time assistance and information to patients, enhancing their telemedicine experience. These chatbots can answer queries, schedule appointments, and even Prompt patients to ensure they stay on top of their medication regimen (Heinzelmann et al., 2005).

6.2. Predictions for the Future of IoT in Healthcare

The IoT has already achieved substantial inroads into various industries, but its Influence on the healthcare sector is poised to be transformative. With the capability to link devices, gather data, and enable real-time monitoring, the integration of IoT in healthcare holds the promise of transforming the way medical services are provided, elevating patient well-being, and elevating the entire healthcare journey.

- **Enhanced Remote Patient Monitoring** - Remote patient monitoring stands out as a leading application of IoT technology in the healthcare sector. In the future, we can expect to see a proliferation of wearable devices & sensors that constantly gather data on patients' vital signs, activity levels, & overall health. These devices will share live data with medical professionals, allowing for early intervention and personalized care plans. Predictive analytics and machine learning algorithms will be employed to identify potential health concerns before they escalate, lowering hospital readmissions and enhancing complete patient health (Surya, 2018).
- **Precision Medicine** - The integration of IoT into healthcare promises to revolutionize precision medicine, enabling the customization of treatments for patients by leveraging their genetic profile, lifestyle choices, and up-to-the-minute health information. Connected devices will enable the continuous monitoring of patients, generating a wealth of data that can be used to customize treatment plans. Artificial intelligence (AI) and machine learning algorithms will analyze this data to pinpoint the optimal treatments, dosages, & interventions for each patient, ushering in a new era of personalized healthcare (Jiang et al., 2017b).
- **Smart Hospitals** - IoT will transform traditional hospitals into smart healthcare facilities. Hospital infrastructure, including medical equipment, beds,

and even building systems, will be interconnected and equipped with sensors. This interconnectedness will enhance hospital efficiency by optimizing resource allocation, improving patient flow, and reducing energy consumption. Patients' experiences within smart hospitals will be more comfortable, with IoT-powered amenities such as voice-activated controls, wayfinding apps, and real-time updates on their care progress.

- **Predictive Healthcare Analytics -** The huge volumes of data produced by IoT devices in healthcare will pave the way for predictive analytics. Healthcare providers will leverage this data to forecast disease outbreaks, manage resources more efficiently, and allocate personnel where they are needed most.

- **Telemedicine and Remote Consultations -** IoT will continue to drive the growth of telemedicine and remote consultations. Patients will have access to an extensive range of medical services through virtual platforms, minimizing the necessity of face-to-face appointments. IoT-enabled devices will provide physicians with real-time patient data during remote consultations, enabling more accurate diagnoses and treatment recommendations (Jin et al., 2020).

- **Data Security and Privacy -** As IoT adoption in healthcare expands, so will concerns about data security and privacy. Safeguarding patient data will become even more critical, and healthcare organizations will invest heavily in strong cybersecurity safeguards and adherence to data privacy regulations such as HIPAA. Innovations like blockchain technology may also be employed to make sure that the integrity & security of patient data, giving patients greater confidence in sharing their health information.

- **Ethical and Regulatory Challenges -** With the rapid evolution of IoT in healthcare, ethical and regulatory challenges will emerge. Questions regarding data ownership, consent, and the ethical handling of patient data will need to be addressed. Additionally, regulators will grapple with updating existing frameworks to keep pace with technological advancements.

7. CONCLUSION

In conclusion, the immense potential of IoT in healthcare and telemedicine presents an exciting opportunity for both healthcare professionals and policymakers to revolutionize the way we deliver and access healthcare services. As we have explored throughout this discussion, IoT technology can enhance patient care, improve diagnostics, streamline operations, and ultimately, save lives.

Healthcare professionals are called upon to embrace the possibilities offered by IoT, leveraging connected devices, wearable technology, and real-time data to provide more personalized and proactive care. By incorporating IoT into their practice, they can enhance patient monitoring, timely identification of health concerns, and remote patient management, ultimately leading to better health outcomes.

Policymakers, on the other hand, must recognize the importance of fostering an environment that encourages the adoption of IoT in healthcare. This includes creating regulations that ensure data privacy and security, incentivizing the development of innovative IoT solutions, & facilitating the integration of these technologies into existing healthcare systems. Additionally, policymakers should invest in digital infrastructure to ensure that underserved populations can also benefit from IoT-enabled telemedicine and remote monitoring.

The convergence of IoT and healthcare has the ability to make healthcare more accessible, efficient, and patient-centric. It can help reduce healthcare costs, alleviate the burden on healthcare facilities, and improve overall healthcare outcomes. However, it will require a collaborative effort between healthcare professionals, policymakers, technology developers, and other stakeholders to harness this potential fully.

In this era of rapid technological advancement, embracing IoT in healthcare and telemedicine is not just a recommendation; it's a call to action. By doing so, we can usher in a new era of healthcare that is more connected, responsive, and inclusive, ultimately enhancing the welfare of people and societies across the globe.

REFERENCES

Aghdam, Z. N., Rahmani, A. M., & Hosseinzadeh, M. (2021). The role of the Internet of Things in healthcare: Future trends and challenges. *Computer Methods and Programs in Biomedicine*, 199, 105903. DOI: 10.1016/j.cmpb.2020.105903 PMID: 33348073

Al-Fuqaha, A., Guizani, M., Mohammadi, M., Aledhari, M., & Ayyash, M. (2015a). Internet of Things: A survey on enabling technologies, protocols, and applications. *IEEE Communications Surveys and Tutorials. IEEE Communications Surveys and Tutorials*, 17(4), 2347–2376. DOI: 10.1109/COMST.2015.2444095

Al-Fuqaha, A., Guizani, M., Mohammadi, M., Aledhari, M., & Ayyash, M. (2015b). Internet of Things: A survey on enabling technologies, protocols, and applications. *IEEE Communications Surveys and Tutorials. IEEE Communications Surveys and Tutorials*, 17(4), 2347–2376. DOI: 10.1109/COMST.2015.2444095

Alshamrani, M. (2022). IoT and artificial intelligence implementations for remote healthcare monitoring systems: A survey. *Journal of King Saud University. Computer and Information Sciences/Ma ala am a Al-malīk Saud : Ùlm Al- asib Wa Al-ma lumat, 34*(8), 4687–4701. DOI: 10.1016/j.jksuci.2021.06.005

Bashshur, R. L. (1995). On the Definition and Evaluation of Telemedicine. *Telemedicine Journal*, 1(1), 19–30. DOI: 10.1089/tmj.1.1995.1.19 PMID: 10165319

Bhatt, C., Dey, N., & Ashour, A. S. (2017). Internet of things and big data technologies for next generation healthcare. In *Studies in big data*. DOI: 10.1007/978-3-319-49736-5

Bollmeier, S. G., Stevenson, E., Finnegan, P., & Griggs, S. K. (2020). Direct to consumer telemedicine: Is healthcare from home best? *Missouri Medicine*, 117(4), 303–309. https://pubmed.ncbi.nlm.nih.gov/32848261/ PMID: 32848261

Chacko, A., & Hayajneh, T. (2018). Security and Privacy Issues with IoT in Healthcare. *EAI Endorsed Transactions on Pervasive Health and Technology*, 0(0), 155079. DOI: 10.4108/eai.13-7-2018.155079

Charles, B. L. (2000). Telemedicine can lower costs and improve access. *PubMed, 54*(4), 66–69. https://pubmed.ncbi.nlm.nih.gov/10915354

Chunara, R., Zhao, Y., Chen, J., Lawrence, K., Testa, P. A., Nov, O., & Mann, D. M. (2020). Telemedicine and healthcare disparities: A cohort study in a large healthcare system in New York City during COVID-19. *Journal of the American Medical Informatics Association : JAMIA*, 28(1), 33–41. DOI: 10.1093/jamia/ocaa217 PMID: 32866264

Davenport, T., & Kalakota, R. (2019). The potential for artificial intelligence in healthcare. *Future Healthcare Journal*, 6(2), 94–98. DOI: 10.7861/futurehosp.6-2-94 PMID: 31363513

Ekeland, A. G., Bowes, A., & Flottorp, S. A. (2010). Effectiveness of telemedicine: A systematic review of reviews. *International Journal of Medical Informatics*, 79(11), 736–771. DOI: 10.1016/j.ijmedinf.2010.08.006 PMID: 20884286

Elhoseny, M., Ramirez-Gonzalez, G., Abu-Elnasr, O. M., Shawkat, S. A., Arunkumar, N., & Farouk, A. (2018). Secure medical data transmission model for IoT-Based healthcare systems. *IEEE Access : Practical Innovations, Open Solutions*, 6, 20596–20608. DOI: 10.1109/ACCESS.2018.2817615

Fuller, A., Fan, Z., Day, C., & Barlow, C. (2020). Digital Twin: Enabling technologies, challenges and open research. *IEEE Access : Practical Innovations, Open Solutions*, 8, 108952–108971. DOI: 10.1109/ACCESS.2020.2998358

Goar, V. K., Yadav, N. S., Chowdhary, C. L., P, K., & Mittal, M. (2021). An IoT and artificial intelligence-based patient care system focused on COVID-19 pandemic. *International Journal of Networking and Virtual Organisations*, 25(3/4), 232. DOI: 10.1504/IJNVO.2021.120169

Haleem, A., Javaid, M., Singh, R. P., & Suman, R. (2021). Telemedicine for healthcare: Capabilities, features, barriers, and applications. *Sensors International*, 2, 100117. DOI: 10.1016/j.sintl.2021.100117 PMID: 34806053

He, S., & Chan, S. G. (2016). Wi-Fi Fingerprint-Based indoor positioning: Recent advances and comparisons. *IEEE Communications Surveys and Tutorials. IEEE Communications Surveys and Tutorials*, 18(1), 466–490. DOI: 10.1109/COMST.2015.2464084

Heinzelmann, P. J., Lugn, N. E., & Kvedar, J. C. (2005). Telemedicine in the future. *Journal of Telemedicine and Telecare*, 11(8), 384–390. DOI: 10.1177/1357633X0501100802 PMID: 16356311

IoT in healthcare and ambient assisted living. (2021). In *Studies in computational intelligence*. DOI: 10.1007/978-981-15-9897-5

Jiang, F., Jiang, Y., Zhi, H., Dong, Y., Li, H., Ma, S., Wang, Y., Dong, Q., Shen, H., & Wang, Y. (2017a). Artificial intelligence in healthcare: Past, present and future. *Stroke and Vascular Neurology*, 2(4), 230–243. DOI: 10.1136/svn-2017-000101 PMID: 29507784

Jiang, F., Jiang, Y., Zhi, H., Dong, Y., Li, H., Ma, S., Wang, Y., Dong, Q., Shen, H., & Wang, Y. (2017b). Artificial intelligence in healthcare: Past, present and future. *Stroke and Vascular Neurology*, 2(4), 230–243. DOI: 10.1136/svn-2017-000101 PMID: 29507784

Jin, M. X., Kim, S. Y., Miller, L. J., Behari, G., & Correa, R. (2020). Telemedicine: Current impact on the future. *Cureus*. Advance online publication. DOI: 10.7759/cureus.9891 PMID: 32968557

Kakhi, K., Alizadehsani, R., Kabir, H. D., Khosravi, A., Nahavandi, S., & Acharya, U. R. (2022). The internet of medical things and artificial intelligence: Trends, challenges, and opportunities. *Biocybernetics and Biomedical Engineering*, 42(3), 749–771. DOI: 10.1016/j.bbe.2022.05.008

Kashani, M. H., Madanipour, M., Nikravan, M., Asghari, P., & Mahdipour, E. (2021). A systematic review of IoT in healthcare: Applications, techniques, and trends. *Journal of Network and Computer Applications*, 192, 103164. DOI: 10.1016/j.jnca.2021.103164

Laplante, P. A., & Laplante, N. (2016). The Internet of Things in Healthcare: Potential applications and challenges. *IT Professional*, 18(3), 2–4. DOI: 10.1109/MITP.2016.42

Losorelli, S. D., Vendra, V., Hildrew, D. M., Woodson, E. A., Brenner, M. J., & Sirjani, D. B. (2021). The future of telemedicine: revolutionizing health care or flash in the Pan? *Otolaryngology and Head and Neck Surgery/Otolaryngology--head and Neck Surgery, 165*(2), 239–243. DOI: 10.1177/0194599820983330

Madakam, S., Ramaswamy, R., & Tripathi, S. (2015). Internet of Things (IoT): A literature review. *Journal of Computer and Communications*, 03(05), 164–173. DOI: 10.4236/jcc.2015.35021

Mathew, P. S., Pillai, A. S., & Palade, V. (2017). Applications of IoT in healthcare. In *Lecture notes on data engineering and communications technologies* (pp. 263–288). DOI: 10.1007/978-3-319-70688-7_11

S, G., L, V., B, R. V., Ss, D., & N, A. (2021). IoT based health monitoring system. *2021 Innovations in Power and Advanced Computing Technologies (i-PACT)*. DOI: 10.1109/i-PACT52855.2021.9696937

Sarhan, F. (2009). Telemedicine in healthcare. 1: Exploring its uses, benefits and disadvantages. *PubMed, 105*(42), 10–13. https://pubmed.ncbi.nlm.nih.gov/19916354

Silva, F. S. D., Neto, E. P., Oliveira, H., Rosario, D., Cerqueira, E., Both, C., Zeadally, S., & Neto, A. V. (2021). A survey on Long-Range Wide-Area Network Technology Optimizations. *IEEE Access : Practical Innovations, Open Solutions*, 9, 106079–106106. DOI: 10.1109/ACCESS.2021.3079095

Son, D., Lee, J., Qiao, S., Ghaffari, R., Kim, J., Lee, J. E., Song, C., Kim, S. J., Lee, D. J., Jun, S. W., Yang, S., Park, M., Shin, J., Do, K., Lee, M., Kang, K., Hwang, C. S., Lu, N., Hyeon, T., & Kim, D. (2014). Multifunctional wearable devices for diagnosis and therapy of movement disorders. *Nature Nanotechnology*, 9(5), 397–404. DOI: 10.1038/nnano.2014.38 PMID: 24681776

Surya, L. (2018). How government can use AI and ML to identify spreading infectious diseases. *Social Science Research Network*. https://autopapers.ssrn.com/sol3/papers.cfm?abstract_id=3785649

Sworna, N. S., Islam, A. M., Shatabda, S., & Islam, S. (2021). Towards development of IoT-ML driven healthcare systems: A survey. *Journal of Network and Computer Applications*, 196, 103244. DOI: 10.1016/j.jnca.2021.103244

Want, R. (2006). An introduction to RFID technology. *IEEE Pervasive Computing*, 5(1), 25–33. DOI: 10.1109/MPRV.2006.2

Yin, Y., Zeng, Y., Chen, X., & Fan, Y. (2016). The internet of things in healthcare: An overview. *Journal of Industrial Information Integration*, 1, 3–13. DOI: 10.1016/j.jii.2016.03.004

KEY TERMS AND DEFINITIONS

IoT: The Internet of Things refers to a group of networks consisting of interlinked devices equipped with sensors, software & technologies to facilitate data transmission or receiving data (Madakam et al., 2015).

LoRaWAN: It stands for Long Range Wide Area Network a kind of Low Power Wide Area Network (LPWAN) that utilizes open source technology & transmits over unlicensed frequency bands (Silva et al., 2021).

M2M: Machine to machine communication refers to the components & applications that facilitate direct communication for devices using any communication channel. i.e. wire or wireless connections (M2M Communications, 2012).

MCUs: MCUs refer to Microcontroller units, intelligent semiconductor ICs that contain processor units, memory modules, communication interfaces & peripherals.

RFID: Radio Frequency Identification technology utilizes radio waves to recognize & track objects, animals, or people (Want, 2006). A wireless communication that uses electromagnetic or electrostatic combination in the radio frequency part of the electromagnetic spectrum to distinctively recognize an entity. i.e. animal, person.

Telemedicine: Telemedicine is the utilization of electronic information & communication tech to support healthcare services when distance separates the patients (Ekeland et al., 2010).

Wearable Devices: Wearable devices are smart gadgets that are created to be worn on the human body consisting of sensors, microprocessors & wireless data transmission capabilities (Son et al., 2014).

Wi-Fi: It is a wireless networking technology that uses radio waves to provide wireless high-speed Internet access following IEEE 802.11x standard (He & Chan, 2016).

Chapter 3
Revolutionizing Healthcare:
IoT Powered Telemedicine Advancements

Venkat Narayana Rao T.

Sreenidhi Institute of Science and Technology, India

M. Stephen

Sreenidhi Institute of Science and Technology, India

Rohan Kolachala

Sreenidhi Institute of Science and Technology, India

ABSTRACT

In an age where healthcare and telemedicine have never been more crucial, the rise of IoT has enhanced free use of healthcare systems around the world. This is accomplished by improving the decision making with the help of accessible data, ensuring that monitoring and consultation of patients is carried out by remote means. In order to efficiently use IoT in healthcare, scalable modelling and effective management of the application plays a critical role. Scalable modelling in healthcare and telemedicine involves the development of systems and that can flexibly respond to changing needs, induce quality, accessibility, and value-for-money. Management of IoT applications in healthcare comes with many challenges such as handling patient data on time, secured medical data, remote, ensure proper amount of medicine is taken by the patient, disease tracking, etc. This chapter aims to guide the readers to understand and develop their own frameworks for the scalable models which adapt to the needs in healthcare and enable readers to explore the potential of IoT in telemedicine.

DOI: 10.4018/979-8-3693-1686-3.ch003

1. INTRODUCTION

1.1 The Significance of Healthcare and Telemedicine

The healthcare business, often known as the medical or health economy, is a broad term for a system of exchange that includes several industries offering products and services for the treatment, care, and prevention of patients in aspects that are preventative, curative, palliative, and rehabilitative. This complex system includes the creation and marketing of goods and services meant to maintain and replenish well-being.

The healthcare industry may be broken down into three main categories in its current form: goods, financing, and services. To meet the healthcare demands of people and communities, further classification crosses several sectors and classes and depends on a varied cadre of highly skilled professionals and paraprofessionals. A healthcare system's efficacy is crucial for both advancing national advancement and relieving family obligations. Developing nations are coming to understand how important healthcare is to their economy and how it directly affects life expectancy. Due in large part to their abundance of highly skilled medical professionals and their unwavering dedication to the healthcare system, some of these countries have become strong competitors. Interestingly, throughout time, the expenses of medical care have decreased significantly in many of these nations (Trivitron Healthcare, 2019) (Haleem, A., et al. 2021) (Karjagi, R., & Jindal).

Telemedicine is defined as the use of a healthcare professional in a remote location to diagnose and treat patients. Using medical applications for fixed periodic visits improves the effectiveness of both healthcare professionals and patients by increasing the chances of follow-up, lowering delays, and boosting patient outcomes. Regular hospital visits can be costly, especially in rural regions, especially because of transport expenses. Fortunately, when telemedicine services are used via video conferencing or other virtual technologies, medical visits can be reduced. In this way, telemedicine saves time and money for both the patient and the health care provider. Additionally, due to its rapid and beneficial properties, it can help hospitals and clinics streamline their workflow. This innovative technology would make monitoring and managing discharged patients' rehabilitation easier. Telemedicine enables clinical services to utilize, information technologies, and video imaging to provide healthcare services at a distance. It also enables patients and doctors to work together on the treatment process. This technology, however, is meant to complement rather than replace physical counselling. Today, this technology provides a safe option for patients who are unable to visit a doctor or stay at home, particularly during a pandemic. In conclusion, both the healthcare industry and telemedicine are an integral part of our society and contribute to its growth.

The growth of the healthcare industry has resulted in a significant decrease in treatment costs, enabling healthcare to reach a wider demographic. This change is especially important for developing countries, because achieving economic development depends on having access to healthcare and longer life expectancies. These nations are actively investing in healthcare infrastructure and developing a pool of highly qualified medical experts because they understand the critical role that healthcare plays in their development.

At the vanguard of industry development, these skilled practitioners use their knowledge to support further progress. The dedication to supporting healthcare is a strategic recognition of its vital role in promoting long-term growth and enhanced quality of life. Because of this, many emerging countries are strengthening the groundwork for sustained economic growth in addition to improving their health-care capacities.

In summary, telemedicine and the healthcare sector are not only essential to our society, but also to its development and advancement, as well as the goal of improving everyone's health and well-being. This chapter explores the various aspects of healthcare and telemedicine in the Internet of Things age, going deep into the core of this revolutionary journey.

1.2 The Role of IoT in Enhancing Healthcare Systems

By rearranging the way that devices and people interact to produce healthcare solutions, the Internet of Things (IoT) is unquestionably changing the healthcare industry. IoT applications benefit patients, families, insurance companies, physicians, and hospitals in the healthcare industry. As doctor-patient consultations have become more convenient and productive, so too have patient participation and satisfaction levels. Furthermore, re-admissions are avoided, and hospital stays are decreased as a result of remote patient monitoring. IoT has a significant influence on improving treatment outcomes and reducing healthcare costs as well. There are a lot of opportunities created by the expansion of IoT items for healthcare. Moreover, the vast amount of data generated by these networked devices has the power to totally change the healthcare industry (Al-Atawi et al., 2022) (Al-kahtani et al., 2022) (Sadek et al., 2022) .

IoT in healthcare is not without its challenges. Concerns regarding data security are raised by the vast amounts of data that IoT-enabled linked devices collect, especially sensitive data. Enough security measures need to be put in place. IoT reveals new aspects of patient care through access to patients' medical data and ongoing health monitoring. Healthcare stakeholders that want to increase revenue, enhance operations, and improve patient satisfaction and health will find this data to be useful. Preparedness to leverage this digital potential will set one apart in a culture growing more interconnected by the day.

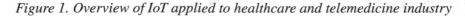

Figure 1. Overview of IoT applied to healthcare and telemedicine industry

Figure 1 gives a simple overview on how IoT is applied in the healthcare and telemedicine industry.

2. SCALABLE MODELLING IN HEALTHCARE AND TELEMEDICINE

2.1 What is Scalable Modelling in Healthcare?

Scalable modelling in healthcare and telemedicine is the use of IoT technology and data-driven modelling approaches to improve the healthcare sector's capacity to deliver care, maximise resource management, and adjust to changing needs. This idea entails gathering and analysing health-related data using networked hardware, sensors, and software. By doing this, healthcare providers will be able to fulfil the industry's growing demand and successfully manage difficulties by expanding their service offerings, providing more individualised treatment, and making educated decisions. (Amyra, 2019) (Healthcare IT Today, 2023) (Nersesian, 2023).

2.2 Advantages of Scalable Modelling

2.2.1 Remote Monitoring

It makes it possible to track patients' conditions remotely by enabling real-time monitoring of their vital signs and health indicators. Managing chronic diseases, providing post-operative care, and keeping an eye on high-risk patients have all benefited greatly from this technology (Eriksson, 2021).

2.2.2 Data Driven Decision Making

To make educated, data-driven decisions in the healthcare industry, scalable modelling uses IoT data. Healthcare professionals can personalize treatments and interventions for each patient by gathering and analysing enormous volumes of patient data, resulting in more individualized and efficient care.

2.2.3 Telemedicine Expansion

Healthcare providers can increase the scope of their telemedicine offerings thanks to the scalability of IoT. IoT devices enable virtual consultations for patients and remote patient data access for doctors, improving access to healthcare services overall and in underprivileged areas.

2.2.4 Predictive Analysis

Healthcare organizations may predict disease outbreaks, optimize resource allocation, and spot trends that could have an impact on public health by using IoT-generated data for predictive analytics.

2.2.5 Reduced Healthcare Costs

By avoiding readmissions to the hospital, enhancing the treatment of chronic diseases, and maximizing resource allocation, scalable modelling using IoT can aid in lowering healthcare expenses. This is particularly important in a healthcare system that is frequently under pressure from rising demand.

2.3 Challenges in Digital Healthcare

2.3.1 Patient Data Protection

Countless sensitive patient data points are produced by IoT devices. The security and privacy of sensitive data must be guaranteed. Stopping unwanted access, data breaches, and data misuse is essential.

2.3.2 Device Compatibility

The healthcare industry employs a vast variety of systems and equipment, frequently from various vendors. It is difficult to ensure interoperability between various devices. To solve this problem, standardization attempts are still being made.

2.3.3 Infrastructure Capacity

Scalability becomes a worry as healthcare systems grow and incorporate more IoT devices, and it's crucial to make sure the infrastructure can handle the rising number of data and devices to avoid performance problems.

2.3.4 Data Accuracy

Data provided by IoT devices might not always be completely correct. To guarantee the accuracy of the data, calibration, routine maintenance, and quality control procedures are required.

2.4 The Real-World Uses of Scalable Modelling in Terms of Health Domain

2.4.1 Wearable Health Devices

Wearables have become widespread, including smartwatches, activity trackers, and medical-grade gadgets like ECG monitors. They continuously track users' fitness and health, making it possible to collect data in real-time.

2.4.2 Remote Patient Monitoring

Scalable IoT technologies have been very beneficial for managing chronic diseases. Patients with illnesses like diabetes, hypertension, or heart disease can monitor their health at home with linked devices, and the data is then sent to healthcare professionals for evaluation (Sternhoff, 2021).

2.4.3 Smart Hospitals

Smart hospital systems can track equipment, regulate energy use, and even monitor patient movements to optimize workflow and decrease wait times. Healthcare facilities are implementing IoT to increase operational efficiency and patient care.

2.4.4 Telemedicine Platforms

Remote consultations and diagnostics are now available because to the proliferation of telemedicine services. During virtual appointments, IoT-enabled platforms give doctors access to patients' health information and vital signs, giving them a complete picture of the patient's health.

2.4.5 Population Health Management

Healthcare organizations can gain a better understanding of the health of their people by utilizing scalable modelling with IoT data. The allocation of resources, preventive care plans, and public health efforts can all benefit from this data.

Figure 2. Framework of a scalable model in healthcare

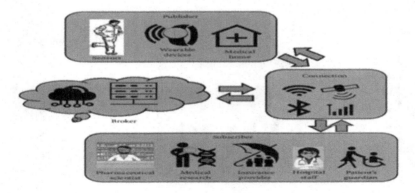

Figure 2 shows a simple framework of a Scalable Model in Healthcare and the applications of IoT in Healthcare Devices.

3. MANAGEMENT OF IOT APPLICATIONS IN HEALTHCARE

3.1 Challenges in Managing IoT Applications in Healthcare

IoT has emerged as a game-changing technology in the healthcare industry, introducing a variety of innovative applications leading to improved patient outcomes and cost-effectiveness. However, it does come with certain challenges which affect the application of these devices (Anonymous, 2022) (Scheibner, Jobin, & Vayena,, 2021) (HealthTech Magazine, 2023) .

3.1.1 Data Security and Privacy Issues

Data breaches can have an extensive number of consequences for both individual users and businesses. Furthermore, if attackers successfully infiltrate users' IoT devices, they will be able to actively watch users' private lives.

Even though IoT is rapidly increasing, the issue of security remains. As the Internet of Things evolves, new applications, particularly in the healthcare industry, will emerge. However, healthcare is tied to personal data, i.e., a patient's privacy and vital health information. As a result, the security of such systems has become an important concern. The graph below shows the variation of data breaches through IoT applications from 2005-2019 as shown in Figure 3.

Figure 3. Data breach in time line

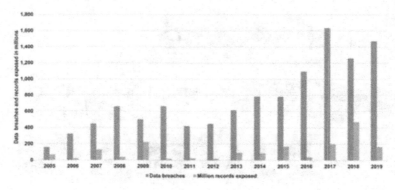

3.1.2 Integration of Multiple Devices and Protocols

Integrating numerous types of devices interferes with IoT development in the healthcare industry. The reason for this stumbling block lies in the fact that the manufacturers of these IoT devices have yet to agree on communication protocols and standards. As a result, each manufacturer develops a unique ecosystem of IoT devices that are incompatible with other manufacturers' devices and apps. There is not one protocol which can be followed and utilized for aggregating data in a scenario like this. This inconsistency delays the process and limits the scope of scalability of IoT in healthcare (FedTech Magazine, 2023) (Hameed et al., 2021) (IEEE, 2022) (Dash, 2020).

3.1.3 Data Overload and Accuracy

It is challenging to combine data for crucial insights and analysis because of the erratic nature of communication and data protocols. Data is received via IoT in large quantities; therefore, to evaluate the data effectively, it must be segmented into smaller subsets without being overly precise. Furthermore, the decision-making process in the hospitality sector may be impacted in the long run by data overload.

3.1.4 Cost of Application

When considering IoT app development for healthcare mobility solutions, one of the most important factors is cost. However, if the IoT solution answers a genuine problem, the expenses are totally justified.

While developing an IoT application will cost you a substantial sum of money and resources, the benefits will be enormous when your company saves time and manpower while improving its operations, generating greater revenue channels, and opening more business opportunities (Rejeb et al., 2022) (Ray, 2018) (Aceto et al., 2020).

3.2 Strategies to Overcome IoT Management Challenges in Healthcare

3.2.1 Securing the Network

The security needs for IoT devices are divided into two categories: cyber security and cyber resilience.

3.2.1.1 Cyber Security

Cyber security is an essential component of any healthcare IoT system because it protects patients' confidential medical data from unauthorised access and tampering Among the top cyber security practices are:

Confidentiality: To keep medical information secret, the IoT system should be structured to prevent unauthorised entities from disclosing it. This involves putting in place encryption techniques and access restrictions that limit access to only authorised users (Qi et al., 2017).

Availability: To guarantee that authorised users always have access to medical data, the IoT system should be built to avoid device malfunctions and operational outages. This may be accomplished using redundancy techniques, such as several backup servers, as well as frequent maintenance and updates (Dhanvijay et al., 2019).

Access Controls: The IoT system should incorporate access controls that define the amount of access based on the user's function to guarantee that various users only have access to the resources they require.

3.2.1.2 Cyber Resiliency

A resilient structure must have specific qualities to assure the system's availability and dependability under all conditions. The following are some of the most important best practices for cyber resilience in healthcare information technology:

Reliability: The system must be able to perform properly in the face of extreme weather, network outages, and other problems (Ratta et al., 2021).

Having autonomy: The system should be able to manage itself and be capable of protecting, configuring, mending, and optimising itself.

Configurability: The system should be able to modify settings so that it can perform successfully in a variety of operating scenarios.

Reparability: The system must be capable of detecting and correcting defects to resume regular functioning.

3.2.2 Enhancing Connectivity

Any disruption in data transmission in a hospital setting might have catastrophic consequences for patients. Because of this, communication with very high dependability and minimal latency is essential; the consequences of losing a connection are too severe to handle.

Highly sophisticated systems and dense device deployments in healthcare networks must operate continuously and without fail. As a result, device designers must include connectivity testing early in the product life cycle, employing strong solutions for hardware, software, and radio frequency evaluations. Effectively testing for signal or power quality concerns helps guarantee that IoMT devices can resist real-world situations and that healthcare organisations do not find connectivity difficulties during an emergency (Mieronkoski et al., 2017).

3.2.3 Operation of IoT Devices Over Time

Battery life is one of the most essential issues for IoMT devices, and for a valid reason. In the healthcare sector, operational consistency is a matter of crucial importance. Device designers may optimise battery runtimes by integrating sensing, processing, control, and communications elements early in manufacturing to analyse their relative power usage and establish a proper balance between functionality and power consumption.

Designers can optimize power usage to enable uninterrupted access to crucial patient data by aiming to prolong the battery life of critically needed healthcare equipment.

3.2.4 Interoperability Between Multiple Devices

In the healthcare IoT, interoperability—a wireless device's capacity to function in the presence of additional devices—is essential for consistent, trustworthy communication. This is particularly critical in healthcare, where interference can lead to connection failures or incorrect data in rescue devices such as IV pumps and pacemakers.

Interoperability testing early in the development of IoMT devices will help avoid these important interference concerns. Before designing, designers must comprehend the interferences and the frequencies, regulations, and signal strengths of the intended environment, as well as the essential functionality for a device's wireless performance, to do effective testing.

3.2.5 Ethical Considerations

To guarantee the appropriate and ethical use of this technology, a number of ethical concerns related to the integration of IoT in healthcare must be addressed. These include:

3.2.5.1 Data Ownership and Control

Clearly defining data ownership and control procedures is essential. Patients ought to be able to control who may access their data and access it themselves. This guarantees people's control over their private health information.

3.2.5.2 Patient Consent

One of the key principles should be patients' approval. Healthcare professionals and tech businesses need to have people's clear and informed consent before using IoT devices to gather their data. Patients should be fully informed about the possible uses, dangers, and advantages of their data as well as who will have access to it.

3.2.5.3 Accountability and Compliance

Following legal and regulatory frameworks like GDPR (General Data Protection Regulation) and HIPAA (Health Insurance Portability and Accountability Act) is essential to using IoT ethically. Compliance guarantees that IT firms and healthcare institutions are responsible for protecting patient data.

3.2.5.4 End-of-Life Data Handling

A specific plan for handling end-of-life data should be in place for healthcare IoT devices. Data should be safely wiped from devices when they are discontinued to keep any leftover information from being accessed.

3.2.5.5 Minimization of Data Collection

In order to respect moral principles, medical professionals should only gather information that is required for diagnosis, treatment, and advancement of patient care. To reduce privacy threats, unnecessary data collecting should be minimised.

3.2.5.6 Continuous Ethical Review

To adjust to changing ethical norms and new issues, IoT systems must undergo periodic ethical evaluations. IoT deployments should be supervised and guided by ethical committees or specialists. In addition to ensuring patient confidence, putting ethical issues first in healthcare IoT encourages the appropriate and advantageous use of technology in healthcare, which eventually improves patient care and well-being as shown in figure 4.

The image below shows the general mapping of interoperability of multiple IoT devices in the healthcare sector. It gives the general idea of the different operations that can be performed in accordance to different devices in order to maximize efficiency and precision (Haghi et al., 2021).

Figure 4. Health care during disaster management

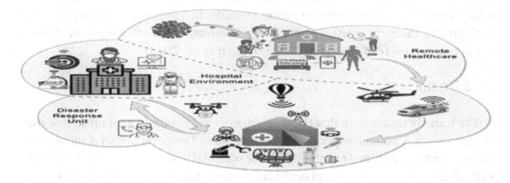

4. CASE STUDIES

4.1 A Case Study on Defibrillator Maintenance in Denmark

In 1962, a non-profit organization called the Danish Heart Foundation was established. "Together we win a healthier and better life for all" is their motto. With over 130.000 members, the Danish Heart Foundation ranks as the second-largest interest group in Denmark for public health. The charity focuses on patient support, cardiovascular disease research, and heart disease prevention.

4.1.1 Background

Studies have shown that many defibrillators are defective. Usually due to lack of maintenance, such as failing to replace electrodes and batteries, is to blame. A single malfunctioning defibrillator could change the odds of survival for a patient experiencing heart failure. This is a significant issue that is getting worse as Denmark's defibrillators age.

4.1.2 Solution

In response to the growing problem, that is the faulty defibrillators, Telenor has developed a ground-breaking response in partnership with Seluxit, the Danish Heart Association, and Hjerteforeningen. This method entails the creation of a digital monitoring system with numerous sensors to provide continuous monitoring of the defibrillator's operational status. The device immediately alerts a service technician when a malfunction is found, enabling quick maintenance. An optical sensor, which visually evaluates the defibrillator's state and power status, is one of the device's major components. The communication component sends a direct message to a platform that instantly notifies a service professional in the event of a breakdown or low power (FedTech Magazine, 2023) (Rejeb et al., 2022).

4.1.3 Result

The remedy makes sure that the defibrillators are regularly kept up so that they function when a patient experiences heart failure. The computerized monitoring system boosts security and eventually has the potential to save more lives. With 20671 defibrillators that have been registered and several unregistered users, the future of the digital monitoring device is very bright.

Over time, it will help to solve the problem of the huge number of defective defibrillators.

4.1.4 Learnings from the Study

This case study serves as an example of how IoT technology can revolutionize telemedicine and healthcare. In addition to resolving a significant issue in Denmark, the creative approach to monitoring and maintaining defibrillators demonstrates the effectiveness of cooperation between public and private organizations in enhancing patient outcomes and saving lives. This IoT solution's successful implementation provides a blueprint for next healthcare applications where technology can significantly improve patient care and safety.

4.2 A Case Study on CardiLink and Westbase.IO Collaboration

CardiLink has made a name for itself as a pioneer in the field of medical technology device monitoring, with a focus on offering fleet management tools to owners of Automated External Defibrillators (AEDs) and international medical device manufacturers. Their cloud based IoT service platform, which presents a cutting-edge method of monitoring medical equipment, is the foundation of their strategy. This platform provides vital information about the location and status of AEDs, as well as immediate alarm alerts about the operation of these life-saving devices. CardiLink also makes sure AEDs follow the most recent medical device regulations, underlining their dedication to patient safety.

4.2.1 Background

Heart failure is the sudden loss of heart function in a person who may or may not have heart disease. It could start suddenly or overlap with different symptoms. If quick measures to save a person's life are not taken, heart failure is fatal and usually ends in death.

However, if CPR is given, a defibrillator shocks a heart, as well as regular heartbeat is established immediately after experiencing heart failure, it may be possible to reverse heart failure (Anonymous, 2022).

A device called an automated external defibrillator (AED) shocks the heart with electricity through the chest. The shock can stop an irregular heartbeat and encourage the return of a regular rhythm. Emergency medical services attempt to revive a victim in the UK, there are about 30,000 OHCAs (out-of-hospital cardiac arrests) every year. Only one in ten people in the UK survive an OHCA, therefore the survival rate is low. Each year, more than 350,000 cardiac arrests take place outside of hospitals in the US. Heart attacks cause about 20% of all fatalities each year in Europe. Heart attacks kill more people worldwide than the combined incidence of prostate cancer, breast cancer, pneumonia, the flu, traffic accidents, HIV, firearms, and house fires.

These statistics demonstrate both the frequency of heart failure and the need of early identification and timely intervention.

4.2.2 Challenge

AEDs are frequently put in public places including malls, theatres, venues, and workplaces where big crowds congregate. AED owners and manufacturers must work to ensure dependable operation.

AEDs require routine maintenance even though they are primarily unattended devices. The problem is that the individual who might have installed the gadget won't be present every day to inspect and evaluate its state of operation. Even when operating well, the equipment still needs to be monitored and subjected to routine safety checks due to its crucial nature.

Sadly, according to several studies, AEDs malfunction occasionally, 25% of the failures were caused by battery problems. This could go unnoticed on a disconnected device until it is most needed. The sad truth is that malfunctioning AEDs can result in fatalities. Therefore, routine inspections are essential and required in many nations.

The COVID-19 pandemic makes things more difficult. It can be logistically difficult to inspect AEDs for issues while numerous facilities are closed.

4.2.3 Solution

The IoT platform from CardiLink provides a complete answer to the problems with AED fleet management. Reliable and secure global managed connectivity from Telenor Connexion supports the service platform, making it easier to manage and monitor AED fleets through prompt alerts and notifications. By doing this, AEDs are kept functional and prepared for use in emergencies.

4.2.3.1 A Subscription-Based Business Model

Each device linked to the service platform is operated by CardiLink through a monthly subscription charge. With this adaptable strategy, the service is tailored to businesses of all sizes and locations, ensuring that it is still available and reasonably priced.

4.2.3.2 Accurate Data Gathering and Analysis

Each connected AED's data is collected, saved, and analysed by the service platform to guarantee compliance with The Medical Device Regulation. When an AED triggers or someone leaves a defined area, CardiLink's solution shines at alerting service workers, planning maintenance or inspections, and contacting security. Additionally, it can notify surrounding emergencies to first aid responders and ask for their assistance (Dang et al., 2019).

4.2.3.3 The Future of Reliable Remote Monitoring

The goal of CardiLink is to utilize data effectively to automate notices from every link in the chain of AED ownership from manufacturers to end-owners. This goal goes beyond safe data transmission. By eliminating the requirement for manual AED monitoring entirely, this automated method dramatically decreases the risk of human mistake, which is a primary point of failure.

4.2.4 Results

Now, CardiLink has deployed bases spanning Asia, Latin America, and Europe in more than twenty countries. Customers have recently requested to add even more gadgets to its platform, like first aid equipment and fire extinguishers, and other medical device makers have signed deals.

Additionally, CardiLink has offered its services to other Heart Safe Cities initiatives worldwide. The initiative's overarching goal is to enhance the proportion of episodes of out-of-hospital cardiac arrest that are successfully managed and prevent fatalities (Bayo-Monton et al., 2018) (Jagadeeswari et al., 2018).

With the help of its service, producers of medical devices can change from delivering only items to solutions based on Service Level Agreements (SLAs). It turned out to be well-liked by both B2B and B2G clients.

CardiLink's solution aids in ensuring that connected AEDs continue to comply with this stringent law in many jurisdictions, both the US and the EU.

Additionally, CardiLink goes above and beyond by providing a "as-a-service" paradigm, that greatly decreases the demands imposed on producers when creating new gadgets. It also provides them with a useful way to connect and update operational units.

4.2.5 Learnings From the Study

In conclusion, the partnership between CardiLink and Westbase.IO represents a radical change in medical technology device monitoring for the healthcare industry. These organizations have proven that the seamless integration of technology can significantly improve the quality of care, device functionality, and regulatory compliance by embracing IoT and utilizing Managed Connectivity. Their collaboration paves the way for upcoming advancements in the sector by serving as an encouraging case study for the academic investigation of IoT applications in healthcare and telemedicine.

4.3 Key Lessons and Implications

In the case studies that came before them, it was shown how telemedicine advances driven by the Internet of Things have transformed healthcare by tackling important problems with the upkeep and administration of life-saving medical equipment. These real-world examples offer insightful knowledge and practical advice that can be used in more general healthcare settings. The main conclusions and ramifications are summarized from these case studies in this section.

4.3.1 Collaboration as a Catalyst for Innovation

The case studies impart important insights on the value of teamwork. Both times, businesses and government agencies collaborated to develop ground-breaking answers to pressing healthcare issues. Cross-sector alliances can spur innovation in healthcare, as demonstrated by the Danish Heart Foundation's cooperation with Telenor, Seluxit, and Hjerteforeningen in Denmark and CardiLink's relationship with Westbase.IO.

> **Case Study 4.1:** The Danish Heart Foundation and its partners showed that they could create a digital defibrillator monitoring system by combining their resources and knowledge. This cooperation was essential in tackling the expanding issue of malfunctioning defibrillators. The clear takeaway from this is that teamwork encourages creativity and makes it easier to find solutions that improve patient care and safety (Verma et al., 2018) (Li et al., 2019).
>
> **Case Study 4.2:** The collaboration between CardiLink and Westbase.IO demonstrated how teamwork may result in the development of an all-inclusive Internet of Things platform for the administration and observation of Automated External Defibrillators (AEDs). They benefited people and healthcare providers worldwide by extending their reach to over twenty nations by utilizing each other's advantages.

4.3.2 IoT Technology: A Game Changer in Healthcare

The two case studies highlight how IoT technology could revolutionize the healthcare industry. Connectivity and IoT-enabled devices were essential in tackling important problems with medical equipment upkeep, real-time monitoring, and regulatory compliance.

> **Case Study 4.1:** The Danish Heart Foundation used sensors and communication components from the Internet of Things (IoT) to monitor the operational status of defibrillators in real time. This could save lives by improving patient safety and ensuring timely maintenance. This example of IoT technology application shows the significant influence it can have on patient outcomes.
>
> **Case Study 4.2:** One excellent illustration of how technology can completely transform the healthcare sector is CardiLink's cloud-based IoT platform. IoT technology guarantees that these life-saving devices are always prepared for action by giving real-time data on the location and status of AEDs and by ensuring compliance with medical device regulatory standards. In the field of

medical device monitoring, the service platform's capacity to automate alerts and notifications is revolutionary.

4.3.3 Patient-Centred Approach

The focus of both case studies is on the patient-centred method of treatment. Enhancing patient outcomes and safety is the main objective of these IoT-powered solutions, especially during emergencies. Healthcare innovation is guided by this patient-centric focus.

Case Study 4.1: The Danish Heart Foundation's approach increases the likelihood of survival for patients suffering from heart failure by ensuring that defibrillators are regularly maintained. Patient safety is prioritized by adopting a proactive approach to device maintenance, which is consistent with the organization's goal of promoting a healthier and better life for everyone.

Case Study 4.2: CardiLink's technology makes sure that AEDs are following medical device standards in addition to monitoring them. The pressing need to preserve lives in situations of cardiac arrest that occur outside of hospitals motivates this strategy. Patient safety is the focus of this creative system, which automates alarms and guarantees that AEDs are in use.

4.3.4 Scalability and Future Possibilities

The scalability of IoT-powered telemedicine solutions is illustrated by both case examples. The healthcare sector has bright futures because these solutions may be tailored for different medical devices and extended across a wider geographic area.

Case Study 4.1: The Danish defibrillator digital monitoring system, which has over 20,000 registered devices and many additional potential users, demonstrates the scalability potential. This solution has the potential to address the nation's pervasive problem of faulty defibrillators, and its effectiveness suggests that there may be more uses for the technology in healthcare.

Case Study 4.2: CardiLink's international expansion and investigation of other medical device categories show how flexible and scalable their IoT platform is. Scalability is attainable since a variety of enterprises and organizations can utilize the platform thanks to its subscription-based revenue model.

4.3.5 Regulatory Compliance and Ethical Considerations

The significance of ethical and regulatory compliance in healthcare IoT applications is emphasized by both case examples. For the sake of patient safety and public confidence, it is imperative that these solutions abide by medical device standards.

> **Case Study 4.1:** Telenor and its partners have created a digital monitoring system that complies with medical device regulations. Following the rules is not only required by law but also morally right, especially when patient lives are involved.
> **Case Study 4.2:** CardiLink's commitment to compliance with The Medical Device Regulation indicates a strong ethical position in offering safe and reliable healthcare solutions. Their capacity to alert emergency personnel and first aid providers further emphasizes the moral importance of prompt action in life-threatening circumstances.
> In conclusion, the takeaways and lessons learned from these case studies highlight the importance of teamwork, the revolutionary potential of IoT technology in healthcare, and the steadfast dedication to patient safety and legal compliance. These observations provide a solid basis for upcoming IoT-enabled healthcare applications that have the potential to greatly improve patient safety and care. A look into the future of a patient-centred, cutting-edge healthcare ecosystem, the case studies present a road map for the wider adoption of IoT-powered telemedicine innovations in healthcare.

5. EMERGING TRENDS AND FUTURE OUTLOOK

Telemedicine enabled by IoT is at the vanguard of healthcare innovation, and it has a bright future ahead of it. It is clear from delving into the newest trends and cutting-edge technologies that this industry has the power to completely transform healthcare as we know it. Here, we examine several significant trends and upcoming initiatives that have the potential to completely transform patient care (Bayo-Monton et al., 2018) (Jagadeeswari et al., 2018).

5.1 AI-Assisted Diagnostics: Transforming Healthcare Delivery

Artificial intelligence (AI) is rapidly becoming a part of the telemedicine foundation. An increasing number of medical practitioners are using AI algorithms to assist them in diagnosing and treating patients. Machine learning and huge datasets are the driving forces behind these systems. AI-assisted diagnosis via telemedicine holds great promise:

5.1.1 Predictive Analysis

AI may evaluate patient data to forecast the course of an illness, assisting medical professionals in creating individualized treatment regimens and interventions.

5.1.2 Image Recognition

To help radiologists make quicker and more accurate diagnoses, AI systems may examine medical images like X-rays and MRIs for irregularities.

5.1.3 Virtual Health Assistants

Chatbots and other AI-driven virtual assistants can help patients in real time by giving them information and support, which eases the workload for medical staff.

The combination of AI and telemedicine has the potential to improve patient outcomes, lower healthcare costs, and increase diagnostic accuracy as the field develops. AI can also help with remote monitoring, warning medical professionals about any problems before they get worse and resulting in more proactive treatment.

5.2 Telehealth for Mental Health: Breaking Down Barriers

With significant ramifications, the integration of telehealth services for mental health is a growing trend. The stigma associated with mental health frequently deters people from getting treatment. This problem is addressed via telehealth, especially when it is coupled with IoT applications:

5.2.1 Therapy Apps and Wearables

People can discreetly monitor their mental health and seek therapeutic care with the help of IoT devices and smartphone apps.

5.2.2 Remote Therapy Sessions

Patients can communicate securely and video call with mental health providers from the comfort of their own homes through teletherapy.

5.2.3 Data Driven Care

Wearables with Internet of Things capabilities can gather information on a patient's vital signs and emotional moods, giving mental health practitioners important new information.

In the field of mental health, the combination of telehealth with IoT has the potential to lower obstacles to care, increase accessibility, and provide continuous assistance for individuals who require it.

5.3 Virtual Reality (VR) in Telemedicine: Transforming the Patient Experience

Another fascinating area of research is the incorporation of virtual reality (VR) into telemedicine. Patients can change their perception of pain and suffering by submerging themselves in a virtual environment thanks to virtual reality technology.

5.3.1 Pain Management

VR is proving to be an effective pain management technique that helps people become distracted from their suffering while receiving treatment or recovering from an injury.

5.3.2 Physical Therapy

Virtual reality (VR) can be utilized to develop stimulating workouts and recovery plans that improve patient results and compliance.

5.3.3 Medical Training

VR training may be realistic and immersive for healthcare professionals, enhancing their knowledge and abilities.

VR-based remote consultations, which allow patients and medical professionals to communicate in a virtual environment and bridge the gap between in-person and distant treatment, may be a feature of telemedicine in the future.

5.4 Blockchain and Secure Health Data Exchange: Enhancing Data Security

It is impossible to overestimate the significance of safe health data interchange as telemedicine develops. The decentralized and secure characteristics of blockchain technology is making waves in the medical field (Verma et al., 2018) (Li et al., 2019):

5.4.1 Patient Data Security

By ensuring the safe exchange and storage of medical records, blockchain helps allay worries about illegal access and data breaches.

5.4.2 Interoperability

Blockchain facilitates data exchange and care coordination by fostering interoperability across different healthcare systems and devices.

5.4.3 Telemedicine Payment Models

Processes for telemedicine payment and reimbursement can be automated and secured with the use of blockchain's smart contracts.

Blockchain technology is being incorporated into telemedicine to protect patient privacy and security and promote confidence in the medical system.

5.5 5G Connectivity and to IoT Integration: Enabling Real-Time Healthcare

Telemedicine is expected to reach new heights with the introduction of 5G networks and the growing integration of IoT devices:

5.5.1 High Speed Connectivity

For real-time telemedicine applications, 5G offers the high-speed, low-latency connectivity needed to ensure lag-free video consultations and data transfer.

5.5.2 IoT Device Proliferation

devices provide for proactive healthcare interventions by enabling remote monitoring of patients' health status and vital signs as they become more commonplace.

5.5.3 Telemedicine in Remote Areas

By bridging the connectivity gap, 5G and IoT enable telemedicine to be available even in underserved and remote locations (Albahri et al., 2021).

Instantaneous, data-rich exchanges that will improve the patient-provider relationship and allow for more effective and efficient healthcare delivery will characterize the future of telemedicine.

6. CONCLUSION

Ultimately, this comprehensive analysis of healthcare and telemedicine in the Internet of Things era emphasizes the significant impact and ground-breaking opportunities that IoT technologies present to the healthcare sector. Healthcare service delivery, patient care, and medical data administration will all be revolutionized by the combination of IoT with telemedicine. This is a paradigm shift. IoT allows real-time data capture and analysis, which improves patient outcomes by empowering healthcare professionals to make prompt, data-driven decisions.

This extraordinary advancement, however, is accompanied by several complicated hurdles. While IoT devices produce vital insights, the sheer volume of data created needs complex data management and integration solutions to minimise data overload and assure the quality of healthcare services. Simultaneously, the increased emphasis on data security, driven by the sensitivity of medical information, necessitates strong encryption, multi-factor authentication, and severe access controls to preserve patient privacy. Furthermore, the ability of IoT for remote monitoring and surveillance necessitates ongoing connectivity and dependable technical assistance to ensure data stream integrity.

While these problems are substantial, the ideas outlined in this chapter provide practical solutions for mitigating and overcoming them. The successful case studies highlighted in this chapter serve as examples of practical application, demonstrating the effectiveness of these tactics in real-world circumstances. These case studies demonstrate that the combination of scalable modelling and effective IoT management in healthcare may not only handle the issues, but also push us closer to the ideal vision of healthcare—an era in which great healthcare is universally available and without limitations.

In conclusion, the combination of healthcare, telemedicine, and IoT represents a revolutionary path towards a future in which healthcare is really efficient, accessible, and open for all persons worldwide. The initiatives and innovations shown in this chapter attest to the potential of IoT technology to improve the healthcare sector. As technology advances and healthcare systems change, the ideas and tactics outlined in this chapter will continue to play an important role in attaining the vision of comprehensive and high-quality healthcare that is not constrained by financial restrictions.

REFERENCES

Aceto, G., Persico, V., & Pescapé, A. (2020). Industry 4.0 and health: Internet of Things, Big Data, and cloud computing for healthcare 4.0. *Journal of Industrial Information Integration*, 18, 18. DOI: 10.1016/j.jii.2020.100129

Al-Atawi, A. A., Khan, F., & Kim, C. G. (2022). Application and Challenges of IoT Healthcare System in COVID-19. *Sensors (Basel)*, 22(19), 7304. DOI: 10.3390/s22197304 PMID: 36236404

Al-kahtani, M. S., Khan, F., & Taekeun, W. (2022). Application of Internet of Things and Sensors in Healthcare. *Sensors (Basel)*, 22(15), 5738. DOI: 10.3390/s22155738 PMID: 35957294

Albahri, A. S., Alwan, J. K., Taha, Z. K., Ismail, S. F., Hamid, R. A., Zaidan, A. A., Albahri, O. S., Zaidan, B. B., Alamoodi, A. H., & Alsalem, M. A. (2021). IoT-based telemedicine for disease prevention and health promotion: state-of-the-Art. *Journal of Network and Computer Applications*, 173, 173. DOI: 10.1016/j.jnca.2020.102873

Amyra. (2019, September 30). IoT in Healthcare: Benefits, Challenges and Applications. Valuecoders - Hire Dedicated Software Development Team.

Anonymous, . (2022, September 30). Publicly funded health care could extend longevity of life. *Journal of Global Health*, 12(4).

Bayo-Monton, J. L., Martinez-Millana, A., Han, W., Fernandez-latas, C., Sun, Y., & Traver, V. (2018). Wearable sensors integrated with Internet of Things for advancing eHealth care. *Sensors (Basel)*, 18(6), 1851. DOI: 10.3390/s18061851 PMID: 29882790

Dang, L. M., Piran, M. J., Han, D., Min, K., & Moon, H. (2019). *A survey on internet of things and cloud computing for healthcare*. Electronics. DOI: 10.3390/electronics8070768

Dash, S. P. (2020). The Impact of IoT in Healthcare: Global Technological Change & The Roadmap to a Networked Architecture in India.

Dhanvijay, M. M., & Patil, S. C. (2019). Internet of Things: A survey of enabling technologies in healthcare and its applications. *Computer Networks*, 153, 113–131. DOI: 10.1016/j.comnet.2019.03.006

Eriksson, N. G. (2021, May 5). The Danish Heart Association: Digital Monitoring of Defibrillators. Telenor IoT.

FedTech Magazine. (2023, October 30). The Role of Blockchain in Secure Health Data Exchange. Retrieved from FedTech Magazine.

Haghi Kashani, M., Madanipour, M., Nikravan, M., Asghari, P., & Mahdipour, E. (2021). A systematic review of IoT in healthcare: Applications, techniques, and trends. *Journal of Network and Computer Applications*, 192, 103164. DOI: 10.1016/j.jnca.2021.103164

Haleem, A., Javaid, M., Singh, R. P., & Suman, R. (2021). Telemedicine for Healthcare: Capabilities, Features, Barriers, and Applications. *Sensors International*, 2(2), 100117. DOI: 10.1016/j.sintl.2021.100117 PMID: 34806053

Hameed, K., Bajwa, I. S., Sarwar, N., Anwar, W., Mushtaq, Z., & Rashid, T. (2021). Integration of 5G and Block-Chain Technologies in Smart Telemedicine Using IoT.

HealthTech Magazine. (2023, October 30). Telehealth and Virtual Reality Expand into Mainstream Care at the VA.

IEEE. (2022, April 28). Connectivity, Wearables and the Evolution of Telemedicine.

Jagadeeswari, V., Subramaniyaswamy, V., Logesh, R., & Vijayakumar, V. (2018). A study on medical Internet of Things and Big Data in personalized healthcare system. *Health Information Science and Systems*, 6(1), 14. DOI: 10.1007/s13755-018-0049-x PMID: 30279984

Karjagi, R., & Jindal, M. IoT in Healthcare Industry | IoT Applications in Healthcare - Wipro.

Li, Q., Zhu, H., Xiong, J., Mo, R., Ying, Z., & Wang, H. (2019). Fine-grained multi-authority access control in IoT-enabled mHealth. *Annales des Télécommunications*, 74(7-8), 74. DOI: 10.1007/s12243-018-00702-6

Mieronkoski, I., Azimi, I., Rahmani, A. M., Aantaa, R., Terävä, V., Liljeberg, P., & Salanterä, S. (2017). The Internet of Things for basic nursing care—A scoping review. *International Journal of Nursing Studies*, 69, 78–90. DOI: 10.1016/j.ijnurstu.2017.01.009 PMID: 28189116

Nersesian, R. (2023, October 21). Council Post: Five Hurdles of Healthcare IoT — and How to Overcome Them. *Forbes*.

Qi, J., Yang, P., Min, G., Amft, O., Dong, F., & Xu, L. (2017). Advanced internet of things for personalised healthcare systems: A survey. *Pervasive and Mobile Computing*, 41, 41. DOI: 10.1016/j.pmcj.2017.06.018

Ratta, P., Kaur, A., Sharma, S., Shabaz, M., & Dhiman, G. (2021). Application of blockchain and Internet of Things in healthcare and medical sector: Applications, challenges, and future perspectives. *Journal of Food Quality*, 2021, 1–20. DOI: 10.1155/2021/7608296

Ray, P. P. (2018). A survey on Internet of Things architectures. *Journal of King Saud University. Computer and Information Sciences*, 30(3), 291–319. DOI: 10.1016/j. jksuci.2016.10.003

Rejeb, A., Rejeb, K., Simske, S., Treiblmaier, H., & Zailani, S. (2022). The big picture on the internet of things and the smart city: A review of what we know and what we need to know. *Internet of Things : Engineering Cyber Physical Human Systems*, 19, 19. DOI: 10.1016/j.iot.2022.100565

Sadek, I., Codjo, J., Rehman, S. U., & Abdulrazak, B. (2022). Security and Privacy in the Internet of Things Healthcare Systems: Toward a Robust Solution in Real-Life Deployment. *Computer Methods and Programs in Biomedicine Update*, 2, 2. DOI: 10.1016/j.cmpbup.2022.100071

Scheibner, J., Jobin, A., & Vayena, E. (2021, February 15). Ethical Issues with Using Internet of Things Devices in Citizen Science Research: A Scoping Review. *Frontiers in Environmental Science*, 9, 9. DOI: 10.3389/fenvs.2021.629649

Sternhoff, J. (2021, April 28). CardiLink: Delivering Lifesaving Connectivity When It's Needed Most. Telenor IoT. Retrieved from iot.telenor.com/iot-case/cardilink/

Trivitron Healthcare. (2019, September 12). How Healthcare Industry Helps in Contributing to the Economy. Trivitron Blog.

Verma, P., & Sood, S. K. (2018). Cloud-centric IoT based disease diagnosis healthcare framework. *Journal of Parallel and Distributed Computing*, 116, 27–38. DOI: 10.1016/j.jpdc.2017.11.018

ENDNOTE

[1] How to Address Security Issues in IoT Devices – Cybersecurity | Healthcare IT Today. (2023, February 28). www.healthcareittoday.com.

Chapter 4
Automatic Irrigation System Using IoT

Guillermo M. Limon-Molina
https://orcid.org/0000-0002-5445
-8928

*Universidad Politécnica de Baja
California, Mexico*

E. Ivette Cota-Rivera
https://orcid.org/0009-0002-6240
-9269

*Universidad Politécnica de Baja
California, Mexico*

Maria E. Raygoza-Limón

*Universidad Politécnica de Baja
California, Mexico*

Fabian N. Murrieta-Rico
https://orcid.org/0000-0001-9829
-3013

*Universidad Politécnica de Baja
California, Mexico*

Jesus Heriberto Orduño-Osuna
https://orcid.org/0009-0004-4850
-7481

*Universidad Politécnica de Baja
California, Mexico*

Roxana Jimenez-Sánchez
https://orcid.org/0009-0002-0061
-7206

*Universidad Politécnica de Baja
California, Mexico*

Miguel E. Bravo-Zanoguera

*Universidad Politécnica de Baja
California, Mexico*

Abelardo Mercado

*Universidad Politécnica de Baja
California, Mexico*

ABSTRACT

Water scarcity is nowadays a global problem, which requires innovative and sustainable solutions to reduce waste. The main uses are in the agricultural sector where in most cases flood irrigation is still used. In a lower degree the domestic use is considered; here the "automated" irrigation is via temporized solenoids that turn on and off the water circulation. These kinds of systems have proved inefficiency due to not considering the real need of water for the plants and cultivations. Considering

DOI: 10.4018/979-8-3693-1686-3.ch004

the above issues, the authors proposed Automatic Irrigation System (AIS) that uses a mobile app and microcontroller to monitor cultivations in real time; this allows the user to take informed decisions to avoid water waste. The proposed system uses moisture and temperature sensors to monitor each type of cultivation needs; with this information the system can work in automatic mode or in manual mode to be activated individually or by sections for maintenance purposes.

INTRODUCTION

According to (United Nations) water is the core of sustainable development and is critical for social and economic development, energy and food production, healthy ecosystems and for human survival. Water is also important for weather adaptation, serving as an important link between society and the environment.

Nearly 71% of the earth's surface is water, but only 2.5% is freshwater and only 0.3% is for human consumption. Therefore, it is important to have innovative and sustainable solutions to reduce water waste.

In agriculture, a good yield of crops is desired, the irrigation systems require constant monitoring, and it is important in areas where water is scarce (Al-Ali et al. 1). Technological advances in agriculture may provide answers to controlling the yield of a crop in response to varying climate conditions (Sassenrath et al., 2008), (García-Ruiz et al., 2020).

With better technology comes better yield, this helps to prevent situations like starvation and malnutrition (Vij et al., 2020). The technology should be available and affordable for being able to reach worldwide; also, technology needs to be sustainable. Every technological implementation should last some years and have to be user friendly, if any system becomes too complex to use people will not invest in them.

To solve water waste problems different solutions were offered in the references such (Al-Ali et al.) where an irrigation system with solar cells was presented. This is a good solution when you also have a problem with the power distribution, but it is well known solar cells are not cheap and the system programming was made in LabVIEW, so it means you require a computer and a LabVIEW license, which is a costly solution (you can have community edition but is not for commercial use).

Another solution (Vij et al., 2020) was presented, in here an agricultural application was implemented where sensor nodes were used each one with a microcontroller. The sensor nodes were equipped with sensors which readings were sent to another microcontroller, which serves as a Gateway node; this is the one with communication to a cloud or server. The article did not show any user interface which means the application was only for data gathering in a scientific way to analyze crops growths, precipitation and relative humidity. This implementation will be a complex solution for average people.

A very similar work is presented in (Nawandar and Satpute, 2019) where a smart irrigation system is presented, with a monitor via web page and the main distinctive feature is the use of Neural Networks and is thought to be used for farm applications, they mention that can be used for greenhouse or garden too, but the layout of the diagrams show otherwise.

The presented work for this chapter is the use of Automatic Irrigation System (AIS) that uses a mobile app and microcontroller to monitor cultivations in real time; this allows the user to take informed decisions to avoid water waste. The proposed system uses moisture and temperature sensors to monitor each type of cultivation needs, with this information the system can work in automatic mode or in manual mode to be activated individually or by sections for maintenance purposes.

METHODS

For the methodology for this case of study the authors used an ESP-32 microcontroller and an Android Application, both microcontroller and the app communicate with each other through a Firebase Database.

The ESP-32 development board has a 2.4 GHz combo chip with Wi-Fi and Bluetooth with low power consumption and it is designed to have power and RF performance (Espressif Systems, 2023). In other words, ESP-32 is a powerful microcontroller and has the capability of being programmed by C Language and Arduino Software.

Nowadays Android OS has better presence compared to IOS, in terms of apps. There are other Operating Systems (OS) but these are the ones used in mobile applications. Android Systems tend to be open source (Jasuja), so it means to create an application is free of charge, also apps can be published everywhere or via Play Store with a unique fee.

Figure 1. Database in json format created in Firebase

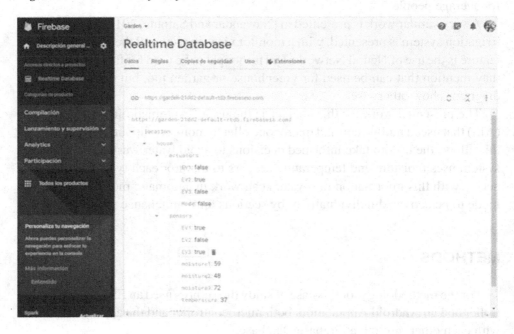

The database (Figure 1) was considered from the beginning to have the need of monitoring three plants with EV1, EV2 and EV3 for the solenoid valve of the individual capability for being irrigated. In addition, a mode field is displayed to control (read or receive instruction) manual or auto setting for the irrigation system. All this information is under the actuators key (field in json format), the intentions of these fields are to send commands from the app to the microcontroller to enable or disable the actuators.

For the sensors' key, the main purpose is to read the sensors from the microcontroller, also the current state of the solenoids for being monitored through the application. In this section Moisture1, Moisture2 and Moisture3 are set to read the moisture of each plant (for the experiment only Moisture1 was used) and then it has the temperature which is the same for all the plants. In addition, EV1, EV2 and EV3 are in this section to be able to read the current state or the solenoids.

As mentioned before the experiment for this study was divided in two parts: ESP-32 programming and the Android Application. An ESP-32-C3-DevKitC-02 was used with Arduino language, two analog inputs and two digital outputs. This microcontroller has 12 bit resolution for the analog inputs, every raw reading has 0-4095 range, used with the maximum attenuation 12 dB is possible to have a reference of 5 volts.

Two digital outputs were used in this experiment, one called LED1 is used to indicate whether a Wi-Fi connection is established and the other output is to activate the solenoid valve (EV1) or pump of the irrigation system. An YL-69 moisture sensor was used along with a LM35 temperature sensor with analog inputs described before.

The system has two modes of operation: Auto (Automatic Mode) and Manual. In Auto mode, the system is constantly monitoring moisture and temperature, with this data the system enables or disables the irrigation water. For Manual Mode the user can enable or disable the water flow, bypassing the sensors' readings. This action can be used for maintenance of the system to check whether the solenoids are working properly and to stop the system if it is required.

In Figure 2 is shown how the whole process of the microcontroller is done. The process starts with ports and Wi-Fi configuring, once completed the program checks the Wi-Fi connection, if a connection is established LED1 is on, and otherwise is off. Then if the microcontroller has a connection the program starts a http get request, if it is successful EV1, EV2, EV3 and mode variables are read from the database, as a reminder only EV1 and mode variables are needed for this experiment.

If the http get request fails, a message is sent to the monitor and the program will end here. In here an area of opportunity is presented, the monitor is not show anywhere is only show if the user connects via USB to the microcontroller, so it can be said is only used right now as a maintenance purpose, so for future implementation the authors can have of signal when the http request fails to be completed. To avoid that problem the microcontroller program has been tested several times and most of the cases when http fails is when the database has been corrupted or changed or when there is no Wi-Fi connection, the last action is shown by LED1 as stated before.

Figure 2. ESP-32 programming algorithm

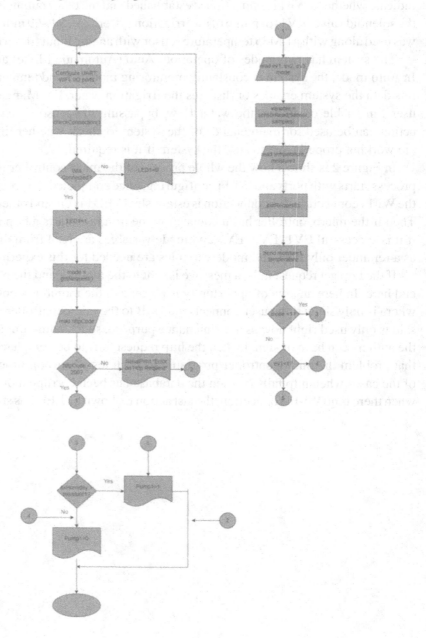

Considering the case when the http get request is completed successfully, our program continues with the sensors´ readings (Moisture and Temperature) via its analog ports, once completed, an http put request is done to send the data through the database. The microcontroller task will always read the sensors and update the database whether or not the program is in Auto or Manual mode.

The next step or the microcontroller program is to ask for the operating mode, if it is Auto mode the program will check if there is enough moisture for the Plant 1, according to the corresponding setting, depending on the type cultivation the moisture level is set in the microcontroller program. So far, this is a fixed data (a constant) for the system. In the future, the author will have a backend program (such a web page) where the technician will set the correct parameters for each plant or cultivation without the need of rewriting the microcontroller program.

For the Manual mode, the system will only be concerned with the desired state of the EV1 (solenoid 1 or pump) and it is here when the program "ends" (starts over).

The other part of the experiment is the Android Application; in this case, this mobile app can serve as a User Interface (UI) of the Irrigation System. The final version of the app will start with a login process via email or by using a google account; in this case of study the authors will show only the demo version, which only has the view of the login activity that will be bypassed by a click of the login button. However, a true login process will need to be implemented for the release version for security purposes that is because the app will be a custom one depending on the real application and only the owner of the garden (or cultivation field) shall have access to.

By having, access administered by Firebase the developer can grant or deny access to the system. That is why the end users should be ones with the full access. The authors prepared only a demo application for the reader or tester to see what the system can do, without worrying about registering an account and memorizing a password.

The Android application as mentioned above, will have a menu for the users to select the main controller of the system, also can choose between a plant catalog which have relevant information about the plants in the garden (or cultivation area) such the name of the crops, moisture needed for the plant to be kept alive and the temperature, and the last selection will have a browser plants if there is the need in the future of adding new crops to the field. For this case of study only the controller and the catalog (in demo mode) are available, the rest will be customizable for the end user.

Figure 3. Android application algorithm

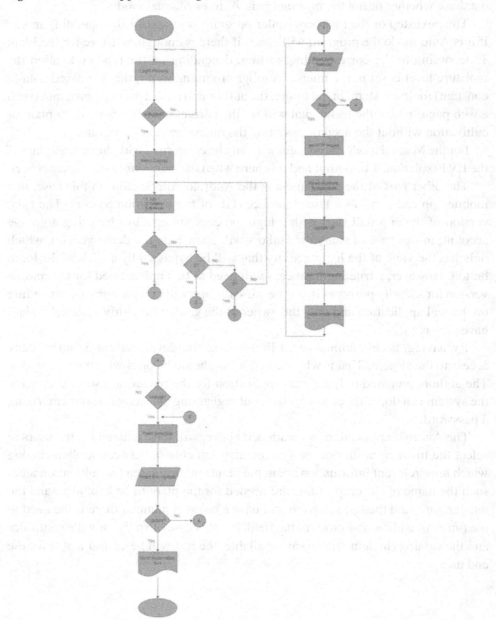

In Figure 3, the Android app algorithm is shown. The process starts with the login process; this can be bypassed as mentioned before to avoid storing sensitive data in this case of study. Once the login process is completed, a menu is shown in which you can select the desired option.

The menu has the following options: *1. Automatic Irrigation System*, which is the main controller of the system and the purpose of this case of study. *2. Catalog*, which will show the end-user relevant information of the plants, for this case of study is demo mode and *three. Browser*, which leads to an internet page with information of new plants to be added to the garden. In addition, this option can have commercial value if redirected to a provider page with option of any purchase to be added to the catalog in the system, but this option is out of the scope right now.

Automatic Irrigation System (AIS) option will wait for the user input whether the Auto or Manual buttons are pressed, if Auto button is pressed the http get request will take place with the intention of reading Moisture and Temperature from the database, with this information the User Interface (UI) will be updated. After this process, the mode variable will be written (via an http put request) to the database to notify the microcontroller, Automatic mode is requested.

If the Manual button is pressed, the user will be prompted to a plant selection with a slider option (Android´s switch button) to enable or disable the water to be irrigated. To perform this action the update button needs to be pressed, when this occurs an http put request will be performed sending the desired EV1 variable value to the database, along with mode variable to notify the microcontroller Manual mode is requested.

RESULTS

In Figure 4, the authors show how the Automatic Irrigation System application for Android OS looks like. On left, the Login window is shown, on the middle the catalog and on right, the main controller view is presented (option 1). The blue box is how the user interface (UI) looks; in there the data read by the sensors are shown. If Manual Mode is active the Moisture Control is shown which you can select the desired plant to be watered, once the update button is pressed, on the bottom the Status is field is presented to display the current mode the system is.

Figure 4. Automatic irrigation system application views

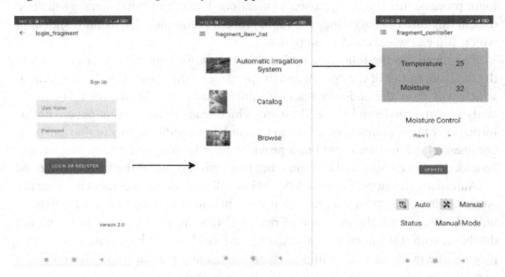

To validate the Irrigation System the authors produce some variations on the variables (temperature and moisture). In Figure 5 the results are shown, on left a temperature the authors manage to lower the temperature and on right a moisture dropping is registered and in there the pump1 (the irrigation) is activated.

Figure 5. Data validation: Temperature variation (left) and Moisture dropping (right)

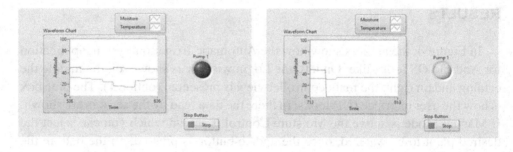

FUTURE WORK

The Automatic Irrigation System presents a low cost solution for reducing water waste. It uses a cheap and powerful microcontroller ESP-32 (cheaper than Arduino) and uses conventional sensors like YL-69 moisture sensor and LM35 temperature sensor.

This research worked well as expected, needed a long term testing and acquired a lot more data, but it worked well in the experiment, has been tested several times for short periods, in the future the experiment will be tested for days and data will be sampled hourly for another paperwork.

There is unfinished work with the mobile application, there are some sections that were not implemented or where are in the demo phase, that is the case the Catalog and Browser options in the main menu. As a reminder, these parts of the mobile application we'll be specific for each customer or user.

So far, temperature feature is only monitored but the main control does not use this data, for a greenhouse application this can be a crucial aspect, but in this experiment was not proposed because the authors does not have any actuator to modify the temperature, for a future implementation, it can be done.

In addition, a backend application will be needed to set parameters of each crop or plant, and to monitor in real time and store data for later use. This application has been thought to be implemented in LabVIEW.

REFERENCES

Al-Ali, A.R. (2019). IoT-solar energy powered smart farm irrigation system. *Journal of Electronic Science and Technology, 17,* 1-14.

García-Ruiz, F. (2020). An integrated system to reduce water consumption in irrigated citrus orchards. *Agricultural Water Management.*

Jasuja, N. (2014). Android vs iOS - Difference and Comparison. *Diffen.* https://www.diffen.com/difference/Android_vs_iOS

Nawandar, N. K., & Satpute, V. R. (2019). IoT based low cost and intelligent module for smart irrigation system. *Computers and Electronics in Agriculture,* 162, 979-990. DOI: 10.1016/j.compag.2019.05.027

Sassenrath, G. F., Heilman, P., Luschei, E., Bennett, G. L., Fitzgerald, G., Klesius, P., Tracy, W., Williford, J. R., & Zimba, P. V. (2008). Technology, complexity and change in agricultural production systems. *Renewable Agriculture and Food Systems,* 23(4), 285–295. DOI: 10.1017/S174217050700213X

Systems, E. (2023). ESP32 Series Datasheet. *Espressif Systems.* https://www.espressif.com/sites/default/files/documentation/esp32_datasheet_en.pdf

Vij, A. IoT and Machine Learning Approaches for Automation of Farm Irrigation System. *International Conference on Computational Intelligence and Data Science,* 167, 1250-1257. DOI: 10.1016/j.procs.2020.03.440

Chapter 5
Study and Analysis of IoT–Based Telemedicine and Remote Patient Monitoring

Ravi Kant Kumar

Department of Computer Science and Engineering, SRM University, India

Sobin C. C.

https://orcid.org/0000-0003-2550-9244

Department of Computer Science and Engineering, SRM University, India

ABSTRACT

As technology continues to advance, the potential for IoT in healthcare (also called IoMT-Internet of Medical Things) is rising day by day. Innovations in telemedicine and remote patient monitoring are helping to improve the healthcare services, making them more accessible and efficient for patients. Contactless health monitoring can ensure better treatment of patients, especially in remote areas. It refers to the interconnection of medical devices, sensors, and systems to the internet. IoMT enables the collection, transmission, and analysis of patient's data in real-time, allowing for remote monitoring and early detection of health. IoMT systems present a promising opportunity for prevention, prediction, and monitoring of emerging infectious diseases. This technology also helps medical professionals make more informed treatment and deliver personalized care to patients. In this study, the authors focus on the emerging developments of IT-based telemedicine and remote patient monitoring including the definition, impact, importance, advantages, challenges, and future of IoT in healthcare.

DOI: 10.4018/979-8-3693-1686-3.ch005

1. INTRODUCTION

The Internet of Things' (IoT) (Madakam, Ramaswamy, & Tripathi, 2015) (Laghari *et al.*, 2021) and Internet of Medical Things (IoMT) (Joyia *et al.*, 2017) rapid development completely reshaped the healthcare sector, especially in health monitoring systems. Real-time and remote health monitoring is made possible by IoT-based health monitoring systems, which make use of sensors, networked devices, and data analytics.

Remote patient monitoring offers several benefits, including early and real-time illness detection, continuous patient monitoring, preventing the worsening of illnesses and premature deaths, lowering hospitalization costs, fewer hospitalizations overall, obtaining more accurate readings while allowing patients to go about their daily lives as usual, improving the efficiency of healthcare services through the use of communication technology, emergency medical care, mobility assistance for patients, emergency care for traffic accidents and other injuries, and the use of non-invasive medical interventions.

Patient monitoring via remote access focuses on many subgroups of patients, such as those with post-surgery chronic disease diagnoses, patients with impairments, or patients having trouble moving about patients, young children, and senior citizens. It is best to have ongoing monitoring for the problems of all these patient groups. The goal of quality healthcare is to enable each patient to live as comfortably and normally as possible.

This study covers a thorough review of the literature on the most recent developments in Internet of Things (IoT)-based health monitoring systems, with an emphasis on significant technological breakthroughs, uses, difficulties, and potential future directions. To present a current overview of the state of the area, the survey draws on a wide range of reliable sources, such as medical industry reports, patents, and academic publications.

Health monitoring systems have advanced significantly because of the IoT's quick adoption in the medical field. The Internet of Things (IoT) introduces a novel paradigm that enables remote control and management of all linked physical devices in intelligent applications, including smart homes, smart cities, and smart healthcare, (Dhanvijay & Patil, 2019). Usually, wearable technology is positioned on the wearer's body directly, within garments, or inside semi-rigid objects like smartwatches, gloves, insoles, and headgear. They can exchange information by utilizing the human body as a transmission channel or by using a suitable transmission medium like Wi-Fi, BLE, or Zigbee (Vijayan *et al.*, 2021) (Aroganam, Manivannan, & Harrison, 2019). Wearable technology records the wearer's long-term physiological and activity data, filters it, and stores it. Wearables might not be able to process data locally because of their constrained computation and storage capacity. They therefore send the collected data to a potential computers or cloud implementation, where the sensor data is analyzed and dissected to provide findings that are meaningfully created, understood, and shown for the user (Jeyaraj *et al.*, 2023) (Xu *et al.*, 2019). Accurate and non-invasive health data collection is made possible in large part by sensor technology. Because of its ease of use and ability to monitor continuously, wearable technology—like fitness trackers and smartwatches—has grown in popularity, (Banaee, Ahmed, & Loutfi, 2013). IoT device seamless connection is made possible by communication protocols like Bluetooth Low Energy (BLE) and Zigbee, which also allow for effective data transfer, (Phillip *et al.*, 2021).

Internet of Things (IoT) devices are a key source of big data in the healthcare industry since they continuously generate data while tracking the health of individuals, or patients. These resources can link different gadgets to give elderly and chronic sickness sufferers a dependable, efficient, and intelligent healthcare service (Abdulmalek *et al.*, 2022). Additionally, to process and analyses the enormous amount of health data created, cloud computing and data analytics techniques have been incorporated into these systems, offering healthcare practitioners actionable insights, (Dash *et al.*, 2019).

IoT-based health monitoring systems have many different and wide-ranging uses. An essential tool that enables healthcare professionals to keep an eye on their patients' health from a distance is remote patient monitoring, which makes it easier to identify abnormalities early and take appropriate action, (Valsalan, Baomar, & Baabood, 2020). IoT-based solutions have also demonstrated promising outcomes in the treatment of chronic diseases, allowing for personalized care plans and lowering readmissions to hospitals, (Taruoco *et al.*, 2012). Individuals are now able to actively control their own health and well-being thanks to the use of IoT-based health monitoring systems in postoperative monitoring, senior care, and health and wellness tracking, (Fernandes, 2022).

IoT-based health monitoring systems confront several difficulties despite their potential advantages. The sensitive nature of health data collected and sent in these systems makes privacy and security issues critical, (Awotunde *et al.*, 2021).

According to Noura, Atiquzzaman, and Gaedke (2019), interoperability problems across various platforms and devices make it difficult to integrate and share data seamlessly. Assuring data quality, dependability, and accessibility requires the use of effective data management techniques to handle the massive amounts of data produced by IoT devices, (Karkouch *et al.*, 2016). Regulatory issues concerning device certifications, healthcare standards, and data privacy must also be considered to guarantee the moral and secure application of IoT technologies in the medical field, (Osama *et al.*, 2023).

Internet of Things-based health monitoring solutions have a bright future ahead of them. Augmenting these systems' accuracy and predictive powers by integration with machine learning and artificial intelligence (AI) algorithms might help identify health issues early and provide tailored therapies, (Thakare, Khire, & Kumbhar, 2022). According Hayyolalam *et al.* (2021), edge computing can provide real-time monitoring and quicker reaction times by addressing bandwidth and latency constraints by processing data closer to the source.

Moreover, the combination of Internet of Things (IoT) devices and health monitoring systems with electronic health records (EHR) and telemedicine platforms can make data exchange and remote consultations smoother, resulting in the delivery of healthcare that is more connected and efficient, (Zhang & Zhang, 2011). In Figure 1, a general architecture of IoT based healthcare system is shown. The architecture describes how a patient's health can be monitored using various sensors, IoT devices and cloud storage and computing. After analyzing the patient's data, a doctor's assistance can also be provided. First patient data is collected through various sensors (Oxygen Level Sensor, Blood Pressure Sensor, Pulse Rate Sensor, Temperature Sensor etc.). Since all the collected data are analog in nature, Analog to Digital converter is required to digitize the data. With the help of cloud storage and computation the enormous amount of data is handled and served.

Figure 1. A general architecture of IOT based telemedicine and healthcare system

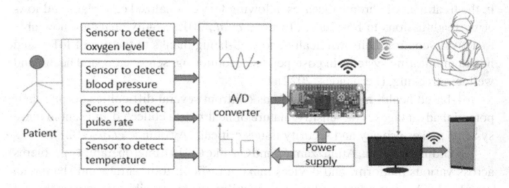

This research study provides a thorough review of the literature on the developments in IoT-based health monitoring systems and telemedicine services. Researchers, healthcare professionals, and industry stakeholders can get useful insights from this study, which examines major technology advances, uses, difficulties, and prospects. IoT technology integration in healthcare has the power to completely change the way that treatment is provided, enhancing patient outcomes, and maximizing resource use. The research community can continue to progress in this subject and realize the full potential of IoT-based health monitoring systems by tackling the obstacles and considering potential future approaches.

2. TECHNOLOGICAL INNOVATIONS

. IoT-based health monitoring systems have evolved because of substantial technological breakthroughs, which have revolutionized patient care and healthcare delivery. Using a wide range of research and industry references, this section explores the major technical advancements that have fueled the growth of these systems.

With the ability to continuously and non-invasively monitor physiological data and vital signs, wearable biosensors have become essential parts of Internet of Things-based health monitoring systems, (Pateraki *et al.*, 2020). These sensors, which include gadgets like temperature sensors (Rai, 2007), blood glucose monitors (Wang & Lee, 2015), and ECG pattern (Agrafioti *et al.*, 2011), provide real-time information on blood pressure, heart rate, glucose levels, and body temperature. This information empowers people to take charge of their health and makes it possible for medical professionals to follow patients from a distance.

To provide smooth data transfer in health monitoring systems, wireless communication technologies must be dependable and efficient. Connectivity and data interchange between wearables, sensors, and centralized healthcare systems are made possible by technologies like 5G, LoRa WAN (Long Range Wide Area Network), Bluetooth, ZigBee, and Wi-Fi, (Verma, Chauhan, & Awasthi, 2023) (Bouazzi *et al.*, 2022). Real-time data transfer is made possible by these communication protocols, which allow healthcare practitioners to monitor patients remotely and react quickly to emergency circumstances.

IoT-based health monitoring systems may now overcome the drawbacks of conventional cloud-centric designs, the combination of edge and fog computing. Fog computing uses only low-end computers, mobile phones, and personal devices, it can offer lower latency than cloud computing. This idea is expanded upon by fog computing, which reduces data transfer to the cloud, improves privacy and security, and uses adjacent edge devices to offer computation and storage capabilities, (Hamdan, Ayyash, & Almajali, 2020) (Mohamed *et al.*, 2021).

IoT-based health tracking devices have more options because to advances in machine learning and artificial intelligence (AI). AI systems can examine vast amounts of medical data to spot trends, forecast the course of diseases, and find abnormalities. Personalized healthcare treatments are made possible by machine learning algorithms, which help healthcare practitioners make decisions by recognizing risk factors. These technologies help provide more accurate diagnoses, better treatment regimens, and better patient outcomes.

To address concerns about data privacy and integrity in Internet of Things (IoT)-based health monitoring systems, blockchain technology (Samuel *et al.*, 2022) offers inherent security and immutability. Blockchain assures consent management and data confidentiality by decentralizing data storage and facilitating safe transactions. Blockchain technology has the potential to transform healthcare by enhancing the security, privacy, and interoperability of health data while putting the patient at the center of the healthcare system. By enhancing the security and efficiency of electronic health records (EHRs) (Chenthara *et al.*, 2020), this technology has the potential to revolutionize the transmission of health information.

The development of IoT-based health monitoring systems has been accelerated by these technical advancements, which include wearable biosensors, wireless communication technologies, edge, and fog computing (Mohamed *et al.*, 2021) (Kharel, Reda, & Shin, 2019), artificial intelligence (Ghazal, 2021), and machine learning (Bharadwaj *et al.*, 2021), and blockchain (Samuel *et al.*, 2022). These systems keep developing by utilizing these breakthroughs, revolutionizing the way healthcare is delivered, increasing patient care, and raising the space for total healthcare results.

Recently, in the era of deep learning and data science, researchers have developed various networks to solve complex computer science problems. Therefore, in the field of healthcare, researchers have come up with several solutions for monitoring health and making telemedicine services effectively by using deep learning approach and IoT devices.

The suggested study in Yu *et al.* (2023), generated an intelligent, sensor-powered remote monitoring system for COVID-19 patients. Accurate data observation is aided by this, and power consumption and effectiveness are also increased. The authors have suggested the POA-RCNN technique which is based on Recurrent Convolutional Neural Network (RCNN) based Puzzle optimization algorithm (POA). This technique is used to process the sensor data, effectively classifying the data as COVID-19 and normal.

Deep Learning-and IoT-Cloud-Based Smart Healthcare Monitoring System (Nancy *et al.*, 2022) has been proposed for the prediction of heart disease. In this work, researchers had suggested Bi-LSTM model for precisely forecasting the severity and risk of heart disease in a patient. The resulting data are delivered to the fuzzy information system (FIS) for the initial classification job.

In the publication Jaiwal *et al.* (2021), authors provide a comparison analysis of several neural network models and an improved method for blindness recognition in retinal pictures, built upon the earlier pre-trained EfficientNet models. This improved EfficientNet-B5 based model outperforms CNN and ResNet50 models when compared to the benchmark dataset of retinal images.

A novel system for smart patient monitoring and recommendations (SPMR) (Motwani, Shukla, & Pawar, 2023) was proposed that combines cloud analytics and deep learning for real-time monitoring of distant patients with chronic illnesses like diabetes and blood pressure. The findings show that the suggested framework predicts the Emergency, Alert, Warning, and Normal cases as well as the Cloud cases.

3. APPLICATIONS OF IOT-BASED HEALTH MONITORING SYSTEMS

The Internet of Things (IoT) has made significant progress in the past several years, opening a platform of possibilities that might completely transform the healthcare industry. The many uses of these systems are examined in this section, along with how they affect many facets of patient care, illness management, and the provision of healthcare. Relevant academic papers and industry reports provide support for the topic.

The most prevalent use of IoT devices in healthcare is remote patient monitoring. Patients who are not physically present at a healthcare institution can have their health metrics, such as heart rate, blood pressure, temperature, and more, automatically collected by IoT devices. This eliminates the need for patients to travel to the doctors or gather the data themselves.

IoT gadgets may assist in constant, automated glucose monitoring of diabetic patients, (Wang & Lee, 2015). The use of human record-keeping is eliminated by glucose monitoring devices, which may also notify patients when their blood sugar levels are dangerous.

Heart rate monitoring (Agrafioti, Hatzinakos, & Anderson, 2011) is now possible with a wide range of tiny Internet of Things devices, allowing patients to wander around as they like while having their hearts constantly watched over.

Another kind of data that has historically been challenging to consistently gather is information regarding patients' overall mood and symptoms of depression, (Moshe et al., 2021). Patients may occasionally be asked how they are feeling by healthcare professionals. These issues can be solved by "Mood-aware" (Tizzano, Spezialetti, & Rossi, 2020) IoT devices. Devices can deduce information about a patient's mental state by gathering and evaluating data, such as blood pressure and heart rate. Even the eye movements of a patient may be tracked by sophisticated Internet of Things sensors used for mood monitoring.

IoT sensors, which continually gather information about Parkinson's symptoms, promise to make this process considerably simpler, (Pasluosta *et al.,* 2015). Simultaneously, the gadgets allow patients to continue their lives in their own homes without being restricted to long stays in hospitals for surveillance.

Attacks from conditions like COPD (Chronic Obstructive Pulmonary Disease) or asthma can occur quickly and without much warning. IoT-enabled inhalers can benefit patients by tracking the frequency of attacks and gathering environmental data to assist medical professionals in determining what precipitated an attack, (Margam, 2024). Furthermore, linked inhalers could notify patients when they misuse or forget to bring their inhaler with them, which puts them at danger of having an attack.

Gathering information from within the human body is usually a disorganized and extremely disruptive process. Ingesting sensors (Zaynidinov *et al.*, 2020) allow for far less intrusive data collection from the digestive and other systems. For example, they provide light on the PH levels in the stomach or assist in identifying the cause of intestinal bleeding. These gadgets need to be readily ingested due to their tiny size. They also need to be able to independently break down or move through the human body without causing any harm. Many businesses are working hard to develop ingestible sensors that satisfy these requirements.

Another technique for passively and non-intrusively gathering heath data is using smart contact lenses, (Seneviratne *et al.*, 2017). In this context, linked contact lenses have been patented by Google, perhaps because they contain micro cameras that enable users to snap photographs with their eyes. Smart glasses promise to transform human eyes into an effective instrument for digital interactions, whether they are utilized for other reasons or to enhance health results.

Internet-connected tiny robots (Banaerjee, Chakraborty, & Rathi, 2020) that are implanted within the body allow surgeons to carry out intricate operations that would be challenging for humans to handle. Simultaneously, robotic operations conducted by tiny IoT devices can minimize the size of incisions needed for surgery, resulting in a less invasive procedure and quicker patient recovery. To execute operations with the least amount of disturbance, these instruments need to be sufficiently tiny and dependable. To make the best choices about the course of an operation, they also need to be able to decipher intricate circumstances within bodies. However, the fact that IoT robots are currently being utilized in surgery proves that these difficulties are manageable.

Managing chronic illnesses is one common use case for Internet of Things-based health monitoring systems. For patients and healthcare professionals, these devices give invaluable insights by enabling continuous monitoring of physiological indicators, medication adherence, and lifestyle choices. Personalized food advice, timely medication administration reminders, and blood glucose monitoring are only a few of the uses of IoT-based systems in the context of diabetes care, (Subramaniyaswamy *et al.*, 2019). Similarly, these systems provide remote monitoring of vital signs, including blood pressure and heart rate, in cardiovascular care, allowing for early anomaly identification and prompt management, (Parati *et al.*, 2009).

The fields of rehabilitation and senior care are important additional application areas. IoT-based health monitoring systems include fall detection, emergency response mechanisms, and remote monitoring of everyday activities as ways to address the problems brought on by an ageing population. By guaranteeing the security and welfare of senior citizens, these programs help to encourage independent life.

Hospital administration and patient monitoring have improved because of the installation of Internet of Things-based health monitoring systems in hospitals and other healthcare institutions. Workflow is optimized, patient safety is improved, and resources are allocated more effectively when real-time tracking of hospital assets, equipment status, and vital signs is possible. In addition, IoT-enabled remote patient monitoring systems enable the prompt identification of worsening symptoms, lowering hospital readmission rates, and enhancing patient outcomes.

IoT-based health monitoring systems have applications in population health management and public health efforts beyond the care of individual patients. IoT based systems make it easier to gather real-time health data from sizable populations. They also monitor environmental elements that may have an impact on health and assist focused treatments. To monitor air quality, follow the development of infectious illnesses, and execute personalized preventative actions, for instance, IoT-based systems have been used, (Mumtaz *et al.*, 2021).

In general, Internet of Things (IoT)-based health monitoring systems have gained traction in a variety of healthcare domains, such as population health, hospital administration, chronic disease management, and senior care. These systems show promise for boosting healthcare delivery, improving patient outcomes, and supporting public health campaigns.

4. CHALLENGES AND LIMITATIONS

Although IoT-based health monitoring systems have a lot of promise, their widespread adoption and successful implementation will require addressing several issues and constraints. Based on research studies and industry reports, this section addresses the major issues facing the field.

Confidentiality and Security of Information

Data precautions and privacy are challenges brought up by the integration of several networked devices and sensors in Internet of Things-based health monitoring systems. Strong security measures are necessary due to the sensitive nature of health data to guard against malicious attacks, unauthorized access, and data breaches,

(Awotunde *et al.,* 2021). To guarantee the integrity and security of patient data, access control methods, encryption techniques, and secure data transfer are crucial.

Standardization and Interoperability

To set a standardization and interoperability a major obstacle is to establish seamless integration and data sharing is the absence of standardized protocols and compatibility among various IoT devices and platforms, (Pathak *et al.*, 2021). The interoperability of IoT-based health monitoring systems is hampered by the variety of devices, communication protocols, and data formats. To improve interoperability across different healthcare settings and enable the smooth integration of devices from multiple manufacturers, it is imperative to develop common standards and frameworks.

Reliability and the Accuracy

Maintaining the data gathered by Internet of Things (IoT) devices is reliable and accurate and is essential for making well-informed healthcare decisions. Technical problems can cause erroneous readings and incorrect data interpretation. These problems include device failures, signal interference, and calibration mistakes, (Selvaraj & Sundaravaradhan, 2020). The accuracy and dependability of IoT-based health monitoring systems must be maintained through calibration processes, routine maintenance, and quality control measures.

Legal and Ethical Challenges

Data ownership, permission, and the appropriate use of personal health information are among the ethical and legal issues that the implementation of Internet of Things-based health monitoring systems brings up, (Gerke, Minssen, & Cohen, 2020). Respecting privacy laws, obtaining informed permission, and using open data management procedures are essential to upholding moral principles and winning the public's confidence in these systems.

Battery Longevity and Energy Consumption

Because batteries have a finite amount of power, many Internets of Things (IoT) devices used in health monitoring systems rely on them. According to research work in Nawaz, Ahmed, and Abbas (2022), maintaining continuous monitoring without frequent battery changes requires optimizing power use and prolonging battery life.

To solve this difficulty, research is being done in the areas of energy harvesting, low-power hardware designs, and efficient energy management strategies.

Scalability and Budget

Scalability is a major challenge as IoT-based health monitoring systems keep growing. As the number of connected devices and users rises, managing large-scale deployments, processing vast amounts of data, and guaranteeing system performance grow more difficult, (Pandey & Litoriya, 2020). Furthermore, there may be financial obstacles to the implementation of these systems in environments with limited resources due to the expense of setting up the infrastructure, purchasing devices, and maintaining them.

Collaboration between researchers, healthcare providers, politicians, and technology companies are necessary to address these obstacles and restrictions. The full promise of IoT-based health monitoring systems to revolutionize healthcare delivery and enhance patient outcomes may be realized by resolving these problems.

5. FUTURE WORK DIRECTION

Healthcare might be significantly transformed by the field of IoT-based health monitoring systems, which is set for additional developments. To influence the creation and use of these systems, this section looks at new trends and potential paths. Recent studies and reports from the industry serve as the foundation for the debate.

The integration of artificial intelligence (AI) and machine learning (ML) methodologies into Internet of Things (IoT)-based health monitoring systems is a viable approach to augmenting the functionalities and efficacy of these systems. AI and ML algorithms can analyze vast amounts of sensor data, spot trends, and produce useful insights for individualized healthcare interventions. Incorporating AI and ML into these systems can enhance real-time decision-making, facilitate predictive analytics, and increase diagnostic accuracy.

The advent of edge computing, which relocates data storage and processing closer to the data source, presents new prospects for Internet of Things (IoT)-based health monitoring systems. Edge computing shortens reaction times, boosts data privacy, and lowers latency by processing data close to the devices at the network edge. Time-sensitive applications may be supported, real-time processing made possible, and network congestion minimized by integrating edge computing with Internet of Things-based health monitoring systems.

IoT-based health monitoring systems are predicted to undergo a substantial evolution with the introduction of sophisticated wearable and implantable devices. Wearable technology offers constant monitoring of vital signs, exercise, and sleep habits. Examples of these devices are smartwatches and fitness trackers. There is promise for long-term monitoring and tailored therapy administration with implantable devices, such as biosensors and smart implants. Real-time feedback, improved data collecting, and individualized healthcare treatments can all be facilitated by integrating these devices with IoT systems.

Blockchain Technology: Blockchain technology has drawn interest due to its potential to solve concerns with data security, privacy, and trust in the healthcare industry. Blockchain can offer a decentralized, immutable ledger for safe data storage, auditability, and access control in the context of Internet of Things-based health monitoring systems. Blockchain-based solutions can improve data integrity, make it possible for stakeholders to share data securely, and make consent management easier.

Analyzing data and using predictive models: By using sophisticated data analytics methods to the massive volumes of data produced by Internet of Things-based health monitoring systems, such as predictive modelling and data-driven decision-making, important insights can be gleaned. It is possible to create predictive models to recognize early indicators of the course of a disease, forecast unfavorable outcomes, and encourage preventative measures. Delivery of healthcare that is more effective and individualized may be made possible by the integration of real-time data analytics capabilities into these systems.

Implications for Ethics, Law, and Society: With the development of Internet of Things (IoT)-based health monitoring systems, it is imperative to tackle the moral, legal, and society consequences of their extensive use. It's important to carefully explore ethical issues pertaining to algorithmic biases, privacy, permission, and data ownership. To guarantee adherence to rules and safeguard patients' rights, legal frameworks need also be put in place. Equity, accessibility, and the possibility of escalating already-existing healthcare inequities are among the societal ramifications of these technologies that must be considered.

More customized, effective, and preventive healthcare is made possible by these promising future avenues for the development of IoT-based health monitoring systems. The achievement of the maximum benefit from these developments depends on ongoing research, interdisciplinary teamwork, and stakeholder involvement.

6. CONCLUSION

In summary, this literature has provided a comprehensive review of the advancements made in Internet of Things-based health monitoring systems. The integration of Internet of Things (IoT) technology with healthcare has rendered real-time and remote monitoring capabilities available, hence transforming the realm of health monitoring. By means of examining current research publications, conference proceedings, and industry reports, this review has illuminated significant technical advancements, uses, obstacles, and forthcoming paths inside the domain. This studies says, IoT-based health monitoring systems have been widely growing and being implemented effectively. But still several issues and constraints are challenging, those must be effectively resolved like regulatory compliance, ethical considerations, data privacy, security, standardization of data formats, communication protocols, interoperability difficulties, and regulatory compliance.

Prospects for research on IoT-based health monitoring systems appear encouraging. Health monitoring will become even more accurate and efficient if sensor technologies, AI, and ML algorithms continue to progress. In IoT-based healthcare systems, the combination of cutting-edge technologies like edge intelligence, fog computing, and 5G networks will enable real-time analytics, low-latency communication, and seamless connection.

In a nutshell, this review of the literature has shed light on the developments, uses, difficulties, and prospects for Internet of Things-based health monitoring systems. IoT technology integration in healthcare has the potential to transform patient care, make early identification and intervention possible, and enhance overall health outcomes.

REFERENCES

Abdulmalek, S., Nasir, A., Jabbar, W. A., Almuhaya, M. A., Bairagi, A. K., Khan, M. A. M., & Kee, S. H. (2022, October). IoT-based healthcare-monitoring system towards improving quality of life: A review. *Health Care*, 10(10), 1993. PMID: 36292441

Agrafioti, F., Hatzinakos, D., & Anderson, A. K. (2011). ECG pattern analysis for emotion detection. *IEEE Transactions on Affective Computing*, 3(1), 102–115. DOI: 10.1109/T-AFFC.2011.28

Aroganam, G., Manivannan, N., & Harrison, D. (2019). Review on wearable technology sensors used in consumer sport applications. *Sensors (Basel)*, 19(9), 1983. DOI: 10.3390/s19091983 PMID: 31035333

Awotunde, J. B., Jimoh, R. G., Folorunso, S. O., Adeniyi, E. A., Abiodun, K. M., & Banjo, O. O. (2021). Privacy and security concerns in IoT-based healthcare systems. In *The fusion of internet of things, artificial intelligence, and cloud computing in health care* (pp. 105–134). Springer International Publishing. DOI: 10.1007/978-3-030-75220-0_6

Banaee, H., Ahmed, M. U., & Loutfi, A. (2013). Data mining for wearable sensors in health monitoring systems: A review of recent trends and challenges. *Sensors (Basel)*, 13(12), 17472–17500. DOI: 10.3390/s131217472 PMID: 24351646

Banerjee, A., Chakraborty, C., & Rathi, M.Sr. (2020). Medical imaging, artificial intelligence, internet of things, wearable devices in terahertz healthcare technologies. In *Terahertz biomedical and healthcare technologies* (pp. 145–165). Elsevier. DOI: 10.1016/B978-0-12-818556-8.00008-2

Bharadwaj, H. K., Agarwal, A., Chamola, V., Lakkaniga, N. R., Hassija, V., Guizani, M., & Sikdar, B. (2021). A review on the role of machine learning in enabling IoT based healthcare applications. *IEEE Access: Practical Innovations, Open Solutions*, 9, 38859–38890. DOI: 10.1109/ACCESS.2021.3059858

Bouazzi, I., Zaidi, M., Usman, M., Shamim, M. Z. M., Gunjan, V. K., & Singh, N. (2022). Future trends for healthcare monitoring system in smart cities using LoRaWAN-based WBAN. *Mobile Information Systems*, 2022, 2022. DOI: 10.1155/2022/1526021

Chenthara, S., Ahmed, K., Wang, H., Whittaker, F., & Chen, Z. (2020). Healthchain: A novel framework on privacy preservation of electronic health records using blockchain technology. *PLoS One*, 15(12), e0243043. DOI: 10.1371/journal.pone.0243043 PMID: 33296379

Dash, S., Shakyawar, S. K., Sharma, M., & Kaushik, S. (2019). Big data in health-care: Management, analysis and future prospects. *Journal of Big Data*, 6(1), 1–25. DOI: 10.1186/s40537-019-0217-0

Dhanvijay, M. M., & Patil, S. C. (2019). Internet of Things: A survey of enabling technologies in healthcare and its applications. *Computer Networks*, 153, 113–131. DOI: 10.1016/j.comnet.2019.03.006

Fernandes, J. G. (2022). Artificial intelligence in telemedicine. In *Artificial Intelligence in Medicine* (pp. 1219–1227). Springer International Publishing. DOI: 10.1007/978-3-030-64573-1_93

Gerke, S., Minssen, T., & Cohen, G. (2020). Ethical and legal challenges of artificial intelligence-driven healthcare. In *Artificial intelligence in healthcare* (pp. 295–336). Academic Press. DOI: 10.1016/B978-0-12-818438-7.00012-5

Ghazal, T. M. (2021). Internet of things with artificial intelligence for health care security. *Arabian Journal for Science and Engineering*.

Hamdan, S., Ayyash, M., & Almajali, S. (2020). Edge-computing architectures for internet of things applications: A survey. *Sensors (Basel)*, 20(22), 6441. DOI: 10.3390/s20226441 PMID: 33187267

Hayyolalam, V., Aloqaily, M., Özkasap, Ö., & Guizani, M. (2021). Edge-assisted solutions for IoT-based connected healthcare systems: A literature review. *IEEE Internet of Things Journal*, 9(12), 9419–9443. DOI: 10.1109/JIOT.2021.3135200

Jaiswal, A. K., Tiwari, P., Kumar, S., Al-Rakhami, M. S., Alrashoud, M., & Ghoneim, A. (2021). Deep learning based smart IoT health system for blindness detection using retina images. *IEEE Access: Practical Innovations, Open Solutions*, 9, 70606–70615. DOI: 10.1109/ACCESS.2021.3078241

Jeyaraj, R., & Balasubramaniam, A., MA, A. K., Guizani, N., & Paul, A. (2023). Resource management in cloud and cloud-influenced technologies for internet of things applications. *ACM Computing Surveys*, 55(12), 1–37. DOI: 10.1145/3571729

Joyia, G. J., Liaqat, R. M., Farooq, A., & Rehman, S. (2017). Internet of medical things (IoMT): Applications, benefits and future challenges in healthcare domain. *Journal of Communication*, 12(4), 240–247.

Karkouch, A., Mousannif, H., Al Moatassime, H., & Noel, T. (2016). Data quality in internet of things: A state-of-the-art survey. *Journal of Network and Computer Applications*, 73, 57–81. DOI: 10.1016/j.jnca.2016.08.002

Kharel, J., Reda, H. T., & Shin, S. Y. (2019). Fog computing-based smart health monitoring system deploying lora wireless communication. *IETE Technical Review*, 36(1), 69–82. DOI: 10.1080/02564602.2017.1406828

Laghari, A. A., Wu, K., Laghari, R. A., Ali, M., & Khan, A. A. (2021). A review and state of art of Internet of Things (IoT). *Archives of Computational Methods in Engineering*, 1–19.

Madakam, S., Ramaswamy, R., & Tripathi, S. (2015). Internet of Things (IoT): A literature review. *Journal of Computer and Communications*, 3(5), 164–173. DOI: 10.4236/jcc.2015.35021

Margam, R. (2024). Smart inhalers: Harnessing iot for precise asthma management. *International Education and Research Journal*, 10.

Mohamed, N., Al-Jaroodi, J., Lazarova-Molnar, S., & Jawhar, I. (2021). Applications of integrated IoT-fog-cloud systems to smart cities: A survey. *Electronics (Basel)*, 10(23), 2918. DOI: 10.3390/electronics10232918

Moshe, I., Terhorst, Y., Opoku Asare, K., Sander, L. B., Ferreira, D., Baumeister, H., Mohr, D. C., & Pulkki-Råback, L. (2021). Predicting symptoms of depression and anxiety using smartphone and wearable data. *Frontiers in Psychiatry*, 12, 625247. DOI: 10.3389/fpsyt.2021.625247 PMID: 33584388

Motwani, A., Shukla, P. K., & Pawar, M. (2023). Novel framework based on deep learning and cloud analytics for smart patient monitoring and recommendation (SPMR). *Journal of Ambient Intelligence and Humanized Computing*, 14(5), 5565–5580. DOI: 10.1007/s12652-020-02790-6

Mumtaz, R., Zaidi, S. M. H., Shakir, M. Z., Shafi, U., Malik, M. M., Haque, A., Mumtaz, S., & Zaidi, S. A. R. (2021). Internet of things (Iot) based indoor air quality sensing and predictive analytic—A COVID-19 perspective. *Electronics (Basel)*, 10(2), 184. DOI: 10.3390/electronics10020184

Nancy, A. A., Ravindran, D., Raj Vincent, P. D., Srinivasan, K., & Gutierrez Reina, D. (2022). Iot-cloud-based smart healthcare monitoring system for heart disease prediction via deep learning. *Electronics (Basel)*, 11(15), 2292. DOI: 10.3390/electronics11152292

Nawaz, M., Ahmed, J., & Abbas, G. (2022). Energy-efficient battery management system for healthcare devices. *Journal of Energy Storage*, 51, 104358. DOI: 10.1016/j.est.2022.104358

Noura, M., Atiquzzaman, M., & Gaedke, M. (2019). Interoperability in internet of things: Taxonomies and open challenges. *Mobile Networks and Applications*, 24(3), 796–809. DOI: 10.1007/s11036-018-1089-9

Osama, M., Ateya, A. A., Sayed, M. S., Hammad, M., Pławiak, P., Abd El-Latif, A. A., & Elsayed, R. A. (2023). Internet of medical things and healthcare 4.0: Trends, requirements, challenges, and research directions. *Sensors (Basel)*, 23(17), 7435. DOI: 10.3390/s23177435 PMID: 37687891

Pandey, P., & Litoriya, R. (2020). Implementing healthcare services on a large scale: Challenges and remedies based on blockchain technology. *Health Policy and Technology*, 9(1), 69–78. DOI: 10.1016/j.hlpt.2020.01.004

Parati, G., Omboni, S., Albini, F., Piantoni, L., Giuliano, A., Revera, M., Illyes, M., & Mancia, G. (2009). Home blood pressure telemonitoring improves hypertension control in general practice. The TeleBPCare study. *Journal of Hypertension*, 27(1), 198–203. DOI: 10.1097/HJH.0b013e3283163caf PMID: 19145785

Pasluosta, C. F., Gassner, H., Winkler, J., Klucken, J., & Eskofier, B. M. (2015). An emerging era in the management of Parkinson's disease: Wearable technologies and the internet of things. *IEEE Journal of Biomedical and Health Informatics*, 19(6), 1873–1881. DOI: 10.1109/JBHI.2015.2461555 PMID: 26241979

Pateraki, M., Fysarakis, K., Sakkalis, V., Spanoudakis, G., Varlamis, I., Maniadakis, M., ... Koutsouris, D. (2020). Biosensors and Internet of Things in smart healthcare applications: Challenges and opportunities. *Wearable and Implantable Medical Devices*, 25-53.

Pathak, N., Misra, S., Mukherjee, A., & Kumar, N. (2021). HeDI: Healthcare device interoperability for IoT-based e-health platforms. *IEEE Internet of Things Journal*, 8(23), 16845–16852. DOI: 10.1109/JIOT.2021.3052066

Philip, N. Y., Rodrigues, J. J., Wang, H., Fong, S. J., & Chen, J. (2021). Internet of Things for in-home health monitoring systems: Current advances, challenges and future directions. *IEEE Journal on Selected Areas in Communications*, 39(2), 300–310. DOI: 10.1109/JSAC.2020.3042421

Rai, V. K. (2007). Temperature sensors and optical sensors. *Applied Physics. B, Lasers and Optics*, 88(2), 297–303. DOI: 10.1007/s00340-007-2717-4

Samuel, O., Omojo, A. B., Mohsin, S. M., Tiwari, P., Gupta, D., & Band, S. S. (2022). An anonymous IoT-Based E-health monitoring system using blockchain technology. *IEEE Systems Journal*.

Selvaraj, S., & Sundaravaradhan, S. (2020). Challenges and opportunities in IoT healthcare systems: A systematic review. *SN Applied Sciences*, 2(1), 139. DOI: 10.1007/s42452-019-1925-y

Seneviratne, S., Hu, Y., Nguyen, T., Lan, G., Khalifa, S., Thilakarathna, K., Hassan, M., & Seneviratne, A. (2017). A survey of wearable devices and challenges. *IEEE Communications Surveys and Tutorials*, 19(4), 2573–2620. DOI: 10.1109/COMST.2017.2731979

Subramaniyaswamy, V., Manogaran, G., Logesh, R., Vijayakumar, V., Chilamkurti, N., Malathi, D., & Senthilselvan, N. (2019). An ontology-driven personalized food recommendation in IoT-based healthcare system. *The Journal of Supercomputing*, 75(6), 3184–3216. DOI: 10.1007/s11227-018-2331-8

Tarouco, L. M. R., Bertholdo, L. M., Granville, L. Z., Arbiza, L. M. R., Carbone, F., Marotta, M., & De Santanna, J. J. C. (2012, June). Internet of Things in healthcare: Interoperatibility and security issues. In *2012 IEEE international conference on communications (ICC)* (pp. 6121-6125). IEEE.

Thakare, V., Khire, G., & Kumbhar, M. (2022). Artificial intelligence (AI) and Internet of Things (IoT) in healthcare: Opportunities and challenges. *ECS Transactions*, 107(1), 7941–7951. DOI: 10.1149/10701.7941ecst

Tizzano, G. R., Spezialetti, M., & Rossi, S. (2020, June). *A deep learning approach for mood recognition from wearable data. In 2020 IEEE international symposium on medical measurements and applications (MeMeA).* IEEE.

Valsalan, P., Baomar, T. A. B., & Baabood, A. H. O. (2020). IoT based health monitoring system. *Journal of Critical Reviews, 7*(4), 739-743.

Verma, H., Chauhan, N., & Awasthi, L. K. (2023). A Comprehensive review of 'Internet of Healthcare Things': Networking aspects, technologies, services, applications, challenges, and security concerns. *Computer Science Review*, 50, 100591. DOI: 10.1016/j.cosrev.2023.100591

Vijayan, V., Connolly, J. P., Condell, J., McKelvey, N., & Gardiner, P. (2021). Review of wearable devices and data collection considerations for connected health. *Sensors (Basel)*, 21(16), 5589. DOI: 10.3390/s21165589 PMID: 34451032

Wang, H. C., & Lee, A. R. (2015). Recent developments in blood glucose sensors. *Yao Wu Shi Pin Fen Xi*, 23(2), 191–200. PMID: 28911373

Xu, M., Qian, F., Zhu, M., Huang, F., Pushp, S., & Liu, X. (2019). Deepwear: Adaptive local offloading for on-wearable deep learning. *IEEE Transactions on Mobile Computing*, 19(2), 314–330. DOI: 10.1109/TMC.2019.2893250

Yu, L., Vijay, M. M., Sunil, J., Vincy, V. A. G., Govindan, V., Khan, M. I., Ali, S., Tamam, N., & Abdullaeva, B. S. (2023). Hybrid deep learning model based smart IOT based monitoring system for Covid-19. *Heliyon*, 9(11), e21150. DOI: 10.1016/j. heliyon.2023.e21150 PMID: 37928011

Zaynidinov, H., Makhmudjanov, S., Rajabov, F., & Singh, D. (2020, November). IoT-enabled mobile device for electrogastrography signal processing. In *International Conference on Intelligent Human Computer Interaction* (pp. 346-356). Cham: Springer International Publishing.

Zhang, X. M., & Zhang, N. (2011, May). An open, secure and flexible platform based on internet of things and cloud computing for ambient aiding living and tele-medicine. In *2011 international conference on computer and management (CAMAN)* (pp. 1-4). IEEE. DOI: 10.1109/CAMAN.2011.5778905

Chapter 6
Comparative Analysis of Detection of Diseases in Apple Tree Leaves Using ResNet and CNN

S. Aditi Apurva

https://orcid.org/0000-0002-1730-8592

Indian Institute of Information Technology, Ranchi, India

ABSTRACT

The modern era has become an era of machine learning as an essential tool for developing IoT (internet of things) application. Machine learning for IoT can be used to depict future trends, detect anomalies, and argument intelligence by ingesting images, videos, and audios. Introducing IoT and machine learning in agricultural has empowered farmers to make and take well informed decision in optimal resource utilization as well as mitigation of pest and disease control. IoT and machine learning has aided in revolutionizing the farming sector. IoT sensors placed in the soil measure parameters like moisture content, pH levels, and nutrient levels. This chapter delves into a comparative analysis of two deep learning architectures, the residual neural network (ResNet), and convolutional neural network (CNN), for detecting diseases in apple tree leaves. By employing these models, the study aims to determine their performance in accurately identifying and classifying diseased apple tree leaves against healthy ones.

DOI: 10.4018/979-8-3693-1686-3.ch006

INTRODUCTION

The modern era has become an era of machine learning as an essential tool for developing IoT (Internet of Things) application. Machine Learning for Internet of Things can be used to depict future trends, detect anomalies and argument intelligence by ingesting images, videos and audios. Introducing Internet of Things and Machine Learning in agricultural has empowered farmers to make and take well informed decision in optimal resource utilization as well as mitigation of pest and disease Control. Internet of Things and machine learning has aided in revolutionizing the farming sector. Internet of Things sensors placed in the soil measure parameters like moisture content, pH levels, and nutrient levels. Machine learning models can analyze these data to predict optimal planting times, irrigation schedules, and nutrient supplementation.

Internet of Things weather stations collect real-time weather data from the farm and with the help of Machine learning models can predict weather patterns, helping farmers make informed decisions about planting, harvesting, and irrigation. Internet of Things devices equipped with cameras and sensors can capture images of crops. Machine learning algorithms can analyze these images to detect early signs of diseases, pests, or nutrient deficiencies. Farmers receive real-time alerts, enabling timely interventions.

Traditionally the farmers used to detect disease and healthy plants manually by extracting the color, texture, and shape features of diseased leaf images (Mahlein *et al.,* 2013) (Yuan *et al.*, 2014) (Qin *et al.,* 2016) (International Journal of Computer Science & Network Security, n.d.) due to which there was a lack in keeping track of the important parameters such as soil type, humidity, temperature amount of macro and micro nutrients in the soil and nutrients requirement of the crop.

Apple cultivation faces considerable challenges due to various diseases affecting its leaves. The accurate and timely detection of diseases in apple plant-leaves will be of paramount importance for ensuring optimal crop health and maximizing agricultural productivity.

This paper aims to contribute a chapter presenting an overview of comparative analysis of Convolutional Neural Networks (CNNs) (Murali & Nagaraju, 2023) (Jianxin, 2017) (Aghdam & Heravi, 2017) (Albawi & Al-Zawi, 2107)with Residual Neural Network (ResNet) (Li & Rai, 2020) (Alsayed & Arif, 2021) for the automated detection of diseases in apple plant leaves.

ResNet, stands for "Residual Network". It is a deep neural network architecture which is designed to address the challenges of training very deep neural networks. It was introduced by Kaiming He et al. in the paper titled "Deep Residual Learning for Image Recognition" in 2015. ResNet is particularly well-known for its success in image classification tasks but has also been applied to various other computer vision tasks and beyond.

Some salient features of Residual Neural Network are:

1. **Residual Blocks:** The core innovation of Residual Neural Network is the use of residual blocks. A residual block is a building block of the network that contains skip connections (also known as shortcut connections). These skip connections enable the network to learn the residual (difference) between the input and output of a block, rather than trying to learn the entire transformation.

2. **Skip Connections:** The skip connections bypass one or more layers in a neural network and add the input to the output. This allows gradients to flow more easily during training, addressing the vanishing gradient problem. Skip connections also make it possible to train very deep networks (e.g., hundreds of layers) without degradation in performance.

3. **Deep Architectures:** Residual Neural Network architectures are very deep, consisting of a large number of layers. Common variants include ResNet-18, ResNet-34, ResNet-50, ResNet-101, and ResNet-152, which differ in terms of their depth and complexity. Deeper networks can capture more complex features and patterns.

4. **Convolutional Layers:** Residual Neural Network primarily uses convolutional layers for feature extraction, making it well-suited for image data. It uses convolutional filters to capture hierarchical features from low level to high-level representations.

5. **Batch Normalization:** Batch normalization is often used in Residual Neural Network architectures to stabilize and accelerate training. It normalizes the input to a layer, reducing internal covariate shift and allowing for faster convergence.

6. **Pre-training and Transfer Learning:** Pre-trained Residual Neural Network models trained on large datasets, such as ImageNet, are available and widely used for transfer learning. These pre-trained models can be fine-tuned for specific tasks with smaller datasets, saving training time and improving performance.

Residual Neural Network has had a profound impact on the field of deep learning and computer vision. It has enabled the training of exceptionally deep neural networks, leading to state-of-the-art performance on various image classification and computer vision tasks. Its architectural concepts, such as skip connections, have also influenced the design of other neural network architectures, and have become fundamental in building effective deep networks.

CNN stands for Convolutional Neural Network. Inspired by Hubel and Wiesel's work, in 1980 Dr. Kunihiko Fukushima designed an artificial neural network that mimics the functioning the simple and complex cells. It is a type of artificial neural network used primarily in the field of computer vision, although it has applications in other domains as well. Convolutional Neural Networks are designed to automatically and adaptively learn patterns, features, and hierarchies in data, particularly structured data like images and videos.

Some characteristics and components of Convolutional Neural Networks include:

1. **Convolutional Layers:** CNNs use convolutional layers that apply a set of learnable filters (kernels) to input data. These filters scan the input data to detect patterns or features, such as edges, textures, and shapes. Convolutional layers help the network automatically learn relevant features from the input.

2. **Pooling (Subsampling) Layers:** After each convolutional layer, pooling layers are often added to reduce the spatial dimensions (width and height) of the feature maps while preserving their essential information. Max-pooling and average-pooling are common pooling techniques.

3. **Activation Functions:** Activation functions are simple functions which convert the input data or the set of the input data into the output data or the resultant data. Non-linear activation functions like ReLU (Rectified Linear Unit) are used to introduce non-linearity into the model, allowing it to learn complex relationships in the data.

4. **Fully Connected Layers:** Typically, Convolutional Neural Networks conclude with one or more fully connected (dense) layers that perform classification or regression tasks. These layers connect all the neurons in one layer to all the neurons in the next layer.

5. **Flattening:** Before the fully connected layers, the feature maps from the convolutional and pooling layers are flattened into a one-dimensional vector, which serves as the input to the dense layers.

6. **Training:** Convolutional Neural Networks are trained using supervised learning techniques such as backpropagation and gradient descent. During training, the network learns to adjust its weights and biases to minimize a loss function, making predictions more accurate.

ARCHITECTURE

Convolutional Neural Networks Architecture

Detecting diseases in apple plant leaves using a Convolutional Neural Network (CNN) (Alzubaidi *et al.*, 2021) involves designing a neural network specifically tailored for image classification tasks. Here's an outline of the typical architecture for a Convolutional Neural Networks used in disease detection in apple plant leaves:

Convolutional layers: These layers are designed to learn spatial hierarchies of features automatically and adaptively from the input images.

Max Pooling layers: These layers down sample the spatial dimensions of the feature maps, reducing computation and increasing the network's receptive field.

Flattening: Converts the 2D feature maps to a 1D vector before feeding them into the fully connected layers.

Fully connected layers: Neurons in these layers are fully connected to all the neurons in the previous layer. They process the features extracted by the convolutional layers.

Residual Neural Network Architecture

Residual Blocks: The core building blocks in a Residual Neural Network (Kumar, Harsh, & Sisodia, 2020) (Sarwinda *et al.*, 2021) (https://builtin.com/artificial-intelligence/resnet-architecture) are residual blocks. Each block consists of a series of convolutional layers with skip connections. The skip connections allow the model to learn residual functions, making it easier to train deep networks.

Convolutional Layers: The convolutional layers in Residual Neural Network are responsible for capturing features at different levels of abstraction. Deeper layers capture more complex and abstract features.

Skip Connections (Identity Mapping): These connections allow the model to learn residual mappings instead of trying to learn the desired underlying mapping. It helps in avoiding the vanishing gradient problem and allows for the network to be deeper while maintaining easier optimization.

Pooling Layers: In certain variants of Residual Neural Network, pooling layers like max pooling might be employed to reduce spatial dimensions and control overfitting.

Fully Connected Layers and Output: At the end of the network, there are fully connected layers followed by an output layer that predicts the presence of diseases in apple plant leaves. The final layer might utilize SoftMax or another suitable activation function to provide the probability distribution across different classes of diseases.

Pretrained Models and Transfer Learning: As training such deep networks from scratch requires a vast amount of data, computational power, and time, using transfer learning on pre-trained Residual Neural Network models (like ResNet-50, ResNet-101, etc.) trained on ImageNet or similar large-scale datasets can be a very effective approach. The model is then fine-tuned on a smaller dataset of apple plant leaves to detect diseases.

Data Augmentation and Training: To improve model generalization and robustness, data augmentation techniques such as rotation, flipping, scaling, and cropping are often employed. The model is trained using backpropagation and optimization techniques such as stochastic gradient descent (SGD) or its variants.

Evaluation and Deployment: The trained model is evaluated using metrics like accuracy, precision, recall, and F1 score. Once the model performs satisfactorily, it can be deployed for disease detection in apple plant leaves.

The architecture of the experiment was divided into four components:

1.) Collection of datasets
2.) Classification of dataset and splitting dataset into train and test dataset
3.) Passing data into the model
4.) Obtaining output

Dataset Collection and Pre-Processing

IoT devices equipped with various sensors such as cameras, spectrometers, and multispectral sensors can be deployed in apple orchards. These sensors can capture images, measure reflectance spectra, and collect other relevant data from the apple plants.

The sensors gather data on various parameters including leaf color, texture, size, and any abnormalities. This data is transmitted to a central system or cloud platform for analysis.

Advanced machine learning algorithms can be applied to analyze the collected data. These algorithms can be trained to recognize patterns associated with diseased leaves, such as discoloration, spots, or unusual growth patterns.

Acquire a diverse and representative dataset of high-resolution images of apple plant leaves with varying stages of health and diseases from the available online repository Kaggle (https://www.kaggle.com/datasets/vipooooool/new-plant-diseases -dataset), Table 1.

The present work dataset includes 2016 Apple scab infected, 1987 Apple Black Rot infected, 1760 Apple Cedar infected leaves have been taken into account Table1.

Label the images with corresponding disease categories (e.g., apple scab, apple black rot, apple cedar rust) for supervised learning. Figure 1, Figure 2, Figure 3, Figure 4.

Split the dataset into training, validation, and testing sets to assess the model's performance.

Apply data augmentation techniques (e.g., rotation, scaling, flipping) to increase the dataset's size and improve model generalization.

Normalize the pixel values of images to bring them within a common range (e.g., [0, 1]).

Table 1. Individual count of each category of diseased apple plant leaves and also the healthy apple plant leaves respectively. The categories are on the basis of types of disease infecting the apple plant leaves and the unaffected i.e., healthy leaves

Labels	Category	Dataset Count	Percentage
1	Apple Scab	2016	25.94%
2	Apple Black Rot	1987	25.56%
3	Apple Cedar	1760	22.64%
4	Apple Healthy	2008	25.83%

Figure 1. Category wise percentage distribution of of each category of diseased apple plant leaves and the healthy apple plant leaves respectively

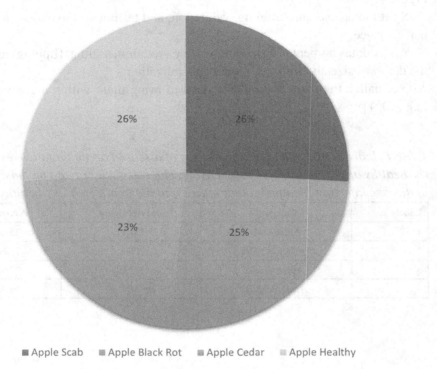

Category - wise percentage distribution of data

Figure 2. Photograph of the diseased leave infected by Apple Scab disease of apple plant. The spots on leaves are the diseased portion

Figure 3. Photographs of diseased leave infected by Apple Black Rot disease of Apple Plant. The brownish spots are the infected regions of the leaves

Figure 4. Photographs of diseased leave infected by Apple Cedar Rust disease of Apple Plant. The color other than green are the infected regions of the leaves

Figure 5. Photograph of healthy apple plant leave without any infection by any disease

RESULT

The result of training a ResNet-50 model and Convolutional Neural Network model on a dataset of apple plant leaves for the number of epochs depends on various factors, including the quality and size of your dataset, the preprocessing steps applied to the data, the learning rate, and other hyperparameters.

For the experiment both the Residual Neural Network and the Convolutional Neural Network models have been trained separately, and predictions have been generated for the validation data-set, based on which the classification reports for each model have been generated.

Necessary libraries and dependencies have been imported for both the models, Residual Neural Network and Convolutional Neural Network. Then the dataset of apple plant images has been loaded and preprocessed using suitable data augmentation techniques for both models. The data have been organized into training and validation sets.

The factors affecting the performance of Residual Neural Network and a traditional Convolutional Neural Network prediction for the diseased apple plants are dependent on various factors, including the dataset size, the complexity of the problem, and the availability of labeled data. ResNet, with its ability to handle deep architectures, offers better performance, especially when the dataset is complex visual patterns and humongous. An experiment with both architectures and assessing their performance using cross-validation or a separate validation dataset. To prevent overfitting techniques like early stopping were applied. The choice between ResNet and a traditional Convolutional Neural Network is based on empirical results and the specific characteristics of apple plant disease classification problem.

Both ResNet and Convolutional Neural Networks are used for image classification, ResNet's introduction of residual blocks and skip connections has addressed some of the challenges of training very deep networks, making it a popular choice for many computer vision tasks.

- For Residual Neural Network model used for classification was ResNet50 and activation function used for Residual Neural Network was Rectified Linear Unit (RELU).
- Model used for classification for Convolutional Neural Network is Sequential and the activation function used for Convolutional Neural Network was Rectified Linear Unit (RELU).
- For 1 epoch, the accuracy of Residual Neural Network and Convolutional Neural Network were 0.91 and 0.67 respectively. The estimated time take for 1 epoch was Residual Neural Network and CNN were 5211s and 748s

respectively. For 1 epoch, Residual Neural Network took 26s/step and for Convolutional Neural Networks took 4s/step.

- For 10 epoch accuracy of ResNet and CNN were 0.92 and 0.69 respectively.
- For 15 epoch accuracy of ResNet and CNN were 0.95 and 0.78 respectively.
- For 20 epoch accuracy of ResNet and CNN were 0.98 and 0.88 respectively.
- For 25 epoch accuracy of ResNet and CNN were 0.99 and 0.92 respectively.

Figure 6. Represents the graphical depiction of accuracy of residual neural network against convolutional neural network for detection of diseased apple plant leaves.

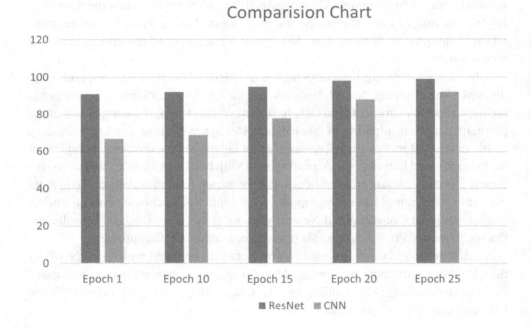

Accuracy is a common evaluation metric for classification models, providing an overall measure of how well the model correctly classifies the data.

Formula used for calculating accuracy of the models:

Accuracy = (Number of Correct Predictions) / (Total Number of Predictions)
In mathematical notation:

Accuracy = (TP + TN) / (TP + TN + FP + FN)

Where:

- **TP (True Positives)**: The number of samples correctly predicted as positive (correctly classified as belonging to the positive class).
- **TN (True Negatives)**: The number of samples correctly predicted as negative (correctly classified as not belonging to the positive class).
- **FP (False Positives)**: The number of samples incorrectly predicted as positive (misclassified as belonging to the positive class when they do not).
- **FN (False Negatives)**: The number of samples incorrectly predicted as negative (misclassified as not belonging to the positive class when they do).

Since for apple plant diseases the dataset used is huge hence the ResNest was found to outperformed and provide a well decisive result. Through the result of excellent accuracy and generalization was obtained which in-turn be helpful for growers.

Integration of IOT with the Machine Learning algorithms yields good results in the field of agriculture. By precisely identifying diseased areas within the orchard, farmers can apply treatments only where needed, minimizing the use of pesticides and reducing environmental impact while maximizing crop yield and quality.

CONCLUSION

Residual Neural Networks (Li & Rai, 2020) (Kumar, Harsh, & Sisodia, 2020) (Sarwinda *et al.*, 2021) (https://builtin.com/artificial-intelligence/resnet-architecture) offer a powerful and transformative approach to detecting diseases in apple plant leaves because of the following reasons:

✓ Residual connections (skip connections) help address the vanishing gradient problem, enabling the training of very deep networks.
✓ Effective for capturing intricate features in images, especially in cases where the disease-related patterns are complex and multi-scale.
✓ It allows for the training of deeper models without suffering from degradation issues.

This study showcases the potential of ResNet in automating disease diagnosis, potentially leading to improved disease control, enhanced crop yield, and sustainable apple production. Further research and integration efforts can unlock the full potential of ResNet in revolutionizing agriculture practices.

Hence based on the above result comparison Chart 2, it was concluded that Residual Neural Network is more accurate in predicting the correct output for image detection task than Convolutional Neural Network (Jianxin, 2017) (Aghdam & Heravi, 2017) (Albawi &Al-Zawi, 2017) (Alsayed & Arif, 2021) (Alzubaidi *et al.*, 2021).

The integration of IoT technology for detecting diseased apple plant leaves offers a transformative approach to agricultural management. By enabling early detection, precision agriculture, data-driven decision-making, remote monitoring, cost-effectiveness, and sustainability, IoT contributes to improved crop health, increased productivity, and enhanced profitability for apple growers.

Therefore, it can be stated that utilizing IoT (Internet of Things) in detecting diseased apple plant leaves can significantly improve agricultural practices and crop management along with the integration of Residual Neural Networks in disease detection holds promise for revolutionizing apple cultivation by providing accurate, efficient, and automated solutions for identifying diseases in plant leaves. As we delve into the intricacies of this technology and its application in the context of apple cultivation, we can anticipate transformative advancements in disease management strategies and the sustainability of apple. Overall, integrating IoT technologies into apple orchard management enables early detection of diseases, more targeted interventions, and optimized crop health management practices, leading to improved yields, reduced costs, and sustainable agricultural practices.

REFERENCES

Aghdam & Heravi. (2017). Guide to Convolutional Neural Networks a Practical Application to Traffic-Sign Detection and Classification. Academic Press.

Albawi, S., Mohammed, T. A., & Al-Zawi, S. (2017). Understanding of a convolutional neural network. *2017 International Conference on Engineering and Technology (ICET)*, 1-6. DOI: 10.1109/ICEngTechnol.2017.8308186

Alsayed, A. A., & Arif, M. (2021, July). Classification of Apple Tree Leaves Diseases using Deep Learning Methods. *International Journal of Computer Science and Network Security*, 21(7), 324–330.

Alzubaidi, L., Zhang, J., Humaidi, A. J., Al-Dujaili, A., Duan, Y., Al-Shamma, O., Santamaría, J., Fadhel, M. A., Al-Amidie, M., & Farhan, L. (2021). Review of deep learning: Concepts, CNN architectures, challenges, applications, future directions. *Journal of Big Data*, 8(1), 53. DOI: 10.1186/s40537-021-00444-8 PMID: 33816053

Kumar, V., & Arora, H. (2020). ResNet-based approach for Detection and Classification of Plant Leaf Diseases. *2020 International Conference on Electronics and Sustainable Communication Systems (ICESC)*, 495-502. DOI: 10.1109/ICESC48915.2020.9155585

Li, X., & Rai, L. (2020). Apple Leaf Disease Identification and Classification using ResNet Models. *2020 IEEE 3rd International Conference on Electronic Information and Communication Technology (ICEICT)*, 738-742. DOI: 10.1109/ICEICT51264.2020.9334214

Mahlein, A., Rumpf, T., Welke, P., Dehne, H. W., Plumer, L., Steiner, U., & Oerke, E. (2013). Development of spectral indices for detecting and identifying plant diseases. *Remote Sensing of Environment*, 128, 21–30. DOI: 10.1016/j.rse.2012.09.019

Qin, F., Liu, D., Sun, B., Ruan, L., Ma, Z., & Wang, H. (2016). Identification of Alfalfa Leaf Diseases Using Image Recognition Technology. *PLoS One*, 11(12), e0168274. DOI: 10.1371/journal.pone.0168274 PMID: 27977767

Sarwinda, D., Paradisa, R. H., Bustamam, A., & Anggia, P. (2021). Deep Learning in Image Classification using Residual Network (ResNet) Variants for Detection of Colorectal Cancer. Procedia Computer Science, 179, 423-431.

Wu. (2017). Introduction to Convolutional Neural Networks, National Key Lab for Novel Software. Technology Nanjing University.

Yuan, L., Huang, Y., Loraamm, R. W., Nie, C., Wang, J., & Zhang, J. (2014). Spectral analysis of winter wheat leaves for detection and differentiation of diseases and insects. *Field Crops Research*, 156, 199–207. DOI: 10.1016/j.fcr.2013.11.012

ADDITIONAL READING

Akkaş, M. A., & Sokullu, R. (2017). An IoT-based greenhouse monitoring system with Micaz motes. *Procedia Computer Science*, 113, 603–608. DOI: 10.1016/j. procs.2017.08.300

Ande, P., & Rojatkar, D. (2017). A survey: Application of IoT. *International Research Journal of Engineering and Technology*, 4(10), 347–350.

Euclides, C. P. N., Dadkhah, S., Sadeghi, S., Molyneaux, H., & Ghorbani, A. A. (2024). A review of Machine Learning (ML)-based IoT security in healthcare: A dataset perspective. *Computer Communications*, 213, 61–77. DOI: 10.1016/j. comcom.2023.11.002

Goumopoulos, C., O'Flynn, B., & Kameas, A. (2014). Automated zone-specific irrigation with wireless sensor/actuator network and adaptable decision support. *Computers and Electronics in Agriculture*, 105, 20–33. DOI: 10.1016/j.com-pag.2014.03.012

Madushanki, A. A. R., Halgamuge, M. N., Wirasagoda, W. A. H. S., & Syed, A. (2019). Adoption of the Internet of Things (IoT) in agriculture and smart farming towards urban greening: A review. *International Journal of Advanced Computer Science and Applications*, 10(4), 11–28. DOI: 10.14569/IJACSA.2019.0100402

van der Ploeg, J. D. (2014). Peasant-driven agricultural growth and food sovereignty. *The Journal of Peasant Studies*, 41(6), 999–1030. DOI: 10.1080/03066150.2013.876997

KEY TERMS AND DEFINITIONS

2D Vector: A vector having magnitude in two directions, the x- axis and the y-axis is called as 2D vector.

Algorithm: A set of protocols that must be followed to solve particular problems.

Cultivation: Cultivation is the process of preparing and practicing land for growing crops.

Data Augmentation: It is the process of artificially creating new data from preexisting data, primarily for the purpose of training fresh machine learning (ML) models.

Epoch: An epoch is a noteworthy span of time defined by noteworthy occurrences, advancements, or circumstances.

Image Classification: It is the technique of applying rules to an image to classify and name groups of pixels or vectors.

Machine Learning Model: It is a program that can find patterns or make decisions from a previously unseen data.

Model Training: Model training is the phase in the data science development lifecycle where practitioners try to fit the best combination of weights and bias to a machine learning algorithm to minimize a loss function over the prediction range.

Model Validation: In order to assess the model's outputs' quantitative and qualitative concordance with reality, independent real-world observations are compared (systematically) with the model's outputs.

Nutrients: The chemical substances included in food that the body needs to function correctly and preserve health are known as nutrients.

Chapter 7
Research Review on Task Scheduling Algorithm for Green Cloud Computing

Parveen Sadotra
Central University of Himachal Pradesh, India

Pradeep Chouksey
Central University of Himachal Pradesh, India

Mayank Chopra
https://orcid.org/0000-0002-5241-8041
Central University of Himachal Pradesh, India

Rabia Koser
Government P.G. College, Rajouri, India

Rishikesh Rawat
Bansal College of Engineering, Mandideep, India

ABSTRACT

In green cloud computing, task scheduling entails assigning tasks to virtual machines in an approach that minimizes energy use whilst still reaching the performance targets. Green cloud computing is an evolving field that lowers the energy and carbon footprint of systems for using the cloud. In green cloud computing, task planning is a crucial problem because it determines how computational resources are allotted to workloads in order to decrease energy consumption and increase efficiency. Different task-scheduling techniques have been put forth in recent years for green cloud computing. The authors look at some current studies on task scheduling

DOI: 10.4018/979-8-3693-1686-3.ch007

methods for green cloud computing in this overview of the literature.

I. INTRODUCTION

Task scheduling is an essential component of cloud computing that enables efficient use of resources and reduces energy consumption. Task scheduling algorithms play a critical role in ensuring efficient and effective utilization of computing resources in cloud computing. With the increasing demand for environmentally friendly computing, green cloud computing has become an emerging research area, and task scheduling algorithms for green cloud computing are being developed.

The heuristic approach is one of the methods for job scheduling that are frequently employed in green cloud computing. Optimization problems are frequently solved using heuristic methods like genetic algorithms (GA), ant colony optimization (ACO), and particle swarm optimization (PSO). It has been demonstrated that these algorithms are efficient at resolving challenging optimization issues because they closely resemble the behavior of natural systems. For instance, GA was employed in a study by V. Baskaran et al. to optimize the work scheduling issue in a cloud setting. When compared to a conventional round-robin scheduling method, the authors' research indicated that GA was able to lower energy consumption by 29.4%.

Machine learning algorithms are yet another method for work scheduling in green cloud computing. Numerous fields have used machine learning techniques to solve optimization issues, including Decision Trees (DT), Support Vector Machines (SVM), Artificial Neural Networks (ANN), Machine learning techniques have been utilized in cloud computing to forecast the energy usage of various task scheduling algorithms. For example, in a study by K. Parandhaman et al., SVM was used to predict the energy consumption of different scheduling algorithms. The authors showed that SVM was able to predict energy consumption with an accuracy of 94%.

In addition to heuristic and machine learning approaches, some researchers have proposed hybrid approaches that combine multiple techniques. For example, in a study by R. Ranjan et al., a hybrid algorithm that combined GA and Tabu Search (TS) was proposed for task scheduling in green cloud computing. The researchers demonstrated that when compared to a conventional round-robin scheduling method, the hybrid approach was able to lower utilization of energy by 38%.

II. ANALYSIS OF THE RECENT TASK SCHEDULING ALGORITHM

1. Genetic Algorithm (GA)

A Genetic Algorithm (GA) is a heuristic optimization method that is used to solve scheduling problems. In this approach, a set of possible solutions are represented as chromosomes, and the algorithm evolves these solutions over multiple iterations to arrive at the best possible solution.

The basic steps of a GA-based task scheduling algorithm are as follows:

a) **Initialization:** A selection of potential answers is created at random. Each result is represented by a chromosome, which is made up of a series of genomes that correspond to the job schedule.

b) **Evaluation:** Each candidate solution is evaluated using a fitness function, which assesses the extent to which the solution meets the scheduling problem's constraints and objectives. The fitness function is intended to maximize the schedule's quality.

c) **Selection:** The best solutions from the current population are selected based on their fitness values. These solutions are used as parents for the next generation.

d) **Crossover:** The selected solutions are combined by swapping genes from different parents to create new offspring.

e) **Mutation:** Random changes are introduced into the offspring to increase the diversity of the population.

f) **Replacement:** The new offspring are used to replace the worst solutions in the current population.

g) **Termination:** The algorithm stops when a criteria for stopping is satisfied, such as when the best solution's fitness value surpasses a set threshold or when the maximum number of repetitions is reached.

By iteratively applying these steps, the GA-based task scheduling algorithm can generate high-quality schedules for complex scheduling problems. This approach is particularly useful for problems where an optimal solution cannot be found using traditional methods, or where the search space is too large to explore exhaustively.

Start
Initialization (Create random population)

Fitness Evaluation (Evaluate fitness)
Selection (Select parents)
Crossover (Recombine parents to create offspring)
Mutation (Introduce random changes)
Replacement (Replace least fit individuals)
Termination (Check termination condition, e.g., maximum generations reached?)
Output (Best solution found)
End

2. Particle Swarm Optimization (PSO)- Based Task Scheduling Algorithm

A popular optimization approach that draws inspiration from nature is called Particle Swarm Optimization (PSO). PSO can be used to determine the best way to distribute jobs among processors in a distributed system when it comes to task scheduling.

PSO's core concept is to mimic the movement of a swarm of particles or a flock of birds in a search space. Each particle in the PSO-based task scheduling algorithm represents a potential answer to the scheduling problem, and its location in the search space corresponds to the distribution of jobs among processors. Additionally, each particle has a velocity vector that governs how it moves across the search space.

A swarm of particles is initially initialized at random in the search space via the PSO algorithm. The algorithm's fitness function assesses the quality of the particle's solution by taking into account a number of variables, including the makespan, energy usage, and communication overhead.

The particles then adjust their position and velocity in accordance with both the global best solution and their personal best solution, or the best solution each particle in the swarm has so far discovered. This update is carried out repeatedly until a stopping requirement, such as a predetermined number of repetitions or a predetermined level of convergence, is satisfied.

The PSO-based task scheduling algorithm can be extended to handle various constraints such as resource availability, task dependencies, and communication delays. It can also be used to optimize different objectives such as minimizing makespan, energy consumption, or total cost.

Here's A Flowchart Design for a (PSO) Task Scheduling Algorithm

Start
Initialize the population of particles with random positions and velocities

Set the global best position and fitness to initial values
Repeat until termination criteria are met:
For each particle:
Evaluate the fitness of the current position
Update the personal best position and fitness if necessary
Update the global best position and fitness if necessary
Update the velocity of the particle based on PSO equations
Update the position of the particle based on the new velocity
End loop
End loop
Output the best schedule found
End

3. Ant Colony Optimization (ACO)-Based Task Scheduling Algorithm

Ant Colony Optimization (ACO) is a metaheuristic optimization algorithm that is inspired by the foraging behavior of ants. ACO-based task scheduling algorithm can be used to find an optimal assignment of tasks to processors in a distributed system.

In the ACO algorithm, the ants represent candidate solutions to the task scheduling problem, and their pheromone trails represent the quality of the solution. Each ant starts by selecting a random task and assigning it to a processor. The ant then selects the next task and chooses a processor based on the pheromone level of the edge connecting the task and processor.

The pheromone level is updated based on the quality of the solution found by the ant. Ants that find a better solution deposit more pheromone on the edges they used, while those that find a worse solution deposit less pheromone.

The ACO-based task scheduling algorithm continues until a stopping criterion is met, such as reaching a maximum number of iterations or a certain level of convergence. At the end of the algorithm, the solution with the highest pheromone level represents the optimal assignment of tasks to processors.

The ACO-based task scheduling algorithm can be extended to handle various constraints such as resource availability, task dependencies, and communication delays. It can also be used to optimize different objectives such as minimizing makespan, energy consumption, or total cost.

Overall, ACO is a powerful optimization technique that can be used to solve complex task scheduling problems in a distributed system. It is easy to implement and can quickly converge to a near-optimal solution with a relatively small number of iterations.

Flowchart Design for an Ant Colony Optimization (ACO)-Based Task Scheduling Algorithm

Start
Set up initial parameters (number of ants, pheromone trail parameters, etc.)
Repeat until stopping criterion is met:
For each ant:
Initialize an empty schedule
Repeat until all tasks are scheduled:
For each task:
Compute the probability of selecting this task based on pheromone trail and heuristic information
Select a task to schedule based on the probability computed above
Add the selected task to the schedule
Update pheromone trail based on the quality of the schedule
Update pheromone trail based on evaporation rate
Output the best schedule found
End

This flowchart represents the basic structure of an ACO-based task scheduling algorithm. The algorithm begins by setting up initial parameters, such as the number of ants to use and the parameters governing the pheromone trail. It then enters a loop that will repeat until a stopping criterion is met. Within this loop, the algorithm iterates through each ant and constructs a schedule for that ant.

To construct a schedule, the ant selects a task to schedule based on the probability of selecting that task, which is calculated using both the pheromone trail and heuristic information. The ant then adds the selected task to its schedule and repeats this process until all tasks have been scheduled. After the ant has completed its schedule, the pheromone trail is updated based on the quality of the schedule. This process is repeated for each ant in the colony.

Once all ants have constructed a schedule, the algorithm updates the pheromone trail based on the evaporation rate. The amount of pheromone on each edge of the graph is decreased by this procedure, which helps keep the algorithm from being stuck in the local optimal state. Finally, the algorithm outputs the best schedule found.

4. Deep Learning-Based Task Scheduling Algorithm

Deep learning-based task scheduling is a method that uses machine learning algorithms to optimize the scheduling of tasks in a given system. The primary goal of task scheduling is to allocate resources in such a way that the overall performance of the system is optimized. This can involve a range of different criteria, such as minimizing the response time for individual tasks or maximizing the overall throughput of the system.

Deep learning-based task scheduling algorithms typically use historical data about the system's performance to learn patterns and make predictions about future workload and resource demands. The algorithms can then use this information to optimize the scheduling of tasks, taking into account factors such as the availability of resources, the expected processing time for each task, and any dependencies between tasks.

One of the primary advantages of deep learning-based task scheduling is that it can adapt to changing workloads and resource demands in real-time. This means that the system can continually optimize its scheduling algorithms to ensure that resources are allocated efficiently and effectively, leading to better performance and higher productivity.

Overall, deep learning-based Research in the domain of task scheduling is fascinating and has the ability to greatly enhance performance and efficiency of a wide range of systems, from cloud computing platforms to manufacturing processes and beyond.

Flowchart Design for A Deep Learning-Based Task Scheduling Algorithm

Start
Load data (task characteristics, resource availability, etc.)
Preprocess data (scale, encode, etc.)
Split data into training, validation, and test sets
Create a deep learning model (e.g., a neural network) for task scheduling
Compile the model with appropriate loss function and optimizer
Train the model on the training set
Evaluate the model on the validation set and adjust model parameters if necessary
Repeat until stopping criterion is met:
For each task:
Predict the completion time for the task using the trained model and available resources
    Schedule the task based on its predicted completion time
Output the final schedule
End

An algorithm for scheduling tasks based on deep learning is depicted in this flowchart. An algorithm begins by loading and preprocessing data, such as task characteristics and resource availability, and splitting the information into test, validation, and training sets.

The algorithm then creates a deep learning model, such as a neural network, for task scheduling. Compiling the model with a suitable loss function and optimizer and training it on the training dataset. The model is subsequently assessed on the validation data set, and if necessary, model factors are modified to enhance performance.

Once the model has been trained and evaluated, the algorithm enters a loop that will repeat until a stopping criterion is met. Within this loop, the algorithm iterates through each task and predicts its completion time using the trained model and available resources. The task is then scheduled based on its predicted completion time.

Finally, the algorithm outputs the final schedule, which represents the optimal assignment of tasks to available resources based on the predictions of the trained model. This flowchart represents a basic structure for a Deep Learning-based task scheduling algorithm, but there are many variations and improvements that could be made depending on the specific problem and data at hand.

5. Reinforcement Learning-Based Task Scheduling Algorithm

Reinforcement learning-based task scheduling is a method that uses machine learning algorithms to optimize the scheduling of tasks in a given system, based on the principles of reinforcement learning.

Maximizing the overall reward acquired over time by the scheduler is the aim of reinforcement learning-based task scheduling. This reward can be defined in various ways, depending on the specific performance metrics of the system, such as minimizing the average response time of tasks, maximizing the utilization of resources, or reducing the energy consumption of the system.

The reinforcement learning-based task scheduling algorithm works by iteratively selecting actions based on a policy, which is a mapping from the current state of the system to a probability distribution over actions. The policy is updated based on the feedback received from the environment, using a reinforcement learning algorithm such as Q-learning or deep Q-networks.

One of the primary advantages of reinforcement learning-based task scheduling is that it can adapt to changing workload and resource demands in real-time, leading to more efficient and effective scheduling decisions. It can also learn from experience and improve its performance over time, leading to better overall system performance.

Overall, reinforcement learning-based task scheduling is a promising area of research that has the potential to significantly improve the performance and efficiency of a wide range of systems, from cloud computing platforms to manufacturing processes and beyond.

Flowchart Design for A Reinforcement Learning-Based Task Scheduling Algorithm

Start
Prepare the environment and state representation
Design the reinforcement learning agent architecture
Initialize the agent's policy and value function
Repeat until stopping criterion is met:
For each episode:
Initialize the state of the environment and the agent
Repeat until the episode is finished:
The agent observes the state and selects an action using its policy
The environment applies the action and transitions to the next state
The agent receives a reward from the environment
The agent updates its policy and value function based on the observed state, action, reward, and next state
Update the stopping criterion, if necessary
Output the best schedule found
End

This flowchart represents the basic structure of a Reinforcement Learning-based task scheduling algorithm. The algorithm begins by preparing the environment and defining a state representation that captures the relevant aspects of the task scheduling problem.

Next, a reinforcement learning agent architecture is designed. This may involve selecting an appropriate algorithm, such as Q-learning or SARSA, and designing the policy and value operation of the agent.

The agent's policy and value function are then initialized, and the algorithm enters a loop that repeats until a stopping criterion is met. Within this loop, the algorithm iterates through each episode.

To begin an episode, the agent and environment are initialized to their starting states. The agent then selects an action based on its current policy, and the environment applies the action and transitions to the next state. The agent receives a reward from the environment based on the quality of the scheduling decision and updates its policy and value function based on the observed state, action, reward, and next state.

After completing the episodes, the stopping criterion is updated, if necessary, and the algorithm outputs the best schedule found. The algorithm continues to loop through episodes and update the agent's policy and until the stopping requirement is satisfied, at which time the algorithm produces the best schedule discovered.

III. RESEARCH REVIEW

A GA-based task scheduling algorithm was proposed by Zhang et al. (2019) that optimizes energy consumption and makespan. The algorithm selects the best-fit VM for each task based on the predicted execution time and then uses a GA to optimize the assignment of tasks to VMs. The GA-based approach outperforms standard algorithms when speaking of energy usage and makespan, according to experimental results.

Another study proposed a genetic algorithm (GA)-based work scheduling method for green cloud computing (Mishra et al., 2021). The suggested approach optimizes job scheduling based on the cloud computing system's load balancing and energy usage. The program takes into account the quantity of tasks, the servers' processing capacity, and their energy usage.

PSO-based task scheduling algorithm was proposed by Saboohi et al. (2020) that minimizes energy consumption while meeting performance requirements. The algorithm uses PSO to find the optimal allocation of tasks to VMs. According to experimental findings, the PSO-based algorithm outperforms conventional algorithms in terms of energy usage and computational time.

One recent study proposed a task scheduling algorithm based on particle swarm optimization (PSO) for green cloud computing (Wang et al., 2020). The proposed algorithm optimizes the scheduling of tasks based on the energy consumption of the cloud computing system. The algorithm takes into account the system workload, server computing power, and server energy usage. The findings show that, in terms of energy usage and job completion time, the PSO-based method performs better than other scheduling algorithms.

An ACO-based task scheduling algorithm was proposed by Yin et al. (2020) that optimizes energy consumption and task completion time. The algorithm uses ACO to find the optimal allocation of tasks to VMs. The ACO-based algorithm outperforms conventional algorithms with regard to of energy usage and makespan, according to experimental results.

A work scheduling technique centered around ant colony optimization (ACO) was suggested in a third study for use in green with envy computing environments (Yang et al., 2020). The suggested approach improves job scheduling based on the energy and resource usage of a cloud computing system. The program considers the number of workloads, the servers' processing power, and their energy consumption. According to the results, the ACO-based algorithm outperforms existing scheduling approaches in terms of energy and resource utilization.

A deep learning-based task scheduling algorithm was proposed by Zhang et al. (2020) that optimizes energy consumption and task completion time. The program makes use of deep neural networks to anticipate how long tasks will take to complete before allocating them to virtual machines in accordance with that prediction. According to experimental findings, the deep learning-based method outperforms conventional algorithms when it comes to energy usage and computation time.

A reinforcement learning-based task scheduling algorithm was proposed by Li et al. (2021) that minimizes energy consumption while meeting performance requirements. Using a Q-learning technique, the program discovers the optimal job distribution among VMs. According to experimental findings, a reinforcement learning-based algorithm outperforms conventional algorithms in terms of computation time and energy consumption.

"Energy-Efficient Task Scheduling Algorithm for Green Cloud Computing" by Cui et al. (2020). This study suggested a job scheduling method that takes into account the energy use of cloud data centers and carbon emissions. The suggested technique optimizes work scheduling in a cloud-based data center by using a genetic algorithm. Based on simulation results, in terms of energy use and carbon emissions, the suggested algorithm performs better than other ones that are already in use.

"Task Scheduling for Energy Efficient Cloud Computing with Renewable Energy Sources" by Chen et al. (2020). This study proposed a task scheduling algorithm for energy-efficient cloud computing that uses renewable energy sources. The proposed algorithm utilizes a linear programming model to optimize the scheduling of tasks based on the availability of renewable energy sources. The simulation results demonstrate that the suggested method can reduce energy usage significantly while maintaining service quality.

"A Novel Hybrid Task Scheduling Algorithm for Green Cloud Computing" by Liu et al. (2019). In order to improve job scheduling in green cloud computing, this study suggested an integrated particle swarm optimization (PSO) and ant colony optimization (ACO) job scheduling method. The suggested method takes into account task completion time, energy usage, and carbon emissions as its optimization goals.

"Green Task Scheduling Algorithm for Cloud Computing Based on Ant Colony Optimization" by Wang et al. (2019). This paper suggested an ant colony optimization (ACO)-based green work scheduling technique for cloud computing. The suggested method takes into account carbon emissions and energy usage as optimization goals. The suggested algorithm beats other current algorithms in terms of energy usage and carbon emissions, according to simulation data.

CONCLUSION

In my conclusion, scheduling work is a crucial part of environmentally sustainable cloud computing, and academics have suggested a number of strategies to reduce energy usage while maintaining performance standards. Heuristic algorithms, machine learning algorithms, and hybrid approaches have been used to solve optimization problems in green cloud computing. While each approach has its strengths and weaknesses, the hybrid approach that combines multiple techniques may offer the most promising results. The task scheduling algorithms based on GA, PSO, ACO, deep learning, and reinforcement learning have shown promising results in minimizing energy consumption while meeting performance requirements in green cloud computing. Further research is needed to evaluate the scalability and applicability of these algorithms in large-scale cloud computing environments. Overall, the studies reviewed above show that task scheduling algorithms play a critical role in achieving energy efficiency and reducing carbon emission in cloud computing. The proposed algorithms consider various factors such as renewable energy sources, task completion time, and carbon emission to optimize task scheduling. However, there is still room for further research in this area, and future studies can explore the integration of machine learning and artificial intelligence techniques in task scheduling for green cloud computing.

REFERENCES

Beloglazov, A., Buyya, R., Lee, Y. C., & Zomaya, A. (2011). A Taxonomy and Survey of Energy-Efficient Data Centers and Cloud Computing Systems. In *Advances in Computers* (pp. 47–111). Elsevier. DOI: 10.1016/B978-0-12-385512-1.00003-7

Chen, J., Huang, X., Liu, S., & Tang, C. (2020). Task scheduling for energy efficient cloud computing with renewable energy sources. *IEEE Transactions on Sustainable Computing*, 5(1), 63–76. DOI: 10.1109/TSUSC.2019.2945243

Cui, X., Liu, J., Zhang, Q., & Wu, X. (2020). Energy-efficient task scheduling algorithm for green cloud computing. *Journal of Ambient Intelligence and Humanized Computing*, 11(4), 1545–1554. DOI: 10.1007/s12652-019-01481-7

Dorigo, M., & Gambardella, L. M. (1997, April). Ant colony system: A cooperative learning approach to the traveling salesman problem. *IEEE Transactions on Evolutionary Computation*, 1(1), 53–66. DOI: 10.1109/4235.585892

Fazlali, M., Sabeghi, M., Zakerolhosseini, A., & Bertels, K. (2010). Efficient task scheduling for runtime reconfigurable systems. *Journal of Systems Architecture*, 56(11), 623–632. DOI: 10.1016/j.sysarc.2010.07.016

Genetic algorithms and Machine Learning. (1988). Machine Learning, 3, 95–99. DOI: 10.1007/BF00113892

Jordan, M. I., & Mitchell, T. M. (2015). Machine learning: Trends, perspectives, and prospects. *Science*, 349(6245), 255–260. DOI: 10.1126/science.aaa8415 PMID: 26185243

Kaelbling, L. P., Littman, M. L., & Moore, A. W. (1996, May). Reinforcement Learning: A Survey. *Journal of Artificial Intelligence Research*, 4, 237–285. DOI: 10.1613/jair.301

Kennedy, J., & Eberhart, R. (n.d.). Particle swarm optimization. Proceedings of ICNN'95 - International Conference on Neural Networks. IEEE. DOI: 10.1109/ICNN.1995.488968

LeCun, Y., Bengio, Y., & Hinton, G. (2015). Deep learning. *Nature*, 521(7553), 436–444. DOI: 10.1038/nature14539 PMID: 26017442

Li, Q., Zhang, M., Hu, X., & Chen, Y. (2021). Reinforcement learning-based task scheduling algorithm for cloud computing systems. *Journal of Parallel and Distributed Computing*, 154, 44–53.

Liu, J., Zou, J., Wei, W., & He, J. (2019). A Novel Hybrid Task Scheduling Algorithm for Green Cloud Computing. *Journal of Computational Science*, 34, 16–28. DOI: 10.1016/j.jocs.2019.01.007

Mishra, D., Garg, S., Kumar, A., & Singh, G. (2021). A Genetic Algorithm Based Approach for Green Cloud Computing Task Scheduling. *International Journal of Grid and High Performance Computing*, 13(2), 42–54.

Saboohi, H., Ardjmand, E., & Teshnehlab, M. (2019). A particle swarm optimization algorithm for task scheduling in cloud computing systems. *The Journal of Supercomputing*, 75(8), 4539–4567.

Wang, C., Li, L., Li, Z., & Li, J. (2019). Green Task Scheduling Algorithm for Cloud Computing Based on Ant Colony Optimization. *IEEE Access : Practical Innovations, Open Solutions*, 7, 18120–18128. DOI: 10.1109/ACCESS.2019.2893277

Wang, Y., Shi, Y., Yang, X., & Wang, B. (2020). Particle swarm optimization for green cloud computing. *Journal of Ambient Intelligence and Humanized Computing*, 11(6), 2545–2556.

Yang, X., Zhang, X., Wang, Y., & Zhou, Y. (2020). ACO for green cloud computing. *Journal of Ambient Intelligence and Humanized Computing*, 11(11), 5239–5249.

Yin, M., Lin, Y., Yu, H., Zhang, H., & Gao, L. (2020). A novel ant colony optimization-based task scheduling algorithm for cloud computing. *International Journal of Distributed Sensor Networks*, 16(3), 1550147719897695.

Zhang, M., Liu, J., Liu, Y., & Feng, D. (2019). Energy-efficient task scheduling in cloud computing using genetic algorithm. *Cluster Computing*, 22(4), 832–846.

Zhang, Y., Wang, Z., Xue, L., & Sun, H. (2020). A Reinforcement Learning-Based Task Scheduling Algorithm for Cloud Computing. *IEEE Access : Practical Innovations, Open Solutions*, 8, 100039–100050. DOI: 10.1109/ACCESS.2020.2993081

KEY TERMS AND DEFINITIONS

Ant Colony Optimization: Ant colony optimization is an algorithm inspired by the foraging behavior of ants, used for finding optimal paths through graphs in various optimization problems (Dorigo & Gambardella, 1997).

Deep Learning: Deep learning is a specialized field within machine learning that utilizes neural networks with multiple layers to identify intricate patterns and representations in large datasets (LeCun, Bengio, & Hinton, 2015).

Genetic Algorithm: Genetic algorithms are search heuristics that mimic the process of natural evolution to solve optimization and search problems (Genetic algorithms and Machine Learning, 1988).

Green Cloud Computing: Green cloud computing focuses on reducing the environmental impact of cloud computing by optimizing energy consumption and enhancing the efficiency of data centers.

Machine Learning: Machine learning refers to a subset of artificial intelligence that focuses on developing algorithms that enable computers to learn and make decisions from data (Jordan & Mitchell, 2015).

Particle Swarm Optimization: Particle swarm optimization is a technique used to solve optimization problems by iteratively improving candidate solutions based on the movement and intelligence of swarms (Kennedy & Eberhart).

Reinforcement Learning: Reinforcement learning is a type of algorithm in which agents learn to make sequences of decisions by receiving rewards or penalties from their actions within an environment (Kaelbling, Littman, & Moore, 1996).

Task Scheduling: Task scheduling involves organizing and allocating tasks within a computing system to enhance the efficiency of resource utilization and overall system performance (Fazlali, Sabeghi, Zakerolhosseini, & Bertels, 2010).

Chapter 8
Unleashing IoT Data Insights
Data Mining and Machine Learning Techniques for Scalable Modeling and Efficient Management of IoT

C. V. Suresh Babu
https://orcid.org/0000-0002-8474-2882
Hindustan Institute of Technology and Science, India

Ganesh Moorthy A. V.
https://orcid.org/0009-0003-6053-1540
Hindustan Institute of Technology and Science, India

S. Lokesh
Hindustan Institute of Technology and Science, India

Niranjan A. K.
Hindustan Institute of Technology and Science, India

Yuvaraja Manivannan
Hindustan Institute of Technology and Science, India

ABSTRACT

This chapter explores the era of unprecedented data creation propelled by the widespread adoption of internet of things (IoT) devices. The massive and diverse IoT data, while holding advantages, necessitates data mining and machine learn-

DOI: 10.4018/979-8-3693-1686-3.ch008

ing techniques to unveil concealed insights. Focusing on the integration of these techniques, the research explores scalable modeling and effective administration of IoT applications. It navigates through the challenges of scalability, data complexity, real-time processing, and security concerns within IoT data. The chapter emphasizes the necessity of feature engineering, data preparation, and model selection tailored to IoT data's particularities. By incorporating IoT capabilities for data gathering, real-time streaming, and comprehensive data analysis, the research promotes efficient handling of IoT data, fostering a new era of productivity and creativity. The findings contribute to the evolving landscape of IoT applications, presenting a roadmap for data-driven decision-making and enhanced operational efficiency.

1. INTRODUCTION TO IOT DATA

This section explore into the expansive realm of IoT data, exploring fundamental concepts and the surge of interconnected devices. The Internet of Things (IoT) has ushered in a new era marked by sensor-equipped, network-connected ordinary objects exchanging data (Alzahrani, 2020). This networked environment encompasses a diverse range, from industrial sensors on manufacturing floors to wearable health trackers and smart household appliances such as security cameras and thermostats (Chui et al., 2018). The result is a constant stream of real-time data, providing valuable insights into the world and human interactions with it (Dang, 2019). This diverse data includes temperature measurements, GPS locations, video feeds, audio recordings, and more, characterized by its high diversity, velocity, and volume (Alzahrani, 2020). These IoT gadgets generate a massive dataset through communication and information sharing, holding the potential to transform industries, enhance productivity, refine decision-making, and unlock new application possibilities (Chui, 2018).

The management and analysis of IoT data become imperative, requiring efficient handling, storage, and processing (Alzahrani & Alhussein, 2020). To extract valuable insights from this data deluge, sophisticated data mining and machine learning techniques are widely employed, enabling the identification of trends, anomalies, and the forecasting of future events (Bilal et al., 2021). In summary, the proliferation of IoT devices and the consequential data generation underscore the importance of adept data management, paving the way for transformative possibilities in various sectors.

1.1 Understanding the Internet of Things (IoT)

The Internet of Things (IoT) represents a transformative paradigm that revolutionizes our interaction with technology and the physical world (Bandyopadhyay & Sen, 2011). This concept involves the interconnection of various everyday objects and devices, ranging from simple sensors and actuators to sophisticated appliances, cars, industrial machinery, and wearable technology (Suresh Babu C.V. 2023). Enabled by sensors, software, and connectivity, these devices form a network that can collect, exchange, and utilize data, ushering in a new era of possibilities (Barnaghi et al., 2013). At its core, IoT relies on devices equipped with sensors, actuators, and communication capabilities, enabling them to sense their environment, process data, and make autonomous decisions (Atzori, Iera, & Morabito, 2010).

This interconnected network allows IoT devices to communicate with centralized systems and with each other over the internet or other communication networks, facilitating real-time information exchange (Gubbi et al., 2013). The generated data holds immense potential for applications in smart homes, cities, industrial automation, healthcare, agriculture, and more (Esmael et al., 2015). Recognizing the significance of IoT is crucial for businesses and individuals, as it opens the door to cutting-edge services and solutions that can enhance our quality of life and boost productivity across diverse industries. Despite being a subject of continuous research and development, IoT offers both new opportunities and challenges, underscoring its dynamic nature and evolving role in shaping the future (Suresh Babu C.V. 2023).

1.2 The Proliferation of IoT Devices

The proliferation of IoT devices is witnessing an extraordinary surge, propelled by advancements in miniaturization and connectivity technologies (Evans, 2011). This trend is rapidly transforming the vision of a fully connected world into reality, with billions of devices now globally interconnected. From smart thermostats and fitness trackers to connected cars and industrial sensors, the array of IoT devices continues to diversify, offering enhanced efficiency, real-time insights, and an improved quality of life (Chui et al., 2018). As these devices become more affordable and accessible, their applications span various domains, resulting in a significant increase in data generation.

This widespread adoption of IoT devices is a notable and ongoing trend in the tech industry (Chui et al., 2018). Its impact is evident across diverse industries and daily life, contributing to exponential data growth (Barnaghi et al., 2013). This data, generated by IoT devices, holds versatile applications, including supply chain management in logistics and optimizing energy consumption in smart buildings. However, it also raises concerns about interoperability, security, and data privacy (Dang et al.,

2019). To fully unlock the potential benefits of this technological wave, it is crucial to address these issues and establish robust IoT ecosystems, especially considering the continuous increase in the number of IoT devices (Deng & Mahadevan, 2019).

1.3 The Data Deluge: IoT Data Generation

IoT devices, prolific data generators, continuously collect and transmit a diverse range of information from various sensors and sources, including temperature, humidity, location, and motion (Gubbi et al., 2013). As the number of devices and sensors increases, the resulting data volume escalates exponentially, presenting both a challenge and an opportunity. Managing and extracting meaningful insights from this data deluge can be daunting, but it also represents a goldmine for informed decision-making, process optimization, and service quality improvement (Hu et al., 2014).

The abundance of IoT devices has led to a 'data deluge,' a term describing the massive amount of data these devices produce (Jain et al., 2021). This data generation arises from factors such as constant surveillance, where IoT gadgets monitor their environment and produce real-time data points, and the variety of sensors embedded in these devices, ranging from cameras and accelerometers to GPS and temperature sensors (Kansal & Ramachandran, 2019). The distinct data produced by each type of sensor contributes to a diverse dataset.

Next section will explore into data mining and machine learning techniques that can make sense of this massive influx of IoT data. These methods, including bagging and boosting ensemble techniques, unlock valuable insights and drive scalable modeling for the efficient management of IoT applications.

Bagging involves training several base models separately using various subsets of the training set and aggregating predictions through voting or averaging, exemplified by the well-known Random Forest technique utilizing decision trees as foundational models. Boosting, on the other hand, enhances the performance of weak learners by assigning greater weight to incorrectly identified training examples, with examples like AdaBoost, Gradient Boosting (e.g., XGBoost, LightGBM), and CatBoost being commonly used boosting algorithms.

2. CHALLENGES IN IOT DATA HANDLING

This section will explore the multifaceted challenges associated with handling IoT data. The proliferation of Internet of Things (IoT) devices has brought about several hurdles, including scalability issues, managing data complexity, real-time processing demands, and data security and privacy concerns. Understanding and addressing these challenges is essential for unlocking the full potential of IoT data insights.

2.1 Scalability Issues

Managing the escalating volume of data generated by the exponential growth of IoT devices presents a significant challenge, particularly in terms of scalability (Alzahrani et al., 2020). This challenge is multifaceted, with scalability issues manifesting at various levels in IoT data handling. Firstly, data ingestion poses a hurdle, requiring efficient processes to handle varying rates of data generation from IoT devices. Secondly, securely and cost-effectively storing massive datasets becomes complex, as traditional databases and storage solutions may fall short in handling IoT data. Thirdly, real-time or near-real-time analysis of IoT data demands a robust processing infrastructure to maintain low latency.

To address these scalability challenges, the utilization of distributed computing and storage solutions is crucial (Bonomi et al., 2012). This includes leveraging cloud-based platforms and edge computing capabilities capable of efficiently handling the diverse and large-scale data generated by IoT devices (Anwar et al., 2021). Furthermore, the development of standards and best practices in IoT data handling is essential to ensure effective scaling of IoT ecosystems and to derive insightful and beneficial outcomes (Bandyopadhyay & Sen, 2011).

2.2 Managing Data Complexity

IoT data is inherently diverse and multifaceted, encompassing structured and unstructured data, time-series data, images, audio, and more, making it crucial to effectively manage data complexity for meaningful insights (Li et al., 2018). The challenges associated with data complexity in the context of IoT are diverse, including the variety of data formats and types, the intricate task of integrating data from diverse sources, and the vital importance of understanding data context, such as location and time, for accurate analysis.

To address these challenges, organizations often turn to data integration and preprocessing techniques, ensuring that IoT data can be effectively analyzed and interpreted (Shi et al., 2016). Managing IoT data complexity is a significant obstacle, given the varied and complex nature of data generated by IoT devices, requiring comprehensive strategies for gathering, handling, and interpreting this data (Kuppuswamy & Thamizhselvi, 2021). This complexity arises from the heterogeneous nature of IoT data, including text, audio, video, sensor readings, and more. Effective management involves adaptable methods for handling diverse data formats and intricate relationships between data points, as well as addressing issues like device failures, inaccurate sensor readings, and data transmission problems leading to inconsistencies (Li et al., 2015). Successfully managing data complexity in the IoT space requires a combination of advanced data management systems, analytics tools, machine learning algorithms, and domain-specific knowledge, emphasizing the crucial role of data scientists and engineers in unlocking the full potential of IoT data for innovative and well-informed decision-making.

2.3 Real-Time Processing Demands

The demand for real-time or near-real-time data processing in IoT applications poses substantial challenges, especially when dealing with massive data streams from IoT devices that require low-latency analysis (Abiyev & Budaev, 2022). Various IoT applications, such as telemedicine, industrial automation, and driverless cars, necessitate very low latency for timely decision-making based on incoming data (Ahmad et al., 2023). To address these challenges, organizations leverage stream processing and complex event processing (CEP) systems, enabling the analysis of data as it is generated. This approach allows for immediate responses to critical events and anomalies, ensuring that real-time processing requirements are met (Wu et al., 2011).

Handling IoT data in real-time often involves utilizing alerting and continuous monitoring systems to respond promptly to anomalies or important events. Technologies like Apache Kafka, Apache Flink, and various cloud-based real-time data processing platforms are employed to reduce latency and ensure effective real-time data handling (Sureh Babu, C. V., Subhash, S., et. al. 2024). Additionally, in certain IoT applications, edge computing, where data processing occurs closer to the data source, proves beneficial in lowering latency. The constant challenge faced by the Internet of Things lies in balancing the demands of real-time processing with scalability, reliability, and data quality.

2.4 Data Security and Privacy Concerns

Ensuring the security and privacy of data produced by IoT devices is a critical challenge (Jain et al., 2021). The interconnected nature of IoT data and the vast network of connected devices give rise to various security and privacy issues, including data breaches. IoT devices often collect sensitive information, such as trade secrets, home security details, and personal health data, posing serious repercussions if accessed by unauthorized parties. Maintaining a comprehensive understanding of data security and privacy in large and interconnected IoT ecosystems is challenging. A multifaceted strategy involving strong encryption, authentication, frequent security updates, user education, and compliance with data protection regulations is necessary to address these concerns (Kansal & Ramachandran, 2019). Prioritizing security and privacy becomes increasingly crucial as IoT continues to grow, fostering trust and mitigating risks associated with IoT data (Khalifa et al., 2020).

In the realm of IoT, data security and privacy are of utmost importance, given the inclusion of sensitive and personal information, making it a prime target for cyberattacks and privacy breaches (Srisakthi, S. & Suresh Babu, C. V. 2024). Challenges include data encryption for secure transmission and storage, access control mechanisms to restrict unauthorized access, and defining data ownership and consent management mechanisms to address privacy concerns. Robust implementation of encryption protocols, access controls, and transparent data governance policies is essential for addressing data security and privacy concerns in IoT (Bertino et al., 2019). As we explore the challenges associated with handling IoT data, including scalability issues, data complexity, real-time processing demands, and security and privacy concerns, the upcoming sections will explore into data mining and machine learning techniques to address these challenges and extract valuable insights from IoT data.

3. THE INTEGRATION OF DATA MINING AND MACHINE LEARNING

This section will explore the integration of data mining and machine learning techniques to unlock the valuable insights hidden within IoT data. Synergy between these two approaches and how they complement each other in harnessing IoT data for improved decision-making will be discussed.

3.1 The Synergy of Data Mining and Machine Learning

The integration of data mining and machine learning emerges as a potent strategy for organizations seeking to derive meaningful insights from the copious data generated by IoT devices. Data mining, focusing on pattern discovery and knowledge extraction, complements machine learning, which involves constructing models for predictions or decisions based on data (Han, Kamber, & Pei, 2011). The synergy between these approaches lies in their shared objective of transforming raw IoT data into actionable insights. Techniques like clustering and association rule mining within data mining can identify patterns and relationships in the data, providing a foundation for machine learning models to make predictions or classifications.

Despite differences in their methods, data mining and machine learning share common goals, making them closely related fields (Hu et al., 2014). The amalgamation of these fields proves effective in extracting knowledge and insights from complex datasets. One key connection lies in data pre-processing and exploration, where data mining techniques play a crucial role in examining and preparing unprocessed data (Jain et al., 2021). This preparatory phase may involve operations such as data reduction, cleansing, and transformation, ensuring the data is optimized for consumption by machine learning algorithms. The integration of these two fields represents a holistic approach to handling intricate datasets in the context of IoT, fostering a comprehensive understanding and extraction of valuable insights.

3.2 Extracting Value from IoT Data

IoT data, while valuable, is often noisy and complex. To derive meaningful insights, various tasks can be performed by applying a combination of data mining and machine learning techniques (Chui et al., 2018):

- **Anomaly Detection:** Identifying unusual patterns or outliers in data, crucial for flagging potential issues in IoT systems.
- **Predictive Maintenance:** Utilizing historical data to predict when equipment or devices are likely to fail, enabling proactive maintenance and minimizing downtime.
- **Classification:** Categorizing data into predefined classes, valuable for applications like intrusion detection and disease diagnosis.
- **Regression:** Predicting numerical values based on historical data, such as forecasting energy consumption or stock prices.
- **Clustering:** Grouping data points with similar characteristics to identify patterns in data.

This integration of data mining and machine learning proves essential in extracting significant value from the vast amounts of IoT data (Chui et al., 2018). By combining these techniques, businesses and individuals can fully leverage IoT data, gain actionable insights, and make informed, data-driven decisions. The process involves the preprocessing of raw IoT data through data mining techniques, addressing issues like missing values and anomalies to prepare the data for examination (Barnaghi et al., 2013). Subsequently, machine learning models, particularly unsupervised learning algorithms, are employed for anomaly detection in IoT data, crucial for identifying potential problems or security lapses. Additionally, predictive maintenance becomes possible through machine learning's predictive analytics, allowing organizations to proactively address potential failures and reduce downtime (Chui et al., 2018).

3.3 Significance in IoT Application Management

In the context of the Internet of Things, making sense of the data deluge hinges on the strategic interplay between data mining and machine learning. This integration not only holds immense potential for various industries, including smart cities, healthcare, manufacturing, and agriculture, but also serves as a catalyst for innovation, streamlined operations, improved decision-making, and expanded product offerings. The transformative power of turning raw IoT data into actionable insights is pivotal for organizations seeking to fully realize the potential of IoT data and propel the ongoing expansion and advancement of IoT applications.

The integration of data mining and machine learning in IoT data analysis has profound implications for IoT application management, empowering organizations to:

- **Enhance Efficiency:** Predicting equipment failures and optimizing resource allocation significantly improves operational efficiency.
- **Reduce Downtime:** Leveraging machine learning models for predictive maintenance reduces downtime and enhances overall equipment reliability.
- **Improve Decision-Making:** Real-time and predictive insights from IoT data enable informed decision-making.
- **Personalize Services:** Analyzing user data from IoT devices allows organizations to provide personalized services and recommendations, enhancing the user experience.
- **Enhance Security:** Data mining and machine learning play a crucial role in identifying security threats and anomalies in real-time, thereby enhancing overall cybersecurity (Babu, C. V. Suresh, and Andrew Simon P. 2024).

4. DATA PREPARATION AND FEATURE ENGINEERING FOR IOT DATA

This section will explore into the critical processes of data preparation and feature engineering as they relate to IoT data. These essential steps are crucial for turning raw IoT data into a format suitable for data mining and machine learning techniques. Various data preprocessing techniques, feature engineering specific to IoT data, and address the challenges associated with handling data variability will be discussed in detail.

4.1 Data Preprocessing Techniques

Efficient data preprocessing is a crucial aspect of handling data from the Internet of Things (IoT), particularly in preparing raw data for analysis with machine learning algorithms. Key methods for IoT data preprocessing include:

- **Data Cleaning:** Identifying and rectifying missing values, outliers, and errors in the data to ensure data quality (Fazle Sadi et al., 2016).
- **Data Transformation:** Normalizing or scaling data to a standard range, enhancing its suitability for analysis and model training (Wei et al., 2019).
- **Data Imputation:** Dealing with missing values by estimating or filling in gaps with appropriate values (Liu et al., 2018).
- **Data Aggregation:** Summarizing data by aggregating values over time intervals or grouping data points (Estrin et al., 2010).

These preprocessing techniques play a pivotal role in improving data quality and consistency, laying the groundwork for more effective analysis of IoT data. Specifically, managing missing values in IoT data, often filled through interpolation and imputation, becomes a critical step in ensuring the completeness and accuracy of the dataset for subsequent machine learning algorithm analysis.

4.2 Feature Engineering for IoT Data

Critical to extracting useful insights from Internet of Things (IoT) data are the essential steps of feature engineering and data preparation (Deng & Mahadevan, 2019). The raw data, fundamental for analysis and machine learning, undergoes a series of transformations to ensure accuracy and completeness. The key processes involved in feature engineering and data preparation for IoT data include:

Data Cleaning: Addressing common issues like missing values, outliers, and inconsistencies in raw IoT data is integral to data cleaning, ensuring the dataset's accuracy and comprehensiveness (Deng & Hoang, 2019).

Feature Engineering: This process involves creating new features or modifying existing ones to enhance machine learning model performance, particularly crucial for IoT data analysis. Some notable feature engineering techniques for IoT data encompass:

- **Temporal Features:** Creating time-based features, such as hourly, daily, or seasonal patterns, to capture temporal dependencies (Xia et al., 2015).

- **Spatial Features:** Incorporating location-based features, such as geographical coordinates or proximity to specific points of interest, to account for spatial dependencies (Kang et al., 2017).
- **Frequency Domain Features:** Transforming time-domain data into the frequency domain to extract cyclic patterns and oscillations (Lopes et al., 2018).
- **Statistical Features:** Generating statistical features like mean, median, and variance to characterize data distribution and variability (Toli et al., 2019).

Effective feature engineering significantly contributes to the accuracy and informativeness of models, leading to improved insights and predictions from IoT data.

4.3 Handling Data Variability

In the realm of the Internet of Things (IoT), the variability of data—ranging from types to production circumstances—is pronounced and demands effective management for insightful analysis (Li et al., 2018). Crucial to handling this variability and extracting meaningful insights are feature engineering and robust data preparation. These procedures, when combined with domain knowledge, address the challenges associated with managing data variability in IoT applications (Li et al., 2018). By transforming unstructured and variable IoT data into a structured and informative dataset, effective data preparation and feature engineering ready the information for analysis and modeling. In the context of the Internet of Things, these procedures play an essential role in obtaining insightful information and making data-driven decisions by effectively handling data variability.

IoT data, often characterized by high variability in dynamic environments and devices, necessitates robust strategies for data analysis:

- **Data Smoothing:** Application of techniques to reduce noise and fluctuations in data, enhancing its suitability for analysis (Chen et al., 2017).
- **Temporal Consistency:** Ensuring temporal consistency by aligning data from different devices or sensors to the same time frame (Bao et al., 2014).
- **Data Quality Checks:** Implementation of checks and anomaly detection methods to identify and address real-time data variability (Alippi et al., 2018).

Effectively managing data variability is integral to ensuring the reliability and accuracy of insights and predictions derived from IoT data.

This section have explored critical steps in data preparation and feature engineering specific to IoT data. Essential techniques include data preprocessing, feature engineering tailored to IoT data, and strategies for addressing data variability, all instrumental in transforming raw data into valuable insights and predictions. For example, in an industrial setting with IoT sensors, occasional spikes or outliers due to sensor malfunctions or external influences can be managed and corrected using data preprocessing techniques like data smoothing and outlier detection. Standardization and normalization techniques further ensure consistency in data units across various manufacturers, facilitating accurate modeling and analysis.

5. MODEL SELECTION FOR IOT DATA

This section will explore the crucial aspect of model selection for IoT data analysis. Model selection is a pivotal step in leveraging data mining and machine learning techniques for IoT applications. The best practices for choosing the right models, considering the unique characteristics of IoT data will be discussed.

5.1 Model Selection Best Practices

Choosing the appropriate model is essential for obtaining meaningful insights from IoT data. Model selection best practices for IoT data encompass the following aspects:

5.1.1 Data Understanding and Exploration

Before selecting a model, it is imperative to thoroughly understand the data. This involves exploring the data, visualizing it, and gaining insights into its characteristics. For IoT data, consider:

- **Data Distribution**: Investigate the distribution of data to determine whether it is Gaussian, skewed, or follows another pattern. This knowledge can influence model selection (Yi et al., 2017).
- **Data Temporality**: Understand how data evolves over time, including trends, seasonality, and cyclic patterns. Temporal data often requires specialized models (Xia et al., 2015).
- **Feature Importance**: Identify which features are most relevant and influential in the data, as this can guide the selection of appropriate models (Kotsiantis et al., 2007).

5.1.2 Problem Type

The type of problem you are addressing with IoT data is a critical factor in model selection. Common problem types include:

- **Regression**: When the goal is to predict numerical values, regression models such as linear regression, decision trees, or support vector regression may be suitable (Wei et al., 2019).
- **Classification**: For tasks involving categorization, classification models like logistic regression, random forests, or neural networks can be effective (Abadi et al., 2016).
- **Anomaly Detection**: When the focus is on identifying anomalies or outliers in data, specialized techniques like isolation forests or one-class SVMs may be appropriate (Liu et al., 2012).

5.1.3 Scalability and Real-Time Processing

IoT data often requires real-time or near-real-time analysis. When selecting models, consider their scalability and efficiency in handling streaming data. Stream processing techniques and online learning algorithms can be advantageous for real-time IoT applications (Carreno et al., 2017).

5.1.4 Model Complexity and Interpretability

The complexity of the model can significantly impact its suitability for IoT data. In some cases, simple models like linear regression or decision trees may be preferred for their interpretability and ease of implementation. Complex models like deep neural networks may be necessary for tasks that demand high accuracy and are not easily solved by simpler methods (Armando et al., 2019).

5.1.5 Regularization and Hyperparameter Tuning

Regularization techniques, such as L1 and L2 regularization, can help prevent overfitting in complex models. Additionally, hyperparameter tuning is crucial for optimizing the model's performance. Techniques like grid search and random search can be employed to fine-tune hyperparameters (Bergstra & Bengio, 2012).

5.1.6 Cross-Validation

Cross-validation is a critical step to assess the performance of selected models. Techniques like k-fold cross-validation can help estimate the model's generalization error and ensure its robustness (Kohavi, 1995).

5.1.7 Ensemble Models

Ensemble models, which combine multiple base models, can enhance predictive accuracy and robustness. Techniques like random forests and gradient boosting are valuable for combining the strength of multiple models (Caruana et al., 2008).

In conclusion, model selection for IoT data is a multidimensional process that involves understanding the data, considering the problem type, scalability, model complexity, and interpretability. Employing regularization, hyperparameter tuning, cross-validation, and potentially ensemble techniques are essential best practices for selecting the right model for IoT data analysis.

Example: Combination of Models for Clustering:

Example: To increase the accuracy of groupings and recommendations, ensembles of clustering models are used in market segmentation for customer targeting and recommendation systems.

Group of Models for Anomaly Detection: For instance, in cybersecurity applications, ensembles of anomaly detection models are used to combine the findings of various anomaly detection algorithms in order to detect intrusions and threats. Multiple Regression Model Ensemble For instance, supply chain management uses ensembles of regression models to forecast demand, and financial forecasting uses them to predict stock prices.

6. REAL-TIME PROCESSING IN IOT APPLICATIONS

This section focuses on the critical importance of real-time processing in IoT applications. Why real-time analysis is crucial, how batch and streaming processing can be effectively integrated are discussed with illustrative use cases that highlight the significance of real-time decision-making in the IoT landscape.

6.1 The Importance of Real-Time Analysis

Real-time processing and analysis are pivotal in Internet of Things (IoT) applications, offering key advantages that significantly enhance IoT ecosystems' functionality and value. The critical importance of real-time analysis in IoT is underscored by the following factors:

Immediate Response: IoT devices often generate real-time data, and real-time analysis enables instant responses, allowing immediate actions or triggering alerts when specific conditions are met. In a smart home, for instance, real-time analysis can swiftly detect a fire or security breach, promptly notifying homeowners.

Fundamental Aspects of Real-time Analysis in IoT:

1. **Immediate Insights:** In IoT environments, particularly in industries like manufacturing, healthcare, and transportation, real-time insights facilitate immediate decision-making and response to critical events (Kambatla et al., 2014).
2. **Predictive Maintenance:** Early detection of anomalies and issues through real-time analysis allows for proactive maintenance scheduling, preventing costly equipment failures (Teh et al., 2017).
3. **Enhanced User Experience:** In consumer-facing IoT applications, real-time data processing personalizes user experiences, adjusting smart home settings or recommending products based on user behavior (Xia et al., 2015).
4. **Safety and Security:** Applications related to safety and security, such as surveillance and emergency response systems, rely on real-time analysis for prompt identification and response to threats (Alippi et al., 2018).

Real-time analysis is not just a technological necessity; it is a strategic asset that ensures the effectiveness and responsiveness of IoT applications across various domains.

6.2 Batch and Streaming Processing Integration

Many Internet of Things (IoT) applications rely on real-time processing to swiftly analyze and respond to incoming data, although real-time processing is not universally suitable for all IoT data. To strike a balance, organizations often integrate batch and real-time processing techniques. The combination of batch and streaming processing is essential to meet the diverse demands of IoT applications. In this integrated approach:

Data Ingestion: IoT devices continuously generate data, which is ingested in real-time using streaming processing platforms like Apache Flink or Kafka.

This integration involves combining the strengths of batch and streaming processing to create a comprehensive solution for IoT applications. Specifically:

1. **Data Ingestion:** Historical data is ingested through batch processing, while streaming processing handles the continuous ingestion of real-time data streams (Carreno et al., 2017).
2. **Data Storage:** Batch-oriented databases or data warehouses store historical data, while real-time data may be stored in distributed systems such as Apache Kafka (Shen et al., 2019).
3. **Data Analysis:** Batch processing is utilized for large-scale analytics and insights generation from historical data, whereas streaming processing enables real-time monitoring and decision-making (Lopes et al., 2018).
4. **Integration:** Tools and platforms like Apache Flink, Apache Spark, and Apache Beam are employed to unify batch and stream processing workflows (Carbone et al., 2015).

This combined approach ensures a flexible and efficient handling of IoT data, accommodating both historical analysis and real-time responsiveness.

6.3 Use Cases for Real-Time Decision-Making

Real-time processing stands as a crucial element in numerous Internet of Things (IoT) applications, facilitating swift decision-making and instantaneous data analysis. This capability proves indispensable in various IoT use cases, including:

1. **Smart City - Traffic Management:** Real-time analysis of data from sensors and cameras optimizes traffic flow, reduces congestion, and enables dynamic control of traffic signals.
2. **Fitness Monitoring:** Wearables provide users with immediate access to real-time data on steps taken, heart rate, and sleep patterns, empowering quick health-related decisions.

In these IoT applications, real-time processing not only enhances productivity but also reduces costs, improves safety, and enables rapid responses to critical events. It plays a pivotal role in the IoT's transformative impact across diverse sectors and applications.

Examining various use cases underscores the significance of real-time decision-making in IoT applications:

- **Smart Cities:** Real-time traffic monitoring and control systems optimize traffic flow, reduce congestion, and enhance urban mobility (Arasteh et al., 2019).
- **Healthcare:** Remote patient monitoring systems leverage real-time data from wearable devices, providing immediate feedback and alerts for healthcare providers and patients (Rajkomar et al., 2018).
- **Manufacturing (IIoT):** Real-time analysis predicts equipment failures and adjusts manufacturing processes in real-time, maximizing efficiency (Schroeder et al., 2017).
- **Agriculture:** Precision agriculture uses real-time data from sensors to optimize irrigation, fertilization, and pest control, resulting in higher crop yields (Bongiovanni et al., 2019).
- **Retail:** Real-time recommendations in online retail platforms analyze user behavior and shopping patterns to offer personalized product suggestions (Rendle et al., 2010).

In conclusion, real-time processing is indispensable for extracting actionable insights from IoT data and enabling immediate decision-making across diverse applications. The integration of batch and streaming processing techniques, along with the adoption of advanced platforms, empowers organizations to fully leverage the benefits of real-time analysis in IoT environments.

Illustration: Quicker Reaction Time - Real-time data processing in autonomous cars enables rapid decision-making based on sensor data, enhancing responsiveness and safety during driving. Forecasting Upkeep - In manufacturing, real-time processing of IoT sensor data aids in identifying anomalies and predicting maintenance needs, minimizing downtime and expensive repairs. Healthcare Surveillance - Healthcare providers can respond promptly to critical health events or deviations from normal conditions through real-time patient data monitoring from wearable IoT devices.

7. DATA SECURITY AND PRIVACY IN IOT DATA

This section will explore into the critical aspects of data security and privacy in the context of IoT data. The sensitivity of IoT data, strategies for ensuring data security in data mining and machine learning, and privacy considerations, with a specific focus on healthcare and smart cities applications are referred (Suresh Babu, C. V., Sivaneshwaran, J., et. al. 2023).

7.1 The Sensitivity of IoT Data

The sensitivity of Internet of Things (IoT) data is a critical concern, given its wide-ranging applications and the potential collection of sensitive, private, or personal information. Considering the significance of data security and privacy, it is imperative to address the following key factors:

1. **Personal Data Collection:** Numerous IoT devices, such as smart wearables and home assistants, gather personal data encompassing location, biometrics, and health metrics. The safeguarding of individual privacy is contingent upon the robust protection of this data.

The sensitivity of IoT data stems from several factors:

- **Personal Information:** Many IoT applications amass personal data, including health details, location information, and biometrics, necessitating a paramount focus on data privacy (Kolias et al., 2017).
- **Security Threats:** Vulnerability to security breaches and cyberattacks is inherent in IoT devices, posing risks when compromised and underscoring the importance of safeguarding individuals (Acar et al., 2019).
- **Protection of Business Secrets:** Industrial IoT applications may involve proprietary information, trade secrets, and intellectual property, demanding stringent protective measures (Petrolo et al., 2017).
- **Regulatory Compliance:** Stringent regulations in various industries govern data privacy and security, with violations potentially resulting in legal consequences and reputational damage (Reich & Monson, 2016).

7.2 Ensuring Data Security in Data Mining and Machine Learning

In the realm of Internet of Things (IoT) data, ensuring data security is imperative for safeguarding sensitive information and maintaining the confidence of stakeholders and users. The following actions are crucial to guarantee IoT data security:

1. **Encryption Measures:**
   o **Data in Transit:** Robust encryption techniques, such as Transport Layer Security (TLS) and Secure Sockets Layer (SSL), are commonly employed to secure data while in transit.
   o **Data at Rest:** Encryption algorithms like AES provide protection for data at rest.

   Securing IoT data within the context of data mining and machine learning involves implementing key strategies:

   - **Data Encryption:** Fundamental to security, encrypting data during storage and transmission prevents unauthorized access (Bertino et al., 2019).
   - **Access Control:** Stringent access controls ensure that only authorized individuals or systems can access and manipulate IoT data (Mishra et al., 2016).
   - **Secure Data Storage:** Using secure storage solutions, such as encrypted databases and blockchain, protects IoT data from physical and digital threats (Conoscenti et al., 2019).
   - **Anomaly Detection:** Employing real-time anomaly detection systems aids in promptly identifying and responding to potential security breaches (Alshehri et al., 2020).
   - **Privacy-Preserving Techniques:** Leveraging techniques like differential privacy and homomorphic encryption enables data analysis while preserving individual privacy (Dwork, 2006).

7.3 Privacy Considerations in Healthcare and Smart Cities

In Internet of Things (IoT) applications, especially within healthcare and smart cities, data security and privacy are paramount due to the involvement of sensitive information. Robust cybersecurity measures are essential to thwart potential cyberattacks and data breaches that could compromise privacy, particularly in smart city systems. Balancing the benefits of IoT in smart cities and healthcare with the imperative to maintain data security and privacy is an ongoing challenge. Achieving this balance requires a combination of technological safeguards, well-defined policies, and ethical considerations to ensure that IoT data serves its intended purposes while upholding individual privacy rights and minimizing the risk of data breaches.

Privacy considerations are notably prominent in IoT data within healthcare and smart city applications:

- **Healthcare:** IoT devices and wearables collect sensitive health data, posing a challenge in balancing data sharing for research with the imperative to protect patient privacy (Fernández-Alemán et al., 2013).
- **Smart Cities:** Surveillance cameras, sensors, and IoT devices in smart cities amass extensive data on citizens, necessitating ethical and secure management of this data (Punetha & Tiwari, 2020).
- **Consent and Transparency:** Critical aspects of protecting privacy include obtaining informed consent and ensuring transparency about data collection and usage (Langheinrich, 2001).
- **Data Anonymization:** Mitigating privacy risks can be achieved by anonymizing data through the removal or obfuscation of personally identifiable information (Machanavajjhala et al., 2007).
- **Secure Data Sharing:** Employing secure data sharing protocols when sharing data for research or public services is crucial to protect sensitive information (Jiang et al., 2014).

In conclusion, safeguarding data security and privacy in IoT data is crucial due to the sensitivity of the involved information. This necessitates a multi-faceted approach, including encryption, access control, secure storage, anomaly detection, and privacy-preserving techniques. Achieving the delicate balance between data utility and individual privacy, particularly in healthcare and smart city applications, is a complex but necessary endeavor (Suresh Babu, C. V., Monika, et. al. 2023).

8. IOT-BASED SOLUTIONS

This section will explore practical IoT-based solutions, focusing on the process of gathering and combining data from IoT devices, streaming data in real time, and how these solutions enhance operational efficiency and lead to significant cost savings in various domains.

8.1 Gathering and Combining Data from IoT Devices

IoT-based solutions, aimed at delivering value and addressing specific use cases, aggregate data from a variety of IoT devices. The process of collecting and consolidating information from these devices involves the following key steps:

● **Data Gathering:** Internet of Things devices rely on diverse sensors to collect data based on their unique functionalities. For instance, sensors measuring temperature, GPS, light, and acceleration generate data specific to their respective characteristics.

This data collection and integration process in IoT-based solutions encompass crucial stages:

- **Data Collection:** Various IoT devices, including sensors, actuators, and wearables, generate substantial data. This data, originating from devices in different locations and settings, is systematically collected (Vermesan et al., 2019).
- **Data Integration:** Different types of IoT devices employing varied communication protocols necessitate integration into a cohesive dataset (Perera et al., 2014).
- **Data Aggregation:** Often, data is aggregated to condense volume and craft meaningful summaries for subsequent analysis (Jara et al., 2017).
- **Data Quality Control:** Ensuring the quality and reliability of IoT data is paramount, as inaccuracies or noisy data can lead to misguided insights (Sun et al., 2018).

8.2 Streaming Data in Real Time

Real-time data streaming is a vital element within IoT-based solutions, playing a pivotal role in facilitating swift decision-making, providing immediate insights, and enabling rapid responses across various applications and industries. Several instances illustrate the diverse applications of real-time data streaming in IoT-based solutions, such as:

● **Automation of Smart Homes - Security:** Homeowners can enhance security through real-time data streaming from IoT cameras and sensors. This allows them to monitor their properties in real time and receive instant alerts in case of potential intruders.

In the context of IoT-based solutions, real-time streaming of data encompasses critical components:

- **Data Ingestion:** IoT data is ingested in real-time as it is generated, often utilizing event-driven architectures for efficient processing (Shi et al., 2017).
- **Processing:** The streaming data is processed as it arrives, facilitating real-time analytics and immediate responses to events (Carreno et al., 2017).
- **Event-Driven Architecture:** Efficient handling of streaming data is achieved through event-driven systems, with platforms like Apache Kafka being commonly employed (Shen et al., 2019).
- **Alerting and Notifications:** Real-time data streams can trigger alerts and notifications based on predefined conditions or thresholds, enhancing responsiveness (Gaber et al., 2016).

8.3 Enhancing Operational Efficiency and Cost Savings

The adoption of Internet of Things (IoT) technologies holds significant potential for enhancing operational efficiency and realizing substantial cost savings across diverse industries. Noteworthy ways in which IoT-based solutions contribute to these objectives include:

- **Predictive Maintenance:** In industrial settings, IoT data is utilized to predict equipment failures and schedule maintenance, thereby reducing downtime and maintenance costs (Schroeder et al., 2017).
- **Energy Management:** IoT-based solutions enable precise monitoring and control of energy usage in buildings, resulting in substantial energy savings (Hu et al., 2018).
- **Inventory Management:** Real-time IoT data optimizes inventory in supply chain and retail, reducing carrying costs and minimizing stockouts (Zhang et al., 2017).
- **Agriculture:** IoT-based solutions enhance agricultural operations by optimizing irrigation, reducing water and fertilizer usage, and increasing crop yields (Bongiovanni et al., 2019; Suresh Babu, C. V., Ganesh, et al., 2023).
- **Smart Cities:** IoT technologies improve urban planning, traffic management, and public services, leading to cost savings and an improved quality of life (Punetha & Tiwari, 2020).

- **Healthcare:** Real-time patient monitoring and telemedicine through IoT devices reduce hospitalization costs and improve patient outcomes (Rajkomar et al., 2018).

In conclusion, IoT-based solutions drive transformative changes by efficiently gathering and combining data from IoT devices, streaming real-time data, and optimizing operational efficiency. These solutions not only enable more efficient operations but also result in substantial cost savings.

Example: For instance, IoT sensors on manufacturing machinery can track real-time machine health, enabling maintenance teams to reduce downtime and costs by predicting when a machine is likely to fail through data analysis.

Intelligent Energy Control in Structures: Energy efficiency in commercial buildings can be maximized by utilizing IoT devices like occupancy sensors, smart lighting controls, and thermostats, adjusting lighting, heating, and cooling based on occupancy and external factors to save significant energy.

9. CONCLUSION

This concluding section will summarize the key takeaways from our exploration of IoT data insights, data mining, and machine learning techniques for scalable modeling and efficient management of IoT applications. The immense potential of data mining and machine learning in the IoT landscape, their role in enabling data-driven decision-making, the importance of embracing scalable modeling, and what lies ahead in the exciting field of IoT data insights are discussed.

9.1 The Potential of Data Mining and Machine Learning in IoT

The Internet of Things has ushered in an era characterized by unprecedented data generation and connectivity. At the forefront of harnessing the potential of this data-rich landscape are data mining and machine learning technologies. Combining these advanced techniques with IoT technology has the enormous potential to revolutionize the utilization and management of the massive amounts of data generated by IoT devices. This powerful synergy enables us to extract actionable insights, fostering innovation and efficiency across various domains. As the Internet of Things ecosystem continues to grow, the importance of data mining and machine learning techniques cannot be overstated, providing the means to maximize the value of IoT data and make informed, data-driven decisions.

9.2 Enabling Data-Driven Decision-Making

Data mining and machine learning techniques serve as the cornerstone for driving data-driven decision-making within IoT applications. These technologies enable organizations to extract valuable insights from the vast array of data produced by the Internet of Things. Through the analysis of IoT data, organizations can gain a deep understanding of operational processes, consumer behavior, equipment health, and more. These insights, in turn, empower informed decision-making, facilitate optimized resource allocation, and enable proactive responses to emerging trends and challenges.

The Internet of Things (IoT) stands as a transformative force, seamlessly connecting the physical and digital realms while generating an unprecedented volume of data. This data, characterized by its high volume, velocity, and variety, holds immense potential to catalyze efficiency and innovation across various industries. Realizing this potential hinge on our ability to effectively leverage the data, paving the way for data-driven excellence in Internet of Things applications.

9.3 Embracing Scalable Modeling for IoT Applications

In the realm of the Internet of Things (IoT), where vast volumes of data are continually generated, scalable modeling plays a pivotal role in extracting actionable insights. Whether applied to predictive maintenance in manufacturing, personalized healthcare monitoring, or optimizing energy consumption in smart buildings, scalable modeling ensures the efficient handling of large and intricate datasets.

The Internet of Things (IoT) serves as a transformative force, seamlessly blending the digital and physical domains and generating unprecedented data quantities. As IoT permeates diverse industries and domains, the necessity for scalable modeling becomes increasingly apparent. This conclusion underscores the crucial importance of embracing scalable modeling approaches in IoT. To harness the full potential of IoT data, businesses must adopt scalable modeling techniques, enabling improved decision-making, streamlined processes, and fostering innovation. As IoT evolves, the adoption of scalable modeling becomes indispensable for unlocking the benefits of this revolutionary technology across various sectors and applications.

9.4 The Road Ahead in IoT Data Insights

The transformative impact of the Internet of Things (IoT) on our interaction with technology will continue to evolve and innovate in the coming years. IoT data insights, already reshaping our technological landscape, hold great promise for businesses and individuals, fostering data-driven decision-making, operational intelligence, and creative solutions that elevate living standards and drive economic expansion.

Looking ahead, the future of IoT data insights is teeming with exciting possibilities, propelled by advancing technology:

- **Edge Computing:** The prevalence of edge computing will rise, enabling data processing and analysis closer to the source, thereby reducing latency and improving real-time decision-making (Shi et al., 2017).
- **Interoperability:** Ongoing efforts to enhance interoperability among diverse IoT devices and platforms will foster more cohesive and standardized data ecosystems (Sundmaeker et al., 2010).
- **AI Integration:** Increased integration of artificial intelligence (AI) techniques into data mining and machine learning will augment the extraction of meaningful insights from IoT data (Chen et al., 2018).
- **Ethical Considerations:** The expansion of IoT data usage will elevate the importance of ethical considerations regarding data privacy, security, and transparency (Barnaghi et al., 2016).
- **Blockchain:** Blockchain technology may play a pivotal role in ensuring data integrity and security within the IoT landscape (Dorri et al., 2017).

In conclusion, the convergence of IoT, data mining, and machine learning is reshaping global industries and domains. The potential for data-driven decision-making, scalable modeling, and continuous advancements in IoT data insights are poised to redefine our way of life and work. Embracing these technologies while considering ethical and security dimensions will be crucial for navigating this data-rich landscape.

Illustration

Example: 5G-Driven IoT: For instance, the introduction of 5G networks will enhance the reliability and speed of IoT data transmission, enabling real-time applications in domains like remote surgery, autonomous vehicles, and augmented reality.

Integration of AI and Machine Learning: As an illustration, AI systems will proficiently evaluate IoT data, leading to advanced predictive analytics, anomaly detection, and intelligent automation in industries such as manufacturing, healthcare, and smart cities.

Edge-Based Computing: For instance, edge devices processing IoT data closer to the source will significantly reduce latency, facilitating instantaneous decision-making. This is exemplified by autonomous cars using edge computing for split-second decisions while driving.

REFERENCES

Abadi, M. (2016). TensorFlow: A system for large-scale machine learning. In *12th USENIX Symposium on Operating Systems Design and Implementation (OSDI 16)* (pp. 265-283).

Abiyev, R. H., & Budaev, N. P. (2022). Artificial intelligence and machine learning in the Internet of Things (IoT): A survey. *Machines (Basel)*, 10(10), 158.

Acar, A. (2019). A survey on security and privacy issues in the Internet of Things. *IEEE Communications Surveys and Tutorials*, 21(1), 234–254.

Ahmad, T., Hakeem, F., Alzahrani, F., & Imran, M. (2023). IoT data mining for real-time traffic congestion prediction and analysis. *IEEE Access : Practical Innovations, Open Solutions*, 11, 8942–8960.

Alippi, C. (2018). Just-in-time prognosis of machine health: A machine learning approach. *IEEE Transactions on Industrial Informatics*, 14(8), 3536–3543.

Alshehri, A. (2020). IoT security: Review, blockchain solutions, and open challenges. *Future Generation Computer Systems*, 107, 1156–1173.

Alzahrani, M., Jararweh, Y., & Alhussein, M. (2020). Data mining and machine learning for internet of things (IoT) security: A systematic literature review. *IEEE Internet of Things Journal*, 7(7), 7069–7094.

Anwar, A., Bilal, K., Qadir, J., & Al-Qadri, A. M. (2021). Data mining and machine learning techniques for efficient management of IoT applications: A systematic literature review. arXiv preprint arXiv:2102.04082.

Arasteh, H. (2019). A comprehensive survey of smart traffic management. *IEEE Transactions on Intelligent Transportation Systems*, 20(12), 4639–4663.

Armando, B. (2019). Machine learning for anomaly detection and inspection. *Robotics and Computer-integrated Manufacturing*, 58, 92–103.

Atzori, L., Iera, A., & Morabito, G. (2010). The Internet of Things: A survey. *Computer Networks*, 54(15), 2787–2805. DOI: 10.1016/j.comnet.2010.05.010

Babu, C. V. S., & Andrew, S. P. (2024). Adaptive AI for Dynamic Cybersecurity Systems: Enhancing Protection in a Rapidly Evolving Digital Landscap. In Zhihan, Lv., & Global, I. G. I. (Eds.), *Principles and Applications of Adaptive Artificial Intelligence* (pp. 52–72). DOI: 10.4018/979-8-3693-0230-9.ch003

Bandyopadhyay, S., & Sen, J. (2011). *Internet of things: Applications and challenges in technology and standardization*. Wiley-IEEE Press.

Bao, J. (2014). An event-based approach for temporal data modeling in sensor networks. *IEEE Transactions on Knowledge and Data Engineering*, 26(5), 1288–1302.

Barnaghi, P. (2016). Smart cities, big data, and open data: A review. In *Handbook of Research on Information Management for Effective and Efficient Services* (pp. 201–230). IGI Global.

Barnaghi, P., Sheth, A., Henson, C., & Modgil, S. (2013). From data streams to knowledge graphs: The semantic web for the internet of things. *IEEE Intelligent Systems*, 28(4), 58–62.

Bergstra, J., & Bengio, Y. (2012). Random search for hyper-parameter optimization. *Journal of Machine Learning Research*, 13(1), 281–305.

Bertino, E. (2019). Data security and privacy in the IoT and edge computing era. *IEEE Cloud Computing*, 6(5), 20–27.

Bongiovanni, R. (2019). A review on the use of IoT in precision agriculture. *Journal of King Saud University. Computer and Information Sciences*.

Bonomi, F. (2012). Fog computing and its role in the Internet of Things. In *Proceedings of the First Edition of the MCC Workshop on Mobile Cloud Computing* (pp. 13-16). DOI: 10.1145/2342509.2342513

C. C. (2016). *Data mining: The textbook*. Springer International Publishing.

Carbone, P. (2015). Apache Flink: Stream and batch processing in a single engine. *A Quarterly Bulletin of the Computer Society of the IEEE Technical Committee on Data Engineering*, 38(4), 28–38.

Carreno, V. A. (2017). Stream-based real-time association rule mining for IoT data streams. *ACM Computing Surveys*, 50(6), 1–41.

Caruana, R (2008). Ensembles of models. *Proceedings of the 21st International Conference on Neural Information Processing Systems*, 22(1), 765-772.

Chen, L. (2017). Data smoothing algorithm in the internet of things for monitoring the quality of chicken meat. *IEEE Internet of Things Journal*, 4(3), 652–659.

Chen, M. (2018). Machine learning for network anomaly detection: A survey. *IEEE Communications Surveys and Tutorials*, 20(3), 1663–1685.

Chui, M., Manyika, J., & Miremadi, M. (2018). *The internet of things: Mapping the value beyond the hype*. McKinsey Global Institute.

Conoscenti, M. (2019). Blockchain for the Internet of Things: A systematic literature review. *IEEE Access : Practical Innovations, Open Solutions*, 7, 45808–45826.

Dang, L. M., Hoang, D. T., & Le, D. N. (2019). A survey on data mining and machine learning techniques for anomaly detection in the internet of things. *Security and Communication Networks*, 2019.

Deng, S., & Mahadevan, S. (2019). *Machine learning in smart manufacturing.* CRC Press.

Dorri, A. (2017). Towards an optimized blockchain for IoT. In *Proceedings of the Second International Conference on Internet of Things, Data and Cloud Computing (ICC'17).*

Dwork, C. (2006). Differential privacy. In International Colloquium on Automata, Languages, and Programming (pp. 1-12). DOI: 10.1007/11787006_1

Esmael, M., Abdelwahab, A., & Awwad, H. H. (2015). Big data analytics: A survey. *Journal of Big Data*, 2(1), 1–37. DOI: 10.1186/s40537-014-0007-7 PMID: 26191487

Estrin, D. (2010). Instrumenting the world with wireless sensor networks. *Proceedings of the IEEE*, 98(11), 1903–1911. DOI: 10.1109/JPROC.2010.2068530

Evans, D. (2011). The Internet of Things: How the Next Evolution of the Internet is Changing Everything. CISCO White Paper.

Fazle Sadi, M. S. (2016). A survey of big data architectures and machine learning algorithms in healthcare. *Journal of King Saud University. Computer and Information Sciences.*

Fernández-Alemán, J. L., Señor, I. C., Lozoya, P. Á. O., & Toval, A. (2013). Security and privacy in electronic health records: A systematic literature review. *Journal of Biomedical Informatics*, 46(3), 541–562. DOI: 10.1016/j.jbi.2012.12.003 PMID: 23305810

Gaber, M. M. (2016). Mining data streams. *ACM Computing Surveys*, 50(3), 1–51.

Gubbi, J., Buyya, R., Marusic, S., & Palaniswami, M. (2013). Internet of Things (IoT): A vision, architectural elements, and future directions. *Future Generation Computer Systems*, 29(7), 1645–1660. DOI: 10.1016/j.future.2013.01.010

Han, J., Kamber, M., & Pei, J. (2011). *Data Mining: Concepts and Techniques.* Morgan Kaufmann.

Hortonworks. (2016). Data stream processing with Hortonworks DataFlow. Hortonworks.

Hu, H., Wen, Y., Chua, T. S., & Li, X. (2014). Toward scalable systems for big data analytics: A survey. *ACM Computing Surveys*, 47(4), 1–63.

Hu, Y. (2018). A review of Internet of Things for smart home: Challenges and solutions. *IEEE Internet of Things Journal*, 5(5), 2973–2989.

Jain, A., Gupta, B. B., & Sharma, B. K. (2021). Data mining techniques and applications in internet of things: A survey. *Future Generation Computer Systems*, 126, 417–433.

Jara, A. J. (2017). Internet of Things in smart cities: A review. *Journal of Computer and Communications*, 5(07), 46–57.

Jiang, W. (2014). A survey of secure wireless communication in the smart grid. *IEEE Transactions on Industrial Informatics*, 10(3), 1738–1746.

Kambatla, K. (2014). Trends in big data analytics. *Journal of King Saud University. Computer and Information Sciences*.

Kang, J. (2017). Location-aware event processing in mobile sensor data analytics. *IEEE Internet of Things Journal*, 4(5), 1279–1292.

Kansal, A., & Ramachandran, M. (2019). Big data mining and machine learning in smart cities: A review. *Journal of Big Data*, 6(1), 26.

Khalifa, M., Khalaf, O. I., & Benkhelifa, E. (2020). A survey of machine learning-based approaches for internet of things security. *Journal of Network and Computer Applications*, 167, 102728.

Kohavi, R. (1995). A study of cross-validation and bootstrap for accuracy estimation and model selection. In *Proceedings of the 14th International Joint Conference on Artificial Intelligence* (Vol. 2, pp. 1137-1143).

Kolias, C., Kambourakis, G., Stavrou, A., & Voas, J. (2017). DDoS in the IoT: Mirai and other botnets. *Computer*, 50(7), 80–84. DOI: 10.1109/MC.2017.201

Kotsiantis, S. B. (2007). Supervised machine learning: A review of classification techniques. *Emerging Artificial Intelligence Applications in Computer Engineering*, 3(1), 3–24.

Kuppuswamy, P., & Thamizhselvi, M. (2021). A survey on data mining techniques and applications in internet of things. *International Journal of Applied Engineering Research: IJAER*, 16(3), 432–438.

Langheinrich, M. (2001). Privacy by design—principles of privacy-aware ubiquitous systems. In *Ubicomp 2001* (pp. 273–291). Ubiquitous Computing. DOI: 10.1007/3-540-45427-6_23

Li, J., Cheng, X., Ding, M., & Xia, Y. (2018). A survey on data mining and machine learning in Internet of Things. *Future Generation Computer Systems*, 87, 631–648.

Li, S., Xu, L., & Zhao, S. (2015). The internet of things: A survey. *Information Systems Frontiers*, 17(2), 243–259. DOI: 10.1007/s10796-014-9492-7

Liu, B. (2018). Handling missing data: A review. *International Journal of Information Management*, 48, 13–31.

Liu, L., & Peng, P. (2016). Survey of data mining techniques for big data. In *Proceedings of the 2016 13th International Conference on Service Systems and Service Management (ICSSS)*

Lopes, F. M. (2018). Time series forecasting based on hidden Markov models. *IEEE Transactions on Industrial Informatics*, 14(3), 1053–1060.

Machanavajjhala, A., Kifer, D., Gehrke, J., & Venkitasubramaniam, M. (2007). l-diversity: Privacy beyond k-anonymity. *ACM Transactions on Knowledge Discovery from Data*, 1(1), 3. DOI: 10.1145/1217299.1217302

Mishra, D. (2016). A survey of access control models in the Internet of Things. *Journal of King Saud University. Computer and Information Sciences*.

Perera, C., Zaslavsky, A., Christen, P., & Georgakopoulos, D. (2014). Sensing as a service model for smart cities supported by Internet of Things. *Transactions on Emerging Telecommunications Technologies*, 25(1), 81–93. DOI: 10.1002/ett.2704

Petrolo, R. (2017). Security of the Internet of Things: A review. *Internet of Things : Engineering Cyber Physical Human Systems*, 1–23.

Punetha, P., & Tiwari, P. (2020). Internet of Things (IoT) and its smart cities applications: A conceptual framework. *Internet of Things : Engineering Cyber Physical Human Systems*, 12, 100269.

Rajkomar, A., Oren, E., Chen, K., Dai, A. M., Hajaj, N., Hardt, M., Liu, P. J., Liu, X., Marcus, J., Sun, M., Sundberg, P., Yee, H., Zhang, K., Zhang, Y., Flores, G., Duggan, G. E., Irvine, J., Le, Q., Litsch, K., & Dean, J. (2018). Scalable and accurate deep learning with electronic health records. *NPJ Digital Medicine*, 1(1), 18. DOI: 10.1038/s41746-018-0029-1 PMID: 31304302

Reich, J., & Monson, J. (2016). The internet of things and cybersecurity: A new framework. *Communications of the ACM*, 59(3), 27–29.

Rendle, S. (2010). Bayesian personalized ranking for non-uniformly sampled items. In *Proceedings of the International Conference on Machine Learning (ICML)* (pp. 1009-1016).

Schroeder, J. L. (2017). Internet of things in logistics and supply chain management: A literature review. *Journal of Enterprise Information Management*, 30(1), 114–129.

Shen, Z. (2019). Real-time big data processing for predictive maintenance in IoT environments. *IEEE Transactions on Industrial Informatics*, 15(3), 1604–1613.

Shi, W., Cao, J., Zhang, Q., Li, Y., & Xu, L. (2017). Edge computing: Vision and challenges. *IEEE Internet of Things Journal*, 3(5), 637–646. DOI: 10.1109/JIOT.2016.2579198

Srisakthi, S., & Suresh Babu, C. V. (2024). Cybersecurity: Protecting Information in a Digital World. In Saeed, S., Azizi, N., Tahir, S., Ahmad, M., & Almuhaideb, A. (Eds.), *Strengthening Industrial Cybersecurity to Protect Business Intelligence* (pp. 1–25). IGI Global. DOI: 10.4018/979-8-3693-0839-4.ch001

Sun, Y. (2018). A survey of big data architectures and machine learning algorithms in healthcare. *Journal of King Saud University. Computer and Information Sciences*.

Sundmaeker, H. (2010). Vision and challenges for realising the Internet of Things. In *European Research Cluster on the Internet of Things*. CERP-IoT.

Sureh Babu, C. V., Subhash, S., Vignesh, M., Jeyavasan, T., & Muthumanikavel, V. (2024). Securing the Cloud: Understanding and Mitigating Data Breaches and Insider Attacks in Cloud Computing Environments. In Goel, P., Pandey, H., Singhal, A., & Agarwal, S. (Eds.), *Analyzing and Mitigating Security Risks in Cloud Computing* (pp. 1–23). IGI Global. DOI: 10.4018/979-8-3693-3249-8.ch001

Suresh Babu, C. V., Ganesh, B. S., Kishoor, T., & Khang, A. (2023). Automatic Irrigation System Using Solar Tracking Device. In Khang, A. (Ed.), *Handbook of Research on AI-Equipped IoT Applications in High-Tech Agriculture* (pp. 239–256). IGI Global. DOI: 10.4018/978-1-6684-9231-4.ch013

Suresh Babu, C. V., Monika, R., Dhanusha, T., Vishnuvaradhanan, K., & Harish, A. (2023). Smart Street Lighting System for Smart Cities Using IoT (LoRa). In Kumar, R., Abdul Hamid, A., & Binti Ya'akub, N. (Eds.), *Effective AI, Blockchain, and E-Governance Applications for Knowledge Discovery and Management* (pp. 78–96). IGI Global. DOI: 10.4018/978-1-6684-9151-5.ch006

Suresh Babu, C. V., & Sivaneshwaran, J. (2023). Controlling Computer Features Through Hand Gesture. In V. Thayananthan (Ed.), AI-Based Digital Health Communication for Securing Assistive Systems (pp. 85-113). IGI Global. DOI: 10.4018/978-1-6684-8938-3.ch005

Teh, Y. W. (2017). Predictive modeling and analytics for equipment health monitoring. *IEEE Transactions on Industrial Informatics*, 13(5), 2282–2291.

Toli, A. (2019). IoT-based data analytics for energy consumption prediction in smart buildings. *Sensors (Basel)*, 19(4), 888. PMID: 30791657

Vermesan, O. (2019). *Internet of Things: Converging Technologies for Smart Environments and Integrated Ecosystems*. River Publishers.

Wei, Y. (2019). Real-time smart grid data analytics for energy theft detection. *IEEE Transactions on Industrial Informatics*, 15(10), 5785–5793.

Wu, D. (2011). A survey of cloud computing and its key techniques. *Journal of Information and Computational Science*, 6(2), 37–51.

Xia, F. (2015). A time-series IoT data cleaning method based on structure learning. *IEEE Transactions on Industrial Informatics*, 11(6), 1504–1511.

Yi, X. (2017). A review of time series data mining. *Theoretical Biology & Medical Modelling*, 14(1), 1–14. PMID: 28100241

Zhang, J. (2017). IoT-based smart rehabilitation system. *IEEE Transactions on Industrial Informatics*, 13(3), 1333–1341.

ADDITIONAL READING

Logambigai, R., & Suresh Babu, C. V. (2024). Blockchain Empowerment for Securing IoT, Sensory Data in Next-Gen Intelligent Systems. In Sharma, S., Prakash, A., & Sugumaran, V. (Eds.), *Developments Towards Next Generation Intelligent Systems for Sustainable Development* (pp. 1–34). IGI Global. DOI: 10.4018/979-8-3693-5643-2.ch001

Sureh Babu, C. V., Sowmi Saltonya, M., Ganapathi, S., & Gunasekar, A. (2024). AIoT Revolution: Transforming Networking Productivity for the Digital Age. In Rezaei, S., & Ansary, A. (Eds.), *Artificial Intelligence of Things (AIoT) for Productivity and Organizational Transition* (pp. 108–143). IGI Global. DOI: 10.4018/979-8-3693-0993-3.ch005

Suresh Babu, C. V., Abhinaba Pal, A., Vinith, A., Muralirajan, V., & Gunasekaran, S. (2024). Enhancing Cloud and IoT Security: Leveraging IoT Technology for Multi-Factor User Authentication. In Ahmed Nacer, A., & Abdmeziem, M. (Eds.), *Emerging Technologies for Securing the Cloud and IoT* (pp. 258–282). IGI Global. DOI: 10.4018/979-8-3693-0766-3.ch011

Suresh Babu, C. V., Anniyappa, C. S., Jampani, S. K., Sai Santhosh, P., Mohith Nithin, I., & Janaki Raam, P. (2024). Interacting With the Future: Smart Tourism Evolution Through IoT and Social Media Strategies. In Ramos, C., Costa, T., Severino, F., & Calisto, M. (Eds.), *Social Media Strategies for Tourism Interactivity* (pp. 41–65). IGI Global. DOI: 10.4018/979-8-3693-0960-5.ch002

Suresh Babu, C. V., Surendar, V., Dheepak, N., Shiraj, S., & Praveen, K. (2024). Revolutionizing Healthcare Harnessing IoT-Integrated Federated Learning for Early Disease Detection and Patient Privacy Preservation. In Lilhore, U., Simaiya, S., Poongodi, M., & Dutt, V. (Eds.), *Federated Learning and Privacy-Preserving in Healthcare AI* (pp. 195–216). IGI Global. DOI: 10.4018/979-8-3693-1874-4.ch013

KEY TERMS AND DEFINITIONS

Cloud Computing Techniques: Methods, algorithms, and technologies employed in cloud computing environments to optimize resource utilization, enhance scalability, ensure data security, and improve performance across a wide range of cloud-based services and applications.

Energy Consumption Prediction: Forecasting future energy usage based on historical consumption patterns, environmental factors, and other relevant variables, enabling utilities and consumers to plan and optimize energy generation, distribution, and consumption strategies.

Energy Theft Detection: The identification of unauthorized or fraudulent activities aimed at tampering with utility meters, diverting energy, or manipulating consumption data, often using advanced analytics and anomaly detection techniques to flag suspicious behavior.

Equipment Health Monitoring: Continuous monitoring and analysis of the operational condition and performance of machinery, equipment, or assets to detect abnormalities, predict failures, and optimize maintenance schedules, thereby minimizing downtime and maximizing productivity.

Hidden Markov Models: Statistical models used to represent sequences of observable events, where the underlying system transitions between a set of hidden states with probabilistic rules, commonly employed in fields such as speech recognition, bioinformatics, and natural language processing.

Hyper-Parameter Optimization: The systematic process of selecting the optimal hyperparameters for a machine learning algorithm, often using techniques such as grid search, random search, or Bayesian optimization to maximize model performance and generalization on unseen data.

IoT Data Cleaning: The process of preprocessing and refining data collected from Internet of Things (IoT) devices to remove noise, errors, and inconsistencies, ensuring the accuracy, reliability, and usability of the data for subsequent analysis and decision-making.

Privacy by Design: A framework that integrates privacy considerations into the design and development of systems, products, and services from the outset, ensuring that privacy is built into the core architecture rather than being an afterthought.

Real-Time Data Analytics: The processing, analysis, and interpretation of data as it is generated or received, allowing for immediate insights and decision-making, commonly used in applications requiring timely responses, such as financial trading, security monitoring, and IoT systems.

Sensing as a Service: A service-oriented approach where sensing capabilities, such as data collection from IoT devices or environmental sensors, are provided on-demand to users as a scalable and accessible service, facilitating real-time monitoring and analysis.

Smart Grid Data Analytics: The application of advanced analytical techniques to data generated by smart grid technologies, aiming to optimize energy distribution, improve efficiency, and enhance grid reliability through insights derived from large-scale data analysis.

Time Series Forecasting: The process of predicting future values based on past observations in sequential order, typically applied to data points recorded at regular intervals over time, such as stock prices, weather patterns, or sales figures.

Ubiquitous Systems: Technological infrastructures characterized by seamless integration and pervasive presence across various environments, enabling continuous and effortless access to computing resources and services from anywhere at any time.

Conclusion

THEMATIC SUMMARY OF THE CHAPTERS

Chapter 1: Predictive and Prescriptive Analytics for IoT: Unlocking Insights

We commence the study in Chapter 1 by exploring how predictive and prescriptive analytics inside IoT frameworks might be revolutionary. It demonstrates how various analytics approaches transform unprocessed Internet of Things data into useful insight. While prescriptive analytics recommends the best course of action to accomplish desired results, predictive analytics uses previous data to estimate future occurrences. This chapter highlights the critical role that advanced analytics play in Internet of Things applications, ranging from smart city resource optimization to industrial IoT equipment failure prediction. These skills are essential for improving operational effectiveness and making well-informed decisions in a variety of industries.

Chapter 2: IoT in Healthcare and Telemedicine - Revolutionizing Patient Care and Medical Practices

Chapter 2 focuses on the significant influence of IoT on telemedicine and healthcare. The chapter examines how IoT technologies, such as preemptive medical treatments, real-time health data collecting, and remote monitoring, are transforming patient care. Wearables and smart medical equipment are examples of IoT devices that continually provide health data that may be evaluated to enhance patient outcomes and expedite the delivery of healthcare. The potential of IoT to increase accessibility, lower healthcare costs, and raise the standard of treatment is highlighted in this chapter, particularly for patients who live in rural or underserved regions.

Chapter 3: Revolutionizing Healthcare - IoT-Powered Telemedicine Advancements

Chapter 3 extends on the topics covered in the previous chapter by emphasizing on the developments in IoT-powered telemedicine. This chapter looks at how IoT technologies are enabling creative ways to monitor patients remotely, conduct teleconsultations, and do remote diagnostics, thereby expanding the possibilities of telemedicine. A new age in healthcare is being ushered in by IoT in telemedicine, where rapid and correct medical answers are made possible by real-time data transfer and continuous patient monitoring. The chapter provides examples of how IoT is enabling telemedicine services to be more effective and scalable while also removing geographical boundaries.

Chapter 4: Automatic Irrigation System Using IoT

In Chapter 4, we shift the spotlight to the agriculture industry and talk about how IoT is being used in autonomous irrigation systems. This chapter shows how IoT may maximize agricultural yields and promote sustainability in agriculture by optimizing water consumption. Farmers may automate irrigation procedures based on accurate data and monitor soil moisture levels in real-time by deploying Internet of Things sensors and actuators. This precision farming method enhances crop health, boosts productivity, and conserves water. The chapter emphasizes how important the Internet of Things is to promoting intelligent farming methods and solving the world's water shortage problem.

Chapter 5: Study and Analysis of IoT-Based Telemedicine and Remote Patient Monitoring

A detailed review of IoT-based telemedicine and remote patient monitoring systems is given in Chapter 5. It looks at several case studies and research findings that show how effective Internet of Things (IoT) is in managing chronic illnesses and providing ongoing healthcare services. Healthcare professionals may make data-driven clinical choices by using IoT devices to monitor patients' vital signs in real-time. Early treatments can greatly enhance patient outcomes in the management of chronic disorders like diabetes and cardiovascular diseases, where this expertise is especially beneficial. The chapter emphasizes how important IoT is to improving the effectiveness and caliber of healthcare services.

Chapter 6: Comparative Analysis of Detection of Diseases in Apple Tree Leaves Using ResNet and CNN

The book digs into the practical application of IoT and machine learning to agriculture in Chapter 6, particularly with regard to the identification of illnesses in apple tree leaves. A comparison between ResNet and Convolutional Neural Networks (CNN) for illness categorization and picture recognition is presented in this chapter. Farmers may reduce crop losses and increase output by early diagnosis and diagnosis of plant diseases by using IoT devices with cameras and sophisticated machine learning algorithms. The chapter provides examples of how machine learning and the Internet of Things might work together to create intelligent agriculture solutions that support sustainable farming methods.

Chapter 7: Research Review on Task Scheduling Algorithm for Green Cloud Computing

Energy efficiency in cloud computing systems is a critical topic that is covered in detail in Chapter 7, especially with regard to Internet of Things applications. This chapter examines many job scheduling algorithms created to maximize energy efficiency and reduce data centers' carbon impact. Requiring effective cloud computing methods is necessary to manage the huge amounts of data generated by IoT deployments in a sustainable manner. The chapter emphasizes the value of green computing techniques and shows how intelligent scheduling algorithms may improve the IoT systems' operational effectiveness and sustainability.

Chapter 8: Unleashing IoT Data Insights: Data Mining and Machine Learning Techniques for Scalable Modeling and Efficient Management of IoT

The last chapter, Chapter 8, explores the data-centric side of IoT, emphasizing machine learning and data mining methods for effective management and scalable modeling. This chapter explores the use of sophisticated data analytics to get insightful information from the massive amounts of data produced by Internet of Things devices. The utilization of data mining and machine learning facilitates the creation of anomaly detection systems, prediction models, and optimization algorithms that improve the scalability and performance of Internet of Things applications. The chapter emphasizes how vital data science is to realizing the Internet of Things' full potential and spurring innovation in a number of industries.

SYNTHESIS OF KEY THEMES AND INSIGHTS

Collectively, the chapters offer a comprehensive perspective on how effective management techniques and scalable models may tackle the opportunities and problems presented by Internet of Things applications. Important ideas that come out of this synthesis are as follows:

1. **Data-Driven Decision Making**: The capacity to extract and interpret data from Internet of Things devices is critical in many fields. The utilization of predictive and prescriptive analytics, together with data mining and machine learning, are crucial instruments in converting unprocessed data into meaningful insights that facilitate decision-making and enhance operational effectiveness.
2. **Scalability and Flexibility**: Scalable designs become essential to handling the growing complexity and volume of data in IoT systems as they develop and grow. Microservices, service-oriented, and modular architectures offer the adaptability and durability required for IoT system scalability.
3. **Cross-Domain Applications**: IoT is applicable in a wide range of industries, including industrial processes, healthcare, and agriculture. Every domain has its own set of possibilities and difficulties, but in order to improve operational effectiveness and efficiency, real-time monitoring, automation, and intelligent decision-making are necessities.
4. **Sustainability and Efficiency**: Effective resource management is a common subject, especially with relation to energy and water. IoT may help with sustainable practices and resource conservation, tackling major global concerns, as demonstrated by green computing and precision agriculture.
5. **Innovative Technological Integration**: IoT integration with other cutting-edge technologies, such edge computing, cloud computing, and artificial intelligence, is spurring innovation and opening up new business prospects. The creation of more intelligent, sensitive, and adaptable systems that can satisfy the varied and changing demands of many industries is made possible by this convergence.

FUTURE DIRECTIONS AND OPPORTUNITIES

The Internet of Things is expected to continue growing and changing in the future. IoT applications will continue to change as a result of emerging trends and technology, which present both new possibilities and difficulties. The following are some possible avenues for further study and advancement:

1. **Edge and Fog Computing**: With the proliferation of IoT devices, decentralized processing and real-time analytics will become increasingly important. Edge and fog computing models reduce latency and bandwidth usage, enabling more responsive and efficient IoT systems that can operate independently of centralized cloud infrastructures.

2. **Artificial Intelligence and Machine Learning**: The integration of AI and machine learning with IoT will continue to enhance the capabilities of smart systems. Advanced algorithms will enable more accurate predictions, anomaly detection, and optimization, further unlocking the potential of IoT data and driving innovation in various sectors.

3. **Blockchain and Security**: Security and privacy remain critical concerns in IoT deployments. Blockchain technology offers promising solutions for enhancing data security, ensuring trusted interactions between devices, and preventing unauthorized access. Future research will explore how blockchain can be integrated with IoT to create more secure and resilient systems.

4. **5G and Beyond**: The rollout of 5G networks will significantly impact IoT by providing faster and more reliable connectivity. This will support the deployment of more complex and data-intensive IoT applications, such as autonomous vehicles, smart cities, and industrial automation. Future advancements in wireless communication will further expand the possibilities for IoT.

5. **Interoperability and Standardization**: As the IoT ecosystem continues to grow, the need for interoperability and standardization will become increasingly important. Developing common frameworks and protocols will facilitate the seamless integration of diverse IoT devices and systems, enhancing their scalability, functionality, and user experience.

To further elucidate the discussions throughout the book, it is beneficial to define some key terms that are foundational to understanding the various concepts and technologies explored.

CONCLUDING REMARKS

The "Scalable Modeling and Efficient Management of IoT Applications" tour has offered a thorough and in-depth examination of all the many aspects of IoT. We have shown that the complex issues presented by IoT deployments can be addressed and the full potential of IoT technology unlocked via scalable designs and effective management approaches. IoT will surely have a revolutionary impact on many different industries as it develops, fostering innovation, improving people's quality of life, and advancing sustainable development. For scholars, practitioners, and policymakers who want to comprehend and harness the potential of IoT, this book is an invaluable resource. Stakeholders can traverse the quickly evolving IoT ecosystem and help design more intelligent, efficient, and sustainable systems by adopting the insights and approaches provided. As the book's editor, we have no doubt that the insights and experiences presented here will spur more IoT research and development. I urge readers to advance the state of the art in scalable modeling and effective management of IoT applications by building on the foundations established in these chapters.

Vinod Kumar

Galgotias University, Greater Noida, India

Gotam Singh Lalotra

Government Degree College, Basohli, India

Compilation of References

Abadi, M. (2016). TensorFlow: A system for large-scale machine learning. In *12th USENIX Symposium on Operating Systems Design and Implementation (OSDI 16)* (pp. 265-283).

Abdulmalek, S., Nasir, A., Jabbar, W. A., Almuhaya, M. A., Bairagi, A. K., Khan, M. A. M., & Kee, S. H. (2022, October). IoT-based healthcare-monitoring system towards improving quality of life: A review. *Health Care*, 10(10), 1993. PMID: 36292441

Abiyev, R. H., & Budaev, N. P. (2022). Artificial intelligence and machine learning in the Internet of Things (IoT): A survey. *Machines (Basel)*, 10(10), 158.

Acar, A. (2019). A survey on security and privacy issues in the Internet of Things. *IEEE Communications Surveys and Tutorials*, 21(1), 234–254.

Aceto, G., Persico, V., & Pescapé, A. (2020). Industry 4.0 and health: Internet of Things, Big Data, and cloud computing for healthcare 4.0. *Journal of Industrial Information Integration*, 18, 18. DOI: 10.1016/j.jii.2020.100129

Adi, E., Anwar, A., Baig, Z., & Zeadally, S. (2020). Machine learning and data analytics for the IoT. *Neural Computing & Applications*, 32(20), 16205–16233. DOI: 10.1007/s00521-020-04874-y

Aghdam & Heravi. (2017). Guide to Convolutional Neural Networks a Practical Application to Traffic-Sign Detection and Classification. Academic Press.

Aghdam, Z. N., Rahmani, A. M., & Hosseinzadeh, M. (2021). The role of the Internet of Things in healthcare: Future trends and challenges. *Computer Methods and Programs in Biomedicine*, 199, 105903. DOI: 10.1016/j.cmpb.2020.105903 PMID: 33348073

Agrafioti, F., Hatzinakos, D., & Anderson, A. K. (2011). ECG pattern analysis for emotion detection. *IEEE Transactions on Affective Computing*, 3(1), 102–115. DOI: 10.1109/T-AFFC.2011.28

Ahmad, T., Hakeem, F., Alzahrani, F., & Imran, M. (2023). IoT data mining for real-time traffic congestion prediction and analysis. *IEEE Access : Practical Innovations, Open Solutions*, 11, 8942–8960.

Al-Ali, A.R. (2019). IoT-solar energy powered smart farm irrigation system. *Journal of Electronic Science and Technology*, *17*, 1-14.

Al-Atawi, A. A., Khan, F., & Kim, C. G. (2022). Application and Challenges of IoT Healthcare System in COVID-19. *Sensors (Basel)*, 22(19), 7304. DOI: 10.3390/s22197304 PMID: 36236404

Albahri, A. S., Alwan, J. K., Taha, Z. K., Ismail, S. F., Hamid, R. A., Zaidan, A. A., Albahri, O. S., Zaidan, B. B., Alamoodi, A. H., & Alsalem, M. A. (2021). IoT-based telemedicine for disease prevention and health promotion: state-of-the-Art. *Journal of Network and Computer Applications*, 173, 173. DOI: 10.1016/j.jnca.2020.102873

Albawi, S., Mohammed, T. A., & Al-Zawi, S. (2017). Understanding of a convolutional neural network. *2017 International Conference on Engineering and Technology (ICET)*, 1-6. DOI: 10.1109/ICEngTechnol.2017.8308186

Al-Fuqaha, A., Guizani, M., Mohammadi, M., Aledhari, M., & Ayyash, M. (2015a). Internet of Things: A survey on enabling technologies, protocols, and applications. *IEEE Communications Surveys and Tutorials. IEEE Communications Surveys and Tutorials*, 17(4), 2347–2376. DOI: 10.1109/COMST.2015.2444095

Alippi, C. (2018). Just-in-time prognosis of machine health: A machine learning approach. *IEEE Transactions on Industrial Informatics*, 14(8), 3536–3543.

Al-kahtani, M. S., Khan, F., & Taekeun, W. (2022). Application of Internet of Things and Sensors in Healthcare. *Sensors (Basel)*, 22(15), 5738. DOI: 10.3390/s22155738 PMID: 35957294

Alsayed, A. A., & Arif, M. (2021, July). Classification of Apple Tree Leaves Diseases using Deep Learning Methods. *International Journal of Computer Science and Network Security*, 21(7), 324–330.

Alshamrani, M. (2022). IoT and artificial intelligence implementations for remote healthcare monitoring systems: A survey. *Journal of King Saud University. Computer and Information Sciences/Ma ala am a Al-malīk Saud : Ùlm Al- asib Wa Al-ma lumat, 34*(8), 4687–4701. DOI: 10.1016/j.jksuci.2021.06.005

Alshehri, A. (2020). IoT security: Review, blockchain solutions, and open challenges. *Future Generation Computer Systems*, 107, 1156–1173.

Alzahrani, M., Jararweh, Y., & Alhussein, M. (2020). Data mining and machine learning for internet of things (IoT) security: A systematic literature review. *IEEE Internet of Things Journal*, 7(7), 7069–7094.

Alzubaidi, L., Zhang, J., Humaidi, A. J., Al-Dujaili, A., Duan, Y., Al-Shamma, O., Santamaría, J., Fadhel, M. A., Al-Amidie, M., & Farhan, L. (2021). Review of deep learning: Concepts, CNN architectures, challenges, applications, future directions. *Journal of Big Data*, 8(1), 53. DOI: 10.1186/s40537-021-00444-8 PMID: 33816053

Amyra. (2019, September 30). IoT in Healthcare: Benefits, Challenges and Applications. Valuecoders - Hire Dedicated Software Development Team.

Anonymous, . (2022, September 30). Publicly funded health care could extend longevity of life. *Journal of Global Health*, 12(4).

Anwar, A., Bilal, K., Qadir, J., & Al-Qadri, A. M. (2021). Data mining and machine learning techniques for efficient management of IoT applications: A systematic literature review. arXiv preprint arXiv:2102.04082.

Arasteh, H. (2019). A comprehensive survey of smart traffic management. *IEEE Transactions on Intelligent Transportation Systems*, 20(12), 4639–4663.

Armando, B. (2019). Machine learning for anomaly detection and inspection. *Robotics and Computer-integrated Manufacturing*, 58, 92–103.

Aroganam, G., Manivannan, N., & Harrison, D. (2019). Review on wearable technology sensors used in consumer sport applications. *Sensors (Basel)*, 19(9), 1983. DOI: 10.3390/s19091983 PMID: 31035333

Atzori, L., Iera, A., & Morabito, G. (2010). The Internet of Things: A survey. *Computer Networks*, 54(15), 2787–2805. DOI: 10.1016/j.comnet.2010.05.010

Awotunde, J. B., Jimoh, R. G., Folorunso, S. O., Adeniyi, E. A., Abiodun, K. M., & Banjo, O. O. (2021). Privacy and security concerns in IoT-based healthcare systems. In *The fusion of internet of things, artificial intelligence, and cloud computing in health care* (pp. 105–134). Springer International Publishing. DOI: 10.1007/978-3-030-75220-0_6

Babu, C. V. S., & Andrew, S. P. (2024). Adaptive AI for Dynamic Cybersecurity Systems: Enhancing Protection in a Rapidly Evolving Digital Landscap. In Zhihan, Lv., & Global, I. G. I. (Eds.), *Principles and Applications of Adaptive Artificial Intelligence* (pp. 52–72). DOI: 10.4018/979-8-3693-0230-9.ch003

Banaee, H., Ahmed, M. U., & Loutfi, A. (2013). Data mining for wearable sensors in health monitoring systems: A review of recent trends and challenges. *Sensors (Basel)*, 13(12), 17472–17500. DOI: 10.3390/s131217472 PMID: 24351646

Bandyopadhyay, S., & Sen, J. (2011). *Internet of things: Applications and challenges in technology and standardization*. Wiley-IEEE Press.

Banerjee, A., Chakraborty, C., & Rathi, M.Sr. (2020). Medical imaging, artificial intelligence, internet of things, wearable devices in terahertz healthcare technologies. In *Terahertz biomedical and healthcare technologies* (pp. 145–165). Elsevier. DOI: 10.1016/B978-0-12-818556-8.00008-2

Bao, J. (2014). An event-based approach for temporal data modeling in sensor networks. *IEEE Transactions on Knowledge and Data Engineering*, 26(5), 1288–1302.

Barnaghi, P. (2016). Smart cities, big data, and open data: A review. In *Handbook of Research on Information Management for Effective and Efficient Services* (pp. 201–230). IGI Global.

Barnaghi, P., Sheth, A., Henson, C., & Modgil, S. (2013). From data streams to knowledge graphs: The semantic web for the internet of things. *IEEE Intelligent Systems*, 28(4), 58–62.

Bashshur, R. L. (1995). On the Definition and Evaluation of Telemedicine. *Telemedicine Journal*, 1(1), 19–30. DOI: 10.1089/tmj.1.1995.1.19 PMID: 10165319

Basu, A. T. A. N. U. (2013). Five pillars of prescriptive analytics success. Analytics Magazine, 8, 12.

Bayo-Monton, J. L., Martinez-Millana, A., Han, W., Fernandez-latas, C., Sun, Y., & Traver, V. (2018). Wearable sensors integrated with Internet of Things for advancing eHealth care. *Sensors (Basel)*, 18(6), 1851. DOI: 10.3390/s18061851 PMID: 29882790

Beloglazov, A., Buyya, R., Lee, Y. C., & Zomaya, A. (2011). A Taxonomy and Survey of Energy-Efficient Data Centers and Cloud Computing Systems. In *Advances in Computers* (pp. 47–111). Elsevier. DOI: 10.1016/B978-0-12-385512-1.00003-7

Bergstra, J., & Bengio, Y. (2012). Random search for hyper-parameter optimization. *Journal of Machine Learning Research*, 13(1), 281–305.

Bertino, E. (2019). Data security and privacy in the IoT and edge computing era. *IEEE Cloud Computing*, 6(5), 20–27.

Bertsimas, D., & Kallus, N. (2020). From predictive to prescriptive analytics. *Management Science*, 66(3), 1025–1044. DOI: 10.1287/mnsc.2018.3253

Bharadwaj, H. K., Agarwal, A., Chamola, V., Lakkaniga, N. R., Hassija, V., Guizani, M., & Sikdar, B. (2021). A review on the role of machine learning in enabling IoT based healthcare applications. *IEEE Access : Practical Innovations, Open Solutions*, 9, 38859–38890. DOI: 10.1109/ACCESS.2021.3059858

Bhatia, J., Italiya, K., Jadeja, K., Kumhar, M., Chauhan, U., Tanwar, S., Bhavsar, M., Sharma, R., Manea, D. L., Verdes, M., & Raboaca, M. S. (2022). An overview of fog data analytics for IoT applications. *Sensors (Basel)*, 23(1), 199. DOI: 10.3390/s23010199 PMID: 36616797

Bhatt, C., Dey, N., & Ashour, A. S. (2017). Internet of things and big data technologies for next generation healthcare. In *Studies in big data*. DOI: 10.1007/978-3-319-49736-5

Bollmeier, S. G., Stevenson, E., Finnegan, P., & Griggs, S. K. (2020). Direct to consumer telemedicine: Is healthcare from home best? *Missouri Medicine*, 117(4), 303–309. https://pubmed.ncbi.nlm.nih.gov/32848261/ PMID: 32848261

Bongiovanni, R. (2019). A review on the use of IoT in precision agriculture. *Journal of King Saud University. Computer and Information Sciences*.

Bonomi, F. (2012). Fog computing and its role in the Internet of Things. In *Proceedings of the First Edition of the MCC Workshop on Mobile Cloud Computing* (pp. 13-16). DOI: 10.1145/2342509.2342513

Bouazzi, I., Zaidi, M., Usman, M., Shamim, M. Z. M., Gunjan, V. K., & Singh, N. (2022). Future trends for healthcare monitoring system in smart cities using LoRaWAN-based WBAN. *Mobile Information Systems*, 2022, 2022. DOI: 10.1155/2022/1526021

C. C. (2016). *Data mining: The textbook*. Springer International Publishing.

Carbone, P. (2015). Apache Flink: Stream and batch processing in a single engine. *A Quarterly Bulletin of the Computer Society of the IEEE Technical Committee on Data Engineering*, 38(4), 28–38.

Carreno, V. A. (2017). Stream-based real-time association rule mining for IoT data streams. *ACM Computing Surveys*, 50(6), 1–41.

Caruana, R (2008). Ensembles of models. *Proceedings of the 21st International Conference on Neural Information Processing Systems*, 22(1), 765-772.

Chacko, A., & Hayajneh, T. (2018). Security and Privacy Issues with IoT in Healthcare. *EAI Endorsed Transactions on Pervasive Health and Technology*, 0(0), 155079. DOI: 10.4108/eai.13-7-2018.155079

Charles, B. L. (2000). Telemedicine can lower costs and improve access. *PubMed, 54*(4), 66–69. https://pubmed.ncbi.nlm.nih.gov/10915354

Chen, J., Huang, X., Liu, S., & Tang, C. (2020). Task scheduling for energy efficient cloud computing with renewable energy sources. *IEEE Transactions on Sustainable Computing*, 5(1), 63–76. DOI: 10.1109/TSUSC.2019.2945243

Chen, L. (2017). Data smoothing algorithm in the internet of things for monitoring the quality of chicken meat. *IEEE Internet of Things Journal*, 4(3), 652–659.

Chen, M. (2018). Machine learning for network anomaly detection: A survey. *IEEE Communications Surveys and Tutorials*, 20(3), 1663–1685.

Chenthara, S., Ahmed, K., Wang, H., Whittaker, F., & Chen, Z. (2020). Health-chain: A novel framework on privacy preservation of electronic health records using blockchain technology. *PLoS One*, 15(12), e0243043. DOI: 10.1371/journal. pone.0243043 PMID: 33296379

Chui, M., Manyika, J., & Miremadi, M. (2018). *The internet of things: Mapping the value beyond the hype*. McKinsey Global Institute.

Chunara, R., Zhao, Y., Chen, J., Lawrence, K., Testa, P. A., Nov, O., & Mann, D. M. (2020). Telemedicine and healthcare disparities: A cohort study in a large healthcare system in New York City during COVID-19. *Journal of the American Medical Informatics Association : JAMIA*, 28(1), 33–41. DOI: 10.1093/jamia/ ocaa217 PMID: 32866264

Conoscenti, M. (2019). Blockchain for the Internet of Things: A systematic literature review. *IEEE Access : Practical Innovations, Open Solutions*, 7, 45808–45826.

Cui, X., Liu, J., Zhang, Q., & Wu, X. (2020). Energy-efficient task scheduling algo-rithm for green cloud computing. *Journal of Ambient Intelligence and Humanized Computing*, 11(4), 1545–1554. DOI: 10.1007/s12652-019-01481-7

Dang, L. M., Hoang, D. T., & Le, D. N. (2019). A survey on data mining and ma-chine learning techniques for anomaly detection in the internet of things. *Security and Communication Networks*, 2019.

Dang, L. M., Piran, M. J., Han, D., Min, K., & Moon, H. (2019). *A survey on in-ternet of things and cloud computing for healthcare*. Electronics. DOI: 10.3390/ electronics8070768

Dash, S. P. (2020). The Impact of IoT in Healthcare: Global Technological Change & The Roadmap to a Networked Architecture in India.

Dash, S., Shakyawar, S. K., Sharma, M., & Kaushik, S. (2019). Big data in health-care: Management, analysis and future prospects. *Journal of Big Data*, 6(1), 1–25. DOI: 10.1186/s40537-019-0217-0

Davenport, T., & Kalakota, R. (2019). The potential for artificial intelligence in healthcare. *Future Healthcare Journal*, 6(2), 94–98. DOI: 10.7861/futurehosp.6-2-94 PMID: 31363513

Deng, S., & Mahadevan, S. (2019). *Machine learning in smart manufacturing.* CRC Press.

Deshpande, P. S., Sharma, S. C., & Peddoju, S. K. (2019). Predictive and Prescriptive Analytics in Big-data Era. In *Security and Data Storage Aspect in Cloud Computing. Studies in Big Data* (Vol. 52). Springer. DOI: 10.1007/978-981-13-6089-3_5

Dhanvijay, M. M., & Patil, S. C. (2019). Internet of Things: A survey of enabling technologies in healthcare and its applications. *Computer Networks*, 153, 113–131. DOI: 10.1016/j.comnet.2019.03.006

Divakar, R., Sowmya, P., Suganya, G., & Primya, T. (2022, March). Prescriptive and Predictive Analysis of Intelligible Big Data. In *2022 6th International Conference on Computing Methodologies and Communication (ICCMC)* (pp. 845-851). IEEE.

Dorigo, M., & Gambardella, L. M. (1997, April). Ant colony system: A cooperative learning approach to the traveling salesman problem. *IEEE Transactions on Evolutionary Computation*, 1(1), 53–66. DOI: 10.1109/4235.585892

Dorri, A. (2017). Towards an optimized blockchain for IoT. In *Proceedings of the Second International Conference on Internet of Things, Data and Cloud Computing (ICC'17).*

Dwork, C. (2006). Differential privacy. In International Colloquium on Automata, Languages, and Programming (pp. 1-12). DOI: 10.1007/11787006_1

Ekeland, A. G., Bowes, A., & Flottorp, S. A. (2010). Effectiveness of telemedicine: A systematic review of reviews. *International Journal of Medical Informatics*, 79(11), 736–771. DOI: 10.1016/j.ijmedinf.2010.08.006 PMID: 20884286

Elhoseny, M., Ramirez-Gonzalez, G., Abu-Elnasr, O. M., Shawkat, S. A., Arun-kumar, N., & Farouk, A. (2018). Secure medical data transmission model for IoT-Based healthcare systems. *IEEE Access : Practical Innovations, Open Solutions*, 6, 20596–20608. DOI: 10.1109/ACCESS.2018.2817615

Eriksson, N. G. (2021, May 5). The Danish Heart Association: Digital Monitoring of Defibrillators. Telenor IoT.

Esmael, M., Abdelwahab, A., & Awwad, H. H. (2015). Big data analytics: A survey. *Journal of Big Data*, 2(1), 1–37. DOI: 10.1186/s40537-014-0007-7 PMID: 26191487

Estrin, D. (2010). Instrumenting the world with wireless sensor networks. *Proceedings of the IEEE*, 98(11), 1903–1911. DOI: 10.1109/JPROC.2010.2068530

Evans, D. (2011). The Internet of Things: How the Next Evolution of the Internet is Changing Everything. CISCO White Paper.

Fazlali, M., Sabeghi, M., Zakerolhosseini, A., & Bertels, K. (2010). Efficient task scheduling for runtime reconfigurable systems. *Journal of Systems Architecture*, 56(11), 623–632. DOI: 10.1016/j.sysarc.2010.07.016

Fazle Sadi, M. S. (2016). A survey of big data architectures and machine learning algorithms in healthcare. *Journal of King Saud University. Computer and Information Sciences*.

FedTech Magazine. (2023, October 30). The Role of Blockchain in Secure Health Data Exchange. Retrieved from FedTech Magazine.

Fernandes, J. G. (2022). Artificial intelligence in telemedicine. In *Artificial Intelligence in Medicine* (pp. 1219–1227). Springer International Publishing. DOI: 10.1007/978-3-030-64573-1_93

Fernández-Alemán, J. L., Señor, I. C., Lozoya, P. Á. O., & Toval, A. (2013). Security and privacy in electronic health records: A systematic literature review. *Journal of Biomedical Informatics*, 46(3), 541–562. DOI: 10.1016/j.jbi.2012.12.003 PMID: 23305810

Frazzetto, D., Nielsen, T. D., Pedersen, T. B., & Šikšnys, L. (2019). Prescriptive analytics: A survey of emerging trends and technologies. *The VLDB Journal*, 28(4), 575–595. DOI: 10.1007/s00778-019-00539-y

Fuller, A., Fan, Z., Day, C., & Barlow, C. (2020). Digital Twin: Enabling technologies, challenges and open research. *IEEE Access : Practical Innovations, Open Solutions*, 8, 108952–108971. DOI: 10.1109/ACCESS.2020.2998358

Gaber, M. M. (2016). Mining data streams. *ACM Computing Surveys*, 50(3), 1–51.

García-Ruiz, F. (2020). An integrated system to reduce water consumption in irrigated citrus orchards. *Agricultural Water Management*.

Genetic algorithms and Machine Learning. (1988). Machine Learning, 3, 95–99. DOI: 10.1007/BF00113892

Gerke, S., Minssen, T., & Cohen, G. (2020). Ethical and legal challenges of artificial intelligence-driven healthcare. In *Artificial intelligence in healthcare* (pp. 295–336). Academic Press. DOI: 10.1016/B978-0-12-818438-7.00012-5

Ghazal, T. M. (2021). Internet of things with artificial intelligence for health care security. *Arabian Journal for Science and Engineering*.

Goar, V. K., Yadav, N. S., Chowdhary, C. L., P, K., & Mittal, M. (2021). An IoT and artificial intelligence-based patient care system focused on COVID-19 pandemic. *International Journal of Networking and Virtual Organisations*, 25(3/4), 232. DOI: 10.1504/IJNVO.2021.120169

Gubbi, J., Buyya, R., Marusic, S., & Palaniswami, M. (2013). Internet of Things (IoT): A vision, architectural elements, and future directions. *Future Generation Computer Systems*, 29(7), 1645–1660. DOI: 10.1016/j.future.2013.01.010

Haleem, A., Javaid, M., Singh, R. P., & Suman, R. (2021). Telemedicine for healthcare: Capabilities, features, barriers, and applications. *Sensors International*, 2, 100117. DOI: 10.1016/j.sintl.2021.100117 PMID: 34806053

Hamdan, S., Ayyash, M., & Almajali, S. (2020). Edge-computing architectures for internet of things applications: A survey. *Sensors (Basel)*, 20(22), 6441. DOI: 10.3390/s20226441 PMID: 33187267

Hameed, K., Bajwa, I. S., Sarwar, N., Anwar, W., Mushtaq, Z., & Rashid, T. (2021). Integration of 5G and Block-Chain Technologies in Smart Telemedicine Using IoT.

Han, J., Kamber, M., & Pei, J. (2011). *Data Mining: Concepts and Techniques*. Morgan Kaufmann.

Hayyolalam, V., Aloqaily, M., Özkasap, Ö., & Guizani, M. (2021). Edge-assisted solutions for IoT-based connected healthcare systems: A literature review. *IEEE Internet of Things Journal*, 9(12), 9419–9443. DOI: 10.1109/JIOT.2021.3135200

HealthTech Magazine. (2023, October 30). Telehealth and Virtual Reality Expand into Mainstream Care at the VA.

Heinzelmann, P. J., Lugn, N. E., & Kvedar, J. C. (2005). Telemedicine in the future. *Journal of Telemedicine and Telecare*, 11(8), 384–390. DOI: 10.1177/1357633X0501100802 PMID: 16356311

He, S., & Chan, S. G. (2016). Wi-Fi Fingerprint-Based indoor positioning: Recent advances and comparisons. *IEEE Communications Surveys and Tutorials*. *IEEE Communications Surveys and Tutorials*, 18(1), 466–490. DOI: 10.1109/COMST.2015.2464084

Hortonworks. (2016). Data stream processing with Hortonworks DataFlow. Hortonworks.

Hu, H., Wen, Y., Chua, T. S., & Li, X. (2014). Toward scalable systems for big data analytics: A survey. *ACM Computing Surveys*, 47(4), 1–63.

Hu, Y. (2018). A review of Internet of Things for smart home: Challenges and solutions. *IEEE Internet of Things Journal*, 5(5), 2973–2989.

IEEE. (2022, April 28). Connectivity, Wearables and the Evolution of Telemedicine.

IoT in healthcare and ambient assisted living. (2021). In *Studies in computational intelligence*. DOI: 10.1007/978-981-15-9897-5

Jagadeeswari, V., Subramaniyaswamy, V., Logesh, R., & Vijayakumar, V. (2018). A study on medical Internet of Things and Big Data in personalized healthcare system. *Health Information Science and Systems*, 6(1), 14. DOI: 10.1007/s13755-018-0049-x PMID: 30279984

Jain, A., Gupta, B. B., & Sharma, B. K. (2021). Data mining techniques and applications in internet of things: A survey. *Future Generation Computer Systems*, 126, 417–433.

Jaiswal, A. K., Tiwari, P., Kumar, S., Al-Rakhami, M. S., Alrashoud, M., & Ghoneim, A. (2021). Deep learning based smart IoT health system for blindness detection using retina images. *IEEE Access: Practical Innovations, Open Solutions*, 9, 70606–70615. DOI: 10.1109/ACCESS.2021.3078241

Jara, A. J. (2017). Internet of Things in smart cities: A review. *Journal of Computer and Communications*, 5(07), 46–57.

Jasuja, N. (2014). Android vs iOS - Difference and Comparison. *Diffen*. https://www.diffen.com/difference/Android_vs_iOS

Jeyaraj, R., & Balasubramaniam, A., MA, A. K., Guizani, N., & Paul, A. (2023). Resource management in cloud and cloud-influenced technologies for internet of things applications. *ACM Computing Surveys*, 55(12), 1–37. DOI: 10.1145/3571729

Jiang, F., Jiang, Y., Zhi, H., Dong, Y., Li, H., Ma, S., Wang, Y., Dong, Q., Shen, H., & Wang, Y. (2017a). Artificial intelligence in healthcare: Past, present and future. *Stroke and Vascular Neurology*, 2(4), 230–243. DOI: 10.1136/svn-2017-000101 PMID: 29507784

Jiang, W. (2014). A survey of secure wireless communication in the smart grid. *IEEE Transactions on Industrial Informatics*, 10(3), 1738–1746.

Jin, M. X., Kim, S. Y., Miller, L. J., Behari, G., & Correa, R. (2020). Telemedicine: Current impact on the future. *Cureus*. Advance online publication. DOI: 10.7759/cureus.9891 PMID: 32968557

Jordan, M. I., & Mitchell, T. M. (2015). Machine learning: Trends, perspectives, and prospects. *Science*, 349(6245), 255–260. DOI: 10.1126/science.aaa8415 PMID: 26185243

Joyia, G. J., Liaqat, R. M., Farooq, A., & Rehman, S. (2017). Internet of medical things (IoMT): Applications, benefits and future challenges in healthcare domain. *Journal of Communication*, 12(4), 240–247.

Kaelbling, L. P., Littman, M. L., & Moore, A. W. (1996, May). Reinforcement Learning: A Survey. *Journal of Artificial Intelligence Research*, 4, 237–285. DOI: 10.1613/jair.301

Kakhi, K., Alizadehsani, R., Kabir, H. D., Khosravi, A., Nahavandi, S., & Acharya, U. R. (2022). The internet of medical things and artificial intelligence: Trends, challenges, and opportunities. *Biocybernetics and Biomedical Engineering*, 42(3), 749–771. DOI: 10.1016/j.bbe.2022.05.008

Kambatla, K. (2014). Trends in big data analytics. *Journal of King Saud University. Computer and Information Sciences*.

Kang, J. (2017). Location-aware event processing in mobile sensor data analytics. *IEEE Internet of Things Journal*, 4(5), 1279–1292.

Kansal, A., & Ramachandran, M. (2019). Big data mining and machine learning in smart cities: A review. *Journal of Big Data*, 6(1), 26.

Karjagi, R., & Jindal, M. IoT in Healthcare Industry | IoT Applications in Healthcare - Wipro.

Karkouch, A., Mousannif, H., Al Moatassime, H., & Noel, T. (2016). Data quality in internet of things: A state-of-the-art survey. *Journal of Network and Computer Applications*, 73, 57–81. DOI: 10.1016/j.jnca.2016.08.002

Kashani, M. H., Madanipour, M., Nikravan, M., Asghari, P., & Mahdipour, E. (2021). A systematic review of IoT in healthcare: Applications, techniques, and trends. *Journal of Network and Computer Applications*, 192, 103164. DOI: 10.1016/j.jnca.2021.103164

Kennedy, J., & Eberhart, R. (n.d.). Particle swarm optimization. Proceedings of ICNN'95 - International Conference on Neural Networks. IEEE. DOI: 10.1109/ICNN.1995.488968

Khalifa, M., Khalaf, O. I., & Benkhelifa, E. (2020). A survey of machine learning-based approaches for internet of things security. *Journal of Network and Computer Applications*, 167, 102728.

Kharel, J., Reda, H. T., & Shin, S. Y. (2019). Fog computing-based smart health monitoring system deploying lora wireless communication. *IETE Technical Review*, 36(1), 69–82. DOI: 10.1080/02564602.2017.1406828

Kohavi, R. (1995). A study of cross-validation and bootstrap for accuracy estimation and model selection. In *Proceedings of the 14th International Joint Conference on Artificial Intelligence* (Vol. 2, pp. 1137-1143).

Kolias, C., Kambourakis, G., Stavrou, A., & Voas, J. (2017). DDoS in the IoT: Mirai and other botnets. *Computer*, 50(7), 80–84. DOI: 10.1109/MC.2017.201

Kotsiantis, S. B. (2007). Supervised machine learning: A review of classification techniques. *Emerging Artificial Intelligence Applications in Computer Engineering*, 3(1), 3–24.

Kumar, V., & Lalotra, G. S. (2023). Blockchain-Enabled Secure Internet of Things. In Research Anthology on Convergence of Blockchain, Internet of Things, and Security (pp. 133-141). IGI Global.

Kumar, V., & Arora, H. (2020). ResNet-based approach for Detection and Classification of Plant Leaf Diseases. *2020 International Conference on Electronics and Sustainable Communication Systems (ICESC)*, 495-502. DOI: 10.1109/ICESC48915.2020.9155585

Kumar, V., & Lalotra, G. S. (2021). predictive model based on supervised machine learning for heart disease diagnosis. In *2021 IEEE International Conference on Technology, Research, and Innovation for Betterment of Society (TRIBES)* (pp. 1-6). IEEE. DOI: 10.1109/TRIBES52498.2021.9751644

Kuppuswamy, P., & Thamizhselvi, M. (2021). A survey on data mining techniques and applications in internet of things. *International Journal of Applied Engineering Research: IJAER*, 16(3), 432–438.

Laghari, A. A., Wu, K., Laghari, R. A., Ali, M., & Khan, A. A. (2021). A review and state of art of Internet of Things (IoT). *Archives of Computational Methods in Engineering*, 1–19.

Lalotra, G. S., Kumar, V., & Rajput, D. S. (2021). Predictive performance analysis of ensemble learners on bcd dataset. In *2021 IEEE International Conference on Technology, Research, and Innovation for Betterment of Society (TRIBES)* (pp. 1-6). IEEE. DOI: 10.1109/TRIBES52498.2021.9751648

Langheinrich, M. (2001). Privacy by design—principles of privacy-aware ubiquitous systems. In *Ubicomp 2001* (pp. 273–291). Ubiquitous Computing. DOI: 10.1007/3-540-45427-6_23

Laplante, P. A., & Laplante, N. (2016). The Internet of Things in Healthcare: Potential applications and challenges. *IT Professional*, 18(3), 2–4. DOI: 10.1109/MITP.2016.42

LeCun, Y., Bengio, Y., & Hinton, G. (2015). Deep learning. *Nature*, 521(7553), 436–444. DOI: 10.1038/nature14539 PMID: 26017442

Lepenioti, K., Bousdekis, A., Apostolou, D., & Mentzas, G. (2020). Prescriptive analytics: Literature review and research challenges. *International Journal of Information Management*, 50, 57–70. DOI: 10.1016/j.ijinfomgt.2019.04.003

Li, X., & Rai, L. (2020). Apple Leaf Disease Identification and Classification using ResNet Models. *2020 IEEE 3rd International Conference on Electronic Information and Communication Technology (ICEICT)*, 738-742. DOI: 10.1109/ICEICT51264.2020.9334214

Li, J., Cheng, X., Ding, M., & Xia, Y. (2018). A survey on data mining and machine learning in Internet of Things. *Future Generation Computer Systems*, 87, 631–648.

Li, Q., Zhang, M., Hu, X., & Chen, Y. (2021). Reinforcement learning-based task scheduling algorithm for cloud computing systems. *Journal of Parallel and Distributed Computing*, 154, 44–53.

Li, Q., Zhu, H., Xiong, J., Mo, R., Ying, Z., & Wang, H. (2019). Fine-grained multi-authority access control in IoT-enabled mHealth. *Annales des Télécommunications*, 74(7-8), 74. DOI: 10.1007/s12243-018-00702-6

Li, S., Xu, L., & Zhao, S. (2015). The internet of things: A survey. *Information Systems Frontiers*, 17(2), 243–259. DOI: 10.1007/s10796-014-9492-7

Liu, B. (2018). Handling missing data: A review. *International Journal of Information Management*, 48, 13–31.

Liu, J., Zou, J., Wei, W., & He, J. (2019). A Novel Hybrid Task Scheduling Algorithm for Green Cloud Computing. *Journal of Computational Science*, 34, 16–28. DOI: 10.1016/j.jocs.2019.01.007

Liu, L., & Peng, P. (2016). Survey of data mining techniques for big data. In *Proceedings of the 2016 13th International Conference on Service Systems and Service Management (ICSSS)*

Lopes, F. M. (2018). Time series forecasting based on hidden Markov models. *IEEE Transactions on Industrial Informatics*, 14(3), 1053–1060.

Losorelli, S. D., Vendra, V., Hildrew, D. M., Woodson, E. A., Brenner, M. J., & Sirjani, D. B. (2021). The future of telemedicine: revolutionizing health care or flash in the Pan? *Otolaryngology and Head and Neck Surgery/Otolaryngology--head and Neck Surgery, 165*(2), 239–243. DOI: 10.1177/0194599820983330

Machanavajjhala, A., Kifer, D., Gehrke, J., & Venkitasubramaniam, M. (2007). l-diversity: Privacy beyond k-anonymity. *ACM Transactions on Knowledge Discovery from Data*, 1(1), 3. DOI: 10.1145/1217299.1217302

Madakam, S., Ramaswamy, R., & Tripathi, S. (2015). Internet of Things (IoT): A literature review. *Journal of Computer and Communications*, 03(05), 164–173. DOI: 10.4236/jcc.2015.35021

Mahlein, A., Rumpf, T., Welke, P., Dehne, H. W., Plumer, L., Steiner, U., & Oerke, E. (2013). Development of spectral indices for detecting and identifying plant diseases. *Remote Sensing of Environment*, 128, 21–30. DOI: 10.1016/j.rse.2012.09.019

Margam, R. (2024). Smart inhalers: Harnessing iot for precise asthma management. *International Education and Research Journal*, 10.

Mathew, P. S., Pillai, A. S., & Palade, V. (2017). Applications of IoT in healthcare. In *Lecture notes on data engineering and communications technologies* (pp. 263–288). DOI: 10.1007/978-3-319-70688-7_11

Memić, B., Hasković Džubur, A., & Avdagić-Golub, E. (2022). Green IoT: Sustainability environment and technologies. Science. *Engineering and Technology*, 2(1), 24–29.

Menezes, B. C., Kelly, J. D., Leal, A. G., & Le Roux, G. C. (2019). Predictive, prescriptive and detective analytics for smart manufacturing in the information age. *IFAC-PapersOnLine*, 52(1), 568–573. DOI: 10.1016/j.ifacol.2019.06.123

Mieronkoski, I., Azimi, I., Rahmani, A. M., Aantaa, R., Terävä, V., Liljeberg, P., & Salanterä, S. (2017). The Internet of Things for basic nursing care—A scoping review. *International Journal of Nursing Studies*, 69, 78–90. DOI: 10.1016/j.ijnurstu.2017.01.009 PMID: 28189116

Mishra, D. (2016). A survey of access control models in the Internet of Things. *Journal of King Saud University. Computer and Information Sciences*.

Mishra, D., Garg, S., Kumar, A., & Singh, G. (2021). A Genetic Algorithm Based Approach for Green Cloud Computing Task Scheduling. *International Journal of Grid and High Performance Computing*, 13(2), 42–54.

Mohamed, N., Al-Jaroodi, J., Lazarova-Molnar, S., & Jawhar, I. (2021). Applications of integrated IoT-fog-cloud systems to smart cities: A survey. *Electronics (Basel)*, 10(23), 2918. DOI: 10.3390/electronics10232918

Moshe, I., Terhorst, Y., Opoku Asare, K., Sander, L. B., Ferreira, D., Baumeister, H., Mohr, D. C., & Pulkki-Råback, L. (2021). Predicting symptoms of depression and anxiety using smartphone and wearable data. *Frontiers in Psychiatry*, 12, 625247. DOI: 10.3389/fpsyt.2021.625247 PMID: 33584388

Motwani, A., Shukla, P. K., & Pawar, M. (2023). Novel framework based on deep learning and cloud analytics for smart patient monitoring and recommendation (SPMR). *Journal of Ambient Intelligence and Humanized Computing*, 14(5), 5565–5580. DOI: 10.1007/s12652-020-02790-6

Mumtaz, R., Zaidi, S. M. H., Shakir, M. Z., Shafi, U., Malik, M. M., Haque, A., Mumtaz, S., & Zaidi, S. A. R. (2021). Internet of things (Iot) based indoor air quality sensing and predictive analytic—A COVID-19 perspective. *Electronics (Basel)*, 10(2), 184. DOI: 10.3390/electronics10020184

Nancy, A. A., Ravindran, D., Raj Vincent, P. D., Srinivasan, K., & Gutierrez Reina, D. (2022). Iot-cloud-based smart healthcare monitoring system for heart disease prediction via deep learning. *Electronics (Basel)*, 11(15), 2292. DOI: 10.3390/electronics11152292

Nawandar, N. K., & Satpute, V. R. (2019). IoT based low cost and intelligent module for smart irrigation system. *Computers and Electronics in Agriculture*, 162, 979-990. DOI: 10.1016/j.compag.2019.05.027

Nawaz, M., Ahmed, J., & Abbas, G. (2022). Energy-efficient battery management system for healthcare devices. *Journal of Energy Storage*, 51, 104358. DOI: 10.1016/j.est.2022.104358

Nersesian, R. (2023, October 21). Council Post: Five Hurdles of Healthcare IoT — and How to Overcome Them. *Forbes*.

Noura, M., Atiquzzaman, M., & Gaedke, M. (2019). Interoperability in internet of things: Taxonomies and open challenges. *Mobile Networks and Applications*, 24(3), 796–809. DOI: 10.1007/s11036-018-1089-9

Onal, A. C., Sezer, O. B., Ozbayoglu, M., & Dogdu, E. (2017). Weather data analysis and sensor fault detection using an extended IoT framework with semantics, big data, and machine learning. In *2017 IEEE International Conference on Big Data (Big Data)* (pp. 2037-2046). IEEE. DOI: 10.1109/BigData.2017.8258150

Osama, M., Ateya, A. A., Sayed, M. S., Hammad, M., Pławiak, P., Abd El-Latif, A. A., & Elsayed, R. A. (2023). Internet of medical things and healthcare 4.0: Trends, requirements, challenges, and research directions. *Sensors (Basel)*, 23(17), 7435. DOI: 10.3390/s23177435 PMID: 37687891

Pandey, P., & Litoriya, R. (2020). Implementing healthcare services on a large scale: Challenges and remedies based on blockchain technology. *Health Policy and Technology*, 9(1), 69–78. DOI: 10.1016/j.hlpt.2020.01.004

Parati, G., Omboni, S., Albini, F., Piantoni, L., Giuliano, A., Revera, M., Illyes, M., & Mancia, G. (2009). Home blood pressure telemonitoring improves hypertension control in general practice. The TeleBPCare study. *Journal of Hypertension*, 27(1), 198–203. DOI: 10.1097/HJH.0b013e3283163caf PMID: 19145785

Pasluosta, C. F., Gassner, H., Winkler, J., Klucken, J., & Eskofier, B. M. (2015). An emerging era in the management of Parkinson's disease: Wearable technologies and the internet of things. *IEEE Journal of Biomedical and Health Informatics*, 19(6), 1873–1881. DOI: 10.1109/JBHI.2015.2461555 PMID: 26241979

Pateraki, M., Fysarakis, K., Sakkalis, V., Spanoudakis, G., Varlamis, I., Maniadakis, M., ... Koutsouris, D. (2020). Biosensors and Internet of Things in smart healthcare applications: Challenges and opportunities. *Wearable and Implantable Medical Devices*, 25-53.

Pathak, N., Misra, S., Mukherjee, A., & Kumar, N. (2021). HeDI: Healthcare device interoperability for IoT-based e-health platforms. *IEEE Internet of Things Journal*, 8(23), 16845–16852. DOI: 10.1109/JIOT.2021.3052066

Pattnaik, P., Mishra, S., & Mishra, B. S. P. (2020). Optimization techniques for intelligent iot applications. *Fog, Edge, and Pervasive Computing in Intelligent IoT Driven Applications*, 311-331.

Perera, C., Zaslavsky, A., Christen, P., & Georgakopoulos, D. (2014). Sensing as a service model for smart cities supported by Internet of Things. *Transactions on Emerging Telecommunications Technologies*, 25(1), 81–93. DOI: 10.1002/ett.2704

Petrolo, R. (2017). Security of the Internet of Things: A review. *Internet of Things : Engineering Cyber Physical Human Systems*, 1–23.

Philip, N. Y., Rodrigues, J. J., Wang, H., Fong, S. J., & Chen, J. (2021). Internet of Things for in-home health monitoring systems: Current advances, challenges and future directions. *IEEE Journal on Selected Areas in Communications*, 39(2), 300–310. DOI: 10.1109/JSAC.2020.3042421

Poornima, S., & Pushpalatha, M. (2020). A survey on various applications of prescriptive analytics. *International Journal of Intelligent Networks*, 1, 76–84. DOI: 10.1016/j.ijin.2020.07.001

Punetha, P., & Tiwari, P. (2020). Internet of Things (IoT) and its smart cities applications: A conceptual framework. *Internet of Things : Engineering Cyber Physical Human Systems*, 12, 100269.

Qi, J., Yang, P., Min, G., Amft, O., Dong, F., & Xu, L. (2017). Advanced internet of things for personalised healthcare systems: A survey. *Pervasive and Mobile Computing*, 41, 41. DOI: 10.1016/j.pmcj.2017.06.018

Qin, F., Liu, D., Sun, B., Ruan, L., Ma, Z., & Wang, H. (2016). Identification of Alfalfa Leaf Diseases Using Image Recognition Technology. *PLoS One*, 11(12), e0168274. DOI: 10.1371/journal.pone.0168274 PMID: 27977767

Raeesi Vanani, I., & Majidian, S. (2021). Prescriptive Analytics in Internet of Things with Concentration on Deep Learning. In García Márquez, F. P., & Lev, B. (Eds.), *Introduction to Internet of Things in Management Science and Operations Research. International Series in Operations Research & Management Science* (Vol. 311). Springer. DOI: 10.1007/978-3-030-74644-5_2

Rai, V. K. (2007). Temperature sensors and optical sensors. *Applied Physics. B, Lasers and Optics*, 88(2), 297–303. DOI: 10.1007/s00340-007-2717-4

Rajkomar, A., Oren, E., Chen, K., Dai, A. M., Hajaj, N., Hardt, M., Liu, P. J., Liu, X., Marcus, J., Sun, M., Sundberg, P., Yee, H., Zhang, K., Zhang, Y., Flores, G., Duggan, G. E., Irvine, J., Le, Q., Litsch, K., & Dean, J. (2018). Scalable and accurate deep learning with electronic health records. *NPJ Digital Medicine*, 1(1), 18. DOI: 10.1038/s41746-018-0029-1 PMID: 31304302

Ratta, P., Kaur, A., Sharma, S., Shabaz, M., & Dhiman, G. (2021). Application of blockchain and Internet of Things in healthcare and medical sector: Applications, challenges, and future perspectives. *Journal of Food Quality*, 2021, 1–20. DOI: 10.1155/2021/7608296

Ray, P. P. (2018). A survey on Internet of Things architectures. *Journal of King Saud University. Computer and Information Sciences*, 30(3), 291–319. DOI: 10.1016/j.jksuci.2016.10.003

Reich, J., & Monson, J. (2016). The internet of things and cybersecurity: A new framework. *Communications of the ACM*, 59(3), 27–29.

Rejeb, A., Rejeb, K., Simske, S., Treiblmaier, H., & Zailani, S. (2022). The big picture on the internet of things and the smart city: A review of what we know and what we need to know. *Internet of Things : Engineering Cyber Physical Human Systems*, 19, 19. DOI: 10.1016/j.iot.2022.100565

Rendle, S. (2010). Bayesian personalized ranking for non-uniformly sampled items. In *Proceedings of the International Conference on Machine Learning (ICML)* (pp. 1009-1016).

S, G., L, V., B, R. V., Ss, D., & N, A. (2021). IoT based health monitoring system. *2021 Innovations in Power and Advanced Computing Technologies (i-PACT)*. DOI: 10.1109/i-PACT52855.2021.9696937

Saboohi, H., Ardjmand, E., & Teshnehlab, M. (2019). A particle swarm optimization algorithm for task scheduling in cloud computing systems. *The Journal of Supercomputing*, 75(8), 4539–4567.

Sadek, I., Codjo, J., Rehman, S. U., & Abdulrazak, B. (2022). Security and Privacy in the Internet of Things Healthcare Systems: Toward a Robust Solution in Real-Life Deployment. *Computer Methods and Programs in Biomedicine Update*, 2, 2. DOI: 10.1016/j.cmpbup.2022.100071

Samuel, O., Omojo, A. B., Mohsin, S. M., Tiwari, P., Gupta, D., & Band, S. S. (2022). An anonymous IoT-Based E-health monitoring system using blockchain technology. *IEEE Systems Journal*.

Sarhan, F. (2009). Telemedicine in healthcare. 1: Exploring its uses, benefits and disadvantages. *PubMed, 105*(42), 10–13. https://pubmed.ncbi.nlm.nih.gov/19916354

Sarwinda, D., Paradisa, R. H., Bustamam, A., & Anggia, P. (2021). Deep Learning in Image Classification using Residual Network (ResNet) Variants for Detection of Colorectal Cancer. Procedia Computer Science, 179, 423-431.

Sassenrath, G. F., Heilman, P., Luschei, E., Bennett, G. L., Fitzgerald, G., Klesius, P., Tracy, W., Williford, J. R., & Zimba, P. V. (2008). Technology, complexity and change in agricultural production systems. *Renewable Agriculture and Food Systems*, 23(4), 285–295. DOI: 10.1017/S174217050700213X

Scheibner, J., Jobin, A., & Vayena, E. (2021, February 15). Ethical Issues with Using Internet of Things Devices in Citizen Science Research: A Scoping Review. *Frontiers in Environmental Science*, 9, 9. DOI: 10.3389/fenvs.2021.629649

Schroeder, J. L. (2017). Internet of things in logistics and supply chain management: A literature review. *Journal of Enterprise Information Management*, 30(1), 114–129.

Selvaraj, S., & Sundaravaradhan, S. (2020). Challenges and opportunities in IoT healthcare systems: A systematic review. *SN Applied Sciences*, 2(1), 139. DOI: 10.1007/s42452-019-1925-y

Seneviratne, S., Hu, Y., Nguyen, T., Lan, G., Khalifa, S., Thilakarathna, K., Hassan, M., & Seneviratne, A. (2017). A survey of wearable devices and challenges. *IEEE Communications Surveys and Tutorials*, 19(4), 2573–2620. DOI: 10.1109/COMST.2017.2731979

Sharma, A. K., Sharma, D. M., Purohit, N., Rout, S. K., & Sharma, S. A. (2022). Analytics Techniques: Descriptive Analytics, Predictive Analytics, and Prescriptive Analytics. In Jeyanthi, P. M., Choudhury, T., Hack-Polay, D., Singh, T. P., & Abujar, S. (Eds.), *Decision Intelligence Analytics and the Implementation of Strategic Business Management. EAI/Springer Innovations in Communication and Computing*. Springer. DOI: 10.1007/978-3-030-82763-2_1

Shen, Z. (2019). Real-time big data processing for predictive maintenance in IoT environments. *IEEE Transactions on Industrial Informatics*, 15(3), 1604–1613.

Shi, W., Cao, J., Zhang, Q., Li, Y., & Xu, L. (2017). Edge computing: Vision and challenges. *IEEE Internet of Things Journal*, 3(5), 637–646. DOI: 10.1109/JIOT.2016.2579198

Silva, F. S. D., Neto, E. P., Oliveira, H., Rosario, D., Cerqueira, E., Both, C., Zeadally, S., & Neto, A. V. (2021). A survey on Long-Range Wide-Area Network Technology Optimizations. *IEEE Access : Practical Innovations, Open Solutions*, 9, 106079–106106. DOI: 10.1109/ACCESS.2021.3079095

Son, D., Lee, J., Qiao, S., Ghaffari, R., Kim, J., Lee, J. E., Song, C., Kim, S. J., Lee, D. J., Jun, S. W., Yang, S., Park, M., Shin, J., Do, K., Lee, M., Kang, K., Hwang, C. S., Lu, N., Hyeon, T., & Kim, D. (2014). Multifunctional wearable devices for diagnosis and therapy of movement disorders. *Nature Nanotechnology*, 9(5), 397–404. DOI: 10.1038/nnano.2014.38 PMID: 24681776

Srisakthi, S., & Suresh Babu, C. V. (2024). Cybersecurity: Protecting Information in a Digital World. In Saeed, S., Azizi, N., Tahir, S., Ahmad, M., & Almuhaideb, A. (Eds.), *Strengthening Industrial Cybersecurity to Protect Business Intelligence* (pp. 1–25). IGI Global. DOI: 10.4018/979-8-3693-0839-4.ch001

Sternhoff, J. (2021, April 28). CardiLink: Delivering Lifesaving Connectivity When It's Needed Most. Telenor IoT. Retrieved from iot.telenor.com/iot-case/cardilink/

Subramaniyaswamy, V., Manogaran, G., Logesh, R., Vijayakumar, V., Chilamkurti, N., Malathi, D., & Senthilselvan, N. (2019). An ontology-driven personalized food recommendation in IoT-based healthcare system. *The Journal of Supercomputing*, 75(6), 3184–3216. DOI: 10.1007/s11227-018-2331-8

Sundmaeker, H. (2010). Vision and challenges for realising the Internet of Things. In *European Research Cluster on the Internet of Things*. CERP-IoT.

Sureh Babu, C. V., Subhash, S., Vignesh, M., Jeyavasan, T., & Muthumanikavel, V. (2024). Securing the Cloud: Understanding and Mitigating Data Breaches and Insider Attacks in Cloud Computing Environments. In Goel, P., Pandey, H., Singhal, A., & Agarwal, S. (Eds.), *Analyzing and Mitigating Security Risks in Cloud Computing* (pp. 1–23). IGI Global. DOI: 10.4018/979-8-3693-3249-8.ch001

Suresh Babu, C. V., & Sivaneshwaran, J. (2023). Controlling Computer Features Through Hand Gesture. In V. Thayananthan (Ed.), AI-Based Digital Health Communication for Securing Assistive Systems (pp. 85-113). IGI Global. DOI: 10.4018/978-1-6684-8938-3.ch005

Suresh Babu, C. V., Ganesh, B. S., Kishoor, T., & Khang, A. (2023). Automatic Irrigation System Using Solar Tracking Device. In Khang, A. (Ed.), *Handbook of Research on AI-Equipped IoT Applications in High-Tech Agriculture* (pp. 239–256). IGI Global. DOI: 10.4018/978-1-6684-9231-4.ch013

Suresh Babu, C. V., Monika, R., Dhanusha, T., Vishnuvaradhanan, K., & Harish, A. (2023). Smart Street Lighting System for Smart Cities Using IoT (LoRa). In Kumar, R., Abdul Hamid, A., & Binti Ya'akub, N. (Eds.), *Effective AI, Blockchain, and E-Governance Applications for Knowledge Discovery and Management* (pp. 78–96). IGI Global. DOI: 10.4018/978-1-6684-9151-5.ch006

Surya, L. (2018). How government can use AI and ML to identify spreading infectious diseases. *Social Science Research Network*. https://autopapers.ssrn.com/sol3/papers.cfm?abstract_id=3785649

Sworna, N. S., Islam, A. M., Shatabda, S., & Islam, S. (2021). Towards development of IoT-ML driven healthcare systems: A survey. *Journal of Network and Computer Applications*, 196, 103244. DOI: 10.1016/j.jnca.2021.103244

Systems, E. (2023). ESP32 Series Datasheet. *Espressif Systems*. https://www.espressif.com/sites/default/files/documentation/esp32_datasheet_en.pdf

Tarouco, L. M. R., Bertholdo, L. M., Granville, L. Z., Arbiza, L. M. R., Carbone, F., Marotta, M., & De Santanna, J. J. C. (2012, June). Internet of Things in healthcare: Interoperatibility and security issues. In *2012 IEEE international conference on communications (ICC)* (pp. 6121-6125). IEEE.

Teh, Y. W. (2017). Predictive modeling and analytics for equipment health monitoring. *IEEE Transactions on Industrial Informatics*, 13(5), 2282–2291.

Thakare, V., Khire, G., & Kumbhar, M. (2022). Artificial intelligence (AI) and Internet of Things (IoT) in healthcare: Opportunities and challenges. *ECS Transactions*, 107(1), 7941–7951. DOI: 10.1149/10701.7941ecst

Tizzano, G. R., Spezialetti, M., & Rossi, S. (2020, June). *A deep learning approach for mood recognition from wearable data. In 2020 IEEE international symposium on medical measurements and applications (MeMeA).* IEEE.

Toli, A. (2019). IoT-based data analytics for energy consumption prediction in smart buildings. *Sensors (Basel)*, 19(4), 888. PMID: 30791657

Trivitron Healthcare. (2019, September 12). How Healthcare Industry Helps in Contributing to the Economy. Trivitron Blog.

Valsalan, P., Baomar, T. A. B., & Baabood, A. H. O. (2020). IoT based health monitoring system. *Journal of Critical Reviews, 7*(4), 739-743.

Vassakis, K., Petrakis, E., & Kopanakis, I. (2018). Big data analytics: Applications, prospects and challenges. Mobile big data: A roadmap from models to technologies, 3-20.

Verma, H., Chauhan, N., & Awasthi, L. K. (2023). A Comprehensive review of 'Internet of Healthcare Things': Networking aspects, technologies, services, applications, challenges, and security concerns. *Computer Science Review*, 50, 100591. DOI: 10.1016/j.cosrev.2023.100591

Verma, P., & Sood, S. K. (2018). Cloud-centric IoT based disease diagnosis healthcare framework. *Journal of Parallel and Distributed Computing*, 116, 27–38. DOI: 10.1016/j.jpdc.2017.11.018

Vermesan, O. (2019). *Internet of Things: Converging Technologies for Smart Environments and Integrated Ecosystems.* River Publishers.

Vij, A.IoT and Machine Learning Approaches for Automation of Farm Irrigation System. *International Conference on Computational Intelligence and Data Science*, 167, 1250-1257. DOI: 10.1016/j.procs.2020.03.440

Vijayan, V., Connolly, J. P., Condell, J., McKelvey, N., & Gardiner, P. (2021). Review of wearable devices and data collection considerations for connected health. *Sensors (Basel)*, 21(16), 5589. DOI: 10.3390/s21165589 PMID: 34451032

Wang, C., Li, L., Li, Z., & Li, J. (2019). Green Task Scheduling Algorithm for Cloud Computing Based on Ant Colony Optimization. *IEEE Access : Practical Innovations, Open Solutions*, 7, 18120–18128. DOI: 10.1109/ACCESS.2019.2893277

Wang, H. C., & Lee, A. R. (2015). Recent developments in blood glucose sensors. *Yao Wu Shi Pin Fen Xi*, 23(2), 191–200. PMID: 28911373

Wang, Y., Shi, Y., Yang, X., & Wang, B. (2020). Particle swarm optimization for green cloud computing. *Journal of Ambient Intelligence and Humanized Computing*, 11(6), 2545–2556.

Want, R. (2006). An introduction to RFID technology. *IEEE Pervasive Computing*, 5(1), 25–33. DOI: 10.1109/MPRV.2006.2

Wei, Y. (2019). Real-time smart grid data analytics for energy theft detection. *IEEE Transactions on Industrial Informatics*, 15(10), 5785–5793.

Wu. (2017). Introduction to Convolutional Neural Networks, National Key Lab for Novel Software. Technology Nanjing University.

Wu, D. (2011). A survey of cloud computing and its key techniques. *Journal of Information and Computational Science*, 6(2), 37–51.

Xia, F. (2015). A time-series IoT data cleaning method based on structure learning. *IEEE Transactions on Industrial Informatics*, 11(6), 1504–1511.

Xu, M., Qian, F., Zhu, M., Huang, F., Pushp, S., & Liu, X. (2019). Deepwear: Adaptive local offloading for on-wearable deep learning. *IEEE Transactions on Mobile Computing*, 19(2), 314–330. DOI: 10.1109/TMC.2019.2893250

Yang, X., Zhang, X., Wang, Y., & Zhou, Y. (2020). ACO for green cloud computing. *Journal of Ambient Intelligence and Humanized Computing*, 11(11), 5239–5249.

Yin, M., Lin, Y., Yu, H., Zhang, H., & Gao, L. (2020). A novel ant colony optimization-based task scheduling algorithm for cloud computing. *International Journal of Distributed Sensor Networks*, 16(3), 1550147719897695.

Yin, Y., Zeng, Y., Chen, X., & Fan, Y. (2016). The internet of things in healthcare: An overview. *Journal of Industrial Information Integration*, 1, 3–13. DOI: 10.1016/j.jii.2016.03.004

Yi, X. (2017). A review of time series data mining. *Theoretical Biology & Medical Modelling*, 14(1), 1–14. PMID: 28100241

Yuan, L., Huang, Y., Loraamm, R. W., Nie, C., Wang, J., & Zhang, J. (2014). Spectral analysis of winter wheat leaves for detection and differentiation of diseases and insects. *Field Crops Research*, 156, 199–207. DOI: 10.1016/j.fcr.2013.11.012

Yu, L., Vijay, M. M., Sunil, J., Vincy, V. A. G., Govindan, V., Khan, M. I., Ali, S., Tamam, N., & Abdullaeva, B. S. (2023). Hybrid deep learning model based smart IOT based monitoring system for Covid-19. *Heliyon*, 9(11), e21150. DOI: 10.1016/j.heliyon.2023.e21150 PMID: 37928011

Zaynidinov, H., Makhmudjanov, S., Rajabov, F., & Singh, D. (2020, November). IoT-enabled mobile device for electrogastrography signal processing. In *International Conference on Intelligent Human Computer Interaction* (pp. 346-356). Cham: Springer International Publishing.

Zhang, X. M., & Zhang, N. (2011, May). An open, secure and flexible platform based on internet of things and cloud computing for ambient aiding living and telemedicine. In *2011 international conference on computer and management (CAMAN)* (pp. 1-4). IEEE. DOI: 10.1109/CAMAN.2011.5778905

Zhang, J. (2017). IoT-based smart rehabilitation system. *IEEE Transactions on Industrial Informatics*, 13(3), 1333–1341.

Zhang, M., Liu, J., Liu, Y., & Feng, D. (2019). Energy-efficient task scheduling in cloud computing using genetic algorithm. *Cluster Computing*, 22(4), 832–846.

Zhang, Y., Wang, Z., Xue, L., & Sun, H. (2020). A Reinforcement Learning-Based Task Scheduling Algorithm for Cloud Computing. *IEEE Access : Practical Innovations, Open Solutions*, 8, 100039–100050. DOI: 10.1109/ACCESS.2020.2993081

Related References

To continue our tradition of advancing information science and technology research, we have compiled a list of recommended IGI Global readings. These references will provide additional information and guidance to further enrich your knowledge and assist you with your own research and future publications.

Beale, R., & André, J. (2017). *Design Solutions and Innovations in Temporary Structures*. Hershey, PA: IGI Global. DOI: 10.4018/978-1-5225-2199-0

Ishii, N., Anami, K., & Knisely, C. W. (2018). *Dynamic Stability of Hydraulic Gates and Engineering for Flood Prevention*. Hershey, PA: IGI Global. DOI: 10.4018/978-1-5225-3079-4

Kumar, A., Patil, P. P., & Prajapati, Y. K. (2018). *Advanced Numerical Simulations in Mechanical Engineering*. Hershey, PA: IGI Global. DOI: 10.4018/978-1-5225-3722-9

Sukhyy, K., Belyanovskaya, E., & Sukhyy, M. (2021). *Basic Principles for Substantiation of Working Pair Choice*. IGI Global. DOI: 10.4018/978-1-7998-4432-7.ch002

Abbasnejad, B., Moeinzadeh, S., Ahankoob, A., & Wong, P. S. (2021). The Role of Collaboration in the Implementation of BIM-Enabled Projects. In Underwood, J., & Shelbourn, M. (Eds.), *Handbook of Research on Driving Transformational Change in the Digital Built Environment* (pp. 27–62). IGI Global. https://doi.org/10.4018/978-1-7998-6600-8.ch002

Abdrabo, A. A. (2018). Egypt's Knowledge-Based Development: Opportunities, Challenges, and Future Possibilities. In Alraouf, A. (Ed.), *Knowledge-Based Urban Development in the Middle East* (pp. 80–101). Hershey, PA: IGI Global. DOI: 10.4018/978-1-5225-3734-2.ch005

Adegbore, A. M., Quadri, M. O., & Oyewo, O. R. (2018). A Theoretical Approach to the Adoption of Electronic Resource Management Systems (ERMS) in Nigerian University Libraries. In Tella, A., & Kwanya, T. (Eds.), *Handbook of Research on Managing Intellectual Property in Digital Libraries* (pp. 292–311). Hershey, PA: IGI Global. DOI: 10.4018/978-1-5225-3093-0.ch015

Afolabi, O. A. (2018). Myths and Challenges of Building an Effective Digital Library in Developing Nations: An African Perspective. In Tella, A., & Kwanya, T. (Eds.), *Handbook of Research on Managing Intellectual Property in Digital Libraries* (pp. 51–79). Hershey, PA: IGI Global. DOI: 10.4018/978-1-5225-3093-0.ch004

Agarwal, P., Kurian, R., & Gupta, R. K. (2022). Additive Manufacturing Feature Taxonomy and Placement of Parts in AM Enclosure. In Salunkhe, S., Hussein, H., & Davim, J. (Eds.), *Applications of Artificial Intelligence in Additive Manufacturing* (pp. 138–176). IGI Global. https://doi.org/10.4018/978-1-7998-8516-0.ch007

Agrawal, R., Sharma, P., & Saxena, A. (2021). A Diamond Cut Leather Substrate Antenna for BAN (Body Area Network) Application. In Singh, V., Dubey, V., Saxena, A., Tiwari, R., & Sharma, H. (Eds.), *Emerging Materials and Advanced Designs for Wearable Antennas* (pp. 54–59). IGI Global. https://doi.org/10.4018/978-1-7998-7611-3.ch004

Ahmad, F., Al-Ammar, E. A., & Alsaidan, I. (2022). Battery Swapping Station: A Potential Solution to Address the Limitations of EV Charging Infrastructure. In Alam, M., Pillai, R., & Murugesan, N. (Eds.), *Developing Charging Infrastructure and Technologies for Electric Vehicles* (pp. 195–207). IGI Global. DOI: 10.4018/978-1-7998-6858-3.ch010

Al-Alawi, A. I., Al-Hammam, A. H., Al-Alawi, S. S., & AlAlawi, E. I. (2021). The Adoption of E-Wallets: Current Trends and Future Outlook. In Albastaki, Y., Razzaque, A., & Sarea, A. (Eds.), *Innovative Strategies for Implementing FinTech in Banking* (pp. 242–262). IGI Global. https://doi.org/10.4018/978-1-7998-3257-7.ch015

Al-Khatri, H., & Al-Atrash, F. (2021). Occupants' Habits and Natural Ventilation in a Hot Arid Climate. In González-Lezcano, R. (Ed.), *Advancements in Sustainable Architecture and Energy Efficiency* (pp. 146–168). IGI Global. https://doi.org/10.4018/978-1-7998-7023-4.ch007

Amer, T. S., & Johnson, T. L. (2017). Information Technology Progress Indicators: Research Employing Psychological Frameworks. In Mesquita, A. (Ed.), *Research Paradigms and Contemporary Perspectives on Human-Technology Interaction* (pp. 168–186). Hershey, PA: IGI Global. DOI: 10.4018/978-1-5225-1868-6.ch008

Amuda, M. O., Lawal, T. F., & Mridha, S. (2021). Microstructure and Mechanical Properties of Silicon Carbide-Treated Ferritic Stainless Steel Welds. In Burstein, L. (Ed.), *Handbook of Research on Advancements in Manufacturing, Materials, and Mechanical Engineering* (pp. 395–411). IGI Global. https://doi.org/10.4018/978-1 -7998-4939-1.ch019

Andreeva, A., & Yolova, G. (2021). Liability in Labor Legislation: New Challenges Related to the Use of Artificial Intelligence. In Vassileva, B., & Zwilling, M. (Eds.), *Responsible AI and Ethical Issues for Businesses and Governments* (pp. 214–232). IGI Global. https://doi.org/10.4018/978-1-7998-4285-9.ch012

Anikeev, V., Gasem, K. A., & Fan, M. (2021). Application of Supercritical Technologies in Clean Energy Production: A Review. In Chen, L. (Ed.), *Handbook of Research on Advancements in Supercritical Fluids Applications for Sustainable Energy Systems* (pp. 792–821). IGI Global. https://doi.org/10.4018/978-1-7998 -5796-9.ch022

Arafat, M. Y., Saleem, I., & Devi, T. P. (2022). Drivers of EV Charging Infrastructure Entrepreneurship in India. In Alam, M., Pillai, R., & Murugesan, N. (Eds.), *Developing Charging Infrastructure and Technologies for Electric Vehicles* (pp. 208–219). IGI Global. https://doi.org/10.4018/978-1-7998-6858-3.ch011

Araujo, A., & Manninen, H. (2022). Contribution of Project-Based Learning on Social Skills Development: An Industrial Engineer Perspective. In Alves, A., & van Hattum-Janssen, N. (Eds.), *Training Engineering Students for Modern Technological Advancement* (pp. 119–145). IGI Global. https://doi.org/10.4018/978-1 -7998-8816-1.ch006

Armutlu, H. (2018). Intelligent Biomedical Engineering Operations by Cloud Computing Technologies. In Kose, U., Guraksin, G., & Deperlioglu, O. (Eds.), *Nature-Inspired Intelligent Techniques for Solving Biomedical Engineering Problems* (pp. 297–317). Hershey, PA: IGI Global. DOI: 10.4018/978-1-5225-4769-3.ch015

Atik, M., Sadek, M., & Shahrour, I. (2017). Single-Run Adaptive Pushover Procedure for Shear Wall Structures. In Plevris, V., Kremmyda, G., & Fahjan, Y. (Eds.), *Performance-Based Seismic Design of Concrete Structures and Infrastructures* (pp. 59–83). Hershey, PA: IGI Global. DOI: 10.4018/978-1-5225-2089-4.ch003

Attia, H. (2021). Smart Power Microgrid Impact on Sustainable Building. In González-Lezcano, R. (Ed.), *Advancements in Sustainable Architecture and Energy Efficiency* (pp. 169–194). IGI Global. https://doi.org/10.4018/978-1-7998-7023-4.ch008

Aydin, A., Akyol, E., Gungor, M., Kaya, A., & Tasdelen, S. (2018). Geophysical Surveys in Engineering Geology Investigations With Field Examples. In Ceryan, N. (Ed.), *Handbook of Research on Trends and Digital Advances in Engineering Geology* (pp. 257–280). Hershey, PA: IGI Global. DOI: 10.4018/978-1-5225-2709-1.ch007

Ayoobkhan, M. U. D., Y., A., J., Easwaran, B., & R., T. (2021). Smart Connected Digital Products and IoT Platform With the Digital Twin. In P. Vasant, G. Weber, & W. Punurai (Ed.), *Research Advancements in Smart Technology, Optimization, and Renewable Energy* (pp. 330-350). IGI Global. https://doi.org/DOI: 10.4018/978-1-7998-3970-5.ch016

Baeza Moyano, D., & González Lezcano, R. A. (2021). The Importance of Light in Our Lives: Towards New Lighting in Schools. In González-Lezcano, R. (Ed.), *Advancements in Sustainable Architecture and Energy Efficiency* (pp. 239–256). IGI Global. https://doi.org/10.4018/978-1-7998-7023-4.ch011

Bailey, E. K. (2017). Applying Learning Theories to Computer Technology Supported Instruction. In Grassetti, M., & Brookby, S. (Eds.), *Advancing Next-Generation Teacher Education through Digital Tools and Applications* (pp. 61–81). Hershey, PA: IGI Global. DOI: 10.4018/978-1-5225-0965-3.ch004

Baker, J. D. (2021). Introduction to Machine Learning as a New Methodological Framework for Performance Assessment. In Bocarnea, M., Winston, B., & Dean, D. (Eds.), *Handbook of Research on Advancements in Organizational Data Collection and Measurements: Strategies for Addressing Attitudes, Beliefs, and Behaviors* (pp. 326–342). IGI Global. https://doi.org/10.4018/978-1-7998-7665-6.ch021

Baklezos, A. T., & Hadjigeorgiou, N. G. (2021). Magnetic Sensors for Space Applications and Magnetic Cleanliness Considerations. In Nikolopoulos, C. (Ed.), *Recent Trends on Electromagnetic Environmental Effects for Aeronautics and Space Applications* (pp. 147–185). IGI Global. https://doi.org/10.4018/978-1-7998-4879-0.ch006

Banerjee, S., Sing, T. Y., Chowdhury, A. R., & Anwar, H. (2018). Let's Go Green: Towards a Taxonomy of Green Computing Enablers for Business Sustainability. In Khosrow-Pour, M. (Ed.), *Green Computing Strategies for Competitive Advantage and Business Sustainability* (pp. 89–109). Hershey, PA: IGI Global. DOI: 10.4018/978-1-5225-5017-4.ch005

Bas, T. G. (2017). Nutraceutical Industry with the Collaboration of Biotechnology and Nutrigenomics Engineering: The Significance of Intellectual Property in the Entrepreneurship and Scientific Research Ecosystems. In Bas, T., & Zhao, J. (Eds.), *Comparative Approaches to Biotechnology Development and Use in Developed and Emerging Nations* (pp. 1–17). Hershey, PA: IGI Global. DOI: 10.4018/978-1-5225-1040-6.ch001

Basham, R. (2018). Information Science and Technology in Crisis Response and Management. In M. Khosrow-Pour, D.B.A. (Ed.), *Encyclopedia of Information Science and Technology, Fourth Edition* (pp. 1407-1418). Hershey, PA: IGI Global. DOI: 10.4018/978-1-5225-2255-3.ch121

Batyashe, T., & Iyamu, T. (2018). Architectural Framework for the Implementation of Information Technology Governance in Organisations. In M. Khosrow-Pour, D.B.A. (Ed.), *Encyclopedia of Information Science and Technology, Fourth Edition* (pp. 810-819). Hershey, PA: IGI Global. DOI: 10.4018/978-1-5225-2255-3.ch070

Behnam, B. (2017). Simulating Post-Earthquake Fire Loading in Conventional RC Structures. In Samui, P., Chakraborty, S., & Kim, D. (Eds.), *Modeling and Simulation Techniques in Structural Engineering* (pp. 425–444). Hershey, PA: IGI Global. DOI: 10.4018/978-1-5225-0588-4.ch015

Bekleyen, N., & Çelik, S. (2017). Attitudes of Adult EFL Learners towards Preparing for a Language Test via CALL. In Tafazoli, D., & Romero, M. (Eds.), *Multiculturalism and Technology-Enhanced Language Learning* (pp. 214–229). Hershey, PA: IGI Global. DOI: 10.4018/978-1-5225-1882-2.ch013

Bentarzi, H. (2021). Fault Tree-Based Root Cause Analysis Used to Study Mal-Operation of a Protective Relay in a Smart Grid. In Recioui, A., & Bentarzi, H. (Eds.), *Optimizing and Measuring Smart Grid Operation and Control* (pp. 289–308). IGI Global. https://doi.org/10.4018/978-1-7998-4027-5.ch012

Bergeron, F., Croteau, A., Uwizeyemungu, S., & Raymond, L. (2017). A Framework for Research on Information Technology Governance in SMEs. In De Haes, S., & Van Gremberger, W. (Eds.), *Strategic IT Governance and Alignment in Business Settings* (pp. 53–81). Hershey, PA: IGI Global. DOI: 10.4018/978-1-5225-0861-8.ch003

Beysens, D. A., Garrabos, Y., & Zappoli, B. (2021). Thermal Effects in Near-Critical Fluids: Piston Effect and Related Phenomena. In Chen, L. (Ed.), *Handbook of Research on Advancements in Supercritical Fluids Applications for Sustainable Energy Systems* (pp. 1–31). IGI Global. https://doi.org/10.4018/978-1-7998-5796-9.ch001

Bhardwaj, M., Shukla, N., & Sharma, A. (2021). Improvement and Reduction of Clustering Overhead in Mobile Ad Hoc Network With Optimum Stable Bunching Algorithm. In Kumar, S., Trivedi, M., Ranjan, P., & Punhani, A. (Eds.), *Evolution of Software-Defined Networking Foundations for IoT and 5G Mobile Networks* (pp. 139–158). IGI Global. https://doi.org/10.4018/978-1-7998-4685-7.ch008

Bhattacharya, A. (2021). Blockchain, Cybersecurity, and Industry 4.0. In Tyagi, A., Rekha, G., & Sreenath, N. (Eds.), *Opportunities and Challenges for Blockchain Technology in Autonomous Vehicles* (pp. 210–244). IGI Global. https://doi.org/10.4018/978-1-7998-3295-9.ch013

Bhuyan, D. (2018). Designing of a Twin Tube Shock Absorber: A Study in Reverse Engineering. In Kumar, K., & Davim, J. (Eds.), *Design and Optimization of Mechanical Engineering Products* (pp. 83–104). Hershey, PA: IGI Global. DOI: 10.4018/978-1-5225-3401-3.ch005

Bhyan, P., Shrivastava, B., & Kumar, N. (2022). Requisite Sustainable Development Contemplating Buildings: Economic and Environmental Sustainability. In Hussain, A., Tiwari, K., & Gupta, A. (Eds.), *Addressing Environmental Challenges Through Spatial Planning* (pp. 269–288). IGI Global. https://doi.org/10.4018/978-1-7998-8331-9.ch014

Blumberg, G. (2021). Blockchains for Use in Construction and Engineering Projects. In Underwood, J., & Shelbourn, M. (Eds.), *Handbook of Research on Driving Transformational Change in the Digital Built Environment* (pp. 179–208). IGI Global. https://doi.org/10.4018/978-1-7998-6600-8.ch008

Bolboaca, A. M. (2021). Considerations Regarding the Use of Fuel Cells in Combined Heat and Power for Stationary Applications. In Badea, G., Felseghi, R., & A chilean, I. (Eds.), *Hydrogen Fuel Cell Technology for Stationary Applications* (pp. 239–275). IGI Global. https://doi.org/10.4018/978-1-7998-4945-2.ch010

Borkar, P. S., Chanana, P. U., Atwal, S. K., Londe, T. G., & Dalal, Y. D. (2021). The Replacement of HMI (Human-Machine Interface) in Industry Using Single Interface Through IoT. In Raut, R., & Mihovska, A. (Eds.), *Examining the Impact of Deep Learning and IoT on Multi-Industry Applications* (pp. 195–208). IGI Global. https://doi.org/10.4018/978-1-7998-7511-6.ch011

Burstein, L. (2021). Simulation Tool for Cable Design. In Burstein, L. (Ed.), *Handbook of Research on Advancements in Manufacturing, Materials, and Mechanical Engineering* (pp. 54–74). IGI Global. https://doi.org/10.4018/978-1-7998-4939-1.ch003

Byker, E. J. (2017). I Play I Learn: Introducing Technological Play Theory. In Martin, C., & Polly, D. (Eds.), *Handbook of Research on Teacher Education and Professional Development* (pp. 297–306). Hershey, PA: IGI Global. DOI: 10.4018/978-1-5225-1067-3.ch016

Calderon, F. A., Giolo, E. G., Frau, C. D., Rengel, M. G., Rodriguez, H., Tornello, M., & Gallucci, R. (2018). Seismic Microzonation and Site Effects Detection Through Microtremors Measures: A Review. In Ceryan, N. (Ed.), *Handbook of Research on Trends and Digital Advances in Engineering Geology* (pp. 326–349). Hershey, PA: IGI Global. DOI: 10.4018/978-1-5225-2709-1.ch009

Calongne, C. M., Stricker, A. G., Truman, B., & Arenas, F. J. (2017). Cognitive Apprenticeship and Computer Science Education in Cyberspace: Reimagining the Past. In Stricker, A., Calongne, C., Truman, B., & Arenas, F. (Eds.), *Integrating an Awareness of Selfhood and Society into Virtual Learning* (pp. 180–197). Hershey, PA: IGI Global. DOI: 10.4018/978-1-5225-2182-2.ch013

Carneiro, A. D. (2017). Defending Information Networks in Cyberspace: Some Notes on Security Needs. In M. Dawson, D. Kisku, P. Gupta, J. Sing, & W. Li (Eds.), *Developing Next-Generation Countermeasures for Homeland Security Threat Prevention* (pp. 354-375). Hershey, PA: IGI Global. https://doi.org/DOI: 10.4018/978-1-5225-0703-1.ch016

Ceryan, N., & Can, N. K. (2018). Prediction of The Uniaxial Compressive Strength of Rocks Materials. In Ceryan, N. (Ed.), *Handbook of Research on Trends and Digital Advances in Engineering Geology* (pp. 31–96). Hershey, PA: IGI Global. DOI: 10.4018/978-1-5225-2709-1.ch002

Ceryan, S. (2018). Weathering Indices Used in Evaluation of the Weathering State of Rock Material. In Ceryan, N. (Ed.), *Handbook of Research on Trends and Digital Advances in Engineering Geology* (pp. 132–186). Hershey, PA: IGI Global. DOI: 10.4018/978-1-5225-2709-1.ch004

Chase, J. P., & Yan, Z. (2017). Affect in Statistics Cognition. In *Assessing and Measuring Statistics Cognition in Higher Education Online Environments: Emerging Research and Opportunities* (pp. 144–187). Hershey, PA: IGI Global. DOI: 10.4018/978-1-5225-2420-5.ch005

Chatterjee, A., Roy, S., & Shrivastava, R. (2021). A Machine Learning Approach to Prevent Cancer. In Rani, G., & Tiwari, P. (Eds.), *Handbook of Research on Disease Prediction Through Data Analytics and Machine Learning* (pp. 112–141). IGI Global. https://doi.org/10.4018/978-1-7998-2742-9.ch007

Chen, H., Padilla, R. V., & Besarati, S. (2017). Supercritical Fluids and Their Applications in Power Generation. In Chen, L., & Iwamoto, Y. (Eds.), *Advanced Applications of Supercritical Fluids in Energy Systems* (pp. 369–402). Hershey, PA: IGI Global. DOI: 10.4018/978-1-5225-2047-4.ch012

Chen, H., Padilla, R. V., & Besarati, S. (2021). Supercritical Fluids and Their Applications in Power Generation. In Chen, L. (Ed.), *Handbook of Research on Advancements in Supercritical Fluids Applications for Sustainable Energy Systems* (pp. 566–599). IGI Global. https://doi.org/10.4018/978-1-7998-5796-9.ch016

Chen, L. (2017). Principles, Experiments, and Numerical Studies of Supercritical Fluid Natural Circulation System. In Chen, L., & Iwamoto, Y. (Eds.), *Advanced Applications of Supercritical Fluids in Energy Systems* (pp. 136–187). Hershey, PA: IGI Global. DOI: 10.4018/978-1-5225-2047-4.ch005

Chen, L. (2021). Principles, Experiments, and Numerical Studies of Supercritical Fluid Natural Circulation System. In Chen, L. (Ed.), *Handbook of Research on Advancements in Supercritical Fluids Applications for Sustainable Energy Systems* (pp. 219–269). IGI Global. https://doi.org/10.4018/978-1-7998-5796-9.ch007

Cifci, M. A. (2021). Optimizing WSNs for CPS Using Machine Learning Techniques. In Luhach, A., & Elçi, A. (Eds.), *Artificial Intelligence Paradigms for Smart Cyber-Physical Systems* (pp. 204–228). IGI Global. https://doi.org/10.4018/978-1-7998-5101-1.ch010

Cimermanova, I. (2017). Computer-Assisted Learning in Slovakia. In Tafazoli, D., & Romero, M. (Eds.), *Multiculturalism and Technology-Enhanced Language Learning* (pp. 252–270). Hershey, PA: IGI Global. DOI: 10.4018/978-1-5225-1882-2.ch015

Cipolla-Ficarra, F. V., & Cipolla-Ficarra, M. (2018). Computer Animation for Ingenious Revival. In Cipolla-Ficarra, F., Ficarra, M., Cipolla-Ficarra, M., Quiroga, A., Alma, J., & Carré, J. (Eds.), *Technology-Enhanced Human Interaction in Modern Society* (pp. 159–181). Hershey, PA: IGI Global. DOI: 10.4018/978-1-5225-3437-2.ch008

Clementi, F., Di Sciascio, G., Di Sciascio, S., & Lenci, S. (2017). Influence of the Shear-Bending Interaction on the Global Capacity of Reinforced Concrete Frames: A Brief Overview of the New Perspectives. In Plevris, V., Kremmyda, G., & Fahjan, Y. (Eds.), *Performance-Based Seismic Design of Concrete Structures and Infrastructures* (pp. 84–111). Hershey, PA: IGI Global. DOI: 10.4018/978-1-5225-2089-4.ch004

Cockrell, S., Damron, T. S., Melton, A. M., & Smith, A. D. (2018). Offshoring IT. In M. Khosrow-Pour, D.B.A. (Ed.), *Encyclopedia of Information Science and Technology, Fourth Edition* (pp. 5476-5489). Hershey, PA: IGI Global. https://doi.org/DOI: 10.4018/978-1-5225-2255-3.ch476

Codinhoto, R., Fialho, B. C., Pinti, L., & Fabricio, M. M. (2021). BIM and IoT for Facilities Management: Understanding Key Maintenance Issues. In Underwood, J., & Shelbourn, M. (Eds.), *Handbook of Research on Driving Transformational Change in the Digital Built Environment* (pp. 209–231). IGI Global. DOI: 10.4018/978-1-7998-6600-8.ch009

Coffey, J. W. (2018). Logic and Proof in Computer Science: Categories and Limits of Proof Techniques. In Horne, J. (Ed.), *Philosophical Perceptions on Logic and Order* (pp. 218–240). Hershey, PA: IGI Global. DOI: 10.4018/978-1-5225-2443-4.ch007

Costa, H. G., Sheremetieff, F. H., & Araújo, E. A. (2022). Influence of Game-Based Methods in Developing Engineering Competences. In Alves, A., & van Hattum-Janssen, N. (Eds.), *Training Engineering Students for Modern Technological Advancement* (pp. 69–88). IGI Global. https://doi.org/10.4018/978-1-7998-8816-1.ch004

Cui, X., Zeng, S., Li, Z., Zheng, Q., Yu, X., & Han, B. (2018). Advanced Composites for Civil Engineering Infrastructures. In Kumar, K., & Davim, J. (Eds.), *Composites and Advanced Materials for Industrial Applications* (pp. 212–248). Hershey, PA: IGI Global. DOI: 10.4018/978-1-5225-5216-1.ch010

Dale, M. (2017). Re-Thinking the Challenges of Enterprise Architecture Implementation. In Tavana, M. (Ed.), *Enterprise Information Systems and the Digitalization of Business Functions* (pp. 205–221). Hershey, PA: IGI Global. DOI: 10.4018/978-1-5225-2382-6.ch009

Dalgıç, S., & Kuşku, İ. (2018). Geological and Geotechnical Investigations in Tunneling. In Ceryan, N. (Ed.), *Handbook of Research on Trends and Digital Advances in Engineering Geology* (pp. 482–529). Hershey, PA: IGI Global. DOI: 10.4018/978-1-5225-2709-1.ch014

Dang, C., & Hihara, E. (2021). Study on Cooling Heat Transfer of Supercritical Carbon Dioxide Applied to Transcritical Carbon Dioxide Heat Pump. In Chen, L. (Ed.), *Handbook of Research on Advancements in Supercritical Fluids Applications for Sustainable Energy Systems* (pp. 451–493). IGI Global. https://doi.org/10.4018/978-1-7998-5796-9.ch013

Das, A., & Mohanty, M. N. (2021). An Useful Review on Optical Character Recognition for Smart Era Generation. In Tyagi, A. (Ed.), *Multimedia and Sensory Input for Augmented, Mixed, and Virtual Reality* (pp. 1–41). IGI Global. https://doi.org/10.4018/978-1-7998-4703-8.ch001

Dash, A. K., & Mohapatra, P. (2021). A Survey on Prematurity Detection of Diabetic Retinopathy Based on Fundus Images Using Deep Learning Techniques. In Saxena, S., & Paul, S. (Eds.), *Deep Learning Applications in Medical Imaging* (pp. 140–155). IGI Global. https://doi.org/10.4018/978-1-7998-5071-7.ch006

de la Varga, D., Soto, M., Arias, C. A., van Oirschot, D., Kilian, R., Pascual, A., & Álvarez, J. A. (2017). Constructed Wetlands for Industrial Wastewater Treatment and Removal of Nutrients. In Val del Río, Á., Campos Gómez, J., & Mosquera Corral, A. (Eds.), *Technologies for the Treatment and Recovery of Nutrients from Industrial Wastewater* (pp. 202–230). Hershey, PA: IGI Global. DOI: 10.4018/978-1-5225-1037-6.ch008

Deb, S., Ammar, E. A., AlRajhi, H., Alsaidan, I., & Shariff, S. M. (2022). V2G Pilot Projects: Review and Lessons Learnt. In Alam, M., Pillai, R., & Murugesan, N. (Eds.), *Developing Charging Infrastructure and Technologies for Electric Vehicles* (pp. 252–267). IGI Global. https://doi.org/10.4018/978-1-7998-6858-3.ch014

Dekhandji, F. Z., & Rais, M. C. (2021). A Comparative Study of Power Quality Monitoring Using Various Techniques. In Recioui, A., & Bentarzi, H. (Eds.), *Optimizing and Measuring Smart Grid Operation and Control* (pp. 259–288). IGI Global. https://doi.org/10.4018/978-1-7998-4027-5.ch011

Demir, K., Çaka, C., Yaman, N. D., İslamoğlu, H., & Kuzu, A. (2018). Examining the Current Definitions of Computational Thinking. In Ozcinar, H., Wong, G., & Ozturk, H. (Eds.), *Teaching Computational Thinking in Primary Education* (pp. 36–64). Hershey, PA: IGI Global. DOI: 10.4018/978-1-5225-3200-2.ch003

Deng, X., Hung, Y., & Lin, C. D. (2017). Design and Analysis of Computer Experiments. In S. Saha, A. Mandal, A. Narasimhamurthy, S. V, & S. Sangam (Eds.), *Handbook of Research on Applied Cybernetics and Systems Science* (pp. 264-279). Hershey, PA: IGI Global. DOI: 10.4018/978-1-5225-2498-4.ch013

Denner, J., Martinez, J., & Thiry, H. (2017). Strategies for Engaging Hispanic/Latino Youth in the US in Computer Science. In Rankin, Y., & Thomas, J. (Eds.), *Moving Students of Color from Consumers to Producers of Technology* (pp. 24–48). Hershey, PA: IGI Global. DOI: 10.4018/978-1-5225-2005-4.ch002

Deperlioglu, O. (2018). Intelligent Techniques Inspired by Nature and Used in Biomedical Engineering. In Kose, U., Guraksin, G., & Deperlioglu, O. (Eds.), *Nature-Inspired Intelligent Techniques for Solving Biomedical Engineering Problems* (pp. 51–77). Hershey, PA: IGI Global. DOI: 10.4018/978-1-5225-4769-3.ch003

Devi, A. (2017). Cyber Crime and Cyber Security: A Quick Glance. In Kumar, R., Pattnaik, P., & Pandey, P. (Eds.), *Detecting and Mitigating Robotic Cyber Security Risks* (pp. 160–171). Hershey, PA: IGI Global. DOI: 10.4018/978-1-5225-2154-9.ch011

Dhaya, R., & Kanthavel, R. (2022). Futuristic Research Perspectives of IoT Platforms. In Jeya Mala, D. (Ed.), *Integrating AI in IoT Analytics on the Cloud for Healthcare Applications* (pp. 258–275). IGI Global. DOI: 10.4018/978-1-7998-9132-1.ch015

Dixit, A. (2018). Application of Silica-Gel-Reinforced Aluminium Composite on the Piston of Internal Combustion Engine: Comparative Study of Silica-Gel-Reinforced Aluminium Composite Piston With Aluminium Alloy Piston. In Kumar, K., & Davim, J. (Eds.), *Composites and Advanced Materials for Industrial Applications* (pp. 63–98). Hershey, PA: IGI Global. DOI: 10.4018/978-1-5225-5216-1.ch004

Doyle, D. J., & Fahy, P. J. (2018). Interactivity in Distance Education and Computer-Aided Learning, With Medical Education Examples. In M. Khosrow-Pour, D.B.A. (Ed.), *Encyclopedia of Information Science and Technology, Fourth Edition* (pp. 5829-5840). Hershey, PA: IGI Global. https://doi.org/DOI: 10.4018/978-1-5225-2255-3.ch507

Dutta, M. M. (2021). Nanomaterials for Food and Agriculture. In Bhat, M., Wani, I., & Ashraf, S. (Eds.), *Applications of Nanomaterials in Agriculture, Food Science, and Medicine* (pp. 75–97). IGI Global. DOI: 10.4018/978-1-7998-5563-7.ch004

Dutta, M. M., & Goswami, M. (2021). Coating Materials: Nano-Materials. In Roy, S., & Bose, G. (Eds.), *Advanced Surface Coating Techniques for Modern Industrial Applications* (pp. 1–30). IGI Global. DOI: 10.4018/978-1-7998-4870-7.ch001

Eklund, P. (2021). Reinforcement Learning in Social Media Marketing. In Christiansen, B., & Škrinjarić, T. (Eds.), *Handbook of Research on Applied AI for International Business and Marketing Applications* (pp. 30–48). IGI Global. https://doi.org/10.4018/978-1-7998-5077-9.ch003

Elias, N. I., & Walker, T. W. (2017). Factors that Contribute to Continued Use of E-Training among Healthcare Professionals. In Topor, F. (Ed.), *Handbook of Research on Individualism and Identity in the Globalized Digital Age* (pp. 403–429). Hershey, PA: IGI Global. DOI: 10.4018/978-1-5225-0522-8.ch018

Elsayed, A. M., Dakkama, H. J., Mahmoud, S., Al-Dadah, R., & Kaialy, W. (2017). Sustainable Cooling Research Using Activated Carbon Adsorbents and Their Environmental Impact. In Kobayashi, T. (Ed.), *Applied Environmental Materials Science for Sustainability* (pp. 186–221). Hershey, PA: IGI Global. DOI: 10.4018/978-1-5225-1971-3.ch009

Ercanoglu, M., & Sonmez, H. (2018). General Trends and New Perspectives on Landslide Mapping and Assessment Methods. In Ceryan, N. (Ed.), *Handbook of Research on Trends and Digital Advances in Engineering Geology* (pp. 350–379). Hershey, PA: IGI Global. DOI: 10.4018/978-1-5225-2709-1.ch010

Faroz, S. A., Pujari, N. N., Rastogi, R., & Ghosh, S. (2017). Risk Analysis of Structural Engineering Systems Using Bayesian Inference. In Samui, P., Chakraborty, S., & Kim, D. (Eds.), *Modeling and Simulation Techniques in Structural Engineering* (pp. 390–424). Hershey, PA: IGI Global. DOI: 10.4018/978-1-5225-0588-4.ch014

Fekik, A., Hamida, M. L., Denoun, H., Azar, A. T., Kamal, N. A., Vaidyanathan, S., Bousbaine, A., & Benamrouche, N. (2022). Multilevel Inverter for Hybrid Fuel Cell/PV Energy Conversion System. In Fekik, A., & Benamrouche, N. (Eds.), *Modeling and Control of Static Converters for Hybrid Storage Systems* (pp. 233–270). IGI Global. https://doi.org/10.4018/978-1-7998-7447-8.ch009

Fekik, A., Hamida, M. L., Houassine, H., Azar, A. T., Kamal, N. A., Denoun, H., Vaidyanathan, S., & Sambas, A. (2022). Power Quality Improvement for Grid-Connected Photovoltaic Panels Using Direct Power Control. In Fekik, A., & Benamrouche, N. (Eds.), *Modeling and Control of Static Converters for Hybrid Storage Systems* (pp. 107–142). IGI Global. https://doi.org/10.4018/978-1-7998-7447-8.ch005

Ferro, G., Minciardi, R., Parodi, L., & Robba, M. (2022). Optimal Charging Management of Microgrid-Integrated Electric Vehicles. In Alam, M., Pillai, R., & Murugesan, N. (Eds.), *Developing Charging Infrastructure and Technologies for Electric Vehicles* (pp. 133–155). IGI Global. https://doi.org/10.4018/978-1-7998-6858-3.ch007

Fisher, R. L. (2018). Computer-Assisted Indian Matrimonial Services. In M. Khosrow-Pour, D.B.A. (Ed.), *Encyclopedia of Information Science and Technology, Fourth Edition* (pp. 4136-4145). Hershey, PA: IGI Global. DOI: 10.4018/978-1-5225-2255-3.ch358

Flumerfelt, S., & Green, C. (2022). Graduate Lean Leadership Education: A Case Study of a Program. In Alves, A., & van Hattum-Janssen, N. (Eds.), *Training Engineering Students for Modern Technological Advancement* (pp. 202–224). IGI Global. https://doi.org/10.4018/978-1-7998-8816-1.ch010

Galiautdinov, R. (2021). Nonlinear Filtering in Artificial Neural Network Applications in Business and Engineering. In Do, Q. (Ed.), *Artificial Neural Network Applications in Business and Engineering* (pp. 1–23). IGI Global. https://doi.org/10.4018/978-1-7998-3238-6.ch001

Gardner-McCune, C., & Jimenez, Y. (2017). Historical App Developers: Integrating CS into K-12 through Cross-Disciplinary Projects. In Rankin, Y., & Thomas, J. (Eds.), *Moving Students of Color from Consumers to Producers of Technology* (pp. 85–112). Hershey, PA: IGI Global. DOI: 10.4018/978-1-5225-2005-4.ch005

Garg, P. K. (2021). The Internet of Things-Based Technologies. In Kumar, S., Trivedi, M., Ranjan, P., & Punhani, A. (Eds.), *Evolution of Software-Defined Networking Foundations for IoT and 5G Mobile Networks* (pp. 37–65). IGI Global. https://doi.org/10.4018/978-1-7998-4685-7.ch003

Garg, T., & Bharti, M. (2021). Congestion Control Protocols for UWSNs. In Goyal, N., Sapra, L., & Sandhu, J. (Eds.), *Energy-Efficient Underwater Wireless Communications and Networking* (pp. 85–100). IGI Global. https://doi.org/10.4018/978-1-7998-3640-7.ch006

Gento, A. M., Pimentel, C., & Pascual, J. A. (2022). Teaching Circular Economy and Lean Management in a Learning Factory. In Alves, A., & van Hattum-Janssen, N. (Eds.), *Training Engineering Students for Modern Technological Advancement* (pp. 183–201). IGI Global. https://doi.org/10.4018/978-1-7998-8816-1.ch009

Ghafele, R., & Gibert, B. (2018). Open Growth: The Economic Impact of Open Source Software in the USA. In Khosrow-Pour, M. (Ed.), *Optimizing Contemporary Application and Processes in Open Source Software* (pp. 164–197). Hershey, PA: IGI Global. DOI: 10.4018/978-1-5225-5314-4.ch007

Ghosh, S., Mitra, S., Ghosh, S., & Chakraborty, S. (2017). Seismic Reliability Analysis in the Framework of Metamodelling Based Monte Carlo Simulation. In Samui, P., Chakraborty, S., & Kim, D. (Eds.), *Modeling and Simulation Techniques in Structural Engineering* (pp. 192–208). Hershey, PA: IGI Global. DOI: 10.4018/978-1-5225-0588-4.ch006

Gikandi, J. W. (2017). Computer-Supported Collaborative Learning and Assessment: A Strategy for Developing Online Learning Communities in Continuing Education. In Keengwe, J., & Onchwari, G. (Eds.), *Handbook of Research on Learner-Centered Pedagogy in Teacher Education and Professional Development* (pp. 309–333). Hershey, PA: IGI Global. DOI: 10.4018/978-1-5225-0892-2.ch017

Gil, M., & Otero, B. (2017). Learning Engineering Skills through Creativity and Collaboration: A Game-Based Proposal. In Alexandre Peixoto de Queirós, R., & Pinto, M. (Eds.), *Gamification-Based E-Learning Strategies for Computer Programming Education* (pp. 14–29). Hershey, PA: IGI Global. DOI: 10.4018/978-1-5225-1034-5.ch002

Gill, J., Ayre, M., & Mills, J. (2017). Revisioning the Engineering Profession: How to Make It Happen! In Gray, M., & Thomas, K. (Eds.), *Strategies for Increasing Diversity in Engineering Majors and Careers* (pp. 156–175). Hershey, PA: IGI Global. DOI: 10.4018/978-1-5225-2212-6.ch008

Gokhale, A. A., & Machina, K. F. (2017). Development of a Scale to Measure Attitudes toward Information Technology. In Tomei, L. (Ed.), *Exploring the New Era of Technology-Infused Education* (pp. 49–64). Hershey, PA: IGI Global. DOI: 10.4018/978-1-5225-1709-2.ch004

Gomes de Gusmão, C. M. (2022). Digital Competencies and Transformation in Higher Education: Upskilling With Extension Actions. In Alves, A., & van Hattum-Janssen, N. (Eds.), *Training Engineering Students for Modern Technological Advancement* (pp. 313–328). IGI Global. https://doi.org/10.4018/978-1-7998-8816-1.ch015A

Goyal, N., Ram, M., & Kumar, P. (2017). Welding Process under Fault Coverage Approach for Reliability and MTTF. In Ram, M., & Davim, J. (Eds.), *Mathematical Concepts and Applications in Mechanical Engineering and Mechatronics* (pp. 222–245). Hershey, PA: IGI Global. DOI: 10.4018/978-1-5225-1639-2.ch011

Gray, M., & Lundy, C. (2017). Engineering Study Abroad: High Impact Strategy for Increasing Access. In Gray, M., & Thomas, K. (Eds.), *Strategies for Increasing Diversity in Engineering Majors and Careers* (pp. 42–59). Hershey, PA: IGI Global. DOI: 10.4018/978-1-5225-2212-6.ch003

Güler, O., & Varol, T. (2021). Fabrication of Functionally Graded Metal and Ceramic Powders Synthesized by Electroless Deposition. In Roy, S., & Bose, G. (Eds.), *Advanced Surface Coating Techniques for Modern Industrial Applications* (pp. 150–187). IGI Global. https://doi.org/10.4018/978-1-7998-4870-7.ch007

Guraksin, G. E. (2018). Internet of Things and Nature-Inspired Intelligent Techniques for the Future of Biomedical Engineering. In Kose, U., Guraksin, G., & Deperlioglu, O. (Eds.), *Nature-Inspired Intelligent Techniques for Solving Biomedical Engineering Problems* (pp. 263–282). Hershey, PA: IGI Global. DOI: 10.4018/978-1-5225-4769-3.ch013

Hafeez-Baig, A., Gururajan, R., & Wickramasinghe, N. (2017). Readiness as a Novel Construct of Readiness Acceptance Model (RAM) for the Wireless Handheld Technology. In Wickramasinghe, N. (Ed.), *Handbook of Research on Healthcare Administration and Management* (pp. 578–595). Hershey, PA: IGI Global. DOI: 10.4018/978-1-5225-0920-2.ch035

Hamida, M. L., Fekik, A., Denoun, H., Ardjal, A., & Bokhtache, A. A. (2022). Flying Capacitor Inverter Integration in a Renewable Energy System. In Fekik, A., & Benamrouche, N. (Eds.), *Modeling and Control of Static Converters for Hybrid Storage Systems* (pp. 287–306). IGI Global. https://doi.org/10.4018/978-1-7998 -7447-8.ch011

Haseski, H. İ., Ilic, U., & Tuğtekin, U. (2018). Computational Thinking in Educational Digital Games: An Assessment Tool Proposal. In Ozcinar, H., Wong, G., & Ozturk, H. (Eds.), *Teaching Computational Thinking in Primary Education* (pp. 256–287). Hershey, PA: IGI Global. DOI: 10.4018/978-1-5225-3200-2.ch013

Hejazi, T., & Akbari, L. (2017). A Multiresponse Optimization Model for Statistical Design of Processes with Discrete Variables. In Ram, M., & Davim, J. (Eds.), *Mathematical Concepts and Applications in Mechanical Engineering and Mechatronics* (pp. 17–37). Hershey, PA: IGI Global. DOI: 10.4018/978-1-5225-1639-2.ch002

Hejazi, T., & Hejazi, A. (2017). Monte Carlo Simulation for Reliability-Based Design of Automotive Complex Subsystems. In Ram, M., & Davim, J. (Eds.), *Mathematical Concepts and Applications in Mechanical Engineering and Mechatronics* (pp. 177–200). Hershey, PA: IGI Global. DOI: 10.4018/978-1-5225-1639-2.ch009

Hejazi, T., & Poursabbagh, H. (2017). Reliability Analysis of Engineering Systems: An Accelerated Life Testing for Boiler Tubes. In Ram, M., & Davim, J. (Eds.), *Mathematical Concepts and Applications in Mechanical Engineering and Mechatronics* (pp. 154–176). Hershey, PA: IGI Global. DOI: 10.4018/978-1-5225-1639-2.ch008

Henao, J., & Sotelo, O. (2018). Surface Engineering at High Temperature: Thermal Cycling and Corrosion Resistance. In Pakseresht, A. (Ed.), *Production, Properties, and Applications of High Temperature Coatings* (pp. 131–159). Hershey, PA: IGI Global. DOI: 10.4018/978-1-5225-4194-3.ch006

Henao, J., Poblano-Salas, C. A., Vargas, F., Giraldo-Betancur, A. L., Corona-Castuera, J., & Sotelo-Mazón, O. (2021). Principles and Applications of Thermal Spray Coatings. In Roy, S., & Bose, G. (Eds.), *Advanced Surface Coating Techniques for Modern Industrial Applications* (pp. 31–70). IGI Global. https://doi.org/10.4018/ 978-1-7998-4870-7.ch002

Hirota, A. (2021). Design of Narrative Creation in Innovation: "Signature Story" and Two Types of Pivots. In Ogata, T., & Ono, J. (Eds.), *Bridging the Gap Between AI, Cognitive Science, and Narratology With Narrative Generation* (pp. 363–376). IGI Global. https://doi.org/10.4018/978-1-7998-4864-6.ch012

Horne-Popp, L. M., Tessone, E. B., & Welker, J. (2018). If You Build It, They Will Come: Creating a Library Statistics Dashboard for Decision-Making. In Costello, L., & Powers, M. (Eds.), *Developing In-House Digital Tools in Library Spaces* (pp. 177–203). Hershey, PA: IGI Global. DOI: 10.4018/978-1-5225-2676-6.ch009

Hrnčič, M. K., Cör, D., & Knez, Ž. (2021). Supercritical Fluids as a Tool for Green Energy and Chemicals. In Chen, L. (Ed.), *Handbook of Research on Advancements in Supercritical Fluids Applications for Sustainable Energy Systems* (pp. 761–791). IGI Global. DOI: 10.4018/978-1-7998-5796-9.ch021

Hu, H., Hu, P. J., & Al-Gahtani, S. S. (2017). User Acceptance of Computer Technology at Work in Arabian Culture: A Model Comparison Approach. In Khosrow-Pour, M. (Ed.), *Handbook of Research on Technology Adoption, Social Policy, and Global Integration* (pp. 205–228). Hershey, PA: IGI Global. DOI: 10.4018/978-1-5225-2668-1.ch011

Ibrahim, O., Erdem, S., & Gurbuz, E. (2021). Studying Physical and Chemical Properties of Graphene Oxide and Reduced Graphene Oxide and Their Applications in Sustainable Building Materials. In González-Lezcano, R. (Ed.), *Advancements in Sustainable Architecture and Energy Efficiency* (pp. 221–238). IGI Global. https://doi.org/10.4018/978-1-7998-7023-4.ch010

Ihianle, I. K., Islam, S., Naeem, U., & Ebenuwa, S. H. (2021). Exploiting Patterns of Object Use for Human Activity Recognition. In Nwajana, A., & Ihianle, I. (Eds.), *Handbook of Research on 5G Networks and Advancements in Computing, Electronics, and Electrical Engineering* (pp. 382–401). IGI Global. https://doi.org/10.4018/978-1-7998-6992-4.ch015

Ijemaru, G. K., Ngharamike, E. T., Oleka, E. U., & Nwajana, A. O. (2021). An Energy-Efficient Model for Opportunistic Data Collection in IoV-Enabled SC Waste Management. In Nwajana, A., & Ihianle, I. (Eds.), *Handbook of Research on 5G Networks and Advancements in Computing, Electronics, and Electrical Engineering* (pp. 1–19). IGI Global. https://doi.org/10.4018/978-1-7998-6992-4.ch001

Islam, A. Y. (2017). Technology Satisfaction in an Academic Context: Moderating Effect of Gender. In Mesquita, A. (Ed.), *Research Paradigms and Contemporary Perspectives on Human-Technology Interaction* (pp. 187–211). Hershey, PA: IGI Global. DOI: 10.4018/978-1-5225-1868-6.ch009

Iwamoto, Y., & Yamaguchi, H. (2021). Application of Supercritical Carbon Dioxide for Solar Water Heater. In Chen, L. (Ed.), *Handbook of Research on Advancements in Supercritical Fluids Applications for Sustainable Energy Systems* (pp. 370–387). IGI Global. https://doi.org/10.4018/978-1-7998-5796-9.ch010

Jamil, G. L., & Jamil, C. C. (2017). Information and Knowledge Management Perspective Contributions for Fashion Studies: Observing Logistics and Supply Chain Management Processes. In Jamil, G., Soares, A., & Pessoa, C. (Eds.), *Handbook of Research on Information Management for Effective Logistics and Supply Chains* (pp. 199–221). Hershey, PA: IGI Global. DOI: 10.4018/978-1-5225-0973-8.ch011

Janakova, M. (2018). Big Data and Simulations for the Solution of Controversies in Small Businesses. In M. Khosrow-Pour, D.B.A. (Ed.), *Encyclopedia of Information Science and Technology, Fourth Edition* (pp. 6907-6915). Hershey, PA: IGI Global. DOI: 10.4018/978-1-5225-2255-3.ch598

Jayapalan, S. (2018). A Review of Chemical Treatments on Natural Fibers-Based Hybrid Composites for Engineering Applications. In Kumar, K., & Davim, J. (Eds.), *Composites and Advanced Materials for Industrial Applications* (pp. 16–37). Hershey, PA: IGI Global. DOI: 10.4018/978-1-5225-5216-1.ch002

Jhawar, A., & Garg, S. K. (2018). Logistics Improvement by Investment in Information Technology Using System Dynamics. In Azar, A., & Vaidyanathan, S. (Eds.), *Advances in System Dynamics and Control* (pp. 528–567). Hershey, PA: IGI Global. DOI: 10.4018/978-1-5225-4077-9.ch017

Kalelioğlu, F., Gülbahar, Y., & Doğan, D. (2018). Teaching How to Think Like a Programmer: Emerging Insights. In Ozcinar, H., Wong, G., & Ozturk, H. (Eds.), *Teaching Computational Thinking in Primary Education* (pp. 18–35). Hershey, PA: IGI Global. DOI: 10.4018/978-1-5225-3200-2.ch002

Kamberi, S. (2017). A Girls-Only Online Virtual World Environment and its Implications for Game-Based Learning. In Stricker, A., Calongne, C., Truman, B., & Arenas, F. (Eds.), *Integrating an Awareness of Selfhood and Society into Virtual Learning* (pp. 74–95). Hershey, PA: IGI Global. DOI: 10.4018/978-1-5225-2182-2.ch006

Kamel, S. H. (2018). The Potential Role of the Software Industry in Supporting Economic Development. In M. Khosrow-Pour, D.B.A. (Ed.), *Encyclopedia of Information Science and Technology, Fourth Edition* (pp. 7259-7269). Hershey, PA: IGI Global. DOI: 10.4018/978-1-5225-2255-3.ch631

Kamel, S., & Rizk, N. (2017). ICT Strategy Development: From Design to Implementation – Case of Egypt. In Howard, C., & Hargiss, K. (Eds.), *Strategic Information Systems and Technologies in Modern Organizations* (pp. 239–257). Hershey, PA: IGI Global. DOI: 10.4018/978-1-5225-1680-4.ch010

Kapetanakis, T. N., Vardiambasis, I. O., Ioannidou, M. P., & Konstantaras, A. I. (2021). Modeling Antenna Radiation Using Artificial Intelligence Techniques: The Case of a Circular Loop Antenna. In Nikolopoulos, C. (Ed.), *Recent Trends on Electromagnetic Environmental Effects for Aeronautics and Space Applications* (pp. 186–225). IGI Global. https://doi.org/10.4018/978-1-7998-4879-0.ch007

Karas, V., & Schuller, B. W. (2021). Deep Learning for Sentiment Analysis: An Overview and Perspectives. In Pinarbasi, F., & Taskiran, M. (Eds.), *Natural Language Processing for Global and Local Business* (pp. 97–132). IGI Global. https://doi.org/10.4018/978-1-7998-4240-8.ch005

Kaufman, L. M. (2022). Reimagining the Magic of the Workshop Model. In Driscoll, T.III, (Ed.), *Designing Effective Distance and Blended Learning Environments in K-12* (pp. 89–109). IGI Global. https://doi.org/10.4018/978-1-7998-6829-3.ch007

Kawata, S. (2018). Computer-Assisted Parallel Program Generation. In M. Khosrow-Pour, D.B.A. (Ed.), *Encyclopedia of Information Science and Technology, Fourth Edition* (pp. 4583-4593). Hershey, PA: IGI Global. DOI: 10.4018/978-1-5225-2255-3.ch398

Kelly, M., Costello, M., Nicholson, G., & O'Connor, J. (2021). The Evolving Integration of BIM Into Built Environment Programmes in a Higher Education Institute. In Underwood, J., & Shelbourn, M. (Eds.), *Handbook of Research on Driving Transformational Change in the Digital Built Environment* (pp. 294–326). IGI Global. https://doi.org/10.4018/978-1-7998-6600-8.ch012

Kesimal, A., Karaman, K., Cihangir, F., & Ercikdi, B. (2018). Excavatability Assessment of Rock Masses for Geotechnical Studies. In Ceryan, N. (Ed.), *Handbook of Research on Trends and Digital Advances in Engineering Geology* (pp. 231–256). Hershey, PA: IGI Global. DOI: 10.4018/978-1-5225-2709-1.ch006

Khari, M., Shrivastava, G., Gupta, S., & Gupta, R. (2017). Role of Cyber Security in Today's Scenario. In Kumar, R., Pattnaik, P., & Pandey, P. (Eds.), *Detecting and Mitigating Robotic Cyber Security Risks* (pp. 177–191). Hershey, PA: IGI Global. DOI: 10.4018/978-1-5225-2154-9.ch013

Knoflacher, H. (2017). The Role of Engineers and Their Tools in the Transport Sector after Paradigm Change: From Assumptions and Extrapolations to Science. In Knoflacher, H., & Ocalir-Akunal, E. (Eds.), *Engineering Tools and Solutions for Sustainable Transportation Planning* (pp. 1–29). Hershey, PA: IGI Global. DOI: 10.4018/978-1-5225-2116-7.ch001

Köse, U. (2017). An Augmented-Reality-Based Intelligent Mobile Application for Open Computer Education. In Kurubacak, G., & Altinpulluk, H. (Eds.), *Mobile Technologies and Augmented Reality in Open Education* (pp. 154–174). Hershey, PA: IGI Global. DOI: 10.4018/978-1-5225-2110-5.ch008

Kose, U. (2018). Towards an Intelligent Biomedical Engineering With Nature-Inspired Artificial Intelligence Techniques. In Kose, U., Guraksin, G., & Deperlioglu, O. (Eds.), *Nature-Inspired Intelligent Techniques for Solving Biomedical Engineering Problems* (pp. 1–26). Hershey, PA: IGI Global. DOI: 10.4018/978-1-5225-4769-3.ch001

Kostić, S. (2018). A Review on Enhanced Stability Analyses of Soil Slopes Using Statistical Design. In Ceryan, N. (Ed.), *Handbook of Research on Trends and Digital Advances in Engineering Geology* (pp. 446–481). Hershey, PA: IGI Global. DOI: 10.4018/978-1-5225-2709-1.ch013

Kumar, N., Basu, D. N., & Chen, L. (2021). Effect of Flow Acceleration and Buoyancy on Thermalhydraulics of sCO2 in Mini/Micro-Channel. In Chen, L. (Ed.), *Handbook of Research on Advancements in Supercritical Fluids Applications for Sustainable Energy Systems* (pp. 161–182). IGI Global. DOI: 10.4018/978-1-7998-5796-9.ch005

Kumari, N., & Kumar, K. (2018). Fabrication of Orthotic Calipers With Epoxy-Based Green Composite. In Kumar, K., & Davim, J. (Eds.), *Composites and Advanced Materials for Industrial Applications* (pp. 157–176). Hershey, PA: IGI Global. DOI: 10.4018/978-1-5225-5216-1.ch008

Kuppusamy, R. R. (2018). Development of Aerospace Composite Structures Through Vacuum-Enhanced Resin Transfer Moulding Technology (VERTMTy): Vacuum-Enhanced Resin Transfer Moulding. In Kumar, K., & Davim, J. (Eds.), *Composites and Advanced Materials for Industrial Applications* (pp. 99–111). Hershey, PA: IGI Global. DOI: 10.4018/978-1-5225-5216-1.ch005

Kurganov, V. A., Zeigarnik, Y. A., & Maslakova, I. V. (2021). Normal and Deteriorated Heat Transfer Under Heating Turbulent Supercritical Pressure Coolants Flows in Round Tubes. In Chen, L. (Ed.), *Handbook of Research on Advancements in Supercritical Fluids Applications for Sustainable Energy Systems* (pp. 494–532). IGI Global. https://doi.org/10.4018/978-1-7998-5796-9.ch014

Lahmiri, S. (2018). Information Technology Outsourcing Risk Factors and Provider Selection. In Gupta, M., Sharman, R., Walp, J., & Mulgund, P. (Eds.), *Information Technology Risk Management and Compliance in Modern Organizations* (pp. 214–228). Hershey, PA: IGI Global. DOI: 10.4018/978-1-5225-2604-9.ch008

Landriscina, F. (2017). Computer-Supported Imagination: The Interplay Between Computer and Mental Simulation in Understanding Scientific Concepts. In Levin, I., & Tsybulsky, D. (Eds.), *Digital Tools and Solutions for Inquiry-Based STEM Learning* (pp. 33–60). Hershey, PA: IGI Global. DOI: 10.4018/978-1-5225-2525-7.ch002

Lara López, G. (2021). Virtual Reality in Object Location. In Negrón, A., & Muñoz, M. (Eds.), *Latin American Women and Research Contributions to the IT Field* (pp. 307–324). IGI Global. https://doi.org/10.4018/978-1-7998-7552-9.ch014

Lee, W. W. (2018). Ethical Computing Continues From Problem to Solution. In M. Khosrow-Pour, D.B.A. (Ed.), *Encyclopedia of Information Science and Technology, Fourth Edition* (pp. 4884-4897). Hershey, PA: IGI Global. DOI: 10.4018/978-1-5225-2255-3.ch423

Li, H., & Zhang, Y. (2021). Heat Transfer and Fluid Flow Modeling for Supercritical Fluids in Advanced Energy Systems. In Chen, L. (Ed.), *Handbook of Research on Advancements in Supercritical Fluids Applications for Sustainable Energy Systems* (pp. 388–422). IGI Global. https://doi.org/10.4018/978-1-7998-5796-9.ch011

Loy, J., Howell, S., & Cooper, R. (2017). Engineering Teams: Supporting Diversity in Engineering Education. In Gray, M., & Thomas, K. (Eds.), *Strategies for Increasing Diversity in Engineering Majors and Careers* (pp. 106–129). Hershey, PA: IGI Global. DOI: 10.4018/978-1-5225-2212-6.ch006

Mabe, L. K., & Oladele, O. I. (2017). Application of Information Communication Technologies for Agricultural Development through Extension Services: A Review. In Tossy, T. (Ed.), *Information Technology Integration for Socio-Economic Development* (pp. 52–101). Hershey, PA: IGI Global. DOI: 10.4018/978-1-5225-0539-6.ch003

Macher, G., Armengaud, E., Kreiner, C., Brenner, E., Schmittner, C., Ma, Z., & Krammer, M. (2018). Integration of Security in the Development Lifecycle of Dependable Automotive CPS. In Druml, N., Genser, A., Krieg, A., Menghin, M., & Hoeller, A. (Eds.), *Solutions for Cyber-Physical Systems Ubiquity* (pp. 383–423). Hershey, PA: IGI Global. DOI: 10.4018/978-1-5225-2845-6.ch015

Mahboub, S. A., Sayed Ali Ahmed, E., & Saeed, R. A. (2021). Smart IDS and IPS for Cyber-Physical Systems. In Luhach, A., & Elçi, A. (Eds.), *Artificial Intelligence Paradigms for Smart Cyber-Physical Systems* (pp. 109–136). IGI Global. https://doi.org/10.4018/978-1-7998-5101-1.ch006

Makropoulos, G., Koumaras, H., Setaki, F., Filis, K., Lutz, T., Montowtt, P., Tomaszewski, L., Dybiec, P., & Järvet, T. (2021). 5G and Unmanned Aerial Vehicles (UAVs) Use Cases: Analysis of the Ecosystem, Architecture, and Applications. In Nwajana, A., & Ihianle, I. (Eds.), *Handbook of Research on 5G Networks and Advancements in Computing, Electronics, and Electrical Engineering* (pp. 36–69). IGI Global. https://doi.org/10.4018/978-1-7998-6992-4.ch003

Manogaran, G., Thota, C., & Lopez, D. (2018). Human-Computer Interaction With Big Data Analytics. In Lopez, D., & Durai, M. (Eds.), *HCI Challenges and Privacy Preservation in Big Data Security* (pp. 1–22). Hershey, PA: IGI Global. DOI: 10.4018/978-1-5225-2863-0.ch001

Margolis, J., Goode, J., & Flapan, J. (2017). A Critical Crossroads for Computer Science for All: "Identifying Talent" or "Building Talent," and What Difference Does It Make? In Rankin, Y., & Thomas, J. (Eds.), *Moving Students of Color from Consumers to Producers of Technology* (pp. 1–23). Hershey, PA: IGI Global. DOI: 10.4018/978-1-5225-2005-4.ch001

Mazzù, M. F., Benetton, A., Baccelloni, A., & Lavini, L. (2022). A Milk Blockchain-Enabled Supply Chain: Evidence From Leading Italian Farms. In De Giovanni, P. (Ed.), *Blockchain Technology Applications in Businesses and Organizations* (pp. 73–98). IGI Global. https://doi.org/10.4018/978-1-7998-8014-1.ch004

Mbale, J. (2018). Computer Centres Resource Cloud Elasticity-Scalability (CRECES): Copperbelt University Case Study. In Aljawarneh, S., & Malhotra, M. (Eds.), *Critical Research on Scalability and Security Issues in Virtual Cloud Environments* (pp. 48–70). Hershey, PA: IGI Global. DOI: 10.4018/978-1-5225-3029-9.ch003

McKee, J. (2018). The Right Information: The Key to Effective Business Planning. In *Business Architectures for Risk Assessment and Strategic Planning: Emerging Research and Opportunities* (pp. 38–52). Hershey, PA: IGI Global. DOI: 10.4018/978-1-5225-3392-4.ch003

Meric, E. M., Erdem, S., & Gurbuz, E. (2021). Application of Phase Change Materials in Construction Materials for Thermal Energy Storage Systems in Buildings. In González-Lezcano, R. (Ed.), *Advancements in Sustainable Architecture and Energy Efficiency* (pp. 1–20). IGI Global. https://doi.org/10.4018/978-1-7998-7023-4.ch001

Mir, M. A., Bhat, B. A., Sheikh, B. A., Rather, G. A., Mehraj, S., & Mir, W. R. (2021). Nanomedicine in Human Health Therapeutics and Drug Delivery: Nanobiotechnology and Nanobiomedicine. In Bhat, M., Wani, I., & Ashraf, S. (Eds.), *Applications of Nanomaterials in Agriculture, Food Science, and Medicine* (pp. 229–251). IGI Global. DOI: 10.4018/978-1-7998-5563-7.ch013

Mohamed, J. H. (2018). Scientograph-Based Visualization of Computer Forensics Research Literature. In Jeyasekar, J., & Saravanan, P. (Eds.), *Innovations in Measuring and Evaluating Scientific Information* (pp. 148–162). Hershey, PA: IGI Global. DOI: 10.4018/978-1-5225-3457-0.ch010

Mohammadzadeh, S., & Kim, Y. (2017). Nonlinear System Identification of Smart Buildings. In Samui, P., Chakraborty, S., & Kim, D. (Eds.), *Modeling and Simulation Techniques in Structural Engineering* (pp. 328–347). Hershey, PA: IGI Global. DOI: 10.4018/978-1-5225-0588-4.ch011

Moreno-Rangel, A., & Carrillo, G. (2021). Energy-Efficient Homes: A Heaven for Respiratory Illnesses. In González-Lezcano, R. (Ed.), *Advancements in Sustainable Architecture and Energy Efficiency* (pp. 49–71). IGI Global. https://doi.org/10.4018/978-1-7998-7023-4.ch003

Muigai, M. N., Mwema, F. M., Akinlabi, E. T., & Obiko, J. O. (2021). Surface Engineering of Materials Through Weld-Based Technologies: An Overview. In Roy, S., & Bose, G. (Eds.), *Advanced Surface Coating Techniques for Modern Industrial Applications* (pp. 247–260). IGI Global. DOI: 10.4018/978-1-7998-4870-7.ch011

Mukherjee, A., Saeed, R. A., Dutta, S., & Naskar, M. K. (2017). Fault Tracking Framework for Software-Defined Networking (SDN). In Singhal, C., & De, S. (Eds.), *Resource Allocation in Next-Generation Broadband Wireless Access Networks* (pp. 247–272). Hershey, PA: IGI Global. DOI: 10.4018/978-1-5225-2023-8.ch011

Mukhopadhyay, A., Barman, T. K., & Sahoo, P. (2018). Electroless Nickel Coatings for High Temperature Applications. In Kumar, K., & Davim, J. (Eds.), *Composites and Advanced Materials for Industrial Applications* (pp. 297–331). Hershey, PA: IGI Global. DOI: 10.4018/978-1-5225-5216-1.ch013

Mukul, M. K., & Bhattaharyya, S. (2017). Brain-Machine Interface: Human-Computer Interaction. In Noughabi, E., Raahemi, B., Albadvi, A., & Far, B. (Eds.), *Handbook of Research on Data Science for Effective Healthcare Practice and Administration* (pp. 417–443). Hershey, PA: IGI Global. DOI: 10.4018/978-1-5225-2515-8.ch018

Mwema, F. M., & Wambua, J. M. (2022). Machining of Poly Methyl Methacrylate (PMMA) and Other Olymeric Materials: A Review. In Kumar, K., Babu, B., & Davim, J. (Eds.), *Handbook of Research on Advancements in the Processing, Characterization, and Application of Lightweight Materials* (pp. 363–379). IGI Global. https://doi.org/10.4018/978-1-7998-7864-3.ch016

Na, L. (2017). Library and Information Science Education and Graduate Programs in Academic Libraries. In Ruan, L., Zhu, Q., & Ye, Y. (Eds.), *Academic Library Development and Administration in China* (pp. 218–229). Hershey, PA: IGI Global. DOI: 10.4018/978-1-5225-0550-1.ch013

Nagpal, G., Bishnoi, G. K., Dhami, H. S., & Vijayvargia, A. (2021). Use of Data Analytics to Increase the Efficiency of Last Mile Logistics for Ecommerce Deliveries. In Patil, B., & Vohra, M. (Eds.), *Handbook of Research on Engineering, Business, and Healthcare Applications of Data Science and Analytics* (pp. 167–180). IGI Global. https://doi.org/10.4018/978-1-7998-3053-5.ch009

Nair, S. M., Ramesh, V., & Tyagi, A. K. (2021). Issues and Challenges (Privacy, Security, and Trust) in Blockchain-Based Applications. In Tyagi, A., Rekha, G., & Sreenath, N. (Eds.), *Opportunities and Challenges for Blockchain Technology in Autonomous Vehicles* (pp. 196–209). IGI Global. https://doi.org/10.4018/978-1-7998-3295-9.ch012

Náprstek, J., & Fischer, C. (2017). Dynamic Stability and Post-Critical Processes of Slender Auto-Parametric Systems. In Plevris, V., Kremmyda, G., & Fahjan, Y. (Eds.), *Performance-Based Seismic Design of Concrete Structures and Infrastructures* (pp. 128–171). Hershey, PA: IGI Global. DOI: 10.4018/978-1-5225-2089-4.ch006

Nath, R., & Murthy, V. N. (2018). What Accounts for the Differences in Internet Diffusion Rates Around the World? In M. Khosrow-Pour, D.B.A. (Ed.), *Encyclopedia of Information Science and Technology, Fourth Edition* (pp. 8095-8104). Hershey, PA: IGI Global. https://doi.org/DOI: 10.4018/978-1-5225-2255-3.ch705

Nautiyal, L., Shivach, P., & Ram, M. (2018). Optimal Designs by Means of Genetic Algorithms. In Ram, M., & Davim, J. (Eds.), *Soft Computing Techniques and Applications in Mechanical Engineering* (pp. 151–161). Hershey, PA: IGI Global. DOI: 10.4018/978-1-5225-3035-0.ch007

Nazir, R. (2017). Advanced Nanomaterials for Water Engineering and Treatment: Nano-Metal Oxides and Their Nanocomposites. In Saleh, T. (Ed.), *Advanced Nanomaterials for Water Engineering, Treatment, and Hydraulics* (pp. 84–126). Hershey, PA: IGI Global. DOI: 10.4018/978-1-5225-2136-5.ch005

Nedelko, Z., & Potocan, V. (2018). The Role of Emerging Information Technologies for Supporting Supply Chain Management. In M. Khosrow-Pour, D.B.A. (Ed.), *Encyclopedia of Information Science and Technology, Fourth Edition* (pp. 5559-5569). Hershey, PA: IGI Global. DOI: 10.4018/978-1-5225-2255-3.ch483

Negrini, L., Giang, C., & Bonnet, E. (2022). Designing Tools and Activities for Educational Robotics in Online Learning. In Eteokleous, N., & Nisiforou, E. (Eds.), *Designing, Constructing, and Programming Robots for Learning* (pp. 202–222). IGI Global. https://doi.org/10.4018/978-1-7998-7443-0.ch010

Ngafeeson, M. N. (2018). User Resistance to Health Information Technology. In M. Khosrow-Pour, D.B.A. (Ed.), *Encyclopedia of Information Science and Technology, Fourth Edition* (pp. 3816-3825). Hershey, PA: IGI Global. DOI: 10.4018/978-1-5225-2255-3.ch331

Nikolopoulos, C. D. (2021). Recent Advances on Measuring and Modeling ELF-Radiated Emissions for Space Applications. In Nikolopoulos, C. (Ed.), *Recent Trends on Electromagnetic Environmental Effects for Aeronautics and Space Applications* (pp. 1–38). IGI Global. https://doi.org/10.4018/978-1-7998-4879-0.ch001

Nogueira, A. F., Ribeiro, J. C., Fernández de Vega, F., & Zenha-Rela, M. A. (2018). Evolutionary Approaches to Test Data Generation for Object-Oriented Software: Overview of Techniques and Tools. In M. Khosrow-Pour, D.B.A. (Ed.), *Incorporating Nature-Inspired Paradigms in Computational Applications* (pp. 162-194). Hershey, PA: IGI Global. https://doi.org/DOI: 10.4018/978-1-5225-5020-4.ch006

Nwajana, A. O., Obi, E. R., Ijemaru, G. K., Oleka, E. U., & Anthony, D. C. (2021). Fundamentals of RF/Microwave Bandpass Filter Design. In Nwajana, A., & Ihianle, I. (Eds.), *Handbook of Research on 5G Networks and Advancements in Computing, Electronics, and Electrical Engineering* (pp. 149–164). IGI Global. https://doi.org/10.4018/978-1-7998-6992-4.ch005

Odagiri, K. (2017). Introduction of Individual Technology to Constitute the Current Internet. In *Strategic Policy-Based Network Management in Contemporary Organizations* (pp. 20–96). Hershey, PA: IGI Global. DOI: 10.4018/978-1-68318-003-6.ch003

Odia, J. O., & Akpata, O. T. (2021). Role of Data Science and Data Analytics in Forensic Accounting and Fraud Detection. In Patil, B., & Vohra, M. (Eds.), *Handbook of Research on Engineering, Business, and Healthcare Applications of Data Science and Analytics* (pp. 203–227). IGI Global. https://doi.org/10.4018/978-1-7998-3053-5.ch011

Ogbodo, E. A. (2021). Comparative Study of Transmission Line Junction vs. Asynchronously Coupled Junction Diplexers. In Nwajana, A., & Ihianle, I. (Eds.), *Handbook of Research on 5G Networks and Advancements in Computing, Electronics, and Electrical Engineering* (pp. 326–336). IGI Global. https://doi.org/10.4018/978-1-7998-6992-4.ch013

Okike, E. U. (2018). Computer Science and Prison Education. In Biao, I. (Ed.), *Strategic Learning Ideologies in Prison Education Programs* (pp. 246–264). Hershey, PA: IGI Global. DOI: 10.4018/978-1-5225-2909-5.ch012

Olelewe, C. J., & Nwafor, I. P. (2017). Level of Computer Appreciation Skills Acquired for Sustainable Development by Secondary School Students in Nsukka LGA of Enugu State, Nigeria. In Ayo, C., & Mbarika, V. (Eds.), *Sustainable ICT Adoption and Integration for Socio-Economic Development* (pp. 214–233). Hershey, PA: IGI Global. DOI: 10.4018/978-1-5225-2565-3.ch010

Orosa, J. A., Vergara, D., Fraguela, F., & Masdías-Bonome, A. (2021). Statistical Understanding and Optimization of Building Energy Consumption and Climate Change Consequences. In González-Lezcano, R. (Ed.), *Advancements in Sustainable Architecture and Energy Efficiency* (pp. 195–220). IGI Global. https://doi.org/10.4018/978-1-7998-7023-4.ch009

Osho, M. B. (2018). Industrial Enzyme Technology: Potential Applications. In Bharati, S., & Chaurasia, P. (Eds.), *Research Advancements in Pharmaceutical, Nutritional, and Industrial Enzymology* (pp. 375–394). Hershey, PA: IGI Global. DOI: 10.4018/978-1-5225-5237-6.ch017

Otunla, A. O., & Amuda, C. O. (2018). Nigerian Undergraduate Students' Computer Competencies and Use of Information Technology Tools and Resources for Study Skills and Habits' Enhancement. In M. Khosrow-Pour, D.B.A. (Ed.), *Encyclopedia of Information Science and Technology, Fourth Edition* (pp. 2303-2313). Hershey, PA: IGI Global. https://doi.org/DOI: 10.4018/978-1-5225-2255-3.ch200

Ouadi, A., & Zitouni, A. (2021). Phasor Measurement Improvement Using Digital Filter in a Smart Grid. In Recioui, A., & Bentarzi, H. (Eds.), *Optimizing and Measuring Smart Grid Operation and Control* (pp. 100–117). IGI Global. https://doi.org/10.4018/978-1-7998-4027-5.ch005

Özçınar, H. (2018). A Brief Discussion on Incentives and Barriers to Computational Thinking Education. In Ozcinar, H., Wong, G., & Ozturk, H. (Eds.), *Teaching Computational Thinking in Primary Education* (pp. 1–17). Hershey, PA: IGI Global. DOI: 10.4018/978-1-5225-3200-2.ch001

Palmer, S., & Hall, W. (2017). An Evaluation of Group Work in First-Year Engineering Design Education. In Tucker, R. (Ed.), *Collaboration and Student Engagement in Design Education* (pp. 145–168). Hershey, PA: IGI Global. DOI: 10.4018/978-1-5225-0726-0.ch007

Pandkar, S. D., & Paatil, S. D. (2021). Big Data and Knowledge Resource Centre. In Dhamdhere, S. (Ed.), *Big Data Applications for Improving Library Services* (pp. 90–106). IGI Global. https://doi.org/10.4018/978-1-7998-3049-8.ch007

Patro, C. (2017). Impulsion of Information Technology on Human Resource Practices. In Ordóñez de Pablos, P. (Ed.), *Managerial Strategies and Solutions for Business Success in Asia* (pp. 231–254). Hershey, PA: IGI Global. DOI: 10.4018/978-1-5225-1886-0.ch013

Patro, C. S., & Raghunath, K. M. (2017). Information Technology Paraphernalia for Supply Chain Management Decisions. In Tavana, M. (Ed.), *Enterprise Information Systems and the Digitalization of Business Functions* (pp. 294–320). Hershey, PA: IGI Global. DOI: 10.4018/978-1-5225-2382-6.ch014

Paul, P. K., & Chatterjee, D. (2018). iSchools Promoting "Information Science and Technology" (IST) Domain Towards Community, Business, and Society With Contemporary Worldwide Trend and Emerging Potentialities in India. In M. Khosrow-Pour, D.B.A. (Ed.), *Encyclopedia of Information Science and Technology, Fourth Edition* (pp. 4723-4735). Hershey, PA: IGI Global. https://doi.org/DOI: 10.4018/978-1-5225-2255-3.ch410

Pavaloiu, A. (2018). Artificial Intelligence Ethics in Biomedical-Engineering-Oriented Problems. In Kose, U., Guraksin, G., & Deperlioglu, O. (Eds.), *Nature-Inspired Intelligent Techniques for Solving Biomedical Engineering Problems* (pp. 219–231). Hershey, PA: IGI Global. DOI: 10.4018/978-1-5225-4769-3.ch010

Pessoa, C. R., & Marques, M. E. (2017). Information Technology and Communication Management in Supply Chain Management. In Jamil, G., Soares, A., & Pessoa, C. (Eds.), *Handbook of Research on Information Management for Effective Logistics and Supply Chains* (pp. 23–33). Hershey, PA: IGI Global. DOI: 10.4018/978-1-5225-0973-8.ch002

Pineda, R. G. (2018). Remediating Interaction: Towards a Philosophy of Human-Computer Relationship. In Khosrow-Pour, M. (Ed.), *Enhancing Art, Culture, and Design With Technological Integration* (pp. 75–98). Hershey, PA: IGI Global. DOI: 10.4018/978-1-5225-5023-5.ch004

Pioro, I., Mahdi, M., & Popov, R. (2017). Application of Supercritical Pressures in Power Engineering. In Chen, L., & Iwamoto, Y. (Eds.), *Advanced Applications of Supercritical Fluids in Energy Systems* (pp. 404–457). Hershey, PA: IGI Global. DOI: 10.4018/978-1-5225-2047-4.ch013

Popat, J., Kakadiya, H., Tak, L., Singh, N. K., Majeed, M. A., & Mahajan, V. (2021). Reliability of Smart Grid Including Cyber Impact: A Case Study. In Singh, R., Singh, A., Dwivedi, A., & Nagabhushan, P. (Eds.), *Computational Methodologies for Electrical and Electronics Engineers* (pp. 163–174). IGI Global. https://doi.org/10.4018/978-1-7998-3327-7.ch013

Qian, Y. (2017). Computer Simulation in Higher Education: Affordances, Opportunities, and Outcomes. In Vu, P., Fredrickson, S., & Moore, C. (Eds.), *Handbook of Research on Innovative Pedagogies and Technologies for Online Learning in Higher Education* (pp. 236–262). Hershey, PA: IGI Global. DOI: 10.4018/978-1-5225-1851-8.ch011

Quiza, R., La Fé-Perdomo, I., Rivas, M., & Ramtahalsing, V. (2021). Triple Bottom Line-Focused Optimization of Oblique Turning Processes Based on Hybrid Modeling: A Study Case on AISI 1045 Steel Turning. In Burstein, L. (Ed.), *Handbook of Research on Advancements in Manufacturing, Materials, and Mechanical Engineering* (pp. 215–241). IGI Global. https://doi.org/10.4018/978-1-7998-4939-1.ch010

Rahman, N. (2018). Environmental Sustainability in the Computer Industry for Competitive Advantage. In Khosrow-Pour, M. (Ed.), *Green Computing Strategies for Competitive Advantage and Business Sustainability* (pp. 110–130). Hershey, PA: IGI Global. DOI: 10.4018/978-1-5225-5017-4.ch006

Rahmani, M. K. (2022). Blockchain Technology: Principles and Algorithms. In Khan, S., Syed, M., Hammad, R., & Bushager, A. (Eds.), *Blockchain Technology and Computational Excellence for Society 5.0* (pp. 16–27). IGI Global. https://doi.org/10.4018/978-1-7998-8382-1.ch002

Raman, A., & Goyal, D. P. (2017). Extending IMPLEMENT Framework for Enterprise Information Systems Implementation to Information System Innovation. In Tavana, M. (Ed.), *Enterprise Information Systems and the Digitalization of Business Functions* (pp. 137–177). Hershey, PA: IGI Global. DOI: 10.4018/978-1-5225-2382-6.ch007

Ramdani, N., & Azibi, M. (2018). Polymer Composite Materials for Microelectronics Packaging Applications: Composites for Microelectronics Packaging. In Kumar, K., & Davim, J. (Eds.), *Composites and Advanced Materials for Industrial Applications* (pp. 177–211). Hershey, PA: IGI Global. DOI: 10.4018/978-1-5225-5216-1.ch009

Rao, A. P., & Reddy, K. S. (2021). Automated Soil Residue Levels Detecting Device With IoT Interface. In Sathiyamoorthi, V., & Elci, A. (Eds.), *Challenges and Applications of Data Analytics in Social Perspectives* (Vol. S, pp. 123–135). IGI Global. https://doi.org/10.4018/978-1-7998-2566-1.ch007

Rapaport, W. J. (2018). Syntactic Semantics and the Proper Treatment of Computationalism. In Danesi, M. (Ed.), *Empirical Research on Semiotics and Visual Rhetoric* (pp. 128–176). Hershey, PA: IGI Global. DOI: 10.4018/978-1-5225-5622-0.ch007

Rezende, D. A. (2018). Strategic Digital City Projects: Innovative Information and Public Services Offered by Chicago (USA) and Curitiba (Brazil). In Lytras, M., Daniela, L., & Visvizi, A. (Eds.), *Enhancing Knowledge Discovery and Innovation in the Digital Era* (pp. 204–223). Hershey, PA: IGI Global. DOI: 10.4018/978-1-5225-4191-2.ch012

Robinson, J., & Beneroso, D. (2022). Project-Based Learning in Chemical Engineering: Curriculum and Assessment, Culture and Learning Spaces. In Alves, A., & van Hattum-Janssen, N. (Eds.), *Training Engineering Students for Modern Technological Advancement* (pp. 1–19). IGI Global. https://doi.org/10.4018/978-1-7998-8816-1.ch001

Rodriguez, A., Rico-Diaz, A. J., Rabuñal, J. R., & Gestal, M. (2017). Fish Tracking with Computer Vision Techniques: An Application to Vertical Slot Fishways. In M. S., & V. V. (Eds.), *Multi-Core Computer Vision and Image Processing for Intelligent Applications* (pp. 74-104). Hershey, PA: IGI Global. https://doi.org/DOI: 10.4018/978-1-5225-0889-2.ch003

Romero, J. A. (2018). Sustainable Advantages of Business Value of Information Technology. In M. Khosrow-Pour, D.B.A. (Ed.), *Encyclopedia of Information Science and Technology, Fourth Edition* (pp. 923-929). Hershey, PA: IGI Global. DOI: 10.4018/978-1-5225-2255-3.ch079

Romero, J. A. (2018). The Always-On Business Model and Competitive Advantage. In Bajgoric, N. (Ed.), *Always-On Enterprise Information Systems for Modern Organizations* (pp. 23–40). Hershey, PA: IGI Global. DOI: 10.4018/978-1-5225-3704-5.ch002

Rosen, Y. (2018). Computer Agent Technologies in Collaborative Learning and Assessment. In M. Khosrow-Pour, D.B.A. (Ed.), *Encyclopedia of Information Science and Technology, Fourth Edition* (pp. 2402-2410). Hershey, PA: IGI Global. DOI: 10.4018/978-1-5225-2255-3.ch209

Roy, D. (2018). Success Factors of Adoption of Mobile Applications in Rural India: Effect of Service Characteristics on Conceptual Model. In Khosrow-Pour, M. (Ed.), *Green Computing Strategies for Competitive Advantage and Business Sustainability* (pp. 211–238). Hershey, PA: IGI Global. DOI: 10.4018/978-1-5225-5017-4.ch010

Rudolf, S., Biryuk, V. V., & Volov, V. (2018). Vortex Effect, Vortex Power: Technology of Vortex Power Engineering. In Kharchenko, V., & Vasant, P. (Eds.), *Handbook of Research on Renewable Energy and Electric Resources for Sustainable Rural Development* (pp. 500–533). Hershey, PA: IGI Global. DOI: 10.4018/978-1-5225-3867-7.ch021

Ruffin, T. R., & Hawkins, D. P. (2018). Trends in Health Care Information Technology and Informatics. In M. Khosrow-Pour, D.B.A. (Ed.), *Encyclopedia of Information Science and Technology, Fourth Edition* (pp. 3805-3815). Hershey, PA: IGI Global. DOI: 10.4018/978-1-5225-2255-3.ch330

Sah, A., Bhadula, S. J., Dumka, A., & Rawat, S. (2018). A Software Engineering Perspective for Development of Enterprise Applications. In Elçi, A. (Ed.), *Handbook of Research on Contemporary Perspectives on Web-Based Systems* (pp. 1–23). Hershey, PA: IGI Global. DOI: 10.4018/978-1-5225-5384-7.ch001

Sahin, H. B., & Anagun, S. S. (2018). Educational Computer Games in Math Teaching: A Learning Culture. In Toprak, E., & Kumtepe, E. (Eds.), *Supporting Multiculturalism in Open and Distance Learning Spaces* (pp. 249–280). Hershey, PA: IGI Global. DOI: 10.4018/978-1-5225-3076-3.ch013

Sahli, Y., Zitouni, B., & Hocine, B. M. (2021). Three-Dimensional Numerical Study of Overheating of Two Intermediate Temperature P-AS-SOFC Geometrical Configurations. In Badea, G., Felseghi, R., & A chilean, I. (Eds.), *Hydrogen Fuel Cell Technology for Stationary Applications* (pp. 186–222). IGI Global. https://doi.org/10.4018/978-1-7998-4945-2.ch008

Sahoo, S. (2018). Laminated Composite Hypar Shells as Roofing Units: Static and Dynamic Behavior. In Kumar, K., & Davim, J. (Eds.), *Composites and Advanced Materials for Industrial Applications* (pp. 249–269). Hershey, PA: IGI Global. DOI: 10.4018/978-1-5225-5216-1.ch011

Sahu, H., & Hungyo, M. (2018). Introduction to SDN and NFV. In Dumka, A. (Ed.), *Innovations in Software-Defined Networking and Network Functions Virtualization* (pp. 1–25). Hershey, PA: IGI Global. DOI: 10.4018/978-1-5225-3640-6.ch001

Sala, N. (2021). Virtual Reality, Augmented Reality, and Mixed Reality in Education: A Brief Overview. In Choi, D., Dailey-Hebert, A., & Estes, J. (Eds.), *Current and Prospective Applications of Virtual Reality in Higher Education* (pp. 48–73). IGI Global. https://doi.org/10.4018/978-1-7998-4960-5.ch003

Salem, A. M., & Shmelova, T. (2018). Intelligent Expert Decision Support Systems: Methodologies, Applications, and Challenges. In Shmelova, T., Sikirda, Y., Rizun, N., Salem, A., & Kovalyov, Y. (Eds.), *Socio-Technical Decision Support in Air Navigation Systems: Emerging Research and Opportunities* (pp. 215–242). Hershey, PA: IGI Global. DOI: 10.4018/978-1-5225-3108-1.ch007

Salunkhe, S., Kanagachidambaresan, G., Rajkumar, C., & Jayanthi, K. (2022). Online Detection and Prediction of Fused Deposition Modelled Parts Using Artificial Intelligence. In Salunkhe, S., Hussein, H., & Davim, J. (Eds.), *Applications of Artificial Intelligence in Additive Manufacturing* (pp. 194–209). IGI Global. https://doi.org/10.4018/978-1-7998-8516-0.ch009

Samal, M. (2017). FE Analysis and Experimental Investigation of Cracked and Un-Cracked Thin-Walled Tubular Components to Evaluate Mechanical and Fracture Properties. In Samui, P., Chakraborty, S., & Kim, D. (Eds.), *Modeling and Simulation Techniques in Structural Engineering* (pp. 266–293). Hershey, PA: IGI Global. DOI: 10.4018/978-1-5225-0588-4.ch009

Samal, M., & Balakrishnan, K. (2017). Experiments on a Ring Tension Setup and FE Analysis to Evaluate Transverse Mechanical Properties of Tubular Components. In Samui, P., Chakraborty, S., & Kim, D. (Eds.), *Modeling and Simulation Techniques in Structural Engineering* (pp. 91–115). Hershey, PA: IGI Global. DOI: 10.4018/978-1-5225-0588-4.ch004

Samarasinghe, D. A., & Wood, E. (2021). Innovative Digital Technologies. In Underwood, J., & Shelbourn, M. (Eds.), *Handbook of Research on Driving Transformational Change in the Digital Built Environment* (pp. 142–163). IGI Global. https://doi.org/10.4018/978-1-7998-6600-8.ch006

Sawant, S. (2018). Deep Learning and Biomedical Engineering. In Kose, U., Guraksin, G., & Deperlioglu, O. (Eds.), *Nature-Inspired Intelligent Techniques for Solving Biomedical Engineering Problems* (pp. 283–296). Hershey, PA: IGI Global. DOI: 10.4018/978-1-5225-4769-3.ch014

Schulenberg, T. (2021). Energy Conversion Using the Supercritical Steam Cycle. In Chen, L. (Ed.), *Handbook of Research on Advancements in Supercritical Fluids Applications for Sustainable Energy Systems* (pp. 659–681). IGI Global. DOI: 10.4018/978-1-7998-5796-9.ch018

Scott, A., Martin, A., & McAlear, F. (2017). Enhancing Participation in Computer Science among Girls of Color: An Examination of a Preparatory AP Computer Science Intervention. In Rankin, Y., & Thomas, J. (Eds.), *Moving Students of Color from Consumers to Producers of Technology* (pp. 62–84). Hershey, PA: IGI Global. DOI: 10.4018/978-1-5225-2005-4.ch004

Sezgin, H., & Berkalp, O. B. (2018). Textile-Reinforced Composites for the Automotive Industry. In Kumar, K., & Davim, J. (Eds.), *Composites and Advanced Materials for Industrial Applications* (pp. 129–156). Hershey, PA: IGI Global. DOI: 10.4018/978-1-5225-5216-1.ch007

Shafaati Shemami, M., & Sefid, M. (2022). Implementation and Demonstration of Electric Vehicle-to-Home (V2H) Application: A Case Study. In Alam, M., Pillai, R., & Murugesan, N. (Eds.), *Developing Charging Infrastructure and Technologies for Electric Vehicles* (pp. 268–293). IGI Global. https://doi.org/10.4018/978-1-7998-6858-3.ch015

Shanmugam, M., Ibrahim, N., Gorment, N. Z., Sugu, R., Dandarawi, T. N., & Ahmad, N. A. (2022). Towards an Integrated Omni-Channel Strategy Framework for Improved Customer Interaction. In Lai, P. (Ed.), *Handbook of Research on Social Impacts of E-Payment and Blockchain Technology* (pp. 409–427). IGI Global. https://doi.org/10.4018/978-1-7998-9035-5.ch022

Sharma, A., & Kumar, S. (2021). Network Slicing and the Role of 5G in IoT Applications. In Kumar, S., Trivedi, M., Ranjan, P., & Punhani, A. (Eds.), *Evolution of Software-Defined Networking Foundations for IoT and 5G Mobile Networks* (pp. 172–190). IGI Global. https://doi.org/10.4018/978-1-7998-4685-7.ch010

Sharma, N., & Kumar, K. (2018). Fabrication of Porous NiTi Alloy Using Organic Binders. In Kumar, K., & Davim, J. (Eds.), *Composites and Advanced Materials for Industrial Applications* (pp. 38–62). Hershey, PA: IGI Global. DOI: 10.4018/978-1-5225-5216-1.ch003

Shivach, P., Nautiyal, L., & Ram, M. (2018). Applying Multi-Objective Optimization Algorithms to Mechanical Engineering. In Ram, M., & Davim, J. (Eds.), *Soft Computing Techniques and Applications in Mechanical Engineering* (pp. 287–301). Hershey, PA: IGI Global. DOI: 10.4018/978-1-5225-3035-0.ch014

Shmelova, T. (2018). Stochastic Methods for Estimation and Problem Solving in Engineering: Stochastic Methods of Decision Making in Aviation. In Kadry, S. (Ed.), *Stochastic Methods for Estimation and Problem Solving in Engineering* (pp. 139–160). Hershey, PA: IGI Global. DOI: 10.4018/978-1-5225-5045-7.ch006

Siero González, L. R., & Romo Vázquez, A. (2017). Didactic Sequences Teaching Mathematics for Engineers With Focus on Differential Equations. In Ramírez-Montoya, M. (Ed.), *Handbook of Research on Driving STEM Learning With Educational Technologies* (pp. 129–151). Hershey, PA: IGI Global. DOI: 10.4018/978-1-5225-2026-9.ch007

Silveira, C., Hir, M. E., & Chaves, H. K. (2022). An Approach to Information Management as a Subsidy of Global Health Actions: A Case Study of Big Data in Health for Dengue, Zika, and Chikungunya. In Lima de Magalhães, J., Hartz, Z., Jamil, G., Silveira, H., & Jamil, L. (Eds.), *Handbook of Research on Essential Information Approaches to Aiding Global Health in the One Health Context* (pp. 219–234). IGI Global. https://doi.org/10.4018/978-1-7998-8011-0.ch012

Sim, M. S., You, K. Y., Esa, F., & Chan, Y. L. (2021). Nanostructured Electromagnetic Metamaterials for Sensing Applications. In Bhat, M., Wani, I., & Ashraf, S. (Eds.), *Applications of Nanomaterials in Agriculture, Food Science, and Medicine* (pp. 141–164). IGI Global. https://doi.org/10.4018/978-1-7998-5563-7.ch009

Simões de Almeida, R., & da Silva, T. (2022). AI Chatbots in Mental Health: Are We There Yet? In Marques, A., & Queirós, R. (Eds.), *Digital Therapies in Psychosocial Rehabilitation and Mental Health* (pp. 226–243). IGI Global. https://doi.org/10.4018/978-1-7998-8634-1.ch011

Simões, A. (2017). Using Game Frameworks to Teach Computer Programming. In Alexandre Peixoto de Queirós, R., & Pinto, M. (Eds.), *Gamification-Based E-Learning Strategies for Computer Programming Education* (pp. 221–236). Hershey, PA: IGI Global. DOI: 10.4018/978-1-5225-1034-5.ch010

Singh, R., & Dutta, S. (2018). Visible Light Active Nanocomposites for Photocatalytic Applications. In Kumar, K., & Davim, J. (Eds.), *Composites and Advanced Materials for Industrial Applications* (pp. 270–296). Hershey, PA: IGI Global. DOI: 10.4018/978-1-5225-5216-1.ch012

Skripov, P. V., Yampol'skiy, A. D., & Rutin, S. B. (2021). High-Power Heat Transfer in Supercritical Fluids: Microscale Times and Sizes. In Chen, L. (Ed.), *Handbook of Research on Advancements in Supercritical Fluids Applications for Sustainable Energy Systems* (pp. 424–450). IGI Global. https://doi.org/10.4018/978-1-7998-5796-9.ch012

Sllame, A. M. (2017). Integrating LAB Work With Classes in Computer Network Courses. In Alphin, H.Jr, Chan, R., & Lavine, J. (Eds.), *The Future of Accessibility in International Higher Education* (pp. 253–275). Hershey, PA: IGI Global. DOI: 10.4018/978-1-5225-2560-8.ch015

Smith-Ditizio, A. A., & Smith, A. D. (2018). Computer Fraud Challenges and Its Legal Implications. In M. Khosrow-Pour, D.B.A. (Ed.), *Encyclopedia of Information Science and Technology, Fourth Edition* (pp. 4837-4848). Hershey, PA: IGI Global. DOI: 10.4018/978-1-5225-2255-3.ch419

Sosnin, P. (2018). Figuratively Semantic Support of Human-Computer Interactions. In *Experience-Based Human-Computer Interactions: Emerging Research and Opportunities* (pp. 244–272). Hershey, PA: IGI Global. DOI: 10.4018/978-1-5225-2987-3.ch008

Sözbilir, H., Özkaymak, Ç., Uzel, B., & Sümer, Ö. (2018). Criteria for Surface Rupture Microzonation of Active Faults for Earthquake Hazards in Urban Areas. In Ceryan, N. (Ed.), *Handbook of Research on Trends and Digital Advances in Engineering Geology* (pp. 187–230). Hershey, PA: IGI Global. DOI: 10.4018/978-1-5225-2709-1.ch005

Stanciu, I. (2018). Stochastic Methods in Microsystems Engineering. In Kadry, S. (Ed.), *Stochastic Methods for Estimation and Problem Solving in Engineering* (pp. 161–176). Hershey, PA: IGI Global. DOI: 10.4018/978-1-5225-5045-7.ch007

Strebkov, D., Nekrasov, A., Trubnikov, V., & Nekrasov, A. (2018). Single-Wire Resonant Electric Power Systems for Renewable-Based Electric Grid. In Kharchenko, V., & Vasant, P. (Eds.), *Handbook of Research on Renewable Energy and Electric Resources for Sustainable Rural Development* (pp. 449–474). Hershey, PA: IGI Global. DOI: 10.4018/978-1-5225-3867-7.ch019

Suri, M. S., & Kaliyaperumal, D. (2022). Extension of Aspiration Level Model for Optimal Planning of Fast Charging Stations. In Fekik, A., & Benamrouche, N. (Eds.), *Modeling and Control of Static Converters for Hybrid Storage Systems* (pp. 91–106). IGI Global. https://doi.org/10.4018/978-1-7998-7447-8.ch004

Susanto, H., Yie, L. F., Setiana, D., Asih, Y., Yoganingrum, A., Riyanto, S., & Saputra, F. A. (2021). Digital Ecosystem Security Issues for Organizations and Governments: Digital Ethics and Privacy. In Mahmood, Z. (Ed.), *Web 2.0 and Cloud Technologies for Implementing Connected Government* (pp. 204–228). IGI Global. https://doi.org/10.4018/978-1-7998-4570-6.ch010

Tallet, E., Gledson, B., Rogage, K., Thompson, A., & Wiggett, D. (2021). Digitally-Enabled Design Management. In Underwood, J., & Shelbourn, M. (Eds.), *Handbook of Research on Driving Transformational Change in the Digital Built Environment* (pp. 63–89). IGI Global. https://doi.org/10.4018/978-1-7998-6600-8.ch003

Tanque, M., & Foxwell, H. J. (2018). Big Data and Cloud Computing: A Review of Supply Chain Capabilities and Challenges. In Prasad, A. (Ed.), *Exploring the Convergence of Big Data and the Internet of Things* (pp. 1–28). Hershey, PA: IGI Global. DOI: 10.4018/978-1-5225-2947-7.ch001

Teixeira, A., Gomes, A., & Orvalho, J. G. (2017). Auditory Feedback in a Computer Game for Blind People. In Issa, T., Kommers, P., Issa, T., Isaías, P., & Issa, T. (Eds.), *Smart Technology Applications in Business Environments* (pp. 134–158). Hershey, PA: IGI Global. DOI: 10.4018/978-1-5225-2492-2.ch007

Tewari, P., Tiwari, P., & Goel, R. (2022). Information Technology in Supply Chain Management. In Garg, V., & Goel, R. (Eds.), *Handbook of Research on Innovative Management Using AI in Industry 5.0* (pp. 165–178). IGI Global. https://doi.org/10.4018/978-1-7998-8497-2.ch011

Thompson, N., McGill, T., & Murray, D. (2018). Affect-Sensitive Computer Systems. In M. Khosrow-Pour, D.B.A. (Ed.), *Encyclopedia of Information Science and Technology, Fourth Edition* (pp. 4124-4135). Hershey, PA: IGI Global. DOI: 10.4018/978-1-5225-2255-3.ch357

Triberti, S., Brivio, E., & Galimberti, C. (2018). On Social Presence: Theories, Methodologies, and Guidelines for the Innovative Contexts of Computer-Mediated Learning. In Marmon, M. (Ed.), *Enhancing Social Presence in Online Learning Environments* (pp. 20–41). Hershey, PA: IGI Global. DOI: 10.4018/978-1-5225-3229-3.ch002

Tripathy, B. K. T. R., S., & Mohanty, R. K. (2018). Memetic Algorithms and Their Applications in Computer Science. In S. Dash, B. Tripathy, & A. Rahman (Eds.), *Handbook of Research on Modeling, Analysis, and Application of Nature-Inspired Metaheuristic Algorithms* (pp. 73-93). Hershey, PA: IGI Global. https://doi.org/DOI: 10.4018/978-1-5225-2857-9.ch004

Tüdeş, Ş., Kumlu, K. B., & Ceryan, S. (2018). Integration Between Urban Planning and Natural Hazards For Resilient City. In Ceryan, N. (Ed.), *Handbook of Research on Trends and Digital Advances in Engineering Geology* (pp. 591–630). Hershey, PA: IGI Global. DOI: 10.4018/978-1-5225-2709-1.ch017

Turulja, L., & Bajgoric, N. (2017). Human Resource Management IT and Global Economy Perspective: Global Human Resource Information Systems. In Khosrow-Pour, M. (Ed.), *Handbook of Research on Technology Adoption, Social Policy, and Global Integration* (pp. 377–394). Hershey, PA: IGI Global. DOI: 10.4018/978-1-5225-2668-1.ch018

Ulamis, K. (2018). Soil Liquefaction Assessment by Anisotropic Cyclic Triaxial Test. In Ceryan, N. (Ed.), *Handbook of Research on Trends and Digital Advances in Engineering Geology* (pp. 631–664). Hershey, PA: IGI Global. DOI: 10.4018/978-1-5225-2709-1.ch018

Unwin, D. W., Sanzogni, L., & Sandhu, K. (2017). Developing and Measuring the Business Case for Health Information Technology. In Moahi, K., Bwalya, K., & Sebina, P. (Eds.), *Health Information Systems and the Advancement of Medical Practice in Developing Countries* (pp. 262–290). Hershey, PA: IGI Global. DOI: 10.4018/978-1-5225-2262-1.ch015

Vadhanam, B. R. S., M., Sugumaran, V., V., V., & Ramalingam, V. V. (2017). Computer Vision Based Classification on Commercial Videos. In M. S., & V. V. (Eds.), *Multi-Core Computer Vision and Image Processing for Intelligent Applications* (pp. 105-135). Hershey, PA: IGI Global. https://doi.org/DOI: 10.4018/978-1-5225-0889-2.ch004

Vairinho, S. (2022). Innovation Dynamics Through the Encouragement of Knowledge Spin-Off From Touristic Destinations. In Ramos, C., Quinteiro, S., & Gonçalves, A. (Eds.), *ICT as Innovator Between Tourism and Culture* (pp. 170–190). IGI Global. https://doi.org/10.4018/978-1-7998-8165-0.ch011

Valente, M., & Milani, G. (2017). Seismic Assessment and Retrofitting of an Under-Designed RC Frame Through a Displacement-Based Approach. In Plevris, V., Kremmyda, G., & Fahjan, Y. (Eds.), *Performance-Based Seismic Design of Concrete Structures and Infrastructures* (pp. 36–58). Hershey, PA: IGI Global. DOI: 10.4018/978-1-5225-2089-4.ch002

Valverde, R., Torres, B., & Motaghi, H. (2018). A Quantum NeuroIS Data Analytics Architecture for the Usability Evaluation of Learning Management Systems. In Bhattacharyya, S. (Ed.), *Quantum-Inspired Intelligent Systems for Multimedia Data Analysis* (pp. 277–299). Hershey, PA: IGI Global. DOI: 10.4018/978-1-5225-5219-2.ch009

Vargas-Bernal, R. (2021). Advances in Electromagnetic Environmental Shielding for Aeronautics and Space Applications. In Nikolopoulos, C. (Ed.), *Recent Trends on Electromagnetic Environmental Effects for Aeronautics and Space Applications* (pp. 80–96). IGI Global. https://doi.org/10.4018/978-1-7998-4879-0.ch003

Vasant, P. (2018). A General Medical Diagnosis System Formed by Artificial Neural Networks and Swarm Intelligence Techniques. In Kose, U., Guraksin, G., & Deperlioglu, O. (Eds.), *Nature-Inspired Intelligent Techniques for Solving Biomedical Engineering Problems* (pp. 130–145). Hershey, PA: IGI Global. DOI: 10.4018/978-1-5225-4769-3.ch006

Vassilis, E. (2018). Learning and Teaching Methodology: "1:1 Educational Computing. In Koutsopoulos, K., Doukas, K., & Kotsanis, Y. (Eds.), *Handbook of Research on Educational Design and Cloud Computing in Modern Classroom Settings* (pp. 122–155). Hershey, PA: IGI Global. DOI: 10.4018/978-1-5225-3053-4.ch007

Verma, S., & Jain, A. K. (2022). A Survey on Sentiment Analysis Techniques for Twitter. In Gupta, B., Peraković, D., Abd El-Latif, A., & Gupta, D. (Eds.), *Data Mining Approaches for Big Data and Sentiment Analysis in Social Media* (pp. 57–90). IGI Global. https://doi.org/10.4018/978-1-7998-8413-2.ch003

Wan, A. C., Zulu, S. L., & Khosrow-Shahi, F. (2021). Industry Views on BIM for Site Safety in Hong Kong. In Underwood, J., & Shelbourn, M. (Eds.), *Handbook of Research on Driving Transformational Change in the Digital Built Environment* (pp. 120–140). IGI Global. https://doi.org/10.4018/978-1-7998-6600-8.ch005

Wexler, B. E. (2017). Computer-Presented and Physical Brain-Training Exercises for School Children: Improving Executive Functions and Learning. In Dubbels, B. (Ed.), *Transforming Gaming and Computer Simulation Technologies across Industries* (pp. 206–224). Hershey, PA: IGI Global. DOI: 10.4018/978-1-5225-1817-4.ch012

Wong, Y. L., & Siu, K. W. (2018). Assessing Computer-Aided Design Skills. In M. Khosrow-Pour, D.B.A. (Ed.), *Encyclopedia of Information Science and Technology, Fourth Edition* (pp. 7382-7391). Hershey, PA: IGI Global. DOI: 10.4018/978-1-5225-2255-3.ch642

Wongsurawat, W., & Shrestha, V. (2018). Information Technology, Globalization, and Local Conditions: Implications for Entrepreneurs in Southeast Asia. In Ordóñez de Pablos, P. (Ed.), *Management Strategies and Technology Fluidity in the Asian Business Sector* (pp. 163–176). Hershey, PA: IGI Global. DOI: 10.4018/978-1-5225-4056-4.ch010

Yang, Y., Zhu, X., Jin, C., & Li, J. J. (2018). Reforming Classroom Education Through a QQ Group: A Pilot Experiment at a Primary School in Shanghai. In Spires, H. (Ed.), *Digital Transformation and Innovation in Chinese Education* (pp. 211–231). Hershey, PA: IGI Global. DOI: 10.4018/978-1-5225-2924-8.ch012

Yardimci, A. G., & Karpuz, C. (2018). Fuzzy Rock Mass Rating: Soft-Computing-Aided Preliminary Stability Analysis of Weak Rock Slopes. In Ceryan, N. (Ed.), *Handbook of Research on Trends and Digital Advances in Engineering Geology* (pp. 97–131). Hershey, PA: IGI Global. DOI: 10.4018/978-1-5225-2709-1.ch003

Yilmaz, R., Sezgin, A., Kurnaz, S., & Arslan, Y. Z. (2018). Object-Oriented Programming in Computer Science. In M. Khosrow-Pour, D.B.A. (Ed.), *Encyclopedia of Information Science and Technology, Fourth Edition* (pp. 7470-7480). Hershey, PA: IGI Global. DOI: 10.4018/978-1-5225-2255-3.ch650

You, K. Y. (2021). Development Electronic Design Automation for RF/Microwave Antenna Using MATLAB GUI. In Nwajana, A., & Ihianle, I. (Eds.), *Handbook of Research on 5G Networks and Advancements in Computing, Electronics, and Electrical Engineering* (pp. 70–148). IGI Global. https://doi.org/10.4018/978-1-7998-6992-4.ch004

Yu, L. (2018). From Teaching Software Engineering Locally and Globally to Devising an Internationalized Computer Science Curriculum. In Dikli, S., Etheridge, B., & Rawls, R. (Eds.), *Curriculum Internationalization and the Future of Education* (pp. 293–320). Hershey, PA: IGI Global. DOI: 10.4018/978-1-5225-2791-6.ch016

Yuhua, F. (2018). Computer Information Library Clusters. In M. Khosrow-Pour, D.B.A. (Ed.), *Encyclopedia of Information Science and Technology, Fourth Edition* (pp. 4399-4403). Hershey, PA: IGI Global. DOI: 10.4018/978-1-5225-2255-3.ch382

Zakaria, R. B., Zainuddin, M. N., & Mohamad, A. H. (2022). Distilling Blockchain: Complexity, Barriers, and Opportunities. In Lai, P. (Ed.), *Handbook of Research on Social Impacts of E-Payment and Blockchain Technology* (pp. 89–114). IGI Global. https://doi.org/10.4018/978-1-7998-9035-5.ch007

Zindani, D., & Kumar, K. (2018). Industrial Applications of Polymer Composite Materials. In Kumar, K., & Davim, J. (Eds.), *Composites and Advanced Materials for Industrial Applications* (pp. 1–15). Hershey, PA: IGI Global. DOI: 10.4018/978-1-5225-5216-1.ch001

Zindani, D., Maity, S. R., & Bhowmik, S. (2018). A Decision-Making Approach for Material Selection of Polymeric Composite Bumper Beam. In Kumar, K., & Davim, J. (Eds.), *Composites and Advanced Materials for Industrial Applications* (pp. 112–128). Hershey, PA: IGI Global. DOI: 10.4018/978-1-5225-5216-1.ch006

Abdulrahman, K. O., Mahamood, R. M., & Akinlabi, E. T. (2022). Additive Manufacturing (AM): Processing Technique for Lightweight Alloys and Composite Material. In K. Kumar, B. Babu, & J. Davim (Ed.), *Handbook of Research on Advancements in the Processing, Characterization, and Application of Lightweight Materials* (pp. 27-48). IGI Global. https://doi.org/10.4018/978-1-7998-7864-3.ch002

Bazeer Ahamed, B., & Periakaruppan, S. (2021). Taxonomy of Influence Maximization Techniques in Unknown Social Networks. In P. Vasant, G. Weber, & W. Punurai (Eds.), *Research Advancements in Smart Technology, Optimization, and Renewable Energy* (pp. 351-363). IGI Global. https://doi.org/10.4018/978-1-7998-3970-5.ch017

Boido, C., Davico, P., & Spallone, R. (2021). Digital Tools Aimed to Represent Urban Survey. In M. Khosrow-Pour D.B.A. (Ed.), *Encyclopedia of Information Science and Technology, Fifth Edition* (pp. 1181-1195). IGI Global. https://doi.org/10.4018/978-1-7998-3479-3.ch082

Carvalho, W. F., & Zarate, L. (2021). Causal Feature Selection. In A. Azevedo & M. Santos (Eds.), *Integration Challenges for Analytics, Business Intelligence, and Data Mining* (pp. 145-160). IGI Global. https://doi.org/10.4018/978-1-7998-5781-5.ch007

Gauttier, S. (2021). A Primer on Q-Method and the Study of Technology. In M. Khosrow-Pour D.B.A. (Eds.), *Encyclopedia of Information Science and Technology, Fifth Edition* (pp. 1746-1756). IGI Global. https://doi.org/10.4018/978-1-7998-3479-3.ch120

Godzhaev, Z., Senkevich, S., Kuzmin, V., & Melikov, I. (2021). Use of the Neural Network Controller of Sprung Mass to Reduce Vibrations From Road Irregularities. In P. Vasant, G. Weber, & W. Punurai (Ed.), *Research Advancements in Smart Technology, Optimization, and Renewable Energy* (pp. 69-87). IGI Global. https://doi.org/10.4018/978-1-7998-3970-5.ch005

Huang, C., Sun, Y., & Fuh, C. (2022). Vehicle License Plate Recognition With Deep Learning. In C. Chen, W. Yang, & L. Chen (Eds.), *Technologies to Advance Automation in Forensic Science and Criminal Investigation* (pp. 161-219). IGI Global. https://doi.org/10.4018/978-1-7998-8386-9.ch009

Ilo, P. I., Nkiko, C., Ugwu, C. I., Ekere, J. N., Izuagbe, R., & Fagbohun, M. O. (2021). Prospects and Challenges of Web 3.0 Technologies Application in the Provision of Library Services. In M. Khosrow-Pour D.B.A. (Ed.), *Encyclopedia of Information Science and Technology, Fifth Edition* (pp. 1767-1781). IGI Global. https://doi.org/10.4018/978-1-7998-3479-3.ch122

Jagdale, S. C., Hable, A. A., & Chabukswar, A. R. (2021). Protocol Development in Clinical Trials for Healthcare Management. In M. Khosrow-Pour D.B.A. (Ed.), *Encyclopedia of Information Science and Technology, Fifth Edition* (pp. 1797-1814). IGI Global. https://doi.org/10.4018/978-1-7998-3479-3.ch124

Jamil, M. I., & Almunawar, M. N. (2021). Importance of Digital Literacy and Hindrance Brought About by Digital Divide. In M. Khosrow-Pour D.B.A. (Ed.), *Encyclopedia of Information Science and Technology, Fifth Edition* (pp. 1683-1698). IGI Global. https://doi.org/10.4018/978-1-7998-3479-3.ch116

Kharb, L., & Singh, P. (2021). Role of Machine Learning in Modern Education and Teaching. In S. Verma & P. Tomar (Ed.), *Impact of AI Technologies on Teaching, Learning, and Research in Higher Education* (pp. 99-123). IGI Global. https://doi.org/10.4018/978-1-7998-4763-2.ch006

Madhu, M. N., Singh, J. G., Mohan, V., & Ongsakul, W. (2021). Transmission Risk Optimization in Interconnected Systems: Risk-Adjusted Available Transfer Capability. In P. Vasant, G. Weber, & W. Punurai (Ed.), *Research Advancements in Smart Technology, Optimization, and Renewable Energy* (pp. 183-199). IGI Global. https://doi.org/10.4018/978-1-7998-3970-5.ch010

Naomi, J. F. M., K., & V., S. (2021). Machine and Deep Learning Techniques in IoT and Cloud. In S. Velayutham (Ed.), *Challenges and Opportunities for the Convergence of IoT, Big Data, and Cloud Computing* (pp. 225-247). IGI Global. https://doi.org/10.4018/978-1-7998-3111-2.ch013

Panchenko, V. (2021). Prospects for Energy Supply of the Arctic Zone Objects of Russia Using Frost-Resistant Solar Modules. In P. Vasant, G. Weber, & W. Punurai (Eds.), *Research Advancements in Smart Technology, Optimization, and Renewable Energy* (pp. 149-169). IGI Global. https://doi.org/10.4018/978-1-7998-3970-5.ch008

Paul, S., & Roy, P. K. (2021). Oppositional Differential Search Algorithm for the Optimal Tuning of Both Single Input and Dual Input Power System Stabilizer. In P. Vasant, G. Weber, & W. Punurai (Eds.), *Research Advancements in Smart Technology, Optimization, and Renewable Energy* (pp. 256-282). IGI Global. https://doi.org/10.4018/978-1-7998-3970-5.ch013

Prabha, V. D., & R., R. (2021). Clinical Decision Support Systems: Decision-Making System for Clinical Data. In G. Rani & P. Tiwari (Eds.), *Handbook of Research on Disease Prediction Through Data Analytics and Machine Learning* (pp. 268-280). IGI Global. https://doi.org/10.4018/978-1-7998-2742-9.ch014

Sadasivam, U. M., & Ganesan, N. (2021). Detecting Fake News Using Deep Learning and NLP. In S. Misra, C. Arumugam, S. Jaganathan, & S. S. (Eds.), *Confluence of AI, Machine, and Deep Learning in Cyber Forensics* (pp. 117-133). IGI Global. https://doi.org/10.4018/978-1-7998-4900-1.ch007

Sakalle, A., Tomar, P., Bhardwaj, H., & Sharma, U. (2021). Impact and Latest Trends of Intelligent Learning With Artificial Intelligence. In S. Verma & P. Tomar (Eds.), *Impact of AI Technologies on Teaching, Learning, and Research in Higher Education* (pp. 172-189). IGI Global. https://doi.org/10.4018/978-1-7998-4763-2.ch011

Usharani, B. (2022). House Plant Leaf Disease Detection and Classification Using Machine Learning. In M. Mundada, S. Seema, S. K.G., & M. Shilpa (Eds.), *Deep Learning Applications for Cyber-Physical Systems* (pp. 17-26). IGI Global. https://doi.org/10.4018/978-1-7998-8161-2.ch002

Wong, S. (2021). Gendering Information and Communication Technologies in Climate Change. In M. Khosrow-Pour D.B.A. (Eds.), *Encyclopedia of Information Science and Technology, Fifth Edition* (pp. 1408-1422). IGI Global. https://doi.org/10.4018/978-1-7998-3479-3.ch096

Abu Doush, I., & Alhami, I. (2018). Evaluating the Accessibility of Computer Laboratories, Libraries, and Websites in Jordanian Universities and Colleges. *International Journal of Information Systems and Social Change*, 9(2), 44–60. DOI: 10.4018/IJISSC.2018040104

Aikhuele, D. (2018). A Study of Product Development Engineering and Design Reliability Concerns. *International Journal of Applied Industrial Engineering*, 5(1), 79–89. DOI: 10.4018/IJAIE.2018010105

Alsharo, M. (2017). Attitudes Towards Cloud Computing Adoption in Emerging Economies. *International Journal of Cloud Applications and Computing*, 7(3), 44–58. DOI: 10.4018/IJCAC.2017070102

Al-Shebeeb, O. A., Rangaswamy, S., Gopalakrishan, B., & Devaru, D. G. (2017). Evaluation and Indexing of Process Plans Based on Electrical Demand and Energy Consumption. *International Journal of Manufacturing, Materials, and Mechanical Engineering*, 7(3), 1–19. DOI: 10.4018/IJMMME.2017070101

Amuda, M. O., Lawal, T. F., & Akinlabi, E. T. (2017). Research Progress on Rheological Behavior of AA7075 Aluminum Alloy During Hot Deformation. *International Journal of Materials Forming and Machining Processes*, 4(1), 53–96. DOI: 10.4018/IJMFMP.2017010104

Anohah, E. (2017). Paradigm and Architecture of Computing Augmented Learning Management System for Computer Science Education. *International Journal of Online Pedagogy and Course Design*, 7(2), 60–70. DOI: 10.4018/IJOPCD.2017040105

Anohah, E., & Suhonen, J. (2017). Trends of Mobile Learning in Computing Education from 2006 to 2014: A Systematic Review of Research Publications. *International Journal of Mobile and Blended Learning*, 9(1), 16–33. DOI: 10.4018/IJMBL.2017010102

Arbaiza, C. S., Huerta, H. V., & Rodriguez, C. R. (2021). Contributions to the Technological Adoption Model for the Peruvian Agro-Export Sector. *International Journal of E-Adoption*, 13(1), 1–17. https://doi.org/10.4018/IJEA.2021010101

Bagdadee, A. H. (2021). A Brief Assessment of the Energy Sector of Bangladesh. *International Journal of Energy Optimization and Engineering*, 10(1), 36–55. DOI: 10.4018/IJEOE.2021010103

Ben Hamida, I., Salah, S. B., Msahli, F., & Mimouni, M. F. (2018). Distribution Network Reconfiguration Using SPEA2 for Power Loss Minimization and Reliability Improvement. *International Journal of Energy Optimization and Engineering*, 7(1), 50–65. DOI: 10.4018/IJEOE.2018010103

Bhaskar, S. V., & Kudal, H. N. (2017). Effect of TiCN and AlCrN Coating on Tribological Behaviour of Plasma-nitrided AISI 4140 Steel. *International Journal of Surface Engineering and Interdisciplinary Materials Science*, 5(2), 1–17. DOI: 10.4018/IJSEIMS.2017070101

Bhatt, G. D., Wang, Z., & Rodger, J. A. (2017). Information Systems Capabilities and Their Effects on Competitive Advantages: A Study of Chinese Companies. *Information Resources Management Journal*, 30(3), 41–57. DOI: 10.4018/IRMJ.2017070103

Brahmane, A. V., & Krishna, C. B. (2021). Rider Chaotic Biography Optimization-driven Deep Stacked Auto-encoder for Big Data Classification Using Spark Architecture: Rider Chaotic Biography Optimization. *International Journal of Web Services Research*, 18(3), 42–62. https://doi.org/10.4018/ijwsr.2021070103

Burcoff, A., & Shamir, L. (2017). Computer Analysis of Pablo Picasso's Artistic Style. *International Journal of Art, Culture and Design Technologies*, 6(1), 1–18. DOI: 10.4018/IJACDT.2017010101

Chiba, Y., Marif, Y., Henini, N., & Tlemcani, A. (2021). Modeling of Magnetic Refrigeration Device by Using Artificial Neural Networks Approach. *International Journal of Energy Optimization and Engineering*, 10(4), 68–76. https://doi.org/10.4018/IJEOE.2021100105

Cortés-Polo, D., Calle-Cancho, J., Carmona-Murillo, J., & González-Sánchez, J. (2017). Future Trends in Mobile-Fixed Integration for Next Generation Networks: Classification and Analysis. *International Journal of Vehicular Telematics and Infotainment Systems*, 1(1), 33–53. DOI: 10.4018/IJVTIS.2017010103

Daus, Y., Kharchenko, V., & Yudaev, I. (2021). Optimizing Layout of Distributed Generation Sources of Power Supply System of Agricultural Object. *International Journal of Energy Optimization and Engineering*, 10(3), 70–84. https://doi.org/10.4018/IJEOE.2021070104

Daus, Y., Kharchenko, V., & Yudaev, I. (2021). Research of Solar Energy Potential of Photovoltaic Installations on Enclosing Structures of Buildings. *International Journal of Energy Optimization and Engineering*, 10(4), 18–34. https://doi.org/10.4018/IJEOE.2021100102

Dhurpate, P. R., & Tang, H. (2021). Quantitative Analysis of the Impact of Inter-Line Conveyor Capacity for Throughput of Manufacturing Systems. *International Journal of Manufacturing, Materials, and Mechanical Engineering*, 11(1), 1–17. https://doi.org/10.4018/IJMMME.2021010101

Dinkar, S., & Deep, K. (2021). A Survey of Recent Variants and Applications of Antlion Optimizer. *International Journal of Energy Optimization and Engineering*, 10(2), 48–73. DOI: 10.4018/IJEOE.2021040103

Drabecki, M. P., & Kułak, K. B. (2021). Global Pandemics on European Electrical Energy Markets: Lessons Learned From the COVID-19 Outbreak. *International Journal of Energy Optimization and Engineering*, 10(3), 24–46. https://doi.org/10.4018/IJEOE.2021070102

El Ghandour, N., Benaissa, M., & Lebbah, Y. (2021). An Integer Linear Programming-Based Method for the Extraction of Ontology Alignment. *International Journal of Information Technology and Web Engineering*, 16(2), 25–44. https://doi.org/10.4018/IJITWE.2021040102

Fernando, P. R., Hamigah, T., Disne, S., Wickramasingha, G. G., & Sutharshan, A. (2018). The Evaluation of Engineering Properties of Low Cost Concrete Blocks by Partial Doping of Sand with Sawdust: Low Cost Sawdust Concrete Block. *International Journal of Strategic Engineering*, 1(2), 26–42. DOI: 10.4018/IJoSE.2018070103

Galli, B. J. (2021). Implications of Economic Decision Making to the Project Manager. *International Journal of Strategic Engineering*, 4(1), 19–32. https://doi.org/10.4018/IJoSE.2021010102

Ghobakhloo, M., & Azar, A. (2018). Information Technology Resources, the Organizational Capability of Lean-Agile Manufacturing, and Business Performance. *Information Resources Management Journal*, 31(2), 47–74. DOI: 10.4018/IRMJ.2018040103

Goswami, J. K., Jalal, S., Negi, C. S., & Jalal, A. S. (2022). A Texture Features-Based Robust Facial Expression Recognition. *International Journal of Computer Vision and Image Processing*, 12(1), 1–15. https://doi.org/10.4018/IJCVIP.2022010103

Hanafizadeh, P., Ghandchi, S., & Asgarimehr, M. (2017). Impact of Information Technology on Lifestyle: A Literature Review and Classification. *International Journal of Virtual Communities and Social Networking*, 9(2), 1–23. DOI: 10.4018/IJVCSN.2017040101

Hasegawa, N., & Takahashi, Y. (2021). Control of Soap Bubble Ejection Robot Using Facial Expressions. *International Journal of Manufacturing, Materials, and Mechanical Engineering*, 11(2), 1–16. https://doi.org/10.4018/IJMMME.2021040101

Hee, W. J., Jalleh, G., Lai, H., & Lin, C. (2017). E-Commerce and IT Projects: Evaluation and Management Issues in Australian and Taiwanese Hospitals. *International Journal of Public Health Management and Ethics*, 2(1), 69–90. DOI: 10.4018/IJPHME.2017010104

Hernandez, A. A. (2017). Green Information Technology Usage: Awareness and Practices of Philippine IT Professionals. *International Journal of Enterprise Information Systems*, 13(4), 90–103. DOI: 10.4018/IJEIS.2017100106

Hernandez, M. A., Marin, E. C., Garcia-Rodriguez, J., Azorin-Lopez, J., & Cazorla, M. (2017). Automatic Learning Improves Human-Robot Interaction in Productive Environments: A Review. *International Journal of Computer Vision and Image Processing*, 7(3), 65–75. DOI: 10.4018/IJCVIP.2017070106

Hond, D., Asgari, H., Jeffery, D., & Newman, M. (2021). An Integrated Process for Verifying Deep Learning Classifiers Using Dataset Dissimilarity Measures. *International Journal of Artificial Intelligence and Machine Learning*, 11(2), 1–21. https://doi.org/10.4018/IJAIML.289536

Ifinedo, P. (2017). Using an Extended Theory of Planned Behavior to Study Nurses' Adoption of Healthcare Information Systems in Nova Scotia. *International Journal of Technology Diffusion*, 8(1), 1–17. DOI: 10.4018/IJTD.2017010101

Ilie, V., & Sneha, S. (2018). A Three Country Study for Understanding Physicians' Engagement With Electronic Information Resources Pre and Post System Implementation. *Journal of Global Information Management*, 26(2), 48–73. DOI: 10.4018/JGIM.2018040103

Ilori, O. O., Adetan, D. A., & Umoru, L. E. (2017). Effect of Cutting Parameters on the Surface Residual Stress of Face-Milled Pearlitic Ductile Iron. *International Journal of Materials Forming and Machining Processes*, 4(1), 38–52. DOI: 10.4018/IJMFMP.2017010103

Imam, M. H., Tasadduq, I. A., Ahmad, A., Aldosari, F., & Khan, H. (2017). Automated Generation of Course Improvement Plans Using Expert System. *International Journal of Quality Assurance in Engineering and Technology Education*, 6(1), 1–12. DOI: 10.4018/IJQAETE.2017010101

Injeti, S. K., & Kumar, T. V. (2018). A WDO Framework for Optimal Deployment of DGs and DSCs in a Radial Distribution System Under Daily Load Pattern to Improve Techno-Economic Benefits. *International Journal of Energy Optimization and Engineering*, 7(2), 1–38. DOI: 10.4018/IJEOE.2018040101

Inoue-Smith, Y. (2017). Perceived Ease in Using Technology Predicts Teacher Candidates' Preferences for Online Resources. *International Journal of Online Pedagogy and Course Design*, 7(3), 17–28. DOI: 10.4018/IJOPCD.2017070102

Kang, H., Kang, Y., & Kim, J. (2022). Improved Fall Detection Model on GRU Using PoseNet. *International Journal of Software Innovation*, 10(2), 1–11. https://doi.org/10.4018/IJSI.289600

Kankam, P. K. (2021). Employing Case Study and Survey Designs in Information Research. *Journal of Information Technology Research*, 14(1), 167–177. https://doi.org/10.4018/JITR.2021010110

Karkalos, N. E., Markopoulos, A. P., & Dossis, M. F. (2017). Optimal Model Parameters of Inverse Kinematics Solution of a 3R Robotic Manipulator Using ANN Models. *International Journal of Manufacturing, Materials, and Mechanical Engineering*, 7(3), 20–40. DOI: 10.4018/IJMMME.2017070102

Khekare, G., & Sheikh, S. (2021). Autonomous Navigation Using Deep Reinforcement Learning in ROS. *International Journal of Artificial Intelligence and Machine Learning*, 11(2), 63–70. https://doi.org/10.4018/IJAIML.20210701.oa4

Khouja, M., Rodriguez, I. B., Ben Halima, Y., & Moalla, S. (2018). IT Governance in Higher Education Institutions: A Systematic Literature Review. *International Journal of Human Capital and Information Technology Professionals*, 9(2), 52–67. DOI: 10.4018/IJHCITP.2018040104

Kiourt, C., Pavlidis, G., Koutsoudis, A., & Kalles, D. (2017). Realistic Simulation of Cultural Heritage. *International Journal of Computational Methods in Heritage Science*, 1(1), 10–40. DOI: 10.4018/IJCMHS.2017010102

Kumar, G. R., Rajyalakshmi, G., & Manupati, V. K. (2017). Surface Micro Patterning of Aluminium Reinforced Composite through Laser Peening. *International Journal of Manufacturing, Materials, and Mechanical Engineering*, 7(4), 15–27. DOI: 10.4018/IJMMME.2017100102

Lakkad, A. K., Bhadaniya, R. D., Shah, V. N., & Lavanya, K. (2021). Complex Events Processing on Live News Events Using Apache Kafka and Clustering Techniques. *International Journal of Intelligent Information Technologies*, 17(1), 39–52. https://doi.org/10.4018/IJIIT.2021010103

Lin, S., Chen, S., & Chuang, S. (2017). Perceived Innovation and Quick Response Codes in an Online-to-Offline E-Commerce Service Model. *International Journal of E-Adoption*, 9(2), 1–16. DOI: 10.4018/IJEA.2017070101

Liu, M., Wang, Y., Xu, W., & Liu, L. (2017). Automated Scoring of Chinese Engineering Students' English Essays. *International Journal of Distance Education Technologies*, 15(1), 52–68. DOI: 10.4018/IJDET.2017010104

Ma, X., Li, X., Zhong, B., Huang, Y., Gu, Y., Wu, M., Liu, Y., & Zhang, M. (2021). A Detector and Evaluation Framework of Abnormal Bidding Behavior Based on Supplier Portrait. *International Journal of Information Technology and Web Engineering*, 16(2), 58–74. https://doi.org/10.4018/IJITWE.2021040104

Mahendramani, G., & Lakshmana Swamy, N. (2018). Effect of Weld Groove Area on Distortion of Butt Welded Joints in Submerged Arc Welding. *International Journal of Manufacturing, Materials, and Mechanical Engineering*, 8(2), 33–44. DOI: 10.4018/IJMMME.2018040103

Meddah, I. H., Remil, N. E., & Meddah, H. N. (2021). Novel Approach for Mining Patterns. *International Journal of Applied Evolutionary Computation*, 12(1), 27–42. https://doi.org/10.4018/IJAEC.2021010103

Mensah, I. K., & Mi, J. (2018). Determinants of Intention to Use Local E-Government Services in Ghana: The Perspective of Local Government Workers. *International Journal of Technology Diffusion*, 9(2), 41–60. DOI: 10.4018/IJTD.2018040103

Mihret, E. T., & Yitayih, K. A. (2021). Operation of VANET Communications: The Convergence of UAV System With LTE/4G and WAVE Technologies. *International Journal of Smart Vehicles and Smart Transportation*, 4(1), 29–51. https://doi.org/10.4018/IJSVST.2021010103

Molina, G. J., Aktaruzzaman, F., Soloiu, V., & Rahman, M. (2017). Design and Testing of a Jet-Impingement Instrument to Study Surface-Modification Effects by Nanofluids. *International Journal of Surface Engineering and Interdisciplinary Materials Science*, 5(2), 43–61. DOI: 10.4018/IJSEIMS.2017070104

Montañés-Del Río, M. Á., Cornejo, V. R., Rodríguez, M. R., & Ortiz, J. S. (2021). Gamification of University Subjects: A Case Study for Operations Management. *Journal of Information Technology Research*, 14(2), 1–29. https://doi.org/10.4018/JITR.2021040101

Moore, R. L., & Johnson, N. (2017). Earning a Seat at the Table: How IT Departments Can Partner in Organizational Change and Innovation. *International Journal of Knowledge-Based Organizations*, 7(2), 1–12. DOI: 10.4018/IJKBO.2017040101

Msomi, V., & Jantjies, B. T. (2021). Correlative Analysis Between Tensile Properties and Tool Rotational Speeds of Friction Stir Welded Similar Aluminium Alloy Joints. *International Journal of Surface Engineering and Interdisciplinary Materials Science*, 9(2), 58–78. https://doi.org/10.4018/IJSEIMS.2021070104

Mykhailyshyn, R., Savkiv, V., Boyko, I., Prada, E., & Virgala, I. (2021). Substantiation of Parameters of Friction Elements of Bernoulli Grippers With a Cylindrical Nozzle. *International Journal of Manufacturing, Materials, and Mechanical Engineering*, 11(2), 17–39. https://doi.org/10.4018/IJMMME.2021040102

Nguyen, T. T., Giang, N. L., Tran, D. T., Nguyen, T. T., Nguyen, H. Q., Pham, A. V., & Vu, T. D. (2021). A Novel Filter-Wrapper Algorithm on Intuitionistic Fuzzy Set for Attribute Reduction From Decision Tables. *International Journal of Data Warehousing and Mining*, 17(4), 67–100. https://doi.org/10.4018/IJDWM.2021100104

Nigam, A., & Dewani, P. P. (2022). Consumer Engagement Through Conditional Promotions: An Exploratory Study. *Journal of Global Information Management*, 30(5), 1–19. https://doi.org/10.4018/JGIM.290364

Oliveira, M., Maçada, A. C., Curado, C., & Nodari, F. (2017). Infrastructure Profiles and Knowledge Sharing. *International Journal of Technology and Human Interaction*, 13(3), 1–12. DOI: 10.4018/IJTHI.2017070101

Otarkhani, A., Shokouhyar, S., & Pour, S. S. (2017). Analyzing the Impact of Governance of Enterprise IT on Hospital Performance: Tehran's (Iran) Hospitals – A Case Study. *International Journal of Healthcare Information Systems and Informatics*, 12(3), 1–20. DOI: 10.4018/IJHISI.2017070101

Padmaja, P., & Marutheswar, G. (2017). Certain Investigation on Secured Data Transmission in Wireless Sensor Networks. *International Journal of Mobile Computing and Multimedia Communications*, 8(1), 48–61. DOI: 10.4018/IJMCMC.2017010104

Panchenko, V. (2021). Photovoltaic Thermal Module With Paraboloid Type Solar Concentrators. *International Journal of Energy Optimization and Engineering*, 10(2), 1–23. https://doi.org/10.4018/IJEOE.2021040101

Pandey, J. M., Garg, S., Mishra, P., & Mishra, B. P. (2017). Computer Based Psychological Interventions: Subject to the Efficacy of Psychological Services. *International Journal of Computers in Clinical Practice*, 2(1), 25–33. DOI: 10.4018/IJCCP.2017010102

Pandey, K., & Datta, S. (2021). Dry Machining of Inconel 825 Superalloys: Performance of Tool Inserts (Carbide, Cermet, and SiAlON). *International Journal of Manufacturing, Materials, and Mechanical Engineering*, 11(4), 26–39. DOI: 10.4018/IJMMME.2021100102

Panneer, R. (2017). Effect of Composition of Fibers on Properties of Hybrid Composites. *International Journal of Manufacturing, Materials, and Mechanical Engineering*, 7(4), 28–43. DOI: 10.4018/IJMMME.2017100103

Pany, C. (2021). Estimation of Correct Long-Seam Mismatch Using FEA to Compare the Measured Strain in a Non-Destructive Testing of a Pressurant Tank: A Reverse Problem. *International Journal of Smart Vehicles and Smart Transportation*, 4(1), 16–28. DOI: 10.4018/IJSVST.2021010102

Paul, P. K. (2018). The Context of IST for Solid Information Retrieval and Infrastructure Building: Study of Developing Country. *International Journal of Information Retrieval Research*, 8(1), 86–100. DOI: 10.4018/IJIRR.2018010106

Paul, S., & Roy, P. (2018). Optimal Design of Power System Stabilizer Using a Novel Evolutionary Algorithm. *International Journal of Energy Optimization and Engineering*, 7(3), 24–46. DOI: 10.4018/IJEOE.2018070102

Plaksina, T., & Gildin, E. (2017). Rigorous Integrated Evolutionary Workflow for Optimal Exploitation of Unconventional Gas Assets. *International Journal of Energy Optimization and Engineering*, 6(1), 101–122. DOI: 10.4018/IJEOE.2017010106

Pushpa, R., & Siddappa, M. (2021). An Optimal Way of VM Placement Strategy in Cloud Computing Platform Using ABCS Algorithm. *International Journal of Ambient Computing and Intelligence*, 12(3), 16–38. https://doi.org/10.4018/IJACI.2021070102

Rahman, N. (2017). Lessons from a Successful Data Warehousing Project Management. *International Journal of Information Technology Project Management*, 8(4), 30–45. DOI: 10.4018/IJITPM.2017100103

Rajh, A., & Pavetic, T. (2017). Computer Generated Description as the Required Digital Competence in Archival Profession. *International Journal of Digital Literacy and Digital Competence*, 8(1), 36–49. DOI: 10.4018/IJDLDC.2017010103

Ramesh, M., Garg, R., & Subrahmanyam, G. V. (2017). Investigation of Influence of Quenching and Annealing on the Plane Fracture Toughness and Brittle to Ductile Transition Temperature of the Zinc Coated Structural Steel Materials. *International Journal of Surface Engineering and Interdisciplinary Materials Science*, 5(2), 33–42. DOI: 10.4018/IJSEIMS.2017070103

Rao, Y. S., Rauta, A. K., Saini, H., & Panda, T. C. (2017). Mathematical Model for Cyber Attack in Computer Network. *International Journal of Business Data Communications and Networking*, 13(1), 58–65. DOI: 10.4018/IJBDCN.2017010105

Raut, R., Priyadarshinee, P., & Jha, M. (2017). Understanding the Mediation Effect of Cloud Computing Adoption in Indian Organization: Integrating TAM-TOE- Risk Model. *International Journal of Service Science, Management, Engineering, and Technology*, 8(3), 40–59. DOI: 10.4018/IJSSMET.2017070103

Rezaie, S., Mirabedini, S. J., & Abtahi, A. (2018). Designing a Model for Implementation of Business Intelligence in the Banking Industry. *International Journal of Enterprise Information Systems*, 14(1), 77–103. DOI: 10.4018/IJEIS.2018010105

Rondon, B. (2021). Experimental Characterization of Admittance Meter With Crude Oil Emulsions. *International Journal of Electronics, Communications, and Measurement Engineering*, 10(2), 51–59. https://doi.org/10.4018/IJECME.2021070104

Safari, M. R., & Jiang, Q. (2018). The Theory and Practice of IT Governance Maturity and Strategies Alignment: Evidence From Banking Industry. *Journal of Global Information Management*, 26(2), 127–146. DOI: 10.4018/JGIM.2018040106

Sahoo, P., & Roy, S. (2017). Tribological Behavior of Electroless Ni-P, Ni-P-W and Ni-P-Cu Coatings: A Comparison. *International Journal of Surface Engineering and Interdisciplinary Materials Science*, 5(1), 1–15. DOI: 10.4018/IJSEIMS.2017010101

Samy, V. S., Pramanick, K., Thenkanidiyoor, V., & Victor, J. (2021). Data Analysis and Visualization in Python for Polar Meteorological Data. *International Journal of Data Analytics*, 2(1), 32–60. https://doi.org/10.4018/IJDA.2021010102

Sanna, A., & Valpreda, F. (2017). An Assessment of the Impact of a Collaborative Didactic Approach and Students' Background in Teaching Computer Animation. *International Journal of Information and Communication Technology Education*, 13(4), 1–16. DOI: 10.4018/IJICTE.2017100101

Sarivougioukas, J., & Vagelatos, A. (2022). Fused Contextual Data With Threading Technology to Accelerate Processing in Home UbiHealth. *International Journal of Software Science and Computational Intelligence*, 14(1), 1–14. https://doi.org/10.4018/IJSSCI.285590

Shaaban, A. A., & Shehata, O. M. (2021). Combining Response Surface Method and Metaheuristic Algorithms for Optimizing SPIF Process. *International Journal of Manufacturing, Materials, and Mechanical Engineering*, 11(4), 1–25. https://doi.org/10.4018/IJMMME.2021100101

Shah, M. Z., Gazder, U., Bhatti, M. S., & Hussain, M. (2018). Comparative Performance Evaluation of Effects of Modifier in Asphaltic Concrete Mix. *International Journal of Strategic Engineering*, 1(2), 13–25. DOI: 10.4018/IJoSE.2018070102

Siddoo, V., & Wongsai, N. (2017). Factors Influencing the Adoption of ISO/IEC 29110 in Thai Government Projects: A Case Study. *International Journal of Information Technologies and Systems Approach*, 10(1), 22–44. DOI: 10.4018/IJITSA.2017010102

Singh, L. K., Khanna, M., Thawkar, S., & Gopal, J. (2021). Robustness for Authentication of the Human Using Face, Ear, and Gait Multimodal Biometric System. *International Journal of Information System Modeling and Design*, 12(1), 39–72. https://doi.org/10.4018/IJISMD.2021010103

Smirnov, A., Ponomarev, A., Shilov, N., Kashevnik, A., & Teslya, N. (2018). Ontology-Based Human-Computer Cloud for Decision Support: Architecture and Applications in Tourism. *International Journal of Embedded and Real-Time Communication Systems*, 9(1), 1–19. DOI: 10.4018/IJERTCS.2018010101

Srilakshmi, R., & Jaya Bhaskar, M. (2021). An Adaptable Secure Scheme in Mobile Ad hoc Network to Protect the Communication Channel From Malicious Behaviours. *International Journal of Information Technology and Web Engineering*, 16(3), 54–73. https://doi.org/10.4018/IJITWE.2021070104

Sukhwani, N., Kagita, V. R., Kumar, V., & Panda, S. K. (2021). Efficient Computation of Top-K Skyline Objects in Data Set With Uncertain Preferences. *International Journal of Data Warehousing and Mining*, 17(3), 68–80. https://doi.org/10.4018/IJDWM.2021070104

Syväjärvi, A., Leinonen, J., Kivivirta, V., & Kesti, M. (2017). The Latitude of Information Management in Local Government: Views of Local Government Managers. *International Journal of Electronic Government Research*, 13(1), 69–85. DOI: 10.4018/IJEGR.2017010105

Terki, A., & Boubertakh, H. (2021). A New Hybrid Binary-Real Coded Cuckoo Search and Tabu Search Algorithm for Solving the Unit-Commitment Problem. *International Journal of Energy Optimization and Engineering*, 10(2), 104–119. https://doi.org/10.4018/IJEOE.2021040105

Verner, C. M., & Sarwar, D. (2021). Avoiding Project Failure and Achieving Project Success in NHS IT System Projects in the United Kingdom. *International Journal of Strategic Engineering*, 4(1), 33–54. https://doi.org/10.4018/IJoSE.2021010103

Verrollot, J., Tolonen, A., Harkonen, J., & Haapasalo, H. J. (2018). Challenges and Enablers for Rapid Product Development. *International Journal of Applied Industrial Engineering*, 5(1), 25–49. DOI: 10.4018/IJAIE.2018010102

Wang, H., Huang, P., & Chen, X. (2021). Research and Application of a Multidimensional Association Rules Mining Method Based on OLAP. *International Journal of Information Technology and Web Engineering*, 16(1), 75–94. https://doi.org/10.4018/IJITWE.2021010104

Wimble, M., Singh, H., & Phillips, B. (2018). Understanding Cross-Level Interactions of Firm-Level Information Technology and Industry Environment: A Multilevel Model of Business Value. *Information Resources Management Journal*, 31(1), 1–20. DOI: 10.4018/IRMJ.2018010101

Wimmer, H., Powell, L., Kilgus, L., & Force, C. (2017). Improving Course Assessment via Web-based Homework. *International Journal of Online Pedagogy and Course Design*, 7(2), 1–19. DOI: 10.4018/IJOPCD.2017040101

Yamada, H. (2021). Homogenization of Japanese Industrial Technology From the Perspective of R&D Expenses. *International Journal of Systems and Service-Oriented Engineering*, 11(2), 24–51. DOI: 10.4018/IJSSOE.2021070102

Yousefi, Y., Gratton, P., & Sarwar, D. (2021). Investigating the Opportunities to Improve the Thermal Performance of a Case Study Building in London. *International Journal of Strategic Engineering*, 4(1), 1–18. https://doi.org/10.4018/IJoSE .2021010101

Zhang, Z., Ma, J., & Cui, X. (2021). Genetic Algorithm With Three-Dimensional Population Dominance Strategy for University Course Timetabling Problem. *International Journal of Grid and High Performance Computing*, 13(2), 56–69. https:// doi.org/10.4018/IJGHPC.2021040104

Aasi, P., Rusu, L., & Vieru, D. (2017). The Role of Culture in IT Governance Five Focus Areas: A Literature Review. *International Journal of IT/Business Alignment and Governance, 8*(2), 42-61. https://doi.org/DOI: 10.4018/IJITBAG.2017070103

De Maere, K., De Haes, S., & von Kutzschenbach, M. (2017). CIO Perspectives on Organizational Learning within the Context of IT Governance. *International Journal of IT/Business Alignment and Governance, 8*(1), 32-47. https://doi.org/ DOI: 10.4018/IJITBAG.2017010103

About the Contributors

Vinod Kumar has received the degree Bachelor of Science (PCM) from University of Allahabad, Uttar Pradesh-India in 2008, Master of Computer Applications in 2011. He has qualified UGC-NET (Computer Science and Applications) in 2013. He did Ph.D. from Maulana Azad National Institute of Technology (MANIT),Bhopal (MP) in 2019. He has worked as a Project Fellow on Project "Network Simulation Testbed at MCTE, MHOW(MP)" in Indian Institute of Information Technology-Allahabad (U.P.) in Collaboration with Military College of Telecommunication Engineering (MCTE), Mhow (MP) funded by Army Technology Board. He has 10+ Years experience in research and teaching. Currently He is working as Assistant Professor in Department of Computer Application, School of Computing Science & Engineering, Galgotias University, Uttar Pradesh, India. He is an active researcher in the field of Web Mining, Machine Learning, Graph Neural Network and Blockchain Technology, Internet of Things.

* * *

C. V. Suresh Babu is a pioneer in content development. A true entrepreneur, he founded Anniyappa Publications, a company that is highly active in publishing books related to Computer Science and Management. Dr. C.V. Suresh Babu has also ventured into SB Institute, a center for knowledge transfer. He holds a Ph.D. in Engineering Education from the National Institute of Technical Teachers Training & Research in Chennai, along with seven master's degrees in various disciplines such as Engineering, Computer Applications, Management, Commerce, Economics, Psychology, Law, and Education. Additionally, he has UGC-NET/SET qualifications in the fields of Computer Science, Management, Commerce, and Education. Currently, Dr. C.V. Suresh Babu is a Professor in the Department of Information Technology at the School of Computing Science, Hindustan Institute of Technology and Science (Hindustan University) in Padur, Chennai, Tamil Nadu, India. For more information, you can visit his personal blog at https://sites.google.com/view/cvsureshbabu/.

Mayank Chopra has received BSc Physics (Hons.) degree from Himachal Pradesh University, India, and MSc Information Technology degree from Central University of Himachal Pradesh, India. Earlier he worked as a resource person in Computer Science & informatics at Central University of Himachal Pradesh, India. His current research interest includes machine learning, UAV, web development, security and data science.

Pradeep Chouksey is an Associate Professor and Head of Department of Computer science and informatics at Central University Himachal Pradesh (H.P.). He has teaching and research experience of more than 16 years. He is actively involved in research with more than 50 presentations, publications and articles in several reputed peer-reviewed international journals, National and international conferences, edited books, etc. He had served as session chair at several National and international conferences. He serves as external examiner for doctoral candidates, external member of doctoral committees, member of board of studies, and academic auditor for various institutions and universities. He also serves as reviewer of papers for various international journals and subject expert for external committees.

E. Ivette Cota-Rivera received a M.Eng. from the Autonomous University of Baja California (UABC, Universidad Autonoma de Baja California). In 2016, she received her Ph.D. in Energy Engineering and is currently working as a pro fessor in the Energy Engineering program at the Polytechnic University of Baja California (UPBC, Universidad Politecnica de Baja California). Her research interests include energy efficiency and sustainability, artificial intelligence, energy science and technology, as well as programming.

Vishal Kumar Gaur is currently working as Dean of Research at Bikaner Technical University, Bikaner. He has wide experience of 17 years as an academician, researcher and in Industry. He has published 46 research papers in international journals (SCI/Scopus/WoS) and presented 41 papers in national/international conferences. He has been editor/authored 13 books including reference, text and edited books of Springer, Singapore, ACM USA and Scholars-Press, Germany. He has published two patents and 3 patents grants in his credit. He supervised 6 Ph.d research scholars in area of cloud computing, software development, Neural Networks and Deep Learning.

Roxana Jiménez Sánchez graduated from the Mexicali Technological Institute, with experience in the public and private sectors in areas related to the analysis of drinking water and wastewater, as well as the safety, hygiene, and environmental management of the industry. Master in Education with specialization in Organizational Development at CETYS University. Teacher of the subject, teaching classes at the secondary, high school, and university levels for 17 years. Project and internship advisor for students in their final semesters at the Polytechnic University of Baja California.

Rabia Koser (MSc- IT, M.Phil) is presently working as Assistant Professor in Higher Education Department, UT of Jammu and Kashmir and presently posted at Govt. P.G. College, Rajouri, Union Territory of J&K. She specializes in Various Programming Languages like C, C++, Java, Software Engineering, Management Information System and Cloud Computing. Furthermore, Prof. Rabia presented and published various research papers on Cyber Forensic and Cyber Security in the leading journals.

Guillermo M. Limon-Molina received ScD degree in Industrial Mechanics from Universidad Autónoma de Baja California, also has a Master and Bachelor Degree in Electronic Engineering, currently works in Mechatronics program from Universidad Politécnica de Baja California. His research interests include automations processes, programming algorithms, mechanical design with CNC systems and machine vision.

Abelardo Mercado Herrera is Doctor of Science and Master of Science from the National Institute of Astrophysics, Optics and Electronics, specializing in Astrophysics, Postdoctorate in Astrophysics from the Institute of Astronomy of the National Autonomous University of Mexico, Electronics Engineer from the Autonomous University of Baja California . He is a specialist in the mathematical-statistical description of stochastic and/or deterministic processes, nonlinear systems, complex systems, chaos theory, among others, as well as their application to physical phenomena such as astronomy, economics, finance, telecommunications, science social etc., in order to determine the underlying dynamics in such processes, and if necessary, their connection with real physical variables and possible prediction. He has worked on the development of various electronic circuits, interfaces and programs to carry out electrical tests in the industry, as well as in scientific instrumentation, applied to telemetry, infrared polarimetry, optics and spectroscopy. He has also specialized in image analysis, measurement techniques and noise reduction.

Fabian N. Murrieta-Rico received B.Eng. and M.Eng. degrees from Instituto Tecnológico de Mexicali (ITM) in 2004 and 2013 respectively. In 2017, he received his PhD in Materials Physics at Centro de Investigación Científica y Educación Superior de Ensenada (CICESE). He has worked as an automation engineer, systems designer, as a university professor, and as postdoctoral researcher at Facultad de Ingeniería, Arquitectura y Diseño from Universidad Autónoma de Baja California (UABC) and at the Centro de Nanociencias y Nanotecnología from Universidad Nacional Autónoma de México (CNyN-UNAM), currently he works as professor at the Universidad Politécnica de Baja California. His research has been published in different journals and presented at international conferences since 2009. He has served as reviewer for different journals, some of them include IEEE Transactions on Industrial Electronics, IEEE Transactions on Instrumentation, Measurement and Sensor Review. His research interests are focused on the field of time and frequency metrology, the design of wireless sensor networks, automated systems and highly sensitive chemical detectors.

Jesús Heriberto Orduño-Osuna obtained a Bachelor's degree in Mechatronics Engineering from the Universidad Politécnica de Baja California (UPBC) and a Master's degree in Computational Sciences and Applied Mathematics from Universidad Internacional de La Rioja, Mexico (UNIR Mexico), where he developed projects in application and research in the area of Machine Learning applied to dynamic systems. He is partially studying a Master's degree in Strategic Administration. He has worked as an engineer in the industry, mainly in the Post-Harvest Automation industry as well as in the manufacturing sector, focusing primarily on automation processes, vision systems, and industrial robotics, among others. Currently, he is a part-time lecturer at the Universidad Politécnica de Baja California and the Universidad del Valle de México, teaching courses in Mechatronics, Manufacturing, Energy, and Computing, contributing to the education of engineers with an innovative and technological focus. His research interests are focused on Machine Learning, Automation, and control of industrial processes, Microcontrollers, and digital signal processing.

Sabyasachi Pramanik is a professional IEEE member. He obtained a PhD in Computer Science and Engineering from Sri Satya Sai University of Technology and Medical Sciences, Bhopal, India. Presently, he is an Associate Professor, Department of Computer Science and Engineering, Haldia Institute of Technology, India. He has many publications in various reputed international conferences, journals, and book chapters (Indexed by SCIE, Scopus, ESCI, etc). He is doing research in the fields of Artificial Intelligence, Data Privacy, Cybersecurity, Network Security, and Machine Learning. He also serves on the editorial boards of several international journals. He is a reviewer of journal articles from IEEE, Springer, Elsevier, Inderscience, IET and IGI Global. He has reviewed many conference papers, has been a keynote speaker, session chair, and technical program committee member at many international conferences. He has authored a book on Wireless Sensor Network. He has edited 8 books from IGI Global, CRC Press, Springer and Wiley Publications.

Rishikesh Rawat, Director, Bansal College of Engineering, Mandideep, is having more than 20 years of academic career in teaching. He obtained his B.E. & M.Tech Degree in Computer Science and Engineering from Maulana Azad National Institute of Technology, Bhopal. He did his PhD degrees in Computer Science and Engineering in the year 2021. He has published more than 20 papers in Journals and Conferences in National and International level. He is the life member of Computer Society of India (CSI) & Indian Society for Technical Education (ISTE).His area of interest includes Distributed System, Theory of Computation & Data Structure.

Maria E. Raygoza-L, Ph.D. in Chemistry and Energy, from Engineering Institute of Universidad Autónoma de Baja California, and a Bachelor of Industrial Engineering with a specialization in Manufacturing, currently works as a full-time professor and researcher at Universidad Politécnica de Baja California and as a Subject Professor at Universidad Autónoma de Baja California, in areas of Energy Engineering and Renewable Energies. Extensive experience in industry, her research interests include renewable energy, energy efficiency, environmental, energy management systems, and integration of public policies for sustainable development.

Parveen Sadotra (MCA, Ph.D, CCSP, CEH, and CCCA) is presently working as a Assistant Professor in Department of Computer Science Informatics, Central University of Himachal Pradesh has definitive experience in the field of computers and Cyber Crime Investigation Training. He specialize in Cyber Security, Ethical Hacking and Cyber Forensics, Furthermore, Dr. Sadotra presented and published various research papers on Cyber Laws, Investigation of cyber crime, Intrusion Detection System, Cyber Security, Web Security, E- Commerce and Cyber Education in the leading journals. He also published a book on Mobile Technologies and Cloud Computing. In addition to this he delivered various Lectures and Presentation in Workshop, Seminar and in capsule Trainings. He has got various Appreciations & Commendations certificates from J&K Police for Working on Cyber Crime.

Venkat T. is Professor, Department of Computer Science and Engineering-IoT, Sreenidhi Institute of Science and Technology, Hyderabad, Telangana, India.

Nagendra Singh Yadav is a Software Testing professional with experience managing remote teams and leading project teams. His background in software testing, technical writing, Research, Author, blogger, and Project management informs his mindful but competitive approach. Nagendra is fueled by his passion for understanding the project requirements and asking from the stakeholders. He considers himself a 'forever student,' eager to build on his academic foundations as a researcher, technical writer, and blogger, and stays in tune with the latest software testing & project management strategies through continued work experience. He is the Global Assistant General Secretary, International Council of Computer Science (ICCS) at Eudoxia Research Centre and holds degrees in M.C.A, B.C.A & a diploma in Blogging and Content Marketing. He has worked with Infosys Limited for 3 years in the field of software validation solutions as a Test Engineer (2016- 2019).

Index

Printed in the United States
by Baker & Taylor Publisher Services